Lofty Dogmas

Lofty Dogmas

Poets on Poetics

EDITED BY

DEBORAH   ANNIE   MAXINE
BROWN   FINCH   KUMIN

THE UNIVERSITY OF ARKANSAS PRESS
Fayetteville • 2005

09   08   07   06   05   5   4   3   2   1

Designed by Liz Lester

☉ The paper used in this publication meets the minimum
requirements of the American National Standard for
Permanence of Paper for Printed Library Materials Z39.48-1984.

LIBRARY OF CONGRESS
CATALOGING-IN-PUBLICATION DATA

   Lofty dogmas : poets on poetics / edited by Deborah Brown,
Annie Finch, Maxine Kumin.
       p.   cm.
   Includes bibliographical references and index.
   ISBN 1-55728-791-0 (cloth : alk. paper)—
ISBN 1-55728-792-9 (pbk. : alk. paper)
     1. Poetics. 2. Poetry—Collections. I. Brown, Deborah,
1948– II. Finch, Annie, 1956– III. Kumin, Maxine, 1925–
   PN1042.L64   2005
   808.1—dc22
                         2005009286

ACKNOWLEDGMENTS

Julia Alvarez, "Housekeeping Cages" from *A Formal Feeling Comes: Poems in Form by Contemporary Women,* edited by Annie Finch (Ashland, OR: Story Line Press, 1994). Reprinted with the permission of the author

Anonymous, ["I crossed the deep sea,"] (excerpt), translated by John Lucas, from Christine Fell, ed., *Egil's Saga* (London: Everyman's Library / J. M. Dent & Sons, 1975). Reprinted with the permission of the translator.

Anonymous, "The Dead Man Asks for a Song," translated by Willard Trask, from *The Unwritten Song, Volume II.* Copyright © 1967 by Willard R. Trask. Reprinted with the permission of Scribner, an imprint of Simon & Schuster Adult Publishing Group.

Matthew Arnold, "The Study of Poetry," in *The Portable Matthew Arnold,* edited by Lionel Trilling (New York: Penguin Books, 1980).

W. H. Auden, excerpts from "Writing," "The Virgin & the Dynamo," and "The Poet & the City" from *The Dyer's Hand and Other Essays.* Copyright 1950, © 1962 by W. H. Auden. Reprinted with the permission of Random House, Inc. and Faber and Faber, Ltd.

Bashō, excerpt from "Kyorai's Conversations with Bashō" from Ryusaku Tsunoda, William Theodore de Bary, and Donald Keene, editors, *Sources of Japanese Tradition, Volume 1,* pp. 326–329. Copyright © 1958 by Columbia University Press. Reprinted with the permission of the publishers.

Charles Bernstein, excerpt from "Against National Poetry Month as Such" (April 1999). First published by The University of Chicago, on their web site, in connection with the publication of *My Way: Speeches and Poems* (Chicago: The University of Chicago Press, 1999). Copyright © 1999 by Charles Bernstein. Reprinted with the permission of the author.

Elizabeth Bishop, letter to John Frederick Nims (October 6, 1979) from *One Art: Letters,* edited by Robert Giroux. Copyright © 1994 by Alice Helen Methfessel. Reprinted with the permission of Farrar, Straus & Giroux, LLC.

William Blake, "A Memorable Fancy," in *Blake, Complete Writings with Variant Readings,* ed. Geoffrey Keynes (New York: Oxford, 1966).

Louise Bogan, excerpt from "The Pleasure of Formal Poetry" from *The Poet's Alphabet* (New York: McGraw-Hill, 1970). Copyright © 1970 by Louise Bogan. Reprinted with the permission of The Estate of Louise Bogan.

Anne Bradstreet, "The Author to Her Book," in *The Complete Works of Anne Bradstreet,* editors Joseph R. McElrath Jr. and Allan P. Robb (Boston: Twayne Publishers, 1981).

Gwendolyn Brooks, excerpt from *The Future of Black Poetry,* an interview with Steve Cape, online: www.wooster.edu./artfuldodge/interviews/brooks.htm.

Callimachus, "Prologue to *The Aetia*" translated by Stanley Lombardo and Diane Raynor, from *Callimachus: Hymns, Epigrams, Selected Fragments.* Copyright © 1988 by The Johns Hopkins University Press. Reprinted with the permission of The Johns Hopkins University Press.

Rafael Campo, excerpt from "Of the Sonnet and Paradoxical Beauties," interview with Joyce Wilson, The Poetry Porch, www.poetryporch.com (1997), reprinted with the permission of the author.

Lewis Carroll, "'Jabberwocky' and Carroll's Interpretations," in *Looking-Glass House, The Annotated Alice,* edited by Martin Gardner (New York: Wings Books, Random House, 1960).

Aimé Césaire, excerpt from *Notebook of a Return To the Native Land,* translated by Clayton Eshelman and Annette Smith. Copyright 1939 by Aimé Césaire, translation copyright © 2001 by Clayton Eshelman and Annette Smith. Reprinted with the permission of Wesleyan University Press.

Theresa Hak Kyung Cha, "Diseuse," from *Dictée* (Berkeley: University of California Press, 2001).

Geoffrey Chaucer, *Troilus and Criseyde,* Book 2, in *Chaucer Complete Works,* edited by Walter Skeat (London: Oxford University Press, 1969).

Lucille Clifton, "when I stand around among poets" from *Quilting: Poems 1987–1990.* Copyright © 1991 by Lucille Clifton. Reprinted with the permission of the author and BOA Editions Ltd.

Judith Ortiz Cofer, excerpt from "And May He Be Bilingual: Notes on Writing, Teaching and Multiculturalism" from *Woman in Front of the Sun: On Becoming a Writer* (Athens: The University of Georgia Press, 2000). Copyright © 2000 by Judith Ortiz Cofer. Reprinted with the permission of the author.

Samuel Taylor Coleridge, Preface to "Kubla Khan, A Vision in a Dream," in *The Selected Poetry and Prose of Samuel Taylor Coleridge,* edited by Donald A. Stauffer (New York: Random House, 1951).

Samuel Taylor Coleridge, *Biographia Literaria* (Dutton, NY: Everyman's Library, 1962).

Hart Crane, excerpts from a letter to Harriet Monroe, from *The Complete Poems and Selected Letters and Prose of Hart Crane.* Copyright © 1966 by Liveright Publishing Corporation. Reprinted with the permission of Liveright Publishing Corporation.

Samuel Daniel, *Selected Poetry and A Defense of Rhyme,* editors Geoffrey G. Hiller and Peter L. Groves (Ashville, NC: Pegasus Press, 1998).

Emily Dickinson, "This was a poet" from *The Complete Poems of Emily Dickinson,* edited by Thomas H. Johnson. Copyright 1945, 1951, © 1955, 1979, 1983 by the President and Fellows of Harvard College. Reprinted with the permission of The Belknap Press of Harvard University Press.

Robert Duncan, from "Ideas on the Meaning of Form," in *Robert Duncan, A Selected Prose,* edited by Robert J. Bertholf (New York: New Directions, 1995).

Moira Egan, "To My Muse, Upon Her Return" from *Cleave* (Washington, DC: Writers' Publishing House, 2004). Reprinted with the permission of the author.

T. S. Eliot, "Tradition and the Individual Talent" and "Hamlet and His Problems" from *Selected Prose of T. S. Eliot*. Reprinted with the permission of Faber & Faber, Ltd.

Ralph Waldo Emerson, "The Poet," in *Selections from Ralph Waldo Emerson An Organic Anthology*, edited by Stephen E. Whicher (Boston: Houghton Mifflin Co., 1957).

Anne Finch, "The Appology," in *The Selected Poems of Anne Finch*, edited by Katharine M. Rogers (New York: Ungar, 1979).

Annie Finch, excerpt from "Coherent Decentering" from *The Body of Poetry: Essays on Women, Form, and the Poetic Self.* Reprinted with the permission of the author and the University of Michigan Press, 2005.

Robert Frost, interview from *Conversations on the Art of Poetry* edited by Cleanth Brooks. Copyright © 1961 by Robert Frost. Reprinted with the permission of Henry Holt and Company, LLC.

Alice Fulton, excerpt from "Of Formal, Free, and Fractal Verse: Singing the Body Electric" from *Feeling as a Foreign Language: The Good Strangeness of Poetry* (St. Paul, Minn.: Graywolf, 1999). Copyright © 1999 by Alice Fulton. Reprinted with the permission of the author.

Jorie Graham, excerpt from the introduction to *The Best American Poetry* (New York: Scribner, 1990). Reprinted with the permission of the author.

Theresa Hak Kyung Cha, "Diseuse," from *Dictée*. Copyright © 1982 by Theresa Hak Kyung Cha. Reprinted with the permission of Berkeley Art Museum.

Donald Hall, excerpt from "Goatfoot, Milktongue, Twinbird: The Infantile Origins of Poetic Form" from *Goatfoot Milktongue Twinbird: Interviews, Essays and Notes on Poetry 1970–1976* (Ann Arbor: The University of Michigan Press, 1978). Reprinted with the permission of the author.

Joy Harjo, excerpt from "The Spiral of Memory" from *The Spiral of Memory: Interviews* (Ann Arbor: The University of Michigan Press, 1996). Reprinted with the permission of the author.

Robert Hass, excerpt from "Listening and Making" from *Twentieth Century Pleasures* (New York: The Ecco Press, 1997). Copyright © 1997 by Robert Hass. Reprinted with the permission of the author.

H.D. (Hilda Doolittle), excerpt from a letter to Norman Holmes Pearson from *Between History and Poetry: The Letters of H. D. and Norman Holmes Pearson*. Copyright © 1997 by the University of Iowa Press. Copyright © 2004 by The Schaffner Family Foundation. Reprinted with the permission of New Directions Publishing Corporation, agents.

Seamus Heaney, "Digging" from *Death of a Naturalist*. Copyright © 1969 by Seamus Heaney. Reprinted with the permission of the author and Farrar, Straus & Giroux, LLC and Faber & Faber, Ltd.

Lyn Hejinian, excerpt from "Formalism" from "The Rejection of Closure" in *Writing/Talks,* edited by Bob Perelmen (Carbondale; Southern Illinois University Press, 1985). Originally in *Poetics Journal* 4 (1984). Reprinted with the permission of the author.

Edward Hirsch, excerpt from "Fending Off the Duende" from *The Demon and the Angel: Searching for the Source of Artistic Inspiration.* Copyright © 2002 by Edward Hirsch. Reprinted with the permission of the author and Harcourt, Inc.

Jane Hirshfield, excerpt from "Poetry as a Vessel of Remembrance" from *Nine Gates: Entering the Mind of Poetry: Essays* (New York: HarperCollins, 1997). Copyright © 1997 by Jane Hirshfield. Reprinted with the permission of the author.

Gerald Manley Hopkins, "Author's Preface" in *The Works of Gerard Manley Hopkins,* with an introduction, unsigned, but attributed to Robert Bridges (Hertfordshire, Great Britain: 1994).

Horace, excerpt from Book Two, Epistle III, "To the Pisos (The Art of Poetry)," translated by David Ferry, from *The Epistles of Horace.* Copyright © 2002 by David Ferry. Reprinted with the permission of the translator and Farrar, Straus, and Giroux, LLC.

Fanny Howe, excerpt from an interview with Daniel Kane, from *Teachers & Writers* 33, no 1 (Sept/Oct 2001). Reprinted with the permission of Fanny Howe.

Langston Hughes, excerpt from "The Negro Artist and the Racial Mountain" from *The Nation* (June 23, 1926). Copyright 1926 by Langston Hughes. Reprinted with the permission of Harold Ober Associates, Incorporated.

Richard Hugo, excerpt from "The Triggering Town" from *The Triggering Town: Lectures and Essays on Poetry and Writing.* Copyright © 1979 by Richard Hugo. Reprinted with the permission of W. W. Norton & Company, Inc.

Richard Jackson, excerpt from "Why Poetry Today?" from a talk delivered at Vilenica Slovenia Conference, 1991. Reprinted with the permission of the author. This selection contains lines by Edvard Kocbek from At the Door of Evening, translated by Tom Lozar. Ljubljana: Aleph, 1990 (bilingual edition). Reprinted with the permission of the translator and J. Gordon Shillingford Publishing.

Randall Jarrell, excerpt from "The Obscurity of the Poet" from *Poetry and the Age* (New York: Alfred A. Knopf, 1953). Reprinted with the permission of Mrs. Mary Jarrell.

Ben Jonson, "A Fit of Rhyme Against Rhyme," in *Elizabethan and Jacobean Poets Marlowe to Marvell,* editors W. H. Auden and Norman Holmes Pearson (New York: The Viking Press, 1950).

John Keats, excerpts from *The Letters of John Keats,* edited by Robert Gittings (New York: Oxford University Press, 1970). Copyright © 1970 by Robert Gittings. Reprinted with the permission of The Society of Authors as Literary Representative of the Estate of Robert Gittings.

Yusef Komunyakaa, excerpt from "Control Is the Mainspring" from *Blue Notes* (Ann Arbor: The University of Michigan Press, 2000). Copyright © 2000 by Yusef Komunyakaa. Reprinted with the permission of the author and the University of Michigan Press.

Richard Kostelanetz, excerpt from *More WordWorks* (Kingston, Rhode Island: Talisman House Publishers, 2001). Copyright © 2001 by Richard Kostelanetz. Reprinted with the permission of the author.

Maxine Kumin, excerpts from "Coming Across: Establishing the Intent of the Poem" and "Closing the Door" from *To Make a Prairie: Essays on Poets, Poetry, and Country Living.* Copyright © 1979 by The University of Michigan. Reprinted with the permission of the author and The University of Michigan Press.

Stanley Kunitz, excerpt from "Table Talk, A Paris Review Interview with Chris Busa" from *Next to Last Things* (Boston: Atlantic Monthly Press, 1985). Copyright © 1985 by Stanley Kunitz. Reprinted with the permission of Stanley Kunitz.

Li-Young Lee, excerpt from an interview with Marie Jordan, from *The Writer's Chronicle* (May / Summer, 2002). Reprinted with permission of the author.

David Lehman, excerpt from "The Prose Poem: An Alternative to Verse" from *Great American Prose Poems: From Poe to Present* (New York: Scribner, 2003). Copyright © 2003 by David Lehman. Reprinted with the permission of Writers' Representatives, Inc. This selection contains Frank O'Hara, excerpt from "Why I Am Not a Painter" from *The Collected Poems of Frank O'Hara.* Copyright © 1956 by Frank O'Hara. Reprinted with the permission of Alfred A. Knopf, a division of Random House, Inc.

Denise Levertov, excerpt from "Horses with Wings" from *New and Selected Essays.* Copyright © 1992 by Denise Levertov. Reprinted with the permission of New Directions Publishing Corporation.

Federico García Lorca, excerpts from "Play and Theory of the Duende," translated by Christopher Mauer. *Juego y teorla del duende* copyright © Herederos de Federico Garcia Lorca, from *Obras Completas* (Galaxia Gutenberg, 1996 edition). Translation copyright © Christopher Mauer and Herederos de Federico García Lorca. All rights reserved. Reprinted with the permission of New Directions Publishing Company and the Estate of Federico García Lorca. For information regarding rights and permissions, please contact lorca@artslaw.co.uk or William Peter Kosmas, 8 Franklin Square, London W14 9UU.

Audre Lorde, "Poetry Is Not a Luxury" from *Sister Outsider: Essays and Speeches.* Copyright © 1982 by Audre Lorde. Reprinted with the permission of The Crossing Press, a division of Ten Speed Press, Berkeley, CA, www.tenspeed.com

Nathaniel Mackey, excerpt from "Cante Moro" from *Paracritical Hinge: Essays, Talks, Notes, Interviews* (Madison: University of Wisconsin Press, 2004). Copyright © 2004. Reprinted with the permission of the author.

Heather McHugh, excerpt from "Moving Means, Meaning Moves" from *Poets Teaching Poets,* edited by Gregory Orr and Ellen Bryant Voight. Copyright © 1993 by Heather McHugh. Reprinted with the permission of the author and University of Michigan Press.

Edna St. Vincent Millay, "I will put Chaos into fourteen lines" from *Collected Poems.* Copyright 1954, © 1982 by Norma Millay Ellis. Reprinted with the permission of Elizabeth Barnett, literary executor.

Czeslaw Milosz, Nobel Lecture (1980) from *Nobel Lectures, Literature 1968–1980.* Copyright © 1980 by The Nobel Foundation. Reprinted with permission.

John Milton, from "Introduction to Paradise Lost," *Complete Poems and Major Prose,* edited by Merritt Y. Hughes, New York: The Odyssey Press, 1957.

Marianne Moore, excerpt from "Feeling and Precision" from *The Complete Prose of Marianne Moore,* edited by Patricia C. Willis. Copyright 1944 by Marianne Moore. Reprinted with the permission of Viking Penguin, a division of Penguin Group (USA) Inc. This selection contains Ludwig Bemelmans, excerpt from *Madeline.* Copyright 1939 by Ludwig Bemelmans, renewed © 1967 by Madeleine Bemelmans and Barbara Bemelmans Marciano. Reprinted with the permission of Viking Penguin, a division of Penguin Young Readers Group, a member of Penguin Group (USA) Inc., 345 Hudson Street, New York, NY 10014. All rights reserved.

Harryette Mullen, excerpt from an interview conducted by Stephen Yenser, from *COMBO: A Journal of Poetry and Poetics* 1. Reprinted with the permission of Stephen Yenser.

Marilyn Nelson, excerpt from "Owning the Masters" from *New Formalism: Poets on Form, Narrative, and Tradition,* edited by Annie Finch (Ashland, Oregon: Story Line Press, 1999). Copyright © 1999 by Marilyn Nelson. Reprinted with the permission of the author.

Howard Nemerov, excerpt from "The Difficulty of Difficult Poetry" from *Reflections on Poetry and Poetics.* Copyright © 1972 by Rutgers, the State University. Reprinted with the permission of Rutgers University Press.

Pablo Neruda, excerpt from "Towards the Splendid City" (Nobel Lecture, December 13, 1971). Copyright © 1971 by The Nobel Foundation. Reprinted with permission.

Naomi Shihab Nye, excerpt from "Lights in the Windows" from *The ALAN Review* 22, no 3 (Spring 1995). Reprinted with the permission of the author.

Frank O'Hara, "Personism" from *The Collected Poems of Frank O'Hara.* Copyright © 1971 by Maureen Granville-Smith, Administratrix of the Estate of Frank O'Hara. Reprinted with the permission of Alfred A. Knopf, a division of Random House, Inc.

Charles Olson, excerpt from "Projective Verse" from *Selected Writings of Charles Olson.* Copyright 1951, © 1966 by Charles Olson. Reprinted with the permission of New Directions Publishing Corporation.

Alicia Ostriker, "Dancing at the Devil's Party," in *Essays on Poetry, Politics and the Erotic* (Ann Arbor: University of Michigan Press, 2000). Reprinted with the permission of the author.

Alicia Ostriker, excerpt from the Preface to *Stealing the Language: The Emergence of Women's Poetry in America* (Boston: Beacon Press, 1986). Copyright © 1986 by Alicia Ostriker. Reprinted with the permission of the author.

Cesare Pavese, "Postscript II: Notes on Certain Unwritten Poems" from *Hard Labor*, translated by William Arrowsmith. Copyright 1943 by Guilio Einaudi editore, Torino. Translation copyright © 1976 by William Arrowsmith. Reprinted with the permission of Viking Penguin, a division of Penguin Group (USA) Inc.

Thomas Love Peacock, *Reply to Shelley, A Defense of Poetry*, in *The Four Ages of Poetry*, edited by John E. Jordan, (Indianapolis: The Bobbs Merrill Co., Inc., 1965).

Po Chu-I, "Madly Singing in the Mountains," translated by Arthur Waley, from *A Hundred and Seventy Chinese Poems* (New York: Alfred A. Knopf, 1919). Copyright 1919 by Arthur Waley. Reprinted with the permission of The Arthur Waley Estate.

Edgar Allan Poe, "The Philosophy of Composition," in *The Complete Poems and Stories of Edgar Allan Poe*, vol. 2, editors Arthur Hobson Quinn and Edward H. O'Neill (New York: Alfred A. Knopf, 1973).

Alexander Pope, from *An Essay on Criticism, A Scolar Press Fascimile*, The Scolar Press Ltd., Yorkshire, England, 1970.

Ezra Pound, "A Few Don'ts by an Imagiste," *Poetry* 1, no. 6 (March 1913). Reprinted with the permission of New Directions Publishing Corporation and Faber & Faber, Ltd.

Adrienne Rich, excerpt from "What would we create" from *What is Found There: Notebooks on Poetry and Politics*. Copyright © 1993 by Adrienne Rich. Reprinted with the permission of the author and W. W. Norton & Company, Inc

Rainer Maria Rilke, "Letter One, February 17, 1903," "Letter Three, April 23, 1903," and "Letter Eight, August 12, 1904" from *Letters to a Young Poet*, translated by M. D. Herter Norton. Copyright 1934, 1954 by W. W. Norton & Company, Inc., renewed © 1962, 1982 by M. D. Herter Norton. Reprinted with the permission of W. W. Norton & Company, Inc.

Lisa Robertson, excerpt from "How Pastoral: A Manifesto" from *XEclogue* (Vancouver: Tsunami Editions, 1993). Reprinted with the permission of the author.

Theodore Roethke, excerpts from "How to Write Like Somebody Else" and "Some Remarks on Rhythm" from *On Poetry and Craft: Selected Prose of Theodore Roethke*. Copyright © 1965, 1972, 2001 by Beatrice Roethke Lushington as administratrix of the estate of Theodore Roethke. Reprinted with the permission of Copper Canyon Press, P. O. Box 271, Port Townsend, WA 98368–0271.

Muriel Rukeyser, excerpt from "The Rare Union: Poetry and Science" from *The Life of Poetry*. Copyright © 1976 by Muriel Rukeyser. Reprinted with the permission of Paris Press.

Sappho, "No Room for Grief," translated by Annie Finch, 2004.

Léopold Sédar Senghor, "Elegy of Midnight" and "Elegy of the Trade Winds," from *The Collected Poetry*, translated by Melvin Dixon, Charlottesville: University of Virginia Press.

William Shakespeare, "Sonnet LV," in *The Complete Sonnets and Poems*, Oxford World's Classics (London: Oxford University Press, 2002).

Percy Bysshe Shelley, "A Defence of Poetry," in *The Four Ages of Poetry*, edited by John E. Jordan (Indianapolis: The Bobbs Merrill Co., Inc., 1965).

Sir Philip Sidney, "Loving in Truth," from *Astrophil and Stella*, in *The Poems of Sir Philip Sidney*, edited by William A. Ringler, Jr. (London: Oxford University Press, 1962).

Barry Spacks, "The Muse" from *The Company of Children*. Copyright © 1969 by Barry Spacks. Reprinted with the permission of the author and Doubleday, a division of Random House, Inc.

Edmund Spenser, "Invocation to the *Faerie Queene*," in *The Complete Poetical Works of Spenser* (Boston: Houghton Mifflin Co., 1908).

Gertrude Stein, excerpt from "Patriarchal Poetry" from *Bee Time Vine, And Other Pieces 1913–1927* (New Haven: Yale University Press, 1953). Reprinted with the permission of the Estate of Gertrude Stein, through its Literary Executor Mr. Sanford Gann, Jr. of Levin & Gann, P.A.

Wallace Stevens, excerpt from "The Noble Rider and the Sound of Words" from *The Necessary Angel: Essays on Reality and the Imagination*. Copyright 1951 by Wallace Stevens. Reprinted with the permission of Alfred A. Knopf, a division of Random House, Inc.

Wislawa Szymborska, excerpt from "The Poet and the World" (Nobel Lecture, 1996), translated by Stanislaw Baranczak and Clare Cavanagh, from *Poems New and Collected 1957–1997*. English translation copyright © 1998 by Stanislaw Baranczak and Clare Cavanagh. Reprinted with the permission of Harcourt, Inc.

Allen Tate, excerpt from "To Whom Is the Poet Responsible?" from *Essays of Four Decades*. Copyright 1952 by Allen Tate. Reprinted with the permission of Ohio University Press/Swallow Press.

Paul Valéry, "The Art of Poetry," translated by Denise Folliot (New York: Vintage Books, Random House, 1961).

Derek Walcott, excerpt from Nobel Lecture (December 7, 1992), from *The Antilles: Fragments of Epic Memory*. Copyright © 1992 by The Nobel Foundation. Reprinted with the permission of Farrar, Straus & Giroux, LLC.

Phillis Wheatley, "On Imagination," in *Poems on Various Subjects, Religious and Moral* (Brooklyn: AMS Press Inc., 1976).

Whitman, Walt, "Preface to *Leaves of Grass*" and "*Song of Myself*, Stanza 2," *Leaves of Grass*, edited by Emory Holloway (Garden City, NY: Doubleday , 1926).

William Carlos Williams, excerpt from "The Poem as a Field of Action" from *Selected Essays of William Carlos Williams*. Copyright 1954 by William Carlos Williams. Reprinted with the permission of New Directions Publishing Corporation.

William Wordsworth, *Preface to Lyrical Ballads, Selected Poetry*, edited by Mark Van Doren, The Modern Library, 1950.

William Butler Yeats, "A General Introduction for My Work," in *Essays and Introductions* (New York: The Macmillan Company, 1961).

To the husbands:

Glen Brand, George Brown, *and* Victor Kumin

"If there is no meaning in it," said the King, "that saves a world of trouble, you know, as we needn't try to find any. And yet I don't know," he went on, spreading out the verses on his knee, and looking at them with one eye; "I seem to see some meaning in them, after all."

—*Lewis Carroll,*
Alice's Adventures
in Wonderland

CONTENTS

PART 2: *Making*

PART 3: *Mapping*

APPRECIATIONS

The editors thank Karol LaCroix, former dean of the University of New Hampshire at Manchester, and the Humanities Division of the university, for grants enabling us to prepare these materials.

We are especially grateful to Ellen Ruggles, administrative assistant at the University of New Hampshire at Manchester, for her faithful work on the manuscript and her unflagging attention to a thousand details and to P. J. Niver, who provided valuable assistance at the start of this project.

We also thank the library staff of the University of New Hampshire at Manchester and especially Heather Walker-White, interlibrary loan librarian, who persisted in tracking down many elusive essays for us.

Thanks also to Fred Courtright, who cheerfully checked and rechecked our sources.

PREFACE

Maxine Kumin

For several years I have been carrying around in my head the idea for a book not unlike the one you are just now opening. In my long shelf-life as a poet I have often been struck—amused, amazed, even made thoughtful—by the sharply opposing views of poets as contemporary as Language poets and as ancient as the Greeks and Romans who were our literary ancestors. The views of the practitioners were what I was after, not those of the detached and theoretical critics. The title I had in my head for this book that did not yet exist was *Lofty Dogmas,* very tongue-in-cheek of me. Why hadn't someone pulled all these essays by poets on poetics together when I needed them, teaching? When I wanted to show students how prejudiced, how flagrantly idiosyncratic, yet how deeply insightful the poets were about their craft? Of the two dozen or more semester-long creative writing seminars I've led, a few stand out as especially gratifying. The students had in common Marianne Moore's impatience "with all this fiddle," but grasped and clung to her image of "imaginary gardens with real toads in them" as a writing lifeline.

One class, all MFA candidates, met at dusk in an upstairs conference room of the library at the University of Miami. (One of the students was married to the head librarian.) There were eleven of us, and every-one always came. I remember that among their own creative assign-ments, these students were invited (required) to write essays on a variety of issues, for example, Hopkins's eccentric metrics, or Denise Levertov's concept of organic form, or the use of caesura in Milton's tightly knit lines . . . not long, formal papers, but enough to force their engagement. When we emerged three hours later into full night, we were still held by "the raw material of poetry in / all its rawness" and found it hard to separate in the parking lot, driving off to our individual destinations as if we were just coming to after a drug-induced sleep. What a boon a book like this would have been then! Undergraduates in my class at Brandeis in the spring of 1975, when I was Hurst Professor, were unspoiled and thirsty. If not innocent of opinion, they were still open to every nuance. Poetry to them was a rich stew, a bouillabaisse inviting them to pick apart and taste its several ingredients: what was an ode, an elegy? What was a sonnet, villanelle, sestina? What made blank verse blank, free verse free? They pored over the shaped poems of May Swenson and George Herbert; they read aloud Frost's and Browning's dramatic monologues and their own often moving early poems. I was awfully proud of them, these bright students, for their sustained interest in technique and their precocious understanding that though poetry begins in self-expression, it inevitably must address formal concerns.

"The mountain labored and brought forth a mouse," Horace admonishes any poet who tries to attain status by imitation or grandiosity or falls into inconsistency. It's a good metaphor to keep in mind as you write, I told them, counterbalanced by Rilke's soothing homilies to Mr. Kappus in *Letters to a Young Poet,* "Works of art are of an infinite loneliness and with nothing so little to be reached as with criticism." Do we all brag about our students' successes, their first-book awards, their plum teaching jobs? The quiet pleasure we take in their books arriving—one, nonfiction, from a former student at Princeton who had been involved in the sanctuary movement protecting illegals in Arizona, came with a note: "Dear Maxine: here is my long poem as promised." But back to the genesis of this book, which is far bigger and better than the one I grumbled over in my head. I first mentioned it to a poet-professor, Deborah Brown, who is my neighbor, give or take ten or so miles, which qualifies as neighborly in New Hampshire. We then appealed to poet Annie Finch, director of the University of Southern Maine's Stonecoast low-residency MFA program, to join us with her considerable expertise as an anthologist. What follows is a running account, only roughly chronological—for sometimes passion dictates that arguments face one another across a gap of years—of poets' essays on the subject of poetics. The main emphasis is on English and American poetry of our own era, with a bit of spice from other cultures for balance, and with some seminal essays and poems from early times. There is some spillage onto more public topics, commercial (i.e. conventional) versus experimental poetry, and the lacunae are numerous. I apologize to every professor and poet who is even now crossly riffling the table of contents and not finding his or her favorite essay by a poet we have omitted. Perhaps this book will invite the gestation of other texts that will fill in the blanks and expatiate further on the desire of poets to write about writing poems.

INTRODUCTION

Poets on Poetics

This book collects statements about poetry by poets. A glance at the table of contents will show that while we have included numerous acknowledged classics, from Horace's "Ars Poetica" to Shelley's "A Defence of Poetry" to Eliot's "Tradition and the Individual Talent," other selections are more eclectic: a shamanistic African song, a contemporary diatribe against National Poetry Month. Our aim has been not to compile a comprehensive history of world poetics, but rather to use our knowledge and instincts as poets to present a stimulating, challenging, and informative collection of remarks in poetry and prose. We hope that this book will at once educate poets and students of poetry in the traditions of the art, and stimulate them to fresh ways of thinking about poetics by showing the great variety of prejudices and convictions that poets hold about poetry.

Texts on the formal craft of poetry and anthologies of contemporary poetics abound, but we feel there is an as yet unmet need for a compilation of poetics by poets from different cultures, periods, and aesthetic schools. While the core of the book is made up of writings by English and American poets over the last two centuries, we have also included contributions from poets far apart in time and space, creating a conversation that ranges from Sappho to Stein, Wordsworth to Walcott, Po Chu-I to Pope. The goal of this inclusiveness has been to show at once the continuity between statements on poetics among poets of some widely differing eras and the persistence of certain ongoing debates over issues of poetics, including questions of diction, form, and the role of the poet.

We see this book as useful for poets of all levels of development and for professors not only in creative-writing courses but in literature courses and introduction to poetry courses. Since we are all poets ourselves, we are especially aware of its importance in the poetry-writing workshop, where it is all too easy for students immersed in the work of their peers to forget the centuries of poets who have struggled with the challenges of writing poetry before them. Our intent is to illuminate poets' doctrines and convictions from era to era, to flesh out the ghosts of bold claims as disparate, say, as Milton's defense of blank verse in the seventeenth century to William Carlos Williams's call for the death of iambic pentameter in the twentieth.

The book is divided into three sections, each of which concentrates on a favorite topic of poets writing on poetry. "Musing" concerns issues of inspiration; "Making," issues of craft, from diction to meter to persona and voice; and "Mapping," the role of poetry and the poet. While organization within each of the three sections is broadly chronological, we have kept these central topics fluid in order to allow for the most unexpected juxtapositions, the maximum cross-pollination between poets. For the benefit of teachers and readers who desire a more structured approach to making such connections, we have included an appendix with a listing of essays arranged according to more specific topics. Headnotes at the beginning of each selection provide background information about the poet and commentary on the significance of the selection. Keeping in mind the book's potential use from the introduction to poetry class at the freshman level to its in-depth use in MFA creative-writing workshops, we have focused in the headnotes on providing a brief biographical sketch that places the poet in his or her literary context. This book is intended to deepen readers' understanding of age-old poetic ideas while at the same time pointing out new directions for thinking about poetry, juxtaposing the familiar and the strange, reconfiguring old boundaries, and shaking up stereotypes.

PART 1
Musing

BARRY SPACKS

The Muse

The Muse came pulling off her gown
and nine feet tall she laid her down
and I at her side a popinjay
with nothing to say. Did she mean to stay?

She smelled like flame; like starch on sweat;
like sperm; like shame; like a launderette.
No one, she said, *has loved me right.*
Day and night. Day and night.

Musing

No art besides poetry has had such attention lavished on its sources of inspiration. The popular legend of the nine Muses, daughters of Mnemosyne (Memory), and the stories of the slopes of Parnassus, the Pierian Spring, and the winged horse Pegasus all testify to the fascination that poetic inspiration holds in the popular mind. Anthropologist Julian Jaynes suggests that poetry, because it combines left-brain linguistic capacity and right-brain rhythmic capacity, effects a unique balance between the unconscious and conscious. On the other hand, Nobel Prize–winning poet Wislawa Szymborska views poetic inspiration as part of the universal human capacity for losing oneself in the joy of a task.

There seem to be as many ways to love the Muse—almost invariably a female spirit for women as well as men poets—as there are poets willing to discuss their infatuation and its origin. Poets can sing endlessly about the wellspring, the source. And still the Muse laments, as does the Muse in Barry Spack's poem, that she has never been "loved right." And still poets wonder whether she will ever favor them again.

So poets have long courted the favor of the Muses, sometimes taking their existence for granted, like Sappho, and sometimes envisioning them in complex detail, like Spenser who, in the invocation to the Muse that opens *The Faerie Queene*, claims to be a humble writer of pastoral ("me, all too meane") who has just now been appointed by the sacred muse to exchange his shepherd's pipe for a trumpet. For some poets, however, inspiration is not an unadulterated good. The Devil who writes the poem Blake sees in his Vision, or the Imagination which seems to hold Phillis Wheatley at its mercy, are just as much a source of inspiration as the beneficent muse of classical antiquity. The less gentle side of the muse inspires Lorca's idea of the duende, which lives "in the remotest mansions of the blood." This spirit has had a powerful hold on twentieth-century poets, calling forth radical changes in forms and smashing old styles with abandon. As Nathaniel Mackey explains, the duende is a complex, ambiguous force, far from the blandly angelic muse that has appeared in so many European paintings.

Sidney and Bradstreet, in their different ways, follow convention in claiming their verse is spontaneous, comes from the heart, and is as natural as childbirth. Joy Harjo describes her poem coming quickly and easily, with the poem's central character standing beside her, urging her on. On the other hand, poets often embrace the challenge of getting their inspiration the hard way. Seamus Heaney, at his desk, has a vision of his grandfather and his father digging potatoes in the old tradition. At the end of his hallmark poem "Digging" he is happy to have defined writing as an agricultural pursuit and to have taken his place in the procession.

As T. S. Eliot's classic essay makes plain, the long line of poets who have formed the canon we revere offers a poet challenge, confirmation, and a heightened sense of where he or she ultimately fits in the tradition. But, he adds, tradition cannot be inherited. It must be earned through the labor of studying past writers. For anyone who wants to continue as a poet past the age of twenty-five, a historical sense is necessary, and not only a sense of the past as past, but also an awareness of it as present in our time and in our literature.

Maxine Kumin's essay distinguishes between the poems that overtake the poet and those that must be brought forth with a more conscious effort. As the Elizabethan Sir Philip Sidney says, often "words come halting forth, wanting Invention's stay." Rarely is it a simple matter of "Fool . . . look in thy heart and write," as he puts it in the disarming ending to this famous sonnet. If a poem or a book of poems is a "child" as Puritan poet Anne Bradstreet would have it, that child may end up being "ill-formed" and the labor can be long and hard.

Still, the image of the lyric poet as a person open to inspiration is an appealing one. Coleridge's "Kubla Khan" was delivered verbatim in an opium dream; many of the Beat Poets revved up on illegal stimulants. Emerson speaks ambiguously of the poet's "unlocking, at all risks, his human doors and suffering the ethereal tides to roll and circulate through him," which, he adds, is the reason "bards love wine, mead, narcotics, coffee, tea, opium." Later, he advises that the poet "should be tipsy with water." The wholehearted embrace of experience that marked Romanticism seemed revolutionary when it manifested itself in Keats's negative capability: in his own words, "when a man is capable of being in uncertainties." Thus the true source of inspiration is a timeless openness, independent of aesthetic movements. It may not be a simple process when a poet is aware of language's psychological and political obstacles, as is Theresa Hak Kyung Cha. To speak Cha's native language, Korean, was punishable by death during thirty-six years of colonization by the Japanese. Cha's book, *Dictée,* is about the difficulty of making poetry when even to speak is a severe challenge. But whatever the obstacles, many poets would no doubt agree with Rilke that the core part of our job is simply to remain quiet enough so that the words of the muse, inspiration, the duende, one's own heart, one's child, one's language, or nature can be heard.

MOIRA EGAN

Moira Egan (1962–) was born in Baltimore, Maryland. Her father, the poet Michael Egan (whose work was published primarily in Ireland) was the first of the family to attend university, but Egan grew up among voracious readers, surrounded by, and in love with, books. At Bryn Mawr she majored in German literature because the idea of studying English seemed too daunting, but eventually she re-found her footing as a poet and went off to Columbia, where James Merrill chose her MFA thesis for the David Craig Austin Prize. After working in New York for many years, the opportunity arose to teach in Greece, and so she followed her muse to that mythopoetic landscape. Currently, she directs the creative-writing program in a public high school in Baltimore.

Cleave, Egan's first book of poems, was published in 2004 and was nominated for the National Book Award. In part due to the influence of her father's formal aesthetic, Egan's work questions the philosophical underpinnings of various received forms, their use either as a naturally supportive foundation for the content of the poem, or as a device to achieve ironic tension between form and content. There has long been a war within her between an "inner formalist" and her free-wheeling, unconventional self: recent poems are, finally, an attempt to work the freedom of thought, the juiciness of language, and the messiness of emotion into and through fixed, as well as interestingly exploded, forms.

To My Muse, Upon Her Return

O Muse,
sweet red jazz juice,
featherboa attitude,

where have you been?
A mystery to me,
your sporadic telegraphy

and how to please
Thee. Now, down on my knees,
most supple supplication, I offer you the keys

to my place. Tell me, what do I do to entice
you to stay and play nice?
In my house I keep no ice,

I tend to fire:
blue sparks along coiled electric wires
and the slow smoke incense of desire.

Is that it? Like love, it's only chemical?
a perfect fit of molecules
one into the other, sweetly nestled?

Big hands in the small of my back,
a kiss so luscious the room turns black
and the ticking of the clock

for a moment stills.
You come, and go, regardless of will.
Tears, libations, heart, what shall I spill

to keep you here with me?
you who make love in normal people,
and in me poetry.

HORACE
(QUINTUS HORATIUS FLACCUS)

As a young man, Horace, Quintus Horatius Flaccus, (65–8 b.c.) studied philosophy in Athens. When civil war broke out, he enlisted in Brutus's army, fighting in the battle of Philippi. Impoverished after this defeat, he came under the wing of Maecenas, a wealthy Roman politician, who became his, as well as Virgil's, patron. Maecenas bought Sabine Farm, a retreat where Horace was then at liberty to write for the rest of his life. Ultimately, Horace, whose often autobiographical works dealt with moral and political issues, became the most celebrated poet of the Augustan Age; Dante listed him third after Homer and Virgil in his *Divine Comedy*. His *Odes* and *Epodes,* descended from Greek lyrics such as Sappho's, were the models for seventeenth-century poets as diverse as Herrick and Marvell.

Ars Poetica is important historically as a major piece of Roman literary criticism and as a practitioner's guide. It is a series of wittily expressed maxims for the guidance of young poets, which set forth Horace's literary theory and his views on formal aspects of craft, both poetic and dramatic. His critical judgments stress the values of proportion, good sense, and decorum. Translated into the vernacular tongues of western Europe, Horace's *Ars Poetica* became the starting point for Renaissance literary criticism.

This selection, taken from the longest of Horace's poems, is found in nearly all manuscripts under the title *Ars Poetica*. Yet the composition is a letter rather than a formal treatise, and Horace himself was probably not responsible for the conventional title. The poem has the discursive and occasionally personal tone of an Epistle but not the completeness, precision, and logical order of a well-constructed treatise. Like other Epistles and Sermones, it is an expression of reflections, suggested by special circumstances, upon an art which concerned one or more of the persons addressed, in this case a father and two sons of the Piso family.

from Book Two, Epistle III, To the Pisos

THE ART OF POETRY:
NOTES FOR ASPIRING POETS AND PLAYWRIGHTS

Suppose some painter had the bright idea
Of sticking a human head on a horse's neck
And covering human nether limbs up with
Assorted feathers so that a beautiful
Woman uptop was an ugly fish below,
And you were invited in to take a look,
How could you possibly manage to keep a straight face?
Dear Pisos, dear friends, a poem's exactly like
Such pictures as those, when the poet's fantasies
Are like a sick man's raving dreams in which
You can't tell head from foot nor what it is
That they're attached to. "Poets and painters," you say,
"Have the right to do whatever they dare to do."
Well, yes. We poets claim that right for ourselves
And recognize that other artists have it.
But it doesn't go so far as mixing up
Savage and civilized, mating tigers and lambs,
Or having serpents get it on with birds.
There are works that begin in genuine nobleness
And therefore make large genuine promises
Yet sometimes they're stuck about with shining purple
Patches that catch the eye: for example, a pause
To tell you all about Diana's grove,
Or "the stream that winds yet hastens through the fields,"
Or to have you admire the far-off scenic Rhine
Or the rainbow you can see when the storm is over.
There are places for things like these, but often not
In the places where they occur. If what you know

Is how to draw the picture of a cypress,
That's not much use if what you're paid to do
Is to paint the picture of a panicked sailor
Swimming away from the sinking wreck of his ship.
Why does what was supposed to turn out to be
A wine jar, when the job began, turn out,
When the pottery wheel stops turning, to be a jug?
In short, whatever the work is supposed to be,
Let it be true to itself, essentially simple.

Father and worthy sons, we poets often
Know what we're aiming at, and often we miss.
I try my best to be terse, and I'm obscure;
I try for mellifluous smoothness, smooth as can be,
And the line comes out as spineless as a worm;
One poet, aiming for grandeur, booms and blusters;
Another one, scared, creeps his way under the storm;
And another, desiring to vary his single theme
In wonderful ways, produces not wonders but monsters—
Dolphins up in the trees, pigs in the ocean.
If you don't know what you're doing you can go wrong
Just out of trying to do your best to do right.
Down near the Aemilian School there's a craftsman's shop
Where he's very good at imitating in bronze
Things like toenails, say, or wavy hair,
But it turns out badly because in fact he isn't
Any good at all at doing the whole body.
If I wanted to write a poem, I'd no more want
To be like him than if I were happy to live with
My nose all crooked and funny, just because
I was praised for my shining dark eyes and lustrous hair.

Aspiring writer, be sure to be careful to pick
Material that you're strong enough to handle;
Give careful consideration to the question
Of what your shoulders can carry and what they can't.
The man who does this will find he doesn't have trouble
Thinking of what to say and in what order.
Order's important: the virtue and beauty of some
Long-promised poem, unless I'm mistaken, often
Depends on the author having judiciously chosen
To say the thing that ought to be said right now,
And keeping other things back for later on,
Favoring one thing over against another.

And furthermore, if you're shrewd about how to do it,
And do it very carefully, you can work it
So that the context makes a word that's worn
From being too familiar seem brand-new;
And if it comes about that you have to invent
New words because your subject's so abstract
Or recondite, you can invent new words
The Cethegi in their loincloths never heard of,
And you'll get away with it, as long as you do it
Circumspectly—you can get by with words
Recently coined if you get them from the Greek,
And if you don't attempt to *over*do it.
Why on earth should Caecilius and Plautus
Be allowed to do what Virgil and Varius aren't?
And why should I be sneered at if I try
To add my little bit, when Ennius and Cato
Gave us new names for things, and doing so made
Our language by what they did so much the richer?
It's always been allowed, and always will be,

To introduce new words, fresh from the mint.
Just as in forests in the changing year
New leaves come in and the oldest drop away,
So is it with words: the old ones die away
And the new ones bloom and prosper in their time.
We and all that we do are bound to die—
The royal work that welcomes in the sea,
Sheltering fleets from storms in man-made bays;
The useless swamp, once fit for nothing but oars,
Now fit for the plow, and nourishing its towns;
The river once the ruiner of fields
Now taught the art of going its harmless way—
All things that mortals do and build are mortal;
How mortal then the glories of our speech.
Words that have fallen away may rise again;
Words now in honor may fall, if Use, which is
The governor of our language, should decide.

And don't begin your poem the way the old
Cyclic "Homeric" poets saw fit to do it:
"I sing of the famous war and Priam's fate."
What's to come out of the mouth of such a boaster?
The mountain labored and brought forth a mouse.
Ridiculous. He does much better who doesn't
Try so hard or make such grandiose claims:
"Muse, tell me about the man who, after Troy,
Witnessed the ways of men in other places. "
His aim is light from smoke, not smoke from fire,
To make the wonders he tells of—Scylla, Charybdis,
Antiphates, the Cyclops—shine more brightly.
To tell Diomedes' story he doesn't think
He has to start with the death of the hero's uncle,
Or start, in telling about the Trojan War,

By telling us how Helen came out of an egg.
He goes right to the point and carries the reader
Into the midst of things, as if known already;
And if there's material that he despairs of presenting
So as to shine for us, he leaves it out;
And he makes his whole poem one. What's true, what's invented,
Beginning, middle, and end, all fit together.

* * *

Poetry wants to instruct or else to delight;
Or, better still, to delight and instruct at once.
As for instruction, make it succinct, so the mind
Can quickly seize on what's being taught and hold it;
Every superfluous word spills out of a full mind.
As for delight, in what you invent stay close
To actuality; your fable shouldn't
Feel free to ask your audience to credit
Just anything whatsoever, no matter what:
Produce no human babies from monsters' bellies.
The elders in the audience reject
The work that yields no profitable wisdom,
The young aristocrats what yields no pleasure.
He who provides to all both profit and pleasure
Wins everybody's vote: his book will bring
Money for bookstore owners and fame across
The seas and down the years to the author himself.

PO CHU-I

Po Chu-I (772–846), a Chinese poet of the Tang dynasty, held a number of government posts and served as president of the Imperial Board of War. Although he had a classical education and was an advisor to the emperor, he was nevertheless banished for arguing against certain repressive government policies, such as the grain tax, which was clearly discriminatory. Deeply concerned with social problems and with questionable religious practices, he wrote over three thousand poems, many of them brief topical verses in clear language. His "Song of Everlasting Regret" records the sufferings of Emperor Ming Huang after the murder of his concubine by rebels; this poem figures in the famous tenth-century Japanese *Tales of Genji* by Murasaki. His sympathy with the oppressed appears in his perhaps best-known poem, "The Charcoal Seller," which describes a life of hard work and of vulnerability to corrupt officials. While he grieved deeply over the death of his mother and his young daughter, he spent three years as a recluse. To critique his poems, he tested them on an old country woman and rejected anything she could not understand.

This selection, "Madly Singing in the Mountains," is a poem in praise of poetry, a lyrical voice raised in a pastoral setting despite or even in tribute to his banishment from the province. In it, Po Chu-I honors his muse and rejoices in the lifelong act of composing poems. In 832, he retired to a monastery where he accepted Buddhist practices that encouraged serenity and peace. "Done adoring it; done loathing it; / So we begin boundless and free," he wrote.

Madly Singing in the Mountains

There is no one among men that has not a special failing:

and my failing consists in writing verses.

I have broken away from the thousand ties of life:

But this infirmity still remains behind.

Each time that I look at a fine landscape:

Each time that I meet a loved friend,

I raise my voice and recite a stanza of poetry

And am glad as though a God had crossed my path.

Ever since the day I was banished to Hsün-yang

Half my time I have lived among the hills.

And often, when I have finished a new poem,

Alone I climb the road to the Eastern Rock.

I lean my body on the banks of white stone:

I pull down with my hands a green cassia branch.

My mad singing startles the valleys and hills:

The apes and birds all come to peep.

Fearing to become a laughing-stock to the world,

I choose a place that is unfrequented by men.

SAPPHO

Sappho (630 b.c.–570 b.c.) is generally considered the greatest early Greek lyric poet. Facts about her life are few. Plato called her "the tenth Muse," a term that has since been applied to numerous women poets down the centuries, reminding us that women were long thought, in Andrew Lang's words, "meant to inspire poetry rather than to create it." She was born into a prosperous family of wine merchants on Lesbos, a major cultural center where women were more educated and had more freedom than elsewhere in Greece. Orphaned at age six, Sappho is thought to have started a school for young women, and eventually became renowned for the poetry she wrote for her circle of friends and students. A lesbian by preference, she had one daughter, Cleis, whose father may have been a merchant named Cercylas.

Sappho wrote in the Aeolic dialect with great skill in a variety of meters, one of which, the Sapphic stanza, is named after her. Her poems are emotionally direct and usually concern the joy, pain, and complications of love. In the third and second centuries b.c., her poetry was edited and collected into nine papyrus books. Her work was revered for several centuries and influenced the Roman poets Catullus, Ovid, and Horace. But the scribes who transcribed papyri into books in the fifth century a.d. ignored her poetry, and sexism caused it to be forgotten until the 1890s. Though only brief, tantalizing fragments of the poems survived this neglect, Sappho remains one of the world's central poets. She was accurate when she wrote of herself and her followers, "I think that someone will remember us in another time." This fragment of a poem, addressed to Cleis with characteristic directness and emotional vividness, shows to what extent the Muses were a regular part of life in Sappho's circle.

No Room for Grief

It is not appropriate, in a household
given to the Muses. No! Lamentation
does not belong here.

Translation by Annie Finch

SIR PHILIP SIDNEY

Sir Philip Sidney (1554–86) was born in Kent of a powerful family. His father was Lord Deputy (governor) of Ireland, his uncle was Queen Elizabeth's favorite, the Earl of Leicester, and his godfather was King Philip II of Spain. He left Oxford before completing his degree and traveled throughout Europe, studying languages, music, and astronomy and serving on several diplomatic missions. On his return to England, he became a leading member of Queen Elizabeth's court and was considered a model of the Renaissance man: dashing, handsome, strong, and brilliant. He exerted a strong influence on English poetry as critic and patron. Most importantly, he encouraged Edmund Spenser, who dedicated *The Shepheardes Calendar* to him.

Sidney's poems were unpublished during his tragically brief lifetime and were circulated only in manuscript, not an uncommon situation for courtier-poets. *Astrophil and Stella,* a sequence of 108 sonnets and eleven songs, was presumably inspired by Sidney's love for Penelope Devereux. However, in 1583, he married Frances Walsingham, the daughter of Sir Francis Walsingham. The famous sonnet reprinted here describes Sidney's views on the sources of inspiration. In emphasizing the importance of the poet's individual "heart," the sonnet is one of the earliest manifestations of the modern view of the poet as a highly sensitive individual, a view which became common in the Romantic period and still reigns today.

Sidney's *The Defence of Poesie* was the first philosophical defense of poetry in English. Sidney makes an ethical argument for the value of literature on the grounds that it teaches the ability to make judgments. And, his argument continues, good judgment in turn leads to wiser action. He may have written this treatise in response to a Puritanical attack on poets, "The School of Abuse," dedicated to him by its author, Stephen Gosson.

Sidney served several years in court, acting as unofficial ambassador to the German emperor and the Prince of Orange, helping Queen Elizabeth recruit allies for a Protestant league. He also served in Parliament before he was dismissed from court, perhaps for opposing Elizabeth's marriage to the Roman Catholic Duke of Anjou. He then stayed with his sister, the poet Mary Sidney Herbert, Countess of Pembroke. At her estate, Wilton, he wrote the prose romance "The

Arcadia," considered by some the first English novel. After being shot in the leg by a musket while fighting the Spanish, he died at the age of thirty-one from gangrene. Mary Herbert combined *The Arcadia* with a later unfinished version and published it after Sidney's death; it is now known as *The Countess of Pembroke's Arcadia*. Mary Herbert also completed Sidney's translation of the Psalms into English in hopes of encouraging England to become a defender of the Protestant faith in Europe.

from Astrophil and Stella

I

Loving in truth, and faine in verse my love to show,
That She, dear She might take some pleasure of my paine:
Pleasure might cause her reade, reading might make her know,
Knowledge might pitie winne, and pitie grace obtaine,
    I sought fit words to paint the blackest face of woe,
Studying inventions fine, her wits to entertaine.
Oft turning others' leaves, to see if thence would flow
Some fresh and fruitful showers upon my sunne-burn'd braine.
    But words came halting forth, wanting Invention's stay,
Invention, Nature's child, fled step-dame Studie's blowes,
And others' feete still seem'd but strangers in my way.
Thus great with child to speake, and helplesse in my throwes,
Biting my trewant pen, beating my selfe for spite,
"Foole," said my Muse to me, "looke in thy heart and write."

EDMUND SPENSER

Edmund Spenser (1552/53–99)was called "prince of poets" by his peers and is often referred to today as a "poet's poet" because of his magnificent ear and intense imagination. Revered by Milton and Keats, he was born in London, England, to a poor family. Schooled in part with charity funds, he earned a BA and MA from Cambridge and soon after began working for the Earl of Leicester. There he met the poet Philip Sidney and others of Queen Elizabeth's court and wrote *The Shepheardes Calendar*. A pastoral, it was the traditional first step for a poet with ambitions to emulate the ancient epic poets.

In 1580 Spenser became secretary to Lord Grey, the lord deputy of Ireland. There he wrote the first three books of *The Faerie Queene*, which Sir Walter Raleigh persuaded him to publish. The poem was immediately popular. Spenser married Elizabeth Boyle in 1594 and wrote the beautiful *Epithalamion* in honor of his wedding. Exiled from Ireland by political uprisings and impoverished, he died in London in 1599. Weeping poets carried his coffin and threw pens and poems into his grave, and he is buried next to Chaucer in Westminster Abbey.

The Faerie Queene, which Spenser intended to be a poem in twelve books after the model of Homer and Virgil, is an allegory of Christian virtues and Arthurian legend, dedicated to Queen Elizabeth and encompassing a panorama of fantastic creatures and tales. The poem is a tour de force because of its complex architecture, its unique language, and the wonderful "Spenserian stanza" he invented for the poem, still used by poets today. The stanza has nine lines. Eight are ten-syllable lines, rhyming ABAB BCBC; the ninth line has twelve syllables and repeats the C rhyme, closing the stanza.

In this invocation, Spenser explains how he has abandoned the pastoral voice of *The Shepheardes Calendar* and asks the blessing of the Muse, Cupid, and Queen Elizabeth (known widely as "the Virgin Queen") on his epic poem. The purposely antique language, one of the poem's chief beauties, is meant to echo the world of Chaucer and the Arthurian tales.

Invocation to the Faerie Queene

1

Lo! I the man, whose Muse whilome did maske,
    As time her taught, in lowly Shepheards weeds,
    Am now enforst a far unfitter taske,
    For trumpets sterne to chaunge mine Oaten reeds,
    And sing of Knights and Ladies gentle deeds;
    Whose prayses having slept in silence long,
    Me, all too meane, the sacred Muse areeds
    To blazon broad emongst her learned throng:
Fierce warres and faithfull loves shall moralize my song.

2

Helpe then, ô holy Virgin chiefe of nine,
    Thy weaker Nouice to performe thy will,
    Lay forth out of thine euerlasting scryne
    The antique rolles, which there lye hidden still,
    Of Faerie knights and fairest Tanaquill,
    Whom that most noble Briton Prince so long
    Sought through the world, and suffered so much ill,
    That I must rue his undeserved wrong:
O helpe thou my weake wit, and sharpen my dull tong.

3

And thou most dreaded impe of highest Jove,
    Faire Venus sonne, that with thy cruell dart
    At that good knight so cunningly didst roue,
    That glorious fire it kindled in his hart,
    Lay now thy deadly Heben bow apart,

And with thy mother milde come to mine ayde:
Come both, and with you bring triumphant Mart,
In loves and gentle jollities arrayd,
After his murdrous spoiles and bloudy rage allayd.

4

And with them eke, ô Goddesse heavenly bright,
Mirrour of grace and Majestie divine,
Great Lady of the greatest Isle, whose light
Like Phoebus lampe throughout the world doth shine,
Shed thy faire beames into my feeble eyne,
And raise my thoughtes too humble and too vile,
To thinke of that true glorious type of thine,
The argument of mine afflicted stile:
The which to heare, vouchsafe, O dearest dread awhile. . . .

WILLIAM BLAKE

William Blake (1757–1827) was born in London where his father ran a hosiery shop. The third of five children, William went to school just long enough to learn to read and write and began writing poetry when he was twelve. Seeing his artistic talent, his father apprenticed him to an engraver. After attending the Royal Academy of Art and rebelling against the rigid atmosphere, he started his own engraving business. In 1782 he married Catherine Boucher, whom he taught to read, write, and draw and who helped him in all his work. *Poetical Sketches* (1783), Blake's first book, was the only one published conventionally during his lifetime. He and Catherine published all his other major poetry, beginning with *Songs of Innocence* (1789), using a method of engraving text and illustration on the same copper plates, which he said was revealed to him in a dream. Blake engraved the words and pictures, usually on a very small scale; Catherine did the printing, hand-colored the pictures, and bound the books.

Blake's paintings and engravings, notably his illustrations of his own poetry, works by Milton, and the Book of Job in the Old Testament are compellingly realistic in their representation of the body and other natural forms. But Blake was a follower of the mystics Emanuel Swedenborg and Jacob Boehme, and from childhood on he saw and talked with angels and depicted them in his artwork. He saw himself as a prophet and deliberately wrote in the style of the Hebrew prophets, championing love and pure liberty, and decrying the rationalist philosophy that justified the oppressions and inequalities brought on by the Industrial Revolution. An ardent sympathizer with revolutionary forces and a friend of Thomas Paine, he incorporated the French and American revolutions into his mythology in the poems *Europe: A Prophecy* and *America: A Prophecy.* His other books include *Songs of Experience* (1794), *The Book of Thel* (1789), *The Book of Urizon* (1794), *The Book of Los* (1795), *Milton* (1804–8), and "Jerusalem" (1804–20). Virtually unknown during his life, he lived in near poverty, died unrecognized, and was dismissed as an eccentric for a long time after his death. Today, however, Blake is venerated as a great artistic figure, and poems such as "Tyger, Tyger," "Jerusalem," and "Auguries of Innocence" are an indelible part of English poetry. *The Marriage of Heaven and Hell* (c. 1790), from which this excerpt is taken, presents, like his other work, a vision in which energy and imagination struggle with the physical and mental forces of oppression and in which direct inspiration is the foundation of truth and value.

from The Marriage of Heaven and Hell

PLATE 6-7
A MEMORABLE FANCY

As I was walking among the fires of hell, delighted with the enjoyments of Genius which to Angels look like torment and insanity . . . I collected some of their Proverbs: thinking that as the sayings used in a nation, mark its character, so the Proverbs of Hell, shew the nature of Infernal wisdom better than any description of buildings or garments.

When I came home; on the abyss of the five senses, where a flat sided steep frowns over the present world. I saw a mighty Devil folded in black clouds, hovering on the sides of the rock, with corroding fires he wrote the following sentence now perceived by the minds of men, and read by them on earth.

How do you know but ev'ry Bird that cuts the airy way,
Is an immense world of delight, clos'd by your senses five?

PLATE 15-17
A MEMORABLE FANCY

I was in a Printing house in Hell and saw the method in which knowledge is transmitted from generation to generation.

In the first chamber was a Dragon-Man, clearing away the rubbish from a cave's mouth; within, a number of Dragons were hollowing the cave.

In the second chamber was a Viper folding round the rock and the cave, and others adorning it with gold silver and precious stones.

In the third chamber was an Eagle with wings and feathers of air: he caused the inside of the cave to be infinite, around were numbers of Eagle like men, who built palaces in the immense cliffs.

In the fourth chamber were Lions of flaming fire raging around and melting the metals into living fluids.

In the fifth chamber were Unnam'd forms, which cast the metals into the expanse.

There they were receiv'd by Men who occupied the sixth chamber, and took the forms of books and were arranged in libraries. . . .

ANNE BRADSTREET

Anne Bradstreet (1612–72) is considered the first poet of note in North America. Although her first sixteen years were spent in a comfortable manor house in the English countryside, she made a three-month long crossing of the Atlantic with her family and settled in the Puritan colony of Massachusetts Bay where her father, Thomas Dudley, participated in governing the new colony. After an early marriage, she gave birth to eight children, all of whom survived, and struggled to adjust to the primitive conditions of her life in the wilderness. Her writing imitated male poetic models, and her first book is full of heroic couplets, elaborate conceits, and extended metaphors. Her later work reflects her experiences living in seventeenth-century New England as a wife, mother, and grandmother.

The Tenth Muse, her first collection, was taken to England and published there by her brother-in-law, without her knowledge, or so she claimed. In fact Anne Bradstreet was adroit at avoiding the criticism she (and her husband) might have received if she had appeared ambitious. Like Anne Hopkins and other intellectual Puritan women, she could have been labeled dangerous and punished by Puritan authorities, who enforced their belief that women should devote their energy to home, family, and God.

In "The Author to Her Book," her prologue to a second edition of *The Tenth Muse,* Bradstreet, comparing her book to a poor, illegitimate, and deformed child, humbly begs that the child be tolerated by its betters. We will never know for sure how strategic Bradstreet's plaintive description really was, but there's no doubt it sounds wittily ironic to readers today.

The Author to Her Book

Thou ill-form'd offspring of my feeble brain,
Who after birth did'st by my side remain,
Till snatcht from thence by friends, less wise than true,
Who thee abroad expos'd to public view,
Made thee in rags, halting to th' press to trudge,
Where errors were not lessened (all may judge).
At thy return my blushing was not small,
My rambling brat (in print) should mother call.
I cast thee by as one unfit for light,
Thy Visage was so irksome in my sight,
Yet being mine own, at length affection would
Thy blemishes amend, if so I could.
I wash'd thy face, but more defects I saw,
And rubbing off a spot, still made a flaw.
I stretcht thy joints to make thee even feet,
Yet still thou run'st more hobbling than is meet.
In better dress to trim thee was my mind,
But nought save home-spun Cloth, i' th' house I find.
In this array, 'mongst Vulgars mayst thou roam.
In Critics' hands, beware thou dost not come,
And take thy way where yet thou art not known.
If for thy Father askt, say, thou hadst none;
And for thy Mother, she alas is poor,
Which caus'd her thus to send thee out of door.

PHILLIS WHEATLEY

The first African American poet to publish a book, Phillis Wheatley (1753–84) was born in West Africa, probably in what is now Senegal. She was stolen by slave-traders at about the age of seven and brought on a slave ship to Boston, where she was purchased by a wealthy tailor, John Wheatley, as a personal slave for his wife Susanna. Phillis Wheatley learned to read and write English from the Wheatleys and studied Latin and Greek. With their support, she read the Bible and the poetry of Milton, Pope, and Gray, and began to write her own poems by the age of thirteen.

Phillis Wheatley was widely recognized as a prodigy after her elegy on the death of the evangelical preacher George Whitfield was published as a broadside in Boston, New York, Philadelphia, and London. Always somewhat frail, she traveled to England with the Wheatleys for relief from her asthma in 1771. She was well received in London, and in 1773, Susanna Wheatley, with the cooperation of Countess of Huntingdon, arranged for a printing there of thirty-nine of Wheatley's poems under the title, *Poems on Various Subjects, Religious and Moral*. The book includes many elegies as well as poems on Christian themes and poems dealing with race, such as the often-anthologized "On Being Brought from Africa to America." Shortly after their return to the United States, both of the Wheatleys died and Phillis Wheatley was freed.

In 1776, Wheatley published a letter and poem in honor of George Washington. In reply, Washington sent an invitation to visit him in Cambridge, stating that he would be "happy to see a person so favored by the muses." Two years later, Wheatley married John Peters, owner of a grocery store. They had three children, but the family was not able to survive financially, and the harsh conditions of poverty contributed to the deaths of the three children. In that climate of war and economic uncertainty, Wheatley had trouble publishing her poems. She tried to find subscribers for a new book that was to include thirty-three new poems and thirteen letters, but could not raise sufficient funds. She died alone in a boarding house at the age of thirty-one. Many of the poems for the proposed second book of poems disappeared after her death and have not been found.

On Imagination

Thy various works, imperial queen, we see,
How bright their forms! how deck'd with pomp by thee!
Thy wond'rous acts in beauteous order stand,
And all attest how potent is thine hand.
From *Helicon's* refulgent heights attend,
Ye sacred choir, and my attempts befriend:
To tell her glories with a faithful tongue,
Ye blooming graces, triumph in my song.

     Now here, now there, the roving *Fancy* flies,
Till some lov'd object strikes her wand'ring eyes,
Whose silken fetters all the senses bind,
And soft captivity involves the mind.

     Imagination! who can sing thy force?
Or who describe the swiftness of thy course?
Soaring through air to find the bright abode,
Th' empyreal palace of the thund'ring God,
We on thy pinions can surpass the wind,
And leave the rolling universe behind:
From star to star the mental optics rove,
Measure the skies, and range the realms above.
There in one view we grasp the mighty whole,
Or with new worlds amaze th' unbounded soul.

     Though *Winter* frowns to *Fancy's* raptur'd eyes
The fields may flourish, and gay scenes arise;
The frozen deeps may break their iron bands,
And bid their waters murmur o'er the sands.
Fair *Flora* may resume her fragrant reign,
And with her flow'ry riches deck the plain;
Sylvanus may diffuse his honours round,
And all the forest may with leaves be crown'd:

Show'rs may descend, and dews their gems disclose,
And nectar sparkle on the blooming rose.

Such is thy pow'r, nor are thine orders vain,
O thou the leader of the mental train:
In full perfection all thy works are wrought,
And thine the sceptre o'er the realms of thought.
Before thy throne the subject-passions bow,
Of subject-passions sov'reign ruler thou;
At thy command joy rushes on the heart,
And through the glowing veins the spirits dart.

Fancy might now her silken pinions try
To rise from earth, and sweep th' expanse on high:
From *Tithon's* bed now might *Aurora* rise,
Her cheeks all glowing with celestial dies,
While a pure stream of light o'erflows the skies.
The monarch of the day I might behold,
And all the mountains tipt with radiant gold,
But I reluctant leave the pleasing views,
Which *Fancy* dresses to delight the *Muse;*
Winter austere forbids me to aspire,
And northern tempests damp the rising fire;
They chill the tides of *Fancy's* flowing sea,
Cease then, my song, cease the unequal lay.

SAMUEL TAYLOR COLERIDGE

Samuel Taylor Coleridge (1772–1834) was born in Devonshire, England, the youngest of ten children. His father died when he was nine, and he was sent to a London charity school where he excelled, met his lifelong friend Charles Lamb, and began writing poems. He attended Cambridge but, after incurring some debts, ran away to join the Light Dragoons using the name Silas Tomkyn Comberbacke. His friends and brothers purchased his discharge, beginning a pattern of financial trouble and rescue that continued throughout his life. With Robert Southey, Coleridge then planned a utopian commune that failed for financial reasons. Coleridge married Southey's fiancée's sister but asked for and obtained a legal separation from her a few years later.

In 1796 Coleridge published his first book, *Poems on Various Subjects*, and another volume, *Poems*, a year later. He also briefly published a liberal political periodical, *The Watchman*. In 1798 he and poet William Wordsworth jointly published *Lyrical Ballads*, an event conventionally credited as the beginning of the English Romantic movement. Soon after, Coleridge traveled to Germany with William and his sister Dorothy Wordsworth to study German. He fell in love with the sister of Wordsworth's future wife, Sara Hutchinson, with whom he wrote and edited a literary and political magazine, *The Friend*. About this time, he began lecturing on literary and political subjects and obtained a reputation as a major Shakespearian critic. By 1810 his friendship with Wordsworth began to decline after a dispute on poetic diction.

In the course of an illness, Coleridge became addicted to opium, and although he made many efforts, he never broke the drug's hold on him. His friend Charles Lamb described him as an "archangel a little damaged." Lamb, along with many other writers of his time, believed that Coleridge had the greatest genius among them. Though it can be argued that Coleridge's career never matched his gifts or his ambitions, his haunting narratives, *The Rime of the Ancient Mariner* and *Christabel*, and such meditative poems as *Frost at Midnight*, hold key places in English poetry. Many other poems—including the famous *Kubla Khan*, written in an opium dream from which he, Coleridge, was awakened by "a man from Porlock," interrupting the poem—forever exist as brilliant fragments. The *Biographia Literaria* is an influential compendium

of Coleridge's thought on many topics, including his relationship with
Wordsworth, the ideals of the Romantic movement, and Coleridge's
spiritual journey. He died in 1834, leaving only books and manuscripts.
He wrote the following lines for his own epitaph:

> A poet lies; or that which once was he.
> O lift one thought in prayer for S. T. C.
> That he, who many a year with toil of breath
> Found Death in Life, may here find Life in Death.

from Preface to Kubla Khan

. . . In the summer of the year 1797, the Author, then in ill health, had
retired to a lonely farmhouse between Porlock and Lynton, on the
Exmoor confines of Somerset and Devonshire. In consequence of a slight
indisposition, an anodyne had been prescribed, from the effects of which
he fell asleep in his chair at the moment he was reading the following sentence, or words of the same substance, in "Purchas's Pilgrimage": "Here
the Khan Kubla commanded a palace to be built, and a stately garden
thereunto. And thus ten miles of fertile ground were inclosed with a wall."
The Author continued for about three hours in a profound sleep, at least
of the external senses, during which time he had the most vivid confidence, that he could not have composed less than from two to three hundred lines; if that indeed can be called composition in which all the images
rose up before him as *things,* with a parallel production of the correspondent expressions, without any sensation or consciousness of effort. On
awaking he appeared to himself to have a distinct recollection of the
whole, and taking his pen, ink, and paper, instantly and eagerly wrote
down the lines that are here preserved. At this moment he was unfortunately called out by a person on business from Porlock, and detained by
him above an hour, and on his return to his room, found, to his no small
surprise and mortification, that though he still retained some value and
dim recollection of the general purport of the vision, yet, with the exception of some eight or ten scattered lines and images, all the rest had passed
away like the images on the surface of a stream into which a stone had
been cast, but alas! without the after restoration of the latter! . . .

JOHN KEATS

John Keats's (1795–1821) tragically short life began near London. His father, a livery-stable keeper, died when Keats was nine. The eldest of four children, Keats attended school in Enfield where he was an honor student and voracious reader who started on his own to translate the *Aeneid*. Keats's mother died when he was fifteen, and her death ended his formal schooling. He remained close to his sister and two brothers but at sixteen was apprenticed to a surgeon-apothecary by his uncles, who had decided he should join the medical profession. After his apprenticeship, Keats was a student at Guy's Hospital, became a Licentiate of the Society of Apothecaries, and spent a year in a London hospital as a junior house surgeon. At about this time, Keats read Spenser's *Faerie Queen* and decided to abandon medicine for literature. His first poem, "Lines in Imitation of Spenser" was written in 1814.

Through Charles Cowden Clarke, the friend who had given him a copy of the *Faerie Queen,* Keats gradually met a group of literary men: Leigh Hunt, Hazlitt, Shelley, and later, Wordsworth, Lamb, and Coleridge. He published a few sonnets in Hunt's periodical, *The Examiner,* and, in 1817, a volume of poems dedicated to Hunt. About this time, Keats began his famous letters to his friends, the only source except his poems for his ideas about poetry. A year later, Keats published *Endymion* to a flood of harsh criticism from conservative London critics, some possibly angered by his friend Hunt's efforts on behalf of romantic literature. *The Quarterly* attacked the poem, while *Blackwood's Magazine* also insulted Keats's social background and his surgeon's profession. Aware of the poem's faults and self-conscious about his early life, Keats almost gave up literature.

Then he suffered a variety of personal and financial difficulties. His brother Tom was seriously ill, and Keats nursed him for three months before his death from tuberculosis, the disease to which Keats had already lost his mother and his sister Fanny. After Tom's death, Keats moved to Hampstead, in part to save money, and worked on *The Fall of Hyperion,* a fragment generally considered brilliant. Keats then became ill himself and, in an effort to ward off the family disease, traveled to the north of England and to Italy in search of a warmer climate. By the end of 1818, having been diagnosed with tuberculosis, Keats fell in love with Fanny Brawne. Many of the poems in his second book, published in 1820, are marked by his sadness at his separation from Fanny and sorrow that his early death as well as his poverty would rob them of marriage and a life together. This book won great critical approval. Keats declined an invitation to join Shelley at Pisa and was buried in the Protestant cemetery in Rome, having written his own epitaph: "Here lies one whose name was writ in water."

from The Letters

LETTER TO BENJAMIN BAILEY, 22 NOVEMBER, 1817

. . . I am certain of nothing but of the holiness of the Heart's affections and the truth of Imagination—What the Imagination seizes as Beauty must be truth—whether it existed before or not—for I have the same Idea of all our Passions as of Love they are all in their sublime, creative of essential Beauty—In a Word, you may know my favorite Speculation by my first Book and the little song I sent in my last—which is a representation from the fancy of the probable mode of operating in these Matters—The Imagination may be compared to Adam's dream— he awoke and found it truth. I am the more zealous in this affair, because I have never yet been able to perceive how anything can be known for truth by consequitive reasoning—and yet it must be—Can it be that even the greatest Philosopher ever arrived at his goal without putting aside numerous objections—However it may be, O for a Life of Sensations rather than of Thoughts! it is "a Vision in the form of Youth" a Shadow of reality to come—and this consideration has further conv[i]nced me for it has come as auxiliary to another favorite Speculation of mine, that we shall enjoy ourselves here after by having what we called happiness on Earth repeated in a finer tone and so repeated—And yet such a fate can only befall those who delight in sensation rather than hunger as you do after Truth—Adam's dream will do here and seems to be a conviction that Imagination and its empyreal reflection is the same as human Life and its spiritual repetition. But as I was saying—the simple imaginative Mind may have its rewards in the repeti[ti]ion of its own silent Working coming continually on the spirit with a fine suddenness—to compare great things with small—have you never by being surprised with an old Melody—in a delicious place—by a delicious voice, felt over again your very speculations and surmises at the time it first operated on your soul—do you not remember forming to yourself the singer's face more beautiful that [than] it was possible and yet with the elevation of the Moment you did not think so—even then you were mounted on the Wings of Imagination so high—that the Prototype must be here after—that delicious face you will see—What a time! I am continually running away from the subject—sure this cannot be exactly the case with complex Mind. . . .

LETTER TO GEORGE AND TOM KEATS, 22, 27 (?) DECEMBER, 1817

. . . I had not a dispute but a disquisition with Dilke, on various subjects; several things dovetailed in my mind, & at once it struck me what quality went to form a Man of Achievement especially in Literature & which Shakespeare posessed [*sic*] so enormously—I mean *Negative Capability*, that is when man is capable of being in uncertainties, Mysteries, doubts, without any irritable reaching after fact & reason—Coleridge, for instance, would let go by a fine isolated verisimilitude caught from the Penetralium of mystery, from being incapable of remaining content with half knowledge. This pursued through Volumes would perhaps take us no further than this, that with a great poet the sense of Beauty overcomes every other consideration, or rather obliterates all consideration. . . .

LETTER TO JOHN TAYLOR, 27 FEBRUARY, 1818

. . . I think Poetry should surprise by a fine excess and not by Singularity—it should strike the Reader as a wording of his own highest thoughts, and appear almost a Remembrance—2nd. Its touches of Beauty should never be half way ther[e] by making the reader breathless instead of content: the rise, the progress, the setting of imagery should like the Sun come natural too him—shine over him and set soberly although in magnificence leaving him in the Luxury of twilight—but it is easier to think what Poetry should be than to write it—and this leads me on to another axiom. That if Poetry comes not as naturally as the Leaves to a tree it had better not come at all. However it may be with me I cannot help looking into new countries with "O for a muse of fire to ascend!"—

if Endymion serves me as a Pioneer perhaps I ought to be content. I have great reason to be content, for thank God I can read and perhaps understand Shakespeare to his depths, and I have, I am sure, many friends, who, if I fail, will attribute any change in my Life and Temper to Humbleness rather than to Pride—to a cowering under the Wings of great Poets rather than to a Bitterness that I am not appreciated. . . .

LETTER RICHARD WOODHOUSE, OCTOBER, 1818

. . . As to the poetical Character itself, (I mean that sort of which, if I am any thing, I am a Member; that sort distinguished from the wordsworthian or egotistical sublime; which is a thing per se and stands alone) it is not itself—it has no self—it is every thing and nothing—It has no character—it enjoys light and shade; it lives in gusto, be it foul or fair, high or low, rich or poor, mean or elevated—It has as much delight in conceiving an Iago as an Imogen. What shocks the virtuous philosopher, delights the camelion [sic] Poet. It does no harm from its relish of the dark side of things any more than from its taste for the bright one; because they both end in speculation. A Poet is the most unpoetical of any thing in existence; because he has no Identity—he is continually in for—and filling some other Body—The Sun, the Moon, the Sea and Men and Women who are creatures of impulse are poetical and have about them an unchangeable attribute—the poet has none; no identity—he is certainly the most unpoetical of all God's Creatures. . . .

In the second place I will speak of my views, and of the life I purpose to myself—I am ambitious of doing the world some good: if I should be spared that may be the work of maturer years—in the interval I will assay to reach to as high a summit in Poetry as the nerve bestowed upon me will suffer. The faint conceptions I have of Poems to come brings the blood frequently into my forehead—All I hope is that I may not lose all interest in human affairs—that the solitary indifference I feel for applause even from the finest Spirits, will not blunt any acuteness of vision I may have. I do not think it will—I feel assured I should write from the mere yearning and fondness I have for the Beautiful even if my night's labours should be burnt every morning and no eye ever shine upon them. . . .

RALPH WALDO EMERSON

Ralph Waldo Emerson (1803–82) was born in Boston, attended Harvard College and Harvard Divinity School, and became a clergyman like his father and many of his ancestors. In 1833, two years after the death of his first wife, while serving as pastor of the Second Unitarian Church of Boston, Emerson lost faith in the sacrament of the Lord's Supper and ultimately resigned his position. He married again in 1835 and settled in Concord, Massachusetts, where he lived the rest of his life.

After European travel that included visits with Samuel Taylor Coleridge and Thomas Carlyle, he became the center of a group of thinkers that included Henry David Thoreau, Margaret Fuller, and Bronson Alcott. They formulated the ideas we know as Transcendentalism, which can be roughly described as an American form of Romanticism asserting the existence of a reality beyond the material world as well as the conviction that each individual has a spark of Divinity, and therefore a moral sense. The Transcendentalists optimistically emphasized the role of intuition, or the heart rather than reason, as the guide to moral and religious life . Emerson become well known as a lecturer on Transcendentalist ideas, and his lectures, later published as essays such as *Self-Reliance* and *The Divinity School Address,* retain the flavor of uplifting sermons and not closely reasoned philosophy. *The Divinity School Address,* the commencement address he gave at Harvard in 1838, celebrated the humanity of Jesus and the divinity of ordinary people. Emerson was attacked in the local press and barred from speaking at Harvard for three decades. However, he garnered many young disciples who formed the Transcendental Club, and his essays, including *The American Scholar,* his 1837 address to the members of Harvard's Phi Beta Kappa Society, were printed and distributed as pamphlets.

Emerson published two collections of essays, *Essays* (1841) and *Essays: Second Series* (1844); the influential *Nature* (1849); *Representative Men* (1850); *English Traits* (1856); and a collection of poems, *Parnassus* (1874). His works insist Americans should break free of European influences and create their own culture and religion: "Why should not we also enjoy an original relation to the Universe?" he asks in *Nature.*

In "The Poet," the essay excerpted here, Emerson discusses the nature of the poet and the poem: the poet is a representative person, the sayer, the namer, while the poem is, famously, "not metres, but a metre-making argument." Emerson's aesthetic ideals influenced such writers as Thoreau and Walt Whitman and, in the twentieth century, Robert Frost, Wallace Stevens, and A. R. Ammons. He remains a major presence and inspiration in American thought.

from The Poet

. . . The poet is the sayer, the namer, and represents beauty. He is a sovereign, and stands on the center. For the world is not painted or adorned, but is from the beginning beautiful; and God has not made some beautiful things, but Beauty is the creator of the universe. Therefore the poet is not any permissive potentate, but is emperor in his own right. Criticism is infested with a cant of materialism, which assumes that manual skill and activity is the first merit of all men, and disparages such as say and do not, overlooking the fact that some men, namely poets, are natural sayers, sent into the world to the end of expression, and confounds them with those whose province is action but who quit it to imitate the sayers. But Homer's words are as costly and admirable to Homer, as Agamemnon's victories are to Agamemnon. The poet does not wait for the hero or the sage, but, as they act and think primarily, so he writes primarily what will and must be spoken, reckoning the others, though primaries also, yet, in respect to him, secondaries and servants; as sitters or models in the studio of a painter, or as assistants who bring building materials to an architect.

For poetry was all written before time was, and whenever we are so finely organized that we can penetrate into that region where the air is music, we hear those primal warblings and attempt to write them down, but we lose ever and anon a word, or a verse and substitute something of our own, and thus miswrite the poem. The men of more delicate ear write down these cadences more faithfully, and these transcripts, though imperfect, become the songs of the nations. For nature is as truly beautiful as it is good, or as it is reasonable, and must as much appear, as it must be done, or be known. Words and deeds are quite indifferent modes of the divine energy. Words are also actions, and actions are a kind of words.

The sign and credentials of the poet are that he announces that which no man foretold. He is the true and only doctor; he knows and tells; he is the only teller of news, for he was present and privy to the appearance which he describes. He is a beholder of ideas and an utterer of the necessary and causal. For we do not speak now of men of poetical talents, or of industry and skill in metre, but of the true poet. I took part in a conversation the other day concerning a recent writer of lyrics, a man of subtle mind, whose head appeared to be a music-box of delicate tunes and rhythms, and whose skill and command of language, we could not sufficiently praise. But when the question arose whether he was not only a lyrist but a poet, we were obliged to confess that he is plainly a contemporary, not an eternal man. He does not stand out of our low limitations, like a Chimborazo under the line, running up from the torrid base through all the climates of the globe, with belts of the herbage of every latitude on its high and mottled sides; but this genius is the landscape-garden of a modern house, adorned with fountains and statues, with well-bred men and women standing and sitting in the walks and terraces. We hear through all the varied music, the ground-tone of conventional life. Our poets are men of talents who sing, and not the children of music. The argument is secondary, the finish of the verses is primary.

For it is not metres, but a metre-making argument, that makes a poem,—a thought so passionate and alive, that like the spirit of a plant or an animal it has an architecture of its own, and adorns nature with a new thing. The thought and the form are equal in the order of time, but in the order of genesis the thought is prior to the form. The poet has a new thought: he has a whole new experience to unfold; he will tell us how it was with him, and all men will be the richer in his fortune. For, the experience of each new age requires a new confession, and the world seems always waiting for its poet. I remember when I was young how much I was moved one morning by tidings that genius had appeared in a youth who sat near me at table. He had left his work, and gone rambling none knew whither, and had written hundreds of lines, but could not tell whether that which was in him was therein told: he could tell nothing but that all was changed,—man, beast, heaven, earth, and sea. How gladly we listened! how credulous! Society seemed to be compromised. We sat in the aurora of a sunrise which was to put out all the stars. Boston seemed to be at twice the distance it had the night before, or was much farther than that. Rome,—what was Rome? Plutarch and Shakespeare were in the yellow leaf, and Homer no more should be heard of. It is much to know that poetry has been written this very day, under this very roof, by your side. What! that wonderful spirit has not expired! These stony moments are still sparkling and animated! I had fancied that the oracles were all silent, and nature had spent her fires, and behold! all night, from every pore, these fine auroras have been streaming. Every one has some interest in the advent of the poet, and no one knows how much it may concern him. We know that the secret of the world is profound, but who or what shall be our interpreter, we know not. A mountain ramble, a new style of face, a new person, may put the key into our hands. Of course, the value of genius to us is in the veracity of its report. Talent may frolic and juggle; genius realizes and adds. Mankind in good earnest have availed so far in understanding themselves and their work, that the foremost watchman on the peak announces his news. It is the truest word ever spoken, and the phrase will be the fittest, most musical and the unerring voice of the world for that time. . . .

It is a secret which every intellectual man quickly learns, that, beyond the energy of his possessed and conscious intellect, he is capable of a new energy (as of an intellect doubled on itself), by abandonment to the nature of things; that, beside his privacy of power as an individual man, there is a great public power on which he can draw, by unlocking, at all risks, his human doors, and suffering the ethereal tides to roll and circulate through him: then he is caught up into the life of the Universe, his speech is thunder, his thought is law, and his words are universally intelligible as the plants and animals. The poet knows that he speaks adequately, then only when he speaks somewhat wildly, or, "with the flower of the mind;" not with the intellect used as an organ, but with the intellect released from all service and suffered to take its direction from its celestial life; or, as the ancients were wont to express themselves, not with intellect alone but with the intellect inebriated by nectar. As the traveler who has lost his way throws his reins on his horse's neck, and trusts to the instinct of the animal to find his road, so must we do with the divine animal who carries us through this world. For if in any manner we can stimulate this instinct, new passages are opened for us into nature, the mind flows into and through things hardest and highest, and the metamorphosis is possible.

This is the reason why bards love wine, mead, narcotics, coffee, tea, opium, the fumes of sandalwood and tobacco, or whatever other procurers of animal exhilaration. All men avail themselves of such means as they can, to add this extraordinary power to their normal powers; and to this end they prize conversation, music, pictures, sculpture, dancing, theatres, traveling, war, mobs, fires, gaming, politics, or love, or science, or animal intoxication,—which are several coarser or finer *quasi*-mechanical substitutes for the true nectar, which is the ravishment of the intellect by coming nearer to the fact. These are auxiliaries to the centrifugal tendency of a man, to his passage out into free space, and they help him to escape the custody of that body in which he is pent up, and of that jail-yard of individual relations in which he is enclosed. Hence a great number of such as were professionally expressors of Beauty, as painters, poets, musicians and actors, have been more than others wont to lead a life of pleasure and indulgence; all but the few who received the true nectar; and, as it was a spurious mode of attaining freedom, as it was an emancipation not into the heavens, but into the freedom of baser places, they were punished for that advantage they won, by a dissipation and deterioration. But never can any advantage be taken of nature by a trick. The spirit of the world, the great calm presence of the Creator, comes not forth to the sorceries of opium or of wine. The sublime vision comes to the pure and simple soul in a clean and chaste body. That is not an inspiration, which we owe to narcotics, but some counterfeit excitement and fury. Milton says that the lyric poet may drink wine and live generously, but the epic poet, he who shall sing of the gods, and their descent unto men, must drink water out of a wooden bowl. For poetry is not "Devil's wine," but God's wine. It is with this as it is with toys. We fill the hands and nurseries of our children with all manner of dolls, drums and horses, withdrawing their eyes from the plain face and sufficing objects of nature, the sun and moon, the animals, the water and stones, which should be their toys. So the poet's habit of living should be set on a key so low and plain that the common influences should delight him. His cheerfulness should be the gift of the sunlight; the air should suffice for his inspiration, and he should be tipsy with water. That spirit which suffices quiet hearts, which seems to come forth to such from every dry knoll of sere grass, from every pine stump, and half-imbedded stone, on which the dull March sun shines, comes forth to the poor and hungry, and such as are of simple taste. If thou fill thy brain with Boston and New York, with fashion and covetousness, and wilt stimulate thy jaded senses with wine and French coffee, thou shalt find no radiance of wisdom in the lonely waste of the pine woods. . . .

RAINER MARIA RILKE

Rainer Maria Rilke (1875–1926) has been credited with transforming German into a poetic language through his dense lyrical style and startling images. He was born in Prague, son of a railway official and a creative mother who introduced him to the arts and often dressed him as the girl she wished she had had. His parents separated when he was nine, and he was sent to a military academy, where he suffered from brutality and constant illness and wrote, "I suffer as Christ suffered." He studied at the universities of Prague, Berlin, and Munich, where he met Lou Andreas-Salomé, a Russian intellectual who, with her husband, strongly influenced Rilke's writing toward mysticism. In 1901 he married the sculptor Klara Westhoff and they had one daughter. When the marriage ended after one year, Rilke worked briefly as secretary to the sculptor Rodin in Paris. There he developed a poetry he called "thing-poems" (*Dinggedichte*), poems which expressed the life of objects, as when the "Archaic Torso of Apollo" is "stuffed with brilliance from inside."

Rilke spent much of his life impoverished, traveling and living with wealthy patrons. He published almost no poetry for a decade before writing *Duino Elegies,* named for the Duino Castle near Trieste, where he was a frequent guest of Princess Marie von Thurn. Rilke is said to have heard the opening line of these elegies, "Who, if I cried out, would hear me among the angels' / hierarchies?" while walking on the rocks above the Mediterranean Sea. Just before completing the elegies in 1923, Rilke wrote *The Sonnets to Orpheus,* one of his best-known book of poems, in an intense three-day spurt of creativity.

When World War I began, Duino Castle was bombed to ruins and Rilke's property was confiscated. He served in the Austrian army and then found a patron in Switzerland, where he remained until his death from leukemia. Legend has it that he died of an infection brought on by the prick of a rose thorn. Rilke's letters—to Marina Tsvetaeva, Rodin, Gide, and others—form an important part of his writings. His *Letters to a Young Poet,* excerpted here, reflect his sense of alienation as a writer and his insistence on the importance of the role of the artist, who must bear witness to his innermost feelings, yet his tone in addressing young Mr. Kappus is always constructive, always eminently positive.

from Letters to a Young Poet

ONE

Paris, February 17, 1903

My Dear Sir:

Your letter only reached me a few days ago. I want to thank you for its great and kind confidence. I can hardly do more. I cannot go into the nature of your verses; for all critical intention is too far from me. With nothing can one approach a work of art so little as with critical words: they always come down to more or less happy misunderstandings. Things are not all so comprehensible and expressible as one would mostly have us believe; most events are inexpressible, taking place in a realm which no word has ever entered, and more inexpressible than all else are works of art, mysterious existences, the life of which, while ours passes away, endures.

After these prefatory remarks, let me only tell you further that your verses have no individual style, although they do show quiet and hidden beginnings of something personal. I feel this most clearly in the last poem, "My Soul." There something of your own wants to come through to word and melody. And in the lovely poem "To Leopardi" there does perhaps grow up a sort of kinship with that great solitary man. Nevertheless the poems are not yet anything on their own account, nothing independent, even the last and the one to Leopardi. Your kind letter, which accompanied them, does not fail to make clear to me various shortcomings which I felt in reading your verses without however being able specifically to name them.

You ask whether your verses are good. You ask me. You have asked others before. You send them to magazines. You compare them with other poems, and you are disturbed when certain editors reject your efforts. Now (since you have allowed me to advise you) I beg you to give up all that. You are looking outward, and that above all you should not do now. Nobody can counsel and help you, nobody. There is only one single way. Go into yourself. Search for the reason that bids you write; find out whether it is spreading out its roots in the deepest places of your heart, acknowledge to yourself whether you would have to die if it were denied you to write. This above all—ask yourself in the stillest hour of your night: *must* I write? Delve into yourself for a deep answer. And if this should be affirmative, if you may meet this earnest question with a strong and simple *"I must,"* then build your life according to this necessity; your life even in its most indifferent and slightest hour must be a sign of this urge and a testimony to it. Then draw near to Nature. Then try, like some first human being, to say what you see and experience and love and lose. Do not write love-poems; avoid at first those forms that are too facile and commonplace: they are the most difficult, for it takes a great, fully matured power to give something of your own where good and even excellent traditions come to mind in quantity. Therefore save yourself from these general themes and seek those which your own everyday life offers you; describe your sorrows and desires, passing thoughts and the belief in some sort of beauty—describe all these with loving, quiet, humble sincerity, and use, to express yourself, the things in your environment, the images from your dreams, and the objects of your memory. If your daily life seems poor, do not blame it; blame yourself, tell yourself that you are not poet enough to call forth its riches; for to the creator there is no poverty and no poor indifferent place. And even if you were in some prison the walls of which let none of the sounds of the world come to your senses—would you not then still have your childhood, that precious, kingly possession, that treasure-house of memories? Turn your attention thither. Try to raise the submerged sensations of that ample past; your personality will grow more firm, your solitude will widen and will become a dusky dwelling past which the noise of others goes by far away.—And if out of this turning inward, out of this absorption into your own world *verses* come, then it will not occur to you to ask anyone whether they are good *verses.* Nor will you try to interest magazines in your poems: for you will see in them your fond natural possession, a fragment and a voice of your life. A work of art is good if it has sprung from necessity. In this nature of its origins lies the judgment of it: there is no other. Therefore, my dear sir, I know no advice for you save this: to go into yourself and test the deeps in which your life takes rise; at its source you will find the answer to the question whether you *must* create. Accept it, just as it sounds, without inquiring into it. Perhaps it will turn out that you are called to be an artist. Then take that destiny upon yourself and bear it, its burden and its greatness without ever asking what recompense might come from outside. For the creator must be a world for himself and find everything in himself and in Nature to whom he has attached himself. . . .

T. S. ELIOT

Thomas Stearns Eliot (1888–1965) was born in St. Louis, Missouri, to a family that believed in the "Law of Service" and inculcated respect for "symbols of Religion, the Community and Education," as Eliot himself wrote. His mother was a writer whose verse drama on Savanarola Eliot later published. He earned a BA and a MA in philosophy at Harvard, where he was influenced by George Santayana and Irving Babbitt. Studying at Oxford on a scholarship, he met Ezra Pound, who became a key supporter of his poetry and encouraged him to remain in England. Ultimately, Eliot became a British citizen and was baptized and confirmed in the Church of England. After his marriage, Eliot worked briefly as a teacher, then in the foreign department of Lloyd's Bank. His marriage to Vivienne Haigh-Wood, who has been called his Muse by recent critics, ended in 1932.

Eliot was an editor of the *Criterion* and expounded his literary views from that podium and in the *Times Literary Supplement* and many other well-known literary journals. His critical essays made his reputation even before his poetry was widely known. Through Bertrand Russell, Eliot became well acquainted with the Bloomsbury group, although his conservative critique of Western civilization differed vastly from theirs in emphasizing order and hierarchy. He described himself as "classicist in literature, Royalist in politics and Anglo-Catholic in religion." But this formula overlooks the daring, experimental nature of Eliot's poetry, accentuated by Pound's editing, and his stance in criticism, which favored the complicated metaphors of the Metaphysical poets over Milton and the Romantics.

The publication of "The Love Song of J. Alfred Prufrock" in 1915 marked not only a turning point in Eliot's career but also the beginning of a new era in American poetry. His subtle ironies, varied levels of diction, juxtapositions of unusual images and shifts in tone without transitions, and mythological and Eastern allusions portray a world of spiritual desolation, sexual disorder, and an unfulfilled quest for regeneration.

An outstanding figure in twentieth-century literature, Eliot was awarded the Nobel Prize in 1948. In the essay we have included, Eliot takes issue with the Wordsworthian concept that poetry is "emotion recollected in tranquility." He stresses the importance to the writer of literary tradition: too much emphasis has been placed on the new and on the individual. To remain a poet "beyond his twenty-fifth year," a writer must seek impersonality at the expense of Romantic ego, and must know the tradition and define himself in relation to it: "No poet, no artist of any art, has his complete meaning alone."

Tradition and the Individual Talent

I

In English writing we seldom speak of tradition, though we occasionally apply its name in deploring its absence. We cannot refer to "the tradition" or to "a tradition"; at most, we employ the adjective in saying that the poetry of So-and-so is "traditional" or even "too traditional." Seldom, perhaps, does the word appear except in a phrase of censure. If otherwise, it is vaguely approbative, with the implication, as to the work approved, of some pleasing archaeological reconstruction. You can hardly make the word agreeable to English ears without this comfortable reference to the reassuring science of archaeology.

Certainly the word is not likely to appear in our appreciations of living or dead writers. Every nation, every race, has not only its own creative, but its own critical turn of mind; and is even more oblivious of the shortcomings and limitations of its critical habits than of those of its creative genius. We know, or think we know, from the enormous mass of critical writing that has appeared in the French language the critical method or habit of the French; we only conclude (we are such unconscious people) that the French are "more critical" than we, and sometimes even plume ourselves a little with the fact, as if the French were the less spontaneous. Perhaps they are; but we might remind ourselves that criticism is as inevitable as breathing, and that we should be none the worse for articulating what passes in our minds when we read a book and feel an emotion about it, for criticizing our own minds in their work of criticism. One of the facts that might come to light in this process is our tendency to insist, when we praise a poet, upon those aspects of his work in which he least resembles anyone else. In these aspects or parts of his work we pretend to find what is individual, what is the peculiar essence of the man.

We dwell with satisfaction upon the poet's difference from his pre-

decessors, especially his immediate predecessors; we endeavour to find
something that can be isolated in order to be enjoyed. Whereas if we
approach a poet without this prejudice we shall often find that not only
the best, but the most individual parts of his work may be those in which
the dead poets, his ancestors, assert their immortality most vigorously.
And I do not mean the impressionable period of adolescence, but the
period of full maturity.

Yet if the only form of tradition, of handing down, consisted in following the ways of the immediate generation before us in a blind or timid
adherence to its successes, "tradition" should positively be discouraged.
We have seen many such simple currents soon lost in the sand; and novelty is better than repetition. Tradition is a matter of much wider significance. It cannot be inherited, and if you want it you must obtain it by
great labour. It involves, in the first place, the historical sense, which we
may call nearly indispensable to anyone who would continue to be a poet
beyond his twenty-fifth year; and the historical sense involves a perception, not only of the pastness of the past, but of its presence; the historical sense compels a man to write not merely with his own generation in
his bones, but with a feeling that the whole of the literature of Europe
from Homer and within it the whole of the literature of his own country has a simultaneous existence and composes a simultaneous order. This
historical sense, which is a sense of the timeless as well as of the temporal and of the timeless and of the temporal together, is what makes a
writer traditional. And it is at the same time what makes a writer most
acutely conscious of his place in time, of his own contemporaneity.

No poet, no artist of any art, has his complete meaning alone. His
significance, his appreciation is the appreciation of his relation to the
dead poets and artists. You cannot value him alone; you must set him,
for contrast and comparison, among the dead. I mean this as a principle
of aesthetic, not merely historical, criticism. The necessity that he shall
conform, that he shall cohere, is not onesided; what happens when a
new work of art is created is something that happens simultaneously to
all the works of art which preceded it. The existing monuments form
an ideal order among themselves, which is modified by the introduction
of the new (the really new) work of art among them. The existing order
is complete before the new work arrives; for order to persist after the
supervention of novelty, the *whole* existing order must be, if ever so

slightly, altered; and so the relations, proportions, values of each work of art toward the whole are readjusted; and this is conformity between the old and the new. Whoever has approved this idea of order, of the form of European, of English literature will not find it preposterous that the past should be altered by the present as much as the present is directed by the past. And the poet who is aware of this will be aware of great difficulties and responsibilities.

In a peculiar sense he will be aware also that he must inevitably be judged by the standards of the past. I say judged, not amputated, by them; not judged to be as good as, or worse or better than, the dead; and certainly not judged by the canons of dead critics. It is a judgment, a comparison, in which two things are measured by each other. To conform merely would be for the new work not really to conform at all; it would not be new, and would therefore not be a work of art. And we do not quite say that the new is more valuable because it fits in; but its fitting in is a test of its value—a test, it is true, which can only be slowly and cautiously applied, for we are none of us infallible judges of conformity. We say: it appears to conform, and is perhaps individual, or it appears individual, and may conform; but we are hardly likely to find that it is one and not the other.

To proceed to a more intelligible exposition of the relation of the poet to the past: he can neither take the past as a lump, an indiscriminate bolus, nor can he form himself wholly on one or two private admirations, nor can he form himself wholly upon one preferred period. The first course is inadmissible, the second is an important experience of youth, and the third is a pleasant and highly desirable supplement. The poet must be very conscious of the main current, which does not at all flow invariably through the most distinguished reputations. He must be quite aware of the obvious fact that art never improves, but that the material of art is never quite the same. He must be aware that the mind of Europe—the mind of his own country—a mind which he learns in time to be much more important than his own private mind—is a mind which changes, and that this change is a development which abandons nothing en route, which does not superannuate either Shakespeare, or Homer, or the rock drawing of the Magdalenian draughtsmen. That this development, refinement perhaps, complication certainly, is not, from the point of view of the artist, any improvement. Perhaps not even an improvement from the point of view of the psychologist or not to the extent which we imagine; perhaps only in the end based upon a complication in economics and machinery. But the difference between the present and the past is that the conscious present is an awareness of the past in a way and to an extent which the past's awareness of itself cannot show.

Someone said: "The dead writers are remote from us because we *know* so much more than they did." Precisely, and they are that which we know.

I am alive to a usual objection to what is clearly part of my programme for the *métier* of poetry. The objection is that the doctrine requires a ridiculous amount of erudition (pedantry), a claim which can be rejected by appeal to the lives of poets in any pantheon. It will even be affirmed that much learning deadens or perverts poetic sensibility. While, however, we persist in believing that a poet ought to know as much as will not encroach upon his necessary receptivity and necessary laziness, it is not desirable to confine knowledge to whatever can be put into a useful shape for examinations, drawing-rooms, or the still more pretentious modes of publicity. Some can absorb knowledge, the more tardy must sweat for it. Shakespeare acquired more essential history from Plutarch than most men could from the whole British Museum. What is to be insisted upon is that the poet must develop or procure the consciousness of the past and that he should continue to develop this consciousness throughout his career.

What happens is a continual surrender of himself as he is at the moment to something which is more valuable. The progress of an artist is a continual self-sacrifice, a continual extinction of personality.

There remains to define this process of depersonalization and its relation to the sense of tradition. It is in this depersonalization that art may be said to approach the condition of science. I shall, therefore, invite you to consider, as a suggestive analogy, the action which takes place when a bit of finely filiated platinum is introduced into a chamber containing oxygen and sulphur dioxide.

II

Honest criticism and sensitive appreciation is directed not upon the poet but upon the poetry. If we attend to the confused cries of the newspaper critics and the susurrus of popular repetition that follows, we shall hear the names of poets in great numbers; if we seek not Blue-book knowledge but the enjoyment of poetry, and ask for a poem, we shall seldom find it. I have tried to point out the importance of the relation of the poem to other poems by other authors, and suggested the conception of poetry as a living whole of all the poetry that has ever been written. The other aspect of this Impersonal theory of poetry is the relation of the poem to its author. And I hinted, by an analogy, that the mind of the mature poet differs from that of the immature one not precisely in any valuation of "personality," not being necessarily more interesting, or having "more to say," but rather by being a more finely perfected medium in which special, or very varied, feelings are at liberty to enter into new combinations.

The analogy was that of the catalyst. When the two gases previously mentioned are mixed in the presence of a filament of platinum, they form sulphurous acid. This combination takes place only if the platinum is present; nevertheless the newly formed acid contains no trace of platinum, and the platinum itself is apparently unaffected: has remained inert, neutral, and unchanged. The mind of the poet is the shred of platinum. It may partly or exclusively operate upon the experience of the man himself; but, the more perfect the artist, the more completely separate in him will be the man who suffers and the mind which creates; the more perfectly will the mind digest and transmute the passions which are its material.

The experience, you will notice, the elements which enter the presence of the transforming catalyst, are of two kinds: emotions and feelings. The effect of a work of art upon the person who enjoys it is an experience different in kind from any experience not of art. It may be formed out of one emotion, or may be a combination of several; and various feelings, inhering for the writer in particular words or phrases or images, may be added to compose the final result. Or great poetry may be made without the direct use of any emotion whatever: composed out of feelings solely. Canto XV of the *Inferno* (Brunetto Latini) is a working up of the emotion evident in the situation; but the effect, though single as that of any work of art, is obtained by considerable complexity of detail. The last quatrain gives an image, a feeling attaching to an image, which "came," which did not develop simply out of what precedes, but which was probably in suspension in the poet's mind until the proper combination arrived for it to add itself to. The poet's mind is in fact a receptacle for seizing and storing up numberless feelings, phrases, images, which remain there until all the particles which can unite to form a new compound are present together.

If you compare several representative passages of the greatest poetry you see how great is the variety of types of combination, and also how completely any semi-ethical criterion of "sublimity" misses the mark. For it is not the "greatness," the intensity, of the emotions, the components, but the intensity of the artistic process, the pressure, so to speak, under which the fusion takes place, that counts. The episode of Paolo and Francesca employs a definite emotion, but the intensity of the poetry is something quite different from whatever intensity in the supposed experience it may give the impression of. It is no more intense, furthermore, than Canto XXVI, the voyage of Ulysses, which has not the direct dependence upon an emotion. Great variety is possible in the process of transmutation of emotion: the murder of *Agamemnon,* or the agony of Othello, gives an artistic effect apparently closer to a possible original than the scenes from Dante. In the *Agamemnon,* the artistic emotion approximates to the emotion of an actual spectator; in *Othello* to the emotion of the protagonist himself. But the difference between art and the event is always absolute; the combination which is the murder of Agamemnon is probably as complex as that which is the voyage of Ulysses. In either case there has been a fusion of elements. The ode of Keats contains a number of feelings which have nothing particular to do with the nightingale, but which the nightingale, partly perhaps because of its attractive name, and partly because of its reputation, served to bring together.

The point of view which I am struggling to attack is perhaps related to the metaphysical theory of the substantial unity of the soul: for my meaning is, that the poet has, not a "personality" to express, but a particular medium, which is only a medium and not a personality, in which impressions and experiences combine in peculiar and unexpected ways. Impressions and experiences which are important for the man may take no place in the poetry, and those which become important in the poetry may play quite a negligible part in the man, the personality.

I will quote a passage which is unfamiliar enough to be regarded with fresh attention in the light—or darkness—of these observations:

And now methinks I could e'en chide myself
For doating on her beauty, though her death
Shall be revenged after no common action.
Does the silkworm expend her yellow labours
For thee? For thee does she undo herself?
Are lordships sold to maintain ladyships
For the poor benefit of a bewildering minute?
Why does yon fellow falsify highways,
And put his life between the judge's lips,
To refine such a thing—keeps horse and men
To beat their valours for her ? . . .

In this passage (as is evident if it is taken in its context) there is a combination of positive and negative emotions: an intensely strong attraction toward beauty and an equally intense fascination by the ugliness which is contrasted with it and which destroys it. This balance of contrasted emotion is in the dramatic situation to which the speech is pertinent, but that situation alone is inadequate to it. This is, so to speak, the structural emotion, provided by the drama. But the whole effect, the dominant tone, is due to the fact that a number of floating feelings, having an affinity to this emotion by no means superficially evident, having combined with it to give us a new art emotion.

It is not in his personal emotions, the emotions provoked by particular events in his life, that the poet is in any way remarkable or interesting. His particular emotions may be simple, or crude, or flat. The emotion in his poetry will be a very complex thing, but not with the complexity of the emotions of people who have very complex or unusual emotions in life. One error, in fact, of eccentricity in poetry is to seek for new human emotions to express; and in this search for novelty in the wrong place it discovers the perverse. The business of the poet is not to find new emotions, but to use the ordinary ones and, in working them up into poetry, to express feelings which are not in actual emotions at all. And emotions which he has never experienced will serve his turn as well as those familiar to him. Consequently, we must believe that "emotion recollected in tranquillity" is an inexact formula. For it is neither emotion, nor recollection, nor without distortion of meaning, tranquillity. It is a concentration, and a new thing resulting from the concentration, of a very great number of experiences which to the practical and active person would not seem to be experiences at all; it is a concentration which does not happen consciously or of deliberation. These experiences are not "recollected," and they finally unite in an atmosphere which is "tranquil" only in that it is a passive attending upon the event. Of course this is not quite the whole story. There is a great deal, in the writing of poetry, which must be conscious and deliberate. In fact, the bad poet is usually unconscious where he ought to be conscious, and conscious where he ought to be unconscious. Both errors tend to make him "personal." Poetry is not a turning loose of emotion, but an escape from emotion; it is not the expression of personality, but an escape from personality. But, of course, only those who have personality and emotions know what it means to want to escape from these things.

III

όδ ενοῖς ῖσως θειότερόν τι καὶ ἀπαθές ἐστιν.

This essay proposes to halt at the frontiers of metaphysics or mysticism, and confine itself to such practical conclusions as can be applied by the responsible person interested in poetry. To divert interest from the poet to the poetry is a laudable aim: for it would conduce to a juster estimation of actual poetry, good and bad. There are many people who appreciate the expression of sincere emotion in verse, and there is a smaller number of people who can appreciate technical excellence. But very few know when there is an expression of *significant* emotion, emotion which has its life in the poem and not in the history of the poet. The emotion of art is impersonal. And the poet cannot reach this impersonality without surrendering himself wholly to the work to be done. And he is not likely to know what is to be done unless he lives in what is not merely the present, but the present moment of the past, unless he is conscious, not of what is dead, but of what is already living.

FEDERICO GARCÍA LORCA

Federico García Lorca (1899–1936) was murdered at the age of thirty-eight by fascists of the Nationalist Party who, winning the Spanish Civil War, inaugurated the dictatorship of Gen. Francisco Franco. As an intellectual, a leftist, and a homosexual, Lorca was designated an enemy of the Nationalists, shot by Franco's men, and thrown into an unmarked grave with two bullfighters and a teacher, a victim of what the Spanish philosopher and novelist Miguel de Unamuno referred to as "the spiritual leprosy of Spain: resentment, envy, hatred for intelligence." His death was used to intimidate others, and his writing was outlawed until 1954; certain bans on his work remained in effect until 1971. Today he is ranked as the greatest Spanish dramatist and poet of the twentieth century. Recently, the pact of silence prevailing since the time of Franco has been revoked, and efforts have been made to exhume and identify the remains of Lorca and others murdered during the Civil War.

The son of a liberal landowner, Lorca grew up near Granada and studied philosophy and law at the University of Granada before turning to theater and poetry at the University of Madrid. Early recognized as a literary genius, Lorca became famous in his twenties with the publication of *The Gypsy Ballads* and his Andalusian tragedies, including *Blood Wedding* and *The House of Bernarda Alba*. He was a member of the Generacion del 27, a group of Spanish artists that included painter Salvador Dali, poet Rafael Alberti, and filmmaker Luis Buñuel. His first theatrical success, *Mariana Pineda* (1929), a historical romance in verse, featured a set designed by Dali. Also in 1929, Lorca moved to New York to study English at Columbia University. Out of this experience came a book of surrealist lyrics published posthumously, *The Poet in New York,* in which he seemed to predict his own assassination.

Lorca may be best known to modern poets for the concept of the duende, which he first developed in a lecture in Havana in 1930. The duende is a spirit of art, but not a kindly one like a muse or an angel. It is a dark force characteristic of Lorca's own writing, and recognized in Andalusia as present in the greatest art. Having nothing to do with surface beauty and form, it is a vibrant energy based on the artist's knowledge of the fact that we die. Duende may be the artist's passionate response to that knowledge. Lorca refers to duende as characteristic of Spanish poetry, but duende may be an essential element in all poetry.

from Play and Theory of the Duende

The muse and angel come from outside us: the angel gives lights, and the muse gives forms (Hesiod learned from her). Loaf of gold or tunic fold: the poet receives norms in his grove of laurel. But one must awaken the duende in the remotest mansions of the blood.

And reject the angel, and give the muse a kick in the seat of the pants, and conquer our fear of the violet smile exhaled by eighteenth-century poetry, and of the great telescope in whose lens the muse, sickened by limits, is sleeping.

The true fight is with the duende.

We know the roads where we can search for God, from the barbarous way of the hermit to the subtle one of the mystic. With a tower like Saint Teresa or with the three ways of Saint John of the Cross. And though we may have to cry out in the voice of Isaiah, "Truly thou art a hidden God," in the end God sends each seeker his first fiery thorns.

But there are neither maps nor exercises to help us find the duende. We only know that he burns the blood like a poultice of broken glass, that he exhausts, that he rejects all the sweet geometry we have learned, that he smashes styles, that he leans on human pain with no consolation and makes Goya (master of the grays, silvers and pinks of the best English painting) work with his fists and knees in horrible bitumens. He strips Moussèn Cinto Verdaguer in the cold of the Pyrenees, or takes Jorge Manrique to watch for death in the wasteland of Ocaña, or dresses Rimbaud's delicate body in the green suit of a saltimbanque, or puts the eyes of a dead fish on the Comte de Lautréamont in the late-night hours of the boulevard.

The great artists of the south of Spain, whether Gypsy or flamenco, whether they sing, dance, or play, know that no emotion is possible unless the duende comes. They may be able to fool people into thinking they have duende—authors and painters and literary fashion-mongers do so every day—but we have only to pay a little attention and not surrender to indifference in order to discover the fraud and chase away their clumsy artifice.

The Andalusian singer Pastora Pavón, *La Niña de los Peines*, dark Hispanic genius whose powers of fantasy are equal to those of Goya or Rafael el Gallo, was once singing in a little tavern in Cadiz. . . .

As though crazy, torn like a medieval mourner, *La Niña de los Peines* leaped to her feet, tossed off a big glass of burning liquor, and began to sing with a scorched throat, without voice, without breath or color, but with duende. She was able to kill all the scaffolding of the song and leave way for a furious, enslaving duende, friend of sand winds, who made the listeners rip their clothes with the same rhythm as do the blacks of the Antilles when, in the "lucumí" rite, they huddle in heaps before the statue of Santa Barbára.

La Niña de los Peines had to tear her voice because she knew she had an exquisite audience, one which demanded not forms but the marrow of forms, pure music, with a body lean enough to stay in the air. She had to rob herself of skill and security, send away her muse and become helpless, that her duende might come and deign to fight her hand-to-hand. And how she sang! Her voice was no longer playing. It was a jet of blood worthy of her pain and her sincerity, and it opened like a ten-fingered hand around the nailed but stormy feet of a Christ by Juan de Juni.

*   *   *

The duende's arrival always means a radical change in forms. It brings to old planes unknown feelings of freshness, with the quality of something newly created, like a miracle, and it produces an almost religious enthusiasm.

In all Arabic music, whether dance, song, or elegy, the duende's arrival is greeted with energetic cries of Allah! Allah!, which is so close to the Olé of the bullfight that who knows if it is not the same thing? And in all the songs of the south of Spain the duende is greeted with sincere cries of ¡Viva Dios!—deep and tender human cry of communication with God by means of the five senses, thanks to the duende, who shakes the body and voice of the dancer. It is a real and poetic evasion of this world, as pure as that of the strange seventeenth-century poet Pedro Soto de Rojas with his seven gardens, or that of John Climacus with his trembling ladder of lamentation.

Naturally, when this evasion succeeds, everyone feels its effects, both the initiate, who sees that style has conquered a poor material, and the unenlightened, who feel some sort of authentic emotion. Years ago, an eighty-year-old woman won first prize at a dance contest in Jerez de la Frontera. She was competing against beautiful women and young girls with waists as supple as water, but all she did was raise her arms, throw back her head, and stamp her foot on the floor. In the gathering of muses and angels—beautiful forms and beautiful smiles—who could have won but her moribund duende, sweeping the ground with its wings of rusty knives.

All arts are capable of duende, but where it finds greatest range, naturally, is in music, dance, and spoken poetry, for these arts require a living body to interpret them, being forms that are born, die, and open their contours against an exact present.

Often the duende of the composer passes into the duende of the interpreter, and at other times, when a composer or poet is no such thing, the interpreter's duende—this is interesting—creates a new marvel that looks like, but is not, the primitive form. This was the case of Eleonora Duse, possessed by duende, who looked for plays that had failed so she could make them triumph thanks to her own inventions, and the case of Paganini, as explained by Goethe, who made one hear deep melodies in vulgar trifles, and the case of a delightful little girl I saw in Puerto de Santa Maria singing and dancing that horrible, corny Italian song "Oh Marí!" with such rhythms, silences, and intention, that she turned the Neapolitan gewgaw into something new and totally unprecedented that could give lifeblood and art to bodies devoid of expressiveness. . . .

The duende . . . Where is the duende? Through the empty arch comes a wind, a mental wind blowing relentlessly over the heads of the dead, in search of new landscapes and unknown accents; a wind that smells of baby's spittle, crushed grass, and jellyfish veil, announcing the constant baptism of newly created things.

EDWARD HIRSCH

Edward Hirsch (1950–) was born in Chicago, Illinois. He received his BA from Grinnell College in Iowa and his PhD in folklore from the University of Pennsylvania. He first taught at Wayne State University and then moved to the University of Houston where he was a professor in the creative writing program for seventeen years. Hirsch is the author of six poetry books, *Lay Back the Darkness* (2003); *On Love* (1998); *Earthly Measures* (1994); *The Night Parade* (1989); *Wild Gratitude* (1986), the winner of the National Book Parade Critics Circle Award; and *For the Sleepwalkers* (1981), which received the Lavan Younger Poets Award from the Academy of American Poets and the Delmore Schwartz Memorial Award from New York University. He has also written three prose books, including *How to Read a Poem and Fall in Love with Poetry* and *The Demon and the Angel: Searching for the Source of Artistic Inspiration*, from which the essay excerpted here is taken. Hirsch has been a frequent contributor to major literary magazines and periodicals, including the *New Yorker, DoubleTake,* and *American Poetry Review* and writes a weekly column on poetry for the *Washington Post Book World*. The fact that his passion for poetry is only matched by his erudition makes him an eloquent spokesperson for poetry in the new century. A lengthy and wide-ranging interview with him, conducted by Tod Marshall, appeared in the *Kenyon Review,* spring 2000. Hirsch's numerous awards include the Prix de Rome, a Guggenheim fellowship, an American Academy of Arts and Letters Award for Literature, and a MacArthur "genius" grant. He is the fourth president of the John Simon Guggenheim Memorial Foundation, the first poet to be named to this post. Hirsch is married and has one son.

from Fending Off the Duende

It seems clear why certain artists want to fend off the irrational splendors of the duende, sometimes to the detriment of their work, but for the sake of their sanity. And yet, "One of the most notable characteristics of the poems of deep song," Lorca explained in a lecture of 1922, "is their almost complete lack of a restrained, middle tone." The duende shuns the middle way, and it avoids works of art that show too much emotional balance and tranquility, feelings tamed entirely to reason, to so-called common sense, which is why it shows up in certain neoclassical poets (such as Walter Savage Landor and Louise Bogan) only when it feels the demonic undertow tugging at their forms, the beating wing of madness passing overhead, the sense that, as the baroque Jesuit poet Tomasso Ceva put it, "Poetry is a dream dreamed in the presence of reason."

Yeats's characterization of Walter Savage Landor in *Per Amica Silentia Lunae* is to the point: "Savage Landor topped us all in calm nobility when his pen was in his hand," he said, "as in the daily violence of his passion when he had laid it down." Yeats is even more explicit in *A Vision*, where he describes Landor as "the most violent of men," who used his intellect "to disengage a visionary image of perfect sanity . . . seen always in the most serene and classic art imaginable."

One senses the rhythm and meter anticipating and trying to prevent the disorder in a range of highly formal modern American poetry, from T. S. Eliot's second book, neutrally entitled *Poems,* and Ezra Pound's *Hugh Selwyn Mauberley,* both published in 1920, to Yvor Winters's strenuously didactic meters and John Crowe Ransom's New Critical ironies in the face of lavish death. (Like Thomas Hardy, his primary model, all Ransom's poems are death-haunted.) Holding texts, stays against ruin. One thinks of J. V. Cunningham, who early on announced that "Good sense and skill / Of madness cured me" ("For My Contemporaries"), but whose later work belies the claim. A demonic spirit unwillingly breaks through such witty, tormented poems as "Interview with Doctor Drink" ("I have a fifth of therapy / In the house, and transference there") and "Montana Fifty Years Ago," a lyric that by dryly yet poignantly reciting the external facts—the storied details—of a woman's life ("Gaunt kept house with her child for the old man / Met at the train") allegorically encapsulates a vanished time and place:

> Nothing was said, nothing was ever said.
> And then the child died and she disappeared.
> This was Montana fifty years ago.

Like Wallace Stevens, L. E. Sissman was Orpheus in a business suit—an advertising executive by day and a poet by night. A recent selection of his poems, *Night Music,* once more reminds us how his work was energized rather than deprived by the onslaught of Hodgkin's disease, an illness he recognized as "routinely fatal" ("Instead of a curtain falling, a curtain rose"); how his first book was charmingly entitled *Dying: An Introduction* (1978); how his wit was challenged and schooled by terror; and how his breezy, seemingly effortless epigrammatic couplets and flexible blank verse lines are weighed down by earthly observations, late knowledge, final illness.

Anthony Hecht's *The Hard Hours* (1968) is one of the books that first crystallized my thinking about how some works of art operate by struggling to fend off the duende. In this collection of modern crisis lyrics, a characteristically urbane, decorous, and stately manner comes up against two recurring dangers or threats: madness and history. The crisis generates from inside the self—the individual at the mercy of his own psychic traumas and wounds—but often that crisis (so severe as to amount to a kind of psychotic breakdown) is generated by a personal impotence in the face of overwhelming external circumstances and forces. American poets have often written as Emersonian individualists, as if the self were an imperial entity that can create and determine not only its own destiny but also history itself, yet in *The Hard Hours* the integrity of that self begins to disintegrate as it is invaded from the outside by forces much larger and stronger than it. Power is real; the individual is neither independent nor immune from the cruelty or authority of others. The self, the house of being, is physically and emotionally vulnerable, and experience is crippling. The Adamic poet has eaten the bitter fruit of history and fallen not only into Time, but also into the political realm of History. . . .

It is against a background of unbearable historical cruelty, of scapegoating and victimization, of compromises and conditions, that we understand how hard one must work to fend off and control what is terrifying and uncontrollable. The traditional ethic of *The Hard Hours*—its sometimes grave, sometimes slangy cadences—provides a conscious way of staying the dangerous irrational. Madness is held off; sanity—at least momentarily—triumphant.

Samuel Johnson is a mountaintop example of a writer whose work is energized by the battle between an overriding common sense and an underlying demonic fury. Johnson called madness "the heaviest of human afflictions" and showed, as his biographer W. Jackson Bate expresses it, "a powerful unconscious need to release nervous tension through order, pattern, or rhythm and keep it from overwhelming the psyche—a need to 'divide up' the welter of subjective feeling and reduce it to manageable units." Bate argues that Johnson, who had suffered a breakdown in his twenties, was constantly on the verge of a nervous collapse for at least a three-year period beginning in 1764. He tells the story of a young artist who went to meet Johnson in his rooms and was so discomfited by the silence at the beginning of their visit that he decided he was in the presence of a "madman," until at last Johnson began to talk and "faith . . . everything he says is as *correct as a second edition.*"

Johnson was terrified that all of his ills were truly "in his head" and once said, "Of all the uncertainties of our present state, the most dreadful and alarming is the uncertain continuance of reason." It is as if the fear of insanity, as well as the need to keep a ferocious grip on logic and reason, drove much of the poignant stoicism of Johnson's work. It also fueled his late prodigious intellectual achievement—his law lectures, his political pamphlets, a new edition of his *Dictionary*, and, especially, the fifty-two *Lives of the English Poets* that are among the triumphs of English critical prose.

It is the hard-fought battle with the duende through formal means, in a formal arena, and not any metrical formulations, that powers such classical and obsessively rational work, from Horace to Paul Valéry, who extolled the pleasures of pure intellect, extreme rationality, and denied the value of enthusiasm for creative concentration. Valéry preferred a state of cool calculation. By contrast, the supremely ironic Byron felt the opposite way and testified to the necessary cathartic release, the power of "enthusiastic" writing. "It comes over me in a kind of rage every now and then," he said, "and then, if I don't write to empty my mind, I go mad." He universalized the experience into a characterization of poetry itself. Poetry, he said,

> is the lava of the imagination whose eruption prevents an earth-quake—they say poets never or rarely *go mad* . . . but are generally so near it—that I cannot help thinking rhyme is so far useful in anticipating & preventing the disorder.

A highly formal and traditional work deepens immeasurably when one feels the primal murkiness threatening to swell up underneath the geometric clarity, the verbal concision, and the ironic wit. The ancient demons are never far from shore. They dwell within the deeps. They move in the ghostly mists. A highly rational art is especially haunting when one feels the struggle *in* the thought, or even underneath the thought; when one senses something dark welling up from below, from the primordial mud; when one recognizes the powerful internal pressure of a mind defending itself against itself.

DONALD HALL

Donald Hall (1928–) was born in New Haven, Connecticut; he was educated at Phillips Exeter Academy, Harvard and Stanford Universities, and at Oxford University. A notably precocious youngster, he wrote throughout his prep school years, attended the Bread Loaf Writers' Conference at the age of sixteen where he first met Robert Frost, and published extensively during his college years. (Among his contemporaries at Harvard were John Ashbery, Robert Bly, Kenneth Koch, Frank O'Hara, and Adrienne Rich.) Early on, his poetry won a number of prizes. After his stint at Stanford where he studied with Yvor Winters, Hall returned to Harvard for three years as a member of the Society of Fellows. During this time he completed his first book, *Exiles and Marriages,* and edited a major anthology with Robert Pack and Louis Simpson, *The New Poets of England and America.* From 1957 to 1975, Hall taught at the University of Michigan. Married to his second wife and former student, the poet Jane Kenyon in 1972, he abandoned his flourishing academic career in Ann Arbor and the couple returned to Hall's deceased grandparents' home in New Hampshire, the now-famous Eagle Pond Farm. From that point on, he has supported himself by writing in a variety of genres: short stories, criticism, journalism, memoir, children's books, plays, and thirteen books of poetry. In addition, as an editor for the University of Michigan Press, he oversaw the publication of sixty-some titles between 1983 and 1996.

Hall is not only a prolific author, he is a survivor. After two colon and liver cancer surgeries followed by chemotherapy, he went into remission in 1994, only to be stunned by the diagnosis of his wife's illness: leukemia. Fifteen agonizing months of the most stringent treatments ensued before Kenyon finally succumbed. Hall's griefstricken poems, *Without,* are perhaps his finest. While the locus for many of his poems is Eagle Pond Farm, his preoccupation is not so much pastoral as it is with the relationship of poetry to society and to the fidelity of the poet's roots in this landscape. *Kicking the Leaves,* 1978, contains new, long poems on such subjects as maple syrup, blackfaced sheep, stone walls, and the search for Hall's grandfather's grave. *The One Day,* a book-length poem celebrating his sixtieth year, received the National Book Critics Circle Award in 1989. The list of his awards is lengthy, including the Lamont Poetry Prize, the Millay Award, two Guggenheim fellowships, the Lenore

Marshall Award, and many others. Hall has remarkably made the transition from professor-poet to major literary figure, in no small part attributable to his workaholic schedule. By 10 a.m. he has already spent four hours at his desk. He dictates five thousand letters a year to his several typists, reads voraciously and broadly, and spends his evenings watching baseball received from his television satellite dish while still woolgathering with pen and paper between innings. An avowed Luddite —the only concession is his dedicated fax—Hall utilizes dictation, a technique that both Henry James and Stendhal relied on heavily.

from Goatfoot, Milktongue, Twinbird: Infantile Origins of Poetic Form

When we pursue the psychic origins of poetic form, we come to the end of the trail. It is deep in the woods, and there is a fire; Twinbird sits quietly, absorbed in the play of flame that leaps and falls; Goatfoot dances by the fire, his eyes reflecting the orange coals, as his lean foot taps the stone. Inside the fire there is a mother and child, made one, the universe of the red coal. This is Milktongue.

1. SOME PREMISES

First, in connection with oppositions:

1. Any quality of poetry can be used for a number of purposes, including opposed purposes. Thus, concentration on technique has often been used to trivialize content, by poets afraid of what they will learn about themselves. But concentration on technique can absorb the attention while unacknowledged material enters the language; so technique can facilitate inspiration.

On the other hand, a poet can subscribe to an antitechnical doctrine of inspiration in a way that simply substitutes one technique for another. Surrealism can become as formulaic as a pastoral elegy.

2. When a poet says he is doing *north,* look and see if he is not actually doing *south.* Chances are that his bent is so entirely *south* that he must swear total allegiance to *north* in order to include the globe.

3. Energy arises from conflict. Without conflict, no energy. Yin and

yang. Dark and light. Pleasure and pain. No synthesis without thesis and antithesis. Conflict of course need not be binary but may include a number of terms.

4. Every present event that moves us deeply connects in our psyches with something (or things) in the past. The analogy is the two pieces of carbon that make an arc light. When they come close enough, the spark leaps across. The one mourning is all mourning; "After the first death, there is no other." This generalization applies to the composition of poems (writing) and to the recomposition of poems (reading).

5. The way out is the same as the way in. To investigate the process of making a poem is not merely an exercise in curiosity or gossip, but an attempt to understand the nature of literature. In the act of reading, the reader undergoes a process—largely without awareness, as the author was largely without intention—which resembles, like a slightly fainter copy of the original, the process of discovery or recovery that the poet went through in her madness or inspiration.

And then, more general:

6. A poem is one inside talking to another inside. It may *also* be reasonable tongue talking to a reasonable ear, but if it is not inside talking to inside, it is not a poem. This inside speaks through the second language of poetry, the unintended language. Sometimes, as in surrealism, the second language is the only language. We have the expression without the song. It is the ancient prong of carbon in the arc light. We all share more when we are five years old than when we are twenty-five; more at five minutes than at fifty years. The second language allows poetry to be universal.

7. *Lyric poetry, typically, has one goal and one message, which is to urge the condition of inwardness, the inside from which its own structure derives.*

2. FORM: THE SENSUAL BODY

There is the old distinction between *vates* and *poiein*. The *poiein*, from the Greek verb for making or doing, becomes the poet—the master of craft, the maker of the labyrinth of epic or tragedy or lyric hymn, tale-teller and spell-binder. The *vates* is bound in a spell. He is the rhapsode Socrates patronizes in *Ion*. In his purest form he utters what he does not understand at all, be he oracle or André Breton. He is the visionary, divinely inspired, who like Blake may take dictation from voices.

But Blake's voices returned to dictate revisions. The more intimately we observe any poet who claims extremes of inspiration or of craftsmanship, the more we realize that such claims are a disguise. There is no *poiein* for the same reason that there is no *vates*. The claims may be serious (they may be the compensatory distortion which allows the poet to write at all) and the claims may affect the looks of the poem—a surrealist poem and a neoclassic imitation of Horace *look* different—but the distinction becomes trivial when we discover the psychic origins of poetic form. . . .

But to begin our search for the psychic origins of poetic form, we must first think of what is usually meant by the word *form,* and then we must look for the reality. So often form is looked upon only as the fulfillment of metrical expectations. Meter is nothing but a loose set of probabilities; it is a trick easily learned; anyone can learn to arrange one hundred-and-forty syllables so that the even syllables are louder than the odd ones, and every tenth syllable rhymes according to a scheme: the object will be a sonnet. But only when you have forgotten the requirements of meter do you begin to write poetry in it. The resolutions of form which ultimately provide the wholeness of a poem—resolutions of syntax, metaphor, diction, and sound—are minute and subtle and vary from poem to poem. They vary from sonnet to sonnet, or, equally and not more greatly, from sonnet to free verse lyric.

Meter is no more seriously binding than the frame we put around a picture. But the *form* of free verse is as binding and as liberating as the *form* of a rondeau. Free verse is simply less predictable. Yeats said that the finished poem made a sound like the click of the lid on a perfectly made box. One-hundred-and-forty syllables, organized into a sonnet, do not necessarily make a click; the same number of syllables, dispersed in asymmetric lines of free verse, will click like a lid if the poem is good. In the sonnet and in the free verse poem, the poet improvises toward that click, and achieves a resolution in unpredictable ways. The rhymes and line-lengths of the sonnet are too gross to contribute greatly to that sense of resolution. The click is our sense of lyric *form.* This pleasure in resolution is Twinbird.

The wholeness and identity of the completed poem, the poem as object in time, the sensual body of the poem—this wholeness depends upon a complex of unpredictable fulfillments. The satisfying resolutions in a sonnet are more subtle than rhyme and meter, and less predictable. The body of sound grows in resolutions like assonance and alliteration, and in near-misses of both; or in the alternations, the going-away and coming-back, of fast and slow, long and short, high and low. The poet— free verse or meter, whatever—may start with lines full of long vowels, glide on diphthong sounds like *eye* and *ay,* move to quick alternative lines of short vowels and clipped consonants, and return in a coda to the long vowels *eye* and *ay.* The assonance is shaped like a saucer.

The requirements of fixity are complex, and the conscious mind seldom deals with them. Any poet who has written metrically can write arithmetically correct iambic pentameter as fast as the hand can move. In improvising toward the click, the poet is mostly aware of what sounds right and what does not. When something persists in not sounding right, the poet can examine it bit by bit—can analyze it—in the attempt to consult knowledge and apply it. . . .

When the experienced reader takes a poem in, the sense of fixity comes also from memory. The reader also has codes in her head. The new poem fulfills the old habits of expectation in some unexpected way. The reader does not know why—unless she bothers to analyze; then probably not fully—she is pleased by the sensual body of the poem. She does not need to know why. The pleasure is sufficient. Since the poet's madness is the reader's madness, the resolution of the mad material is the reader's resolution as well as the poet's. The way in is the same as the way out.

Whatever else we may say of a poem we admire, it exists as a sensual body. It is beautiful and pleasant, manifest content aside, like a worn stone that is good to touch, or like a shape of flowers arranged or accidental. This sensual body reaches us through our mouths, which are warm in the love of vowels held together, and in the muscles of our legs, which as in dance tap the motion and pause of linear and syntactic structure. These pleasures are Milktongue and Goatfoot. . . .

The *vates* feels that he speaks from the unconscious (or with the voice of God), and the *poiein* that he makes all these wholenesses of shape on purpose. Both of them disguise the truth. All poets are *poiein* and *vates.* The *poiein* comes from the memory of reading, and the *vates* from the imprint of infancy. The sensual body of the poem derives most obviously from memory of reading, but ultimately leads us back further—to the most primitive psychic origins of poetic form.

3. CONFLICT MAKES ENERGY

People frequently notice that poetry concerns itself with unpleasant subjects: death, deprivation, loneliness, despair, abandonment—if love then the death of love. Of course there are happy poems, but in English poetry there are few which are happy through and through—and those few tend to be light, short, pleasant, and forgettable. Memorable happy poems have a portion of blackness in them. Over all—Keats, Blake, Donne, Yeats, Eliot, Shakespeare, Wordsworth—there is more dark than light, more elegy than celebration. There is no great poem in our language which is simply happy. . . .

Energy arises from conflict.

(A) The sensual body of a poem is a pleasure separate from any message the poem may contain.

(B) If the poem contains a message which is pleasurable (a word I have just substituted for *happy*), then the two pleasures walk agreeably together for a few feet, and collapse into a smiling lethargy. The happy poem sleeps in the sun.

(C) If the message of the poem, on the whole, is terrifying—that They flee from me, that one time did me seek; that I am sick, I must die, that On Margate Sands / I can connect / Nothing with nothing; that Things fall apart, the center will not hold—then pain of message and pleasure of body copulate in a glorious conflict-dance of energy. This alternation of pleasure and pain is so swift as to seem simultaneous, to *be* simultaneous in the complexity both of creation and reception, a fused circle of yin and yang, a oneness in diversity.

The pain is clear to anyone. The pleasure is clear (dear) to anyone who loves poems. If we acknowledge the pleasure of the sensual body of the poem, we can see why painful poems are best: conflict makes energy and resolves our suffering into ambivalent living tissue. If human nature is necessarily ambivalent, then the structure of the energetic poem resembles the structure of human nature.

The sensual body, in poems, is not simply a compensation for the pain of the message. It is considerably more important, and more central to the nature of poetry. When we pursue the psychic origins of our satisfaction with poetic form, we come to the end of the trail. It is deep in the woods, and there is a fire; Twinbird sits quietly, absorbed in the play of flame that leaps and falls; Goatfoot dances by the fire, his eyes reflecting the orange coals, as his lean foot taps the stone. Inside the fire there is a mother and child, made one, the universe of the red coal. This is Milktongue.

4. GOATFOOT, MILKTONGUE, TWINBIRD

. . . As Milktongue mouths the noises it curls around, the rest of the infant's body plays in pleasure also. His fists open and close spasmodically. His small bowed legs, no good for walking, contract and expand in a rhythmic beat. He has begun the dance, his muscles move like his heartbeat, and Goatfoot improvises his circle around the fire. His whole body throbs and thrills with pleasure. The first parts of his body which he notices are his hands; then his feet. The strange birds fly at his head, waver, and pause. After a while he perceives that there are two of them. They begin to act when he wishes them to act, and since the *mental* creates the *physical*, Twinbird is the first magic he performs. He examines these independent / dependent twin birds. They are exactly alike. And they are exactly unalike, mirror images of each other, the perfection of opposite-same. Twinbird. . . .

Civilized humans gradually cut away the autistic component in their speech. Goatfoot survives in the dance, Twinbird in rhyme and resolution of dance and noise. Milktongue hides itself more. It ties us to the mother so obviously that men are ashamed of it. Tribal society was unashamed and worshipped Milktongue in religion and history. Among the outcast in modern society, Milktongue sometimes endures in language, as it does in the American black speech. In Ireland where the mother (and the Virgin) are still central, Milktongue prevails in the love of sweet speech. Probably, in most of the modern world, Milktongue exists only in smoking, eating, and drinking; and in oral sexuality.

But Milktongue and Goatfoot and Twinbird have always lived in the lyric poem, for poet and for reader. They are the ancestors, and they remain the psychic origins of poetic form, primitive both personally (back to the crib) and historically (back to the fire in front of the cave). They keep pure the sensual pleasure that is the dark secret shape of the poem. We need an intermediary to deal with them, for a clear reason: Goatfoot and Milktongue and Twinbird, like other figures that inhabit the forest, are wholly preverbal. They live before words. . . .

From the earliest times, poetry has existed in order to retrieve, to find again, and to release. In the poet who writes the poem, in the reader who lives it again, in the ideas, the wit, the images, the doctrines, the exhortations, the laments and the cries of joy, the lost forest struggles to be born again inside the word. The life of urge and instinct, that rages and coos, kicks and frolics, as it chooses only without choosing—this life is the life the poem grows from, and reconstitutes.

H.D.

H.D. (1886–1961) was born Hilda Doolittle in Bethlehem, Pennsylvania, a center of the Moravian religion of which her mother was a strict practitioner. Her father was an astronomer. H.D. attended Bryn Mawr where she met her lifelong friend Marianne Moore. Later, at the University of Pennsylvania she became friends with Ezra Pound. In 1911 she moved to England and became a permanent expatriate. In London she met the novelist Richard Aldington and married him in 1913, the same year her first poems were published in *Poetry Magazine* under the name "H.D. Imagiste," an idea of Pound's, who thought her poetry perfectly represented imagist principles (see Pound's essay in this volume). She published her first book of poems, *Sea Garden,* in 1916; it would be followed by thirteen more books of poems and nine of prose.

H.D. spent the rest of her life living and traveling in Europe, especially Greece. In 1918 in Cornwall, she met her lifelong partner, the writer Bryher (Annie Ellerman, who had named herself after an island she loved). H.D. had a daughter, Perdita, by Cecil Gray in 1919, the year her father and brother died and her marriage ended. When Bryher started a film company with her second husband and became involved in film, H.D. appeared in two of their films in 1927 and 1930. Her books of poetry from this time, with Greek classical themes and in the Imagist style, include *Hymen* (1921) and *Hippolytus Temporizes* (1927). In 1933 she moved to Vienna and began psychoanalysis with Freud, the subject of her memoir *Tribute to Freud* (1956). During World War II she lived with Bryher and wrote the three-volume series *Trilogy,* which moved her away from Imagism and to a more ambitious, visionary poetry, though her style remained spare and strongly imagistic. After the war she suffered a mental breakdown but continued to write prolifically. Her epic masterpiece *Helen in Egypt* was published in 1961, the year she died of a stroke. Although she won the Gold Medal from the American Academy of Arts and Letters and other awards, her work was never widely appreciated during her lifetime, perhaps because the deeply feminist aspects of her later and most ambitious work were ahead of their time. The letter reprinted here brilliantly defends the importance of a poetics of the imagination and spirit in an age of overwhelming external changes: H.D. explains that if she is thought guilty of escapism, it results from "a wish to make real to myself what is most real."

from Letter to Norman Holmes Pearson

French Line
S.S. Normandie
December 12 [1937]
New York City

. . . That was and is still, I believe with many, the final indictment of this sort of poetry.

We don't live. We don't see life. And so on.

In order to speak adequately of my poetry and its aims, I must, you see, drag in a whole deracinated epoc[h]. Perhaps specifically, I might say that the house next door was struck another night. We came home and simply waded through glass, which wind from now unshuttered windows, made the house, a barn, an unprotected dug-out. What does that sort of shock do to the mind, the imagination—not solely of myself, but of an epoc[h]? One of the group found some pleasure in the sight of the tilted shelves and the books tumbled, on the floor. He gave a decisive football kick with his army boot to the fattest volume. It happened actually to be Browning. He demanded dramatically, "what is the use of all this—now?" To me, *Fortu* and the *yellow melon flower* answered by existing. They were in other space, other dimension, never so clear as at that very moment. The *unexpected isle in the far seas* remained. Remains.

Life?

Poetry?

Times and places?

"Leda" was done at the same time as "Lethe." Lotus-land, all this. It is nostalgia for a lost land. I call it Hellas. I might, psychologically just as well, have listed the Casco Bay islands off the coast of Maine but I called my islands Rhodes, Samos and Cos. They are symbols. And symbolically, the first island of memory was dredged away or lost, like a miniature Atlantis. It was a thickly wooded island in the Lehigh River and believe it or not, was named actually, Calypso's island. . . .

The "lost" world of the classics and the neo-classics is the world of childhood. "What are the islands to me?" This, I suppose—an inner region of defence, escape, these are the poems of escapism—if there is any such word. And of memory, suppressed memory, maybe. (And what about the mother of the Muses? Mnemosyne, if I remember.) Actual memory, repressed memory, desire to escape, desire to create (music), intellectual curiosity, a wish to make real to myself what is most real, the fragrant pages of the early Greek poets, to tear, if it be even the barest fragment of vibrant electric parchment from hands not always worthy to touch, fingers whose sterile "intellectuality" is so often an inverted curse of Midas—these are some of the ingredients of my poetry. . . .

MAXINE KUMIN

Maxine Kumin (1925–) is the author of fifteen books of poetry and four essay collections. Her fourth book of poems, *Up Country,* won the Pulitzer Prize; *Looking for Luck* won the Poets' Prize. She also holds the Aiken Taylor Award, an American Academy of Arts and Letters Award, the Ruth Lilly Prize, and the Harvard Medal for the Arts. A former Consultant in Poetry to the Library of Congress before that post was renamed Poet Laureate, she lives on a horse farm in New Hampshire, the setting for many of her poems. Central to them is a vision of nature and the place of humans in the natural world. Frequently, she convicts us of cruelty towards others, especially animals, and of a heedless destruction of the environment. Her family, a large web of connections, has provided material for another group of poems she refers to as "tribal."

A self-declared formalist, Kumin is most comfortable, as she points out in these selections, with the paradoxical freedom working in form conveys. She describes her "tools"—typewriter and pen at that time, though she has since converted to the computer—the need she feels for psychic distance from the emotion of the poem, and her insistence on enough specificity and narrative to carry the freight of the poem. A disgruntled student called this attention to detail "furniture"; Kumin liked this term so much that she added it to "geography" and "chronology," her other bywords for a successful poem.

In 1998 she survived a life-threatening accident and has since published a memoir of her recovery, *Inside the Halo and Beyond: Anatomy of a Recovery,* and two collections of poems, *The Long Marriage* and *Jack and Other New Poems.* According to poet Philip Booth, Kumin has outrun the limits of her generation by trusting those elements which are most strongly individual in her work. Women readers in particular respond to her earthy humor, to her attention to women as mothers, daughters, friends, and mentors and to her loyalty to women writers.

from Coming Across:
Establishing the Intent of the Poem

How do poems begin? Who really knows? "How do I love you, let me count the ways" is probably as good an answer as any. The impulse to build a poem may be something amorphous, inchoate, vague yet persistent as a floating sense of unease. It may be an emotion as specific as anger, as explicit as the sex drive, as necessary as food. The poet may start with a fact or feeling. She may be the kind of writer who knows from the outset what she is aiming at, or she may be the kind who at the moment of particularly heightened tension in a peculiar aura seizes her chaos or prickly perception and seeks to interpret it, make some sort of order out of it, never knowing really where the muse will lead her.

I think most poets have had both kinds of experience—the immediate palpable need to get a poem down whole, and the other, formless but equally valid urge to follow wherever the words and feelings lead. Once in a great while the "given" poem comes along, the *don*, the gift, a poem that flows easily. It proceeds onto the page as if it had been shaped by the seraphim up there on the golden pavement and lightly handed down to the poet simply to record. It is like admitting to having had an earthly visitation to get such a poem—three times in ten years this has happened to me—and each time I was totally unprepared for the event. Much more often there is the sweat and wrestle of tearing the poem out of experience and struggling to get it into being. . . .

Intent, as I read it, is something larger than the simple event or plot of the poem. I have a lot of narrow prejudices in this connection. I'm not very often satisfied with a straight imagist poem. For me a poem must go beyond its setting or its particular to say outright or by subtle suggestion something about the human universal condition. If the gift without the giver is bare, the poem without the concept is emaciated, merely a skeleton. I want, I am hungry for something elusive I can only call *realization*.

I don't know another word for it except maybe to say that what I want of a poem is that it arouse in me a sympathetic response to its authenticity.

from Closing the Door

. . . I confess that I am growing rather curmudgeonly on the issue of endings, wanting as I do some definitive and actual sense of closure. If not the slam of the door at the end of the poem, which Oscar Williams speaks of, then at least the click of the bolt in the jamb. My bête noire is the poem that ends by simply falling off the page in an accident of imbalance, so that the reader, poor fish, doesn't actually know the poem has ended. She turns the page in expectation of further enlightenment, only to be caught red-fingered with the title of the next poem coldly sizing her up.

Nor does it matter, I think, whether we are talking about the vatic, oracular poet whose poems come in a kind of seizure as Blake's did, or as Richard Eberhart's do, or whether we are talking about the carefully crafted poems which A. E. Housman carried around for weeks in his head before writing them down, something Richard Wilbur also does (as he says, "in a state of warm self-indulgence"), or as I imagine John Crowe Ransom did. A poem may be written at one sitting or it may lie around in a pile of thoughts for months or years before coming to being. The finished poem, whatever its wellspring, has been raised to its highest intensity, has passed the fulcrum, the hinge part if you will, and now comes to its conclusion. It has always seemed to me that some lapses can be forgiven the poet if she finishes well, just as they can be forgiven the lover. I will of course be accused by some of having fallen victim to a bad case of formalism, as if to end well or to end declaratively were a disease of technical cunning. I can only plead, if this be technical cunning, make the most of it. . . .

ALICIA OSTRIKER

Alicia Ostriker has published ten volumes of poetry in the course of a distinguished career as a professor of English at Rutgers University. She has received fellowships from the Guggenheim and Rockefeller Foundations, as well as from the National Foundation for the Arts. She won the Willliam Carlos Williams Award in 1986 for *The Imaginary Lover; The Crack in Everything* was a National Book Award finalist in 1996 and won both the Paterson Poetry Prize and the San Francisco State Poetry Center Award; *The Little Space: Poems Selected and New 1968–1998* was a National Book Award and a Lenore Marshall finalist.

Ostriker's work often pursues both personal and political themes. An early book, *The Mother/Child Papers* (1980) deals with issues of love and violence during the Vietnam War. In *The Volcano Sequence* (2002) the volcano can be seen as metaphor for the poet's angers, for her ongoing quarrel with God, and for her unspoken anger with her mother, a conflict ultimately resolved late in her mother's life. God is a major presence in the volcano poems; raised in an atheistic Jewish household, Ostriker has become increasingly engaged with questions of religion and history. *The Nakedness of the Fathers: Biblical Visions and Revisions* (1994) combines prose and poetry, Midrash and autobiography, in a set of re-readings of the Hebrew Bible.

In addition to being a scholar of Blake and the Bible, Ostriker is a highly regarded feminist critic. With the publication of *Writing Like a Woman* (1982), *Stealing the Language: The Emergence of Women's Poetry in America* (1986), and *Dancing at the Devil's Party: Essays on Poetry, Politics and the Erotic* (2000), she has taken her place in the forefront of contemporary women authors who support and explore what she calls "the poetics of ardor."

from Stealing the Language

FROM THE INTRODUCTION

. . . The idea that women writers have been imprisoned in an "oppressor's language" which denies them access to authoritative expression is a common thread throughout this book, and I suggest the variety of strategies women use to subvert and overcome this denial. . . . I consider a major strategy—revisionist mythmaking—as a means of exploring and attempting to transform the self and the culture. Myths are the sanctuaries of language where our meanings for "male" and "female" are stored; to rewrite them from a female point of view is to discover new possibilities for meaning. . . .

FROM CHAPTER 4: HERR GOD, HERR LUCIFER: ANGER, VIOLENCE, AND POLARIZATION

. . . To begin, it is clear that the women's poetry movement coincides with an outpouring of what we can call victimization writing. Men in victimization poems embody a cultural script in which masculine power, intrinsically violent and tyrannical, dominates the concentric worlds of personal life and society, supported by myths of superior male rationality and, ultimately, male divinity. Women in victimization poems submit, angrily complying in their own powerlessness, as if three centuries had scarcely altered the confession of Shakespeare's Kate that a woman's man is "Thy lord, thy life, the keeper, / Thy head, the sovereign." Typically, victimization writing is clear, powerful, and accessible, deploying familiar gendered scenarios—relying, for the most part, on our ability to recognize the gendered gestures and rhetoric built into our culture.

Second, as a partial consequence of women's discovery of female victimization, we have an immense explosion of violence in women's poetry today, an articulation of a need which may indeed have been buried for three thousand years. Much of this writing is highly inventive in its deployment of gender-saturated metaphor and profoundly subversive both in its exploration of prohibited emotion and in its attack on our culture's systemic phallocentricity, that potent combination of might and right ascribed to the deity and his sons. The release of fantasy in these poems is a striking example of the volcanic return of the repressed. What has been less often recognized is that the violence in women's poems is directed as often against the self as against what Adrienne Rich calls the oppressor, and that here too we have the bringing into literary consciousness of elements long present and long denied in our psychic and cultural netherworlds. . . .

FROM CHAPTER 6: THIEVES OF LANGUAGE: WOMEN POETS AND REVISIST MYTHOLOGY

... The recognition that the faces in mythology may be our own faces which we "must explore" to gain knowledge of myth's inner meanings and our own, has been crucial. As we approach our own time, women's mythological poems demonstrate increasing self-consciousness, increasing irony, and increasing awareness that the poet may not only say "Sappho" or "Ariadne" when the culture does not permit her to say "I" but may also deviate from or explicitly challenge the meanings attributed to mythic figures and tales. She may keep the name but change the game, and here is where revisionist mythology comes in.

Since 1960 one can count over a dozen major works (poem sequences, long poems, or whole books) of revisionist myth published by American women, and one cannot begin to count the individual poems in which familiar figures from male tradition emerge altered. These poems generically assume the high literary status that myth confers and that women writers have often been denied because they write "personally" or "confessionally." But in them the old stories are changed, changed utterly, by female knowledge of female experience, so that they can no longer stand as foundations of collective male fantasy or as the pillars sustaining phallocentric "high" culture. Instead, they are corrections; they are representations of what women find divine and demonic in themselves; they are retrieved images of what women have collectively and historically suffered; in some cases they are instructions for survival. ...

The poems surveyed in this chapter have several characteristics in common. First, they treat existing texts as fenceposts, surrounding the terrain of mythic truth, but by no means identical to it. In other words, they are enactments of feminist antiauthoritarianism opposed to the patriarchal praxis of reifying texts. As Adrienne Rich declares in her definition of women's "writing as re-vision," "Re-vision—the act of looking back, of seeing with fresh eyes, of entering an old text from a new critical direction—is for women more than a chapter in cultural history; it is an act of survival." Knowledge throughout women's mythmaking is achieved through personal, intuitive, and subjective means. It is never to be derived from prior authority and is always to be tested within the self. This is not to say that the poems, or the truths they represent, are merely private. As we have already seen, the private-public distinction is one that contemporary women poets tend to resist and attempt to dissolve in favor of a personal-communal continuum. As in women's love poems, the tacit assumption in women's myth poems is that the self in its innermost reaches is plural. The "I" is a "we," the myth contains and conveys common knowledge. The effectiveness of these poems rests on their power to release meanings that were latent but imprisoned all along in the stories we thought we knew.

Second, most of these poems involve reevaluations of social, political, and philosophical values, particularly those most enshrined in occidental literature, such as the glorification of conquest and the faith that the cosmos is—must be—hierarchically ordered with earth and body on the bottom and mind and spirit on the top. By the same token, none of these writers concerns herself with the achievement of immortality. On the contrary, the desire to live eternally tends to be mockingly deconstructed by women poets as a corollary of male aggressiveness and need for control.

Third, the work of women mythmakers is conspicuously different from the modernist mythmaking of Yeats, Pound, Eliot, and Auden because it contains no trace of nostalgia, no faith that the past is a repository of truth, goodness, or desirable social organization. Prufrock may yearn to be Hamlet, but what woman would want to be Ophelia? What woman's soul would seek monuments of its own magnificence in Byzantium? While the myth of a Golden Age has exerted incalculable pressure in the shaping of western literature and its attitude toward history, the revisionist woman poet does not care if the hills of Arcady are dead. Or rather, she does not believe they are dead. Far from representing history as a decline or bemoaning disjunctions of past and present, her poems insist that past and present are, for better or worse, essentially the same. H.D.'s concept of the "palimpsest" seems to be the norm, along with a treatment of time that effectively flattens it so that the past is not then but now.

Fourth, degree of revisionism correlates with formal experiment. This is important not only because new meanings must generate new forms—when we have a new form in art we can assume we have a new meaning—but because the strategies of defamiliarization draw attention to the discrepancies between traditional concepts and the conscious mental and emotional activity of female re-vision. As it accentuates its argument to make clear that there *is* an argument, that an act of theft is occurring, feminist revisionism differs from Romantic revisionism, although in other respects, such as its stress on personal feeling, it is similar. . . .

from Dancing at the Devil's Party

FROM III. CHANGING THE MUSIC

. . . Presumably in response to our culture's identification of femininity with pliability, many of the best women poets use what I call an exoskeletal style: hard, steely, implacably ironic. This is a multipurpose device. It makes the condescending label "poetess" impossible, as it is conspicuously and exaggeratedly antisentimental. It is useful for satire and parody. It is a kind of formal shell like the armor on so many of Marianne Moore's beasts, a sign of the need for self-protection on the part of the vulnerable. Unlike Moore (or more recently Amy Clampitt), however, these poets do not pretend to be charming eccentrics. Often this style is used to challenge the neutrality of the reader, addressing a "you" who is perceived as an antagonist or lover-antagonist and whose role the reader is forced to play. . . .

Women's poems are not of course necessarily written from within the dominant literary language. A powerful resource for poets lucky enough to have access to it is Black English, with its repertoire of cadences and phrases lifted from field hollers, spirituals, gospel, and blues on its musical side, as well as the King James Bible, high-energy preaching, and verbal rituals like rapping and the dozens on its oratorical side. The artful mimesis of "uneducated" speech has been a strategy of social criticism since *Huckleberry Finn*, first because it lets us enjoy the pleasure of breaking school rules (we all know in our hearts that rules are in the service of the rulers; to obey them is to accede to social structures for which grammatical structures are the gateway), second because it pits lively imagery against dry abstraction, humor against precept, the play of improvisation and the body's rhythms against the strictures of prior form.

NATHANIEL MACKEY

Nathaniel Mackey (1947–) was born in Miami, Florida, of half Bahamian ancestry. His parents separated when he was four, and he moved to California with his mother and siblings. He became interested in music early, first in church music and then, as a teenager, jazz. In an interview with Christopher Funkhouser, Mackey said, "Why I didn't take up an instrument and become a musician is a mystery to me." At Princeton University he studied literature, receiving his BA in 1969, followed by his PhD from Stanford University in 1975. He began to edit the innovative literary magazine *Hambone* in 1974, and since 1979 he has been professor of English at the University of California, Santa Cruz. Known as a scholar of jazz and African, Latin American, and Caribbean mythologies and histories, he hosts a weekly radio show, *Tanganyika Strut*, featuring eclectic juxtapositions of African American and world music. Now a chancellor of the Academy of American Poets, Mackey has received recognition from the National Poetry Series and won a Whiting Award. Father of three children, he married Pascale Gaitet in 1991.

Mackey's books of poetry include *Four for Trane* (1978), *Eroding Witness* (1985), *School of Udhra* (1993), and *Song of the Andoumboulou: 18-20* (1994). His prose includes a book of criticism, *Discrepant Engagement: Dissonance, Cross-Culturality, and Experimental Writing* (1993), and two books of fiction, *Bedouin Hornbook* (1986) and *Djbot Baghostus's Run* (1993). He co-edited the anthology, *Moment's Notice: Jazz in Poetry and Prose* (1993). A compact disc recording of poems read with musical accompaniment titled *Strick: Song of the Andoumboulou 16-25* was released in 1995.

Mackey's poetry is influenced by the open form poetics of Amiri Baraka, Robert Duncan, and Charles Olson and at the same time explores correspondences across African, Latin American, and Caribbean cultures. His work, infused with history, meditation, and musical phrasing, shows that the poetry and music of many cultures are closely intertwined. In the excerpt below from *Cante Moro*, Mackey connects the passionate sources of poetic inspiration as described by Neruda with powerful themes in African culture.

from Cante Moro

. . . In his lecture "Theory and Function of the *Duende*," Lorca tells us: "The dark and quivering *duende* that I am talking about is a descendant of the merry daemon of Socrates." The madness, then . . . is not ultimately a surrealist simulation drawn from a clinical model in a program of systematic alienation but, past that state, means to return to the divine madness of daemonic inspiration, the speaking more than one knew, that Plato tells us his master, Socrates, thought to be at once the power and the dementia of the poet in his art. . . .

It is a taking over of one's voice by another voice. This wooing of another voice, an alternate voice, that is so important to *duende* has as one of its aspects or analogies in poetry that state of entering the language in such a way that one is into an area of implication, resonance, and connotation that is manifold, many-meaninged, polysemous. One has worked beyond oneself. It is as if the language itself takes over. Something beyond the will, the conscious design or desire of the poet, is active, something that goes beyond univocal, unequivocal control. . . .

My work has a pronounced relationship to music. I was always struck by Louis Zukofsky's definition of poetry as a function whose lower limit is speech and whose upper limit is song. He uses the integral sign from calculus to suggest that we are integrating that lower limit, speech, and that upper limit, song. Poetry is an integral function. But even before I came across Zukovsky's formulation of it, I heard poetry as a musical deployment of language, the music peculiar to language, language bordering on song, speech bordering on song. . . .

One of the striking things about the blues tradition is the way the instrument becomes that other, alternate voice. Everyone talks about the speechlike qualities of the instruments as they are played in African-American music. Built into that is some kind of dissatisfaction with—if not critique of—the limits of conventionally articulate speech, verbal speech. One of the reasons the music so often goes over into nonspeech— moaning, humming, shouts, nonsense lyrics, scat—is to say, among other things, that the realm of conventionally articulate speech is not sufficient for saying what needs to be said. We are often making that same assertion in poetry. This is one of the reasons that in poetry we seek out that "trouble of an unbound reference" about which Duncan writes, as well as one of the reasons this music has been so attractive, so instructive, such an inspiration to poets. . . .

SEAMUS HEANEY

Seamus Heany (1939–), the oldest of nine children, grew up on a small farm called Mossbawn in County Derry, Ireland, where his father, a taciturn man, was a cattle dealer. His mother, he has said, was always ready to speak out, and Heaney interprets this inner tension between speech and silence, this "quarrel with himself" as a trait that he inherited from his parents.

As a small child Heaney observed, without understanding their importance, American troops stationed at a nearby airfield where they were preparing for the Normandy invasion in World War II. Reflecting back, he sees himself caught between "history and ignorance," another step in his poetic development. Although the family moved away from Mossbawn when the poet was only fourteen, rural County Derry remains the "country of the mind" where so much of Heaney's work is rooted. He spoke of leaving the farm as moving from "the earth of farm labour to the heaven of education."

At Catholic boarding school in Derry, forty miles from home, Heaney studied Latin and Irish. Later, at Queen's University in Belfast—yet another remove from Mossbawn—he studied Anglo-Saxon. His early work draws linguistically from the Anglo-Saxon note in English, with a strongly stressed and packed line. Later, there are echoes of Dante and Virgil to be found in *Station Island* (1984) and *Seeing Things* (1991). Heaney also undertook translations from the Middle Irish in *Sweeney Astray* (1982). His Gaelic heritage remains central to his work, both politically and culturally.

In the mid-'60s, Heaney was active in a Northern Irish group of writers with whom he shared the fate of having been born into a deeply divided society. The religious and political differences of his country darkened Heaney's work in the '70s and immersed him in the ongoing question of the poet's responsibility to the wider world. The issue of social obligation balanced against the poet's creative freedom runs through his prose essay collections, most notably *The Government of the Tongue* (1988) and *The Redress of Poetry* (1995). Field Day, an Irish theater company founded in 1980 by Brian Friel and Stephen Rea to bring the crisis in politics into artistic focus through plays and pamphlets, deeply involved Heaney from the outset. His version of Sophocles' play *Philoctetes* toured Ireland in 1990 under the title *The Cure at Troy*.

Heaney and his wife Marie spent 1970–71 at Berkeley, where the poet was a visiting lecturer; this visit culminated in Heaney's decision to resign his post at Queen's University and become a full-time freelance writer. In 1982, he accepted the position of Boylston Professor of Rhetoric and Oratory at Harvard, but resigned from it in 1996. He returns occasionally to Harvard as poet-in-residence, but makes his home in Dublin where he continues to be active in the promotion of artistic and educational causes.

The honors bestowed on Heaney are many, including membership in the American Academy of Arts and Letters, and the Nobel Prize in Literature in 1995. He is the author of thirteen collections of poems— *Opened Ground* (1999) was a New York Times Notable Book of the Year—and five essay collections as well as one play. "Digging," the poem reprinted here, is drawn from his first book and is emblematic of his preoccupation with his country heritage.

Digging

Between my finger and my thumb
The squat pen rests; snug as a gun.

Under my window, a clean rasping sound
When the spade sinks into gravelly ground:
My father, digging. I look down

Till his straining rump among the flowerbeds
Bends low, comes up twenty years away
Stooping in rhythm through potato drills
Where he was digging.

The coarse boot nestled on the lug, the shaft
Against the inside knee was levered firmly.
He rooted out tall tops, buried the bright edge deep

To scatter new potatoes that we picked,
Loving their cool hardness in our hands.

By God, the old man could handle a spade.
Just like his old man.

My grandfather cut more turf in a day
Than any other man on Toner's bog.
Once I carried him milk in a bottle
Corked sloppily with paper. He straightened up
To drink it, then fell to right away
Nicking and slicing neatly, heaving sods
Over his shoulder, going down and down
For the good turf. Digging.

The cold smell of potato mould, the squelch and slap
Of soggy peat, the curt cuts of an edge
Through living roots awaken in my head.
But I've no spade to follow men like them.
Between my finger and my thumb
The squat pen rests.
I'll dig with it.

JOY HARJO

Joy Harjo (1951–) was born in Tulsa, Oklahoma, of mixed French and Cherokee and Creek Native American heritage. She was enrolled at birth as a member of the Creek tribe, and is a member of the Muscogee Creek Nation of Oklahoma. She is also a member of the Tulluhasse Wakokaye Ceremonial Grounds. She graduated from the University of New Mexico with a BA in poetry and received her MFA in creative writing from the University of Iowa. Her ethnic background permeates her poetry and prose, celebrating the Southwest and specifically Oklahoma, her "prairie of words."

She has become a powerful voice in the Native American renaissance that includes such figures as N. Scott Momaday and Leslie Marmon Silko. Her numerous poetry collections—*How We Became Human: New and Selected Poems; A Map to the Next World; The Woman Who Fell From the Sky*—have garnered many significant awards, including an American Book Award, the William Carlos Williams Award, the American Indian Distinguished Achievement in the Arts Award, and the Delmore Schwartz Memorial Award. Her subjects include the Native American's devastating confrontation with whites, as well as the topics that concern all poets, like love, death, and transformation. Transformation of hatred to love is a major theme. Harjo depends on repetition as a key poetic technique; she herself considers it an acknowledgment of ceremony rather than simply a device. Perhaps no other poet in this collection is more deeply rooted in her cultural past.

Her work is woman-identified and often portrays powerful, nearly mythic female characters. Her six major books focus on the idea of survival of the individual and of the Native Americans as a people, rather than emphasizing political correctness. She also performs her poetry and plays saxophone with her band, including "tribal-jazz-reggae" to enthusiastic audiences. Her new solo CD is *Native Joy for Real*. In addition, she writes movie scripts, makes films, writes for television, and has done educational broadcasting on public radio. She has two grown children, lives in Honolulu, Hawaii, and is a professor at UCLA.

from The Spiral of Memory

THE CREATIVE PROCESS

The Woman Hanging
from the Thirteenth Floor Window

She is the woman hanging from the 13th floor
window. Her hands are pressed white against the
concrete moulding of the tenement building. She
hangs from the 13th floor window in east Chicago,
with a swirl of birds over her head. They could
be a halo, or a storm of glass waiting to crush her.

She thinks she will be set free.

The woman hanging from the 13th floor window
on the east side of Chicago is not alone.
She is a woman of children, of the baby, Carlos,
and of Margaret, and of Jimmy who is the oldest.
She is her mother's daughter and her father's son.
She is several pieces between the two husbands
she has had. She is all the women of the apartment
building who stand watching her, watching themselves.

When she was young she ate wild rice on scraped down
plates in warm wood rooms. It was in the farther
north and she was the baby then. They rocked her.

She sees Lake Michigan lapping at the shores of
herself. It is a dizzy hole of water and the rich
live in tall glass houses at the edge of it. In some
places Lake Michigan speaks softly, here, it just sputters
and butts itself against the asphalt. She sees

other buildings just like hers. She sees other
women hanging from many-floored windows
counting their lives in the palms of their hands
and in the palms of their children's hands.

She is the woman hanging from the 13th floor window
on the Indian side of town. Her belly is soft from
her children's births, her worn levis swing down below
her waist, and then her feet, and then her heart.
She is dangling.

The woman hanging from the 13th floor hears voices.
They come to her in the night when the lights have gone
dim. Sometimes they are little cats mewing and scratching
at the door, sometimes they are her grandmother's voice,
and sometimes they are gigantic men of light whispering
to her to get up, to get up, to get up. That's when she wants
to have another child to hold onto in the night, to be able
to fall back into dreams.

And the woman hanging from the 13th floor window
hears other voices. Some of them scream out from below
for her to jump, they would push her over. Others cry softly
from the sidewalks, pull their children up like flowers and gather
them into their arms. They would help her, like themselves.

But she is the woman hanging from the 13th floor window,
and she knows she is hanging by her own fingers, her
own skin, her own thread of indecision.

She thinks of Carlos, of Margaret, of Jimmy.
She thinks of her father, and of her mother.
She thinks of all the women she has been, of all
the men. She thinks of the color of her skin, and

of Chicago streets, and of waterfalls and pines.
She thinks of moonlight nights, and of cool spring storms.
Her mind chatters like neon and northside bars.
She thinks of the 4 a.m. lonelinesses that have folded
her up like death, discordant, without logical and
beautiful conclusion. Her teeth break off at the edges.
She would speak.

The woman hangs from the 13th floor window crying for
the lost beauty of her own life. She sees the
sun falling west over the grey plane of Chicago.
She thinks she remembers listening to her own life
break loose, as she falls from the 13th floor
window on the east side of Chicago,
or as she climbs back up to claim herself again.

How did this poem begin?

This poem began two years before I began writing it, during a trip to Chicago to visit friends, see the King Tut exhibit and look for other Indians. I found the Chicago Indian Center at nearly dusk. It could have been any other urban Indian center, the same part of the city, a color like lost dreams, air tasting like a borrowed hope, and always the ragged pool tables where kids acting twice their age shoot pool downhill all day.

One particular image stayed with me for two years, and it probably wasn't exactly what I saw, but changed, transformed with living. And it wasn't the most significant image I remember, or it didn't appear to be, but something about that one small room, hardly anyone in it, a western window with no curtains, maybe a few toothless venetian blinds, and a rocking chair, especially that bony rocking chair with stuffing coming out of the padding, and the sun falling behind a horizon of skyscrapers, triggered the poem, the story in it.

What still strikes me about the remembering is not knowing whether "for real" anyone had been rocking in that rocking chair, but everytime I remember it I remember a young woman nursing a baby, or an old man with a greasy paper sack on his knee, softly breathing: or two kids rocking it hard and being warned to slow down; or that old woman at forty who watched the sunset as receding light across the floor; or the other one laughing at her sister's terrible jokes; or anyone I may have seen or not seen in that rocking chair.

The woman hanging from the thirteenth floor window could have been in that chair, just hours before, letting that steady rhythm calm her, a heartbeat against wood, trying to dream her own regeneration, so that any kind of hopelessness wouldn't be overwhelming.

Out of this the poem took root, two years before the actual writing began.

I wrote the poem one afternoon as I sat at my desk in my office at the Institute of American Indian Arts in Santa Fe, after I pulled out a sheaf of papers one of which had a note on it about the Chicago Indian Center, something quickly scribbled about the rocking chair, that room.

It was probably one of the quicker poems I have written, in terms of getting its basic structure down, the basic line of it. And unusual in the sense that I kept feeling her there, standing behind me, urging me on. . . .

RICHARD HUGO

Richard Hugo (1923–82) was born in White Center, a working-class suburb south of Seattle. His father abandoned him, and his teenage mother took him to live with her rigid parents. It was a Depression-era childhood. In his autobiography *The Real West Marginal Way* he reports that he was "subjected to gratuitous beatings" as well as silent, undemonstrative affection. Although his newly remarried mother and stepfather did not take him to live with them, Hugo assumed his stepfather's name. Hugo played baseball throughout high school and semipro ball in the city leagues. At nineteen, he was drafted into, or volunteered for—accounts differ on this matter—World War II, where he served as a bombardier, flying thirty-five combat missions and attaining the rank of first lieutenant in 1945. After his discharge, Hugo returned to White Center and continued to play in the semipro leagues while attending the University of Washington, majoring in creative writing. He studied with Theodore Roethke and acquired his MFA in 1952. That same year, he married Barbara Williams and was hired by Boeing as a technical writer, a job he held for thirteen years. He admired Wallace Stevens, who wrote his poems while serving as vice president of an insurance company and wondered, in *The Real West Marginal Way* if he could "be that tough . . . while all around me were people who didn't know or care." His first book of poems, *A Run of Jacks,* appeared in 1961. In 1963 he and his wife traveled to Italy, a trip that provided material for *Good Luck in Cracked Italian* (1969). The couple separated in 1964 and two years later divorced.

Hugo then took a position as visiting lecturer at the University of Montana in Missoula. A period of emotional turmoil and heavy drinking ensued but he went on to be an associate professor at Montana, visiting poet at the University of Iowa, holder of the Roethke chair at the University of Washington, and ultimately the director of the creative writing program at Montana from 1971 to 1982. In 1973 he met Ripley Schemm Hansen; they married the following year and he moved in with her and her two children on her property near Rattlesnake Creek, where assorted dogs and Ripley's two quarter horses, unfenced, coexisted. It was a period of domestic happiness. Hugo produced several more poetry books; his essays, *The Triggering Town,* from which this excerpt is taken; a novel, *Death and the Good Life;* and his autobiography. In 1977 he became editor of the Yale Younger Poets Series. His friendships were many. They included a circle of Northwest writers, Carolyn Kizer, Madeline DeFrees, Jim Welch, and William Stafford, who encouraged one another, in the words of Hugo's poem, "Making Certain It Goes On." Hugo died suddenly of leukemia in 1982.

from The Triggering Town

You hear me make extreme statements like "don't communicate" and "there is no reader." While these statements are meant as said, I presume when I make them that you *can* communicate and can write clear English sentences. I caution against communication because once language exists only to convey information, it is dying.

Let's take language that exists to communicate—the news story. In a news story the words are there to give you information about the event. Even if the reporter has a byline, anyone might have written the story, and quite often more than one person has by the time it is printed. Once you have the information, the words seem unimportant. Valéry said they dissolve, but that's not quite right. Anyway, he was making a finer distinction, one between poetry and prose that in the reading of English probably no longer applies. That's why I limited our example to news articles. By understanding the words of a news article you seem to deaden them.

In the news article the relation of the words to the subject (triggering subject since there is no other unless you can provide it) is a strong one. The relation of the words to the writer is so weak that for our purposes it isn't worth consideration. Since the majority of your reading has been newspapers, you are used to seeing language function this way. When you write a poem these relations must reverse themselves. That is, the relation of the words to the subject must weaken and the relation of the words to the writer (you) must take on strength.

This is probably the hardest thing about writing poems. It may be a problem with every poem, at least for a long time. Somehow you must switch your allegiance from the triggering subject to the words. For our purposes I'll use towns as examples. The poem is always in your hometown, but you have a better chance of finding it in another. The reason for that, I believe, is that the stable set of knowns that the poem needs to anchor on is less stable at home than in the town you've just seen for the first time. At home, not only do you know that the movie house wasn't always there, or that the grocer is a newcomer who took over after the former grocer committed suicide, you have complicated emotional responses that defy sorting out. With the strange town, you can assume all knowns are stable, and you owe the details nothing emotionally. However, not just any town will do. Though you've never seen it before, it must be a town you've lived in all your life. You must take emotional possession of the town and so the town must be one that, for personal reasons I can't understand, you feel is your town. In some mysterious way that you need not and probably won't understand, the relationship is based on fragments of information that are fixed—and if you need knowns that the town does not provide, no trivial concerns such as loyalty to truth, a nagging consideration had you stayed home, stand in the way of your introducing them as needed by the poem. It is easy to turn the gas station attendant into a drunk. Back home it would have been difficult because he had a drinking problem.

Once these knowns sit outside the poem, the imagination can take off from them and if necessary can return. You are operating from a base. . . .

> That silo, filled with chorus girls and grain
> burned down last night and grew back tall.
> The grain escaped to the river. The girls ran
> crying to the moon. When we knock, the metal
> gives a hollow ring—

O.K. I'm just fooling around. (God, I'm even rhyming.) It looks like the news I got an hour ago was bad, but note the silo replaced itself and we might still fill it again. Note also that now the town has a river and that when I got fancy and put those girls on the moon I got back down to earth in a hurry and knocked on something real. Actually I'm doing all this because I like "l" sounds, "silo" "filled" "girls" "tall" "metal" "hollow," and I like "n" sounds, "grain" "burned" "down" "ran" "moon," "ring," and I like "k" sounds, "back" "knock." Some critic, I think Kenneth Burke, would say I like "k" sounds because my name is Dick.

In this case I imagined the town, but an imagined town is at least as real as an actual town. If it isn't you may be in the wrong business. Our triggering subjects, like our words, come from obsessions we must submit to, whatever the social cost. It can be hard. It can be worse forty years from now if you feel you could have done it and didn't. It is narcissistic, vain, egotistical, unrealistic, selfish, and hateful to assume emotional ownership of a town or a word. It is also essential.

This gets us to a somewhat tricky area. Please don't take this too seriously, but for purposes of discussion we can consider two kinds of poets, public and private. Let's use as examples Auden and Hopkins. The distinction (not a valid one, I know, but good enough for us right now) doesn't lie in the subject matter. That is, a public poet doesn't necessarily write on public themes and the private poet on private or personal ones. The distinction lies in the relation of the poet to the language. With the public poet the intellectual and emotional contents of the words are the same for the reader as for the writer. With the private poet, and most good poets of the last century or so have been private poets, the words, at least certain key words, mean something to the poet they don't mean to the reader. A sensitive reader perceives this relation of poet to word and in a way that relation—the strange way the poet emotionally possesses his vocabulary—is one of the mysteries and preservative forces of the art. With Hopkins this is evident in words like "dappled," "stippled," and "pied." In Yeats, "gyre." In Auden, no word is more his than yours.

The reason that distinction doesn't hold, of course, is that the majority of words in any poem are public—that is, they mean the same to writer and reader. That some words are the special property of a poet implies how he feels about the world and about himself, and chances are he often fights impulses to sentimentality. A public poet must always be more intelligent than the reader, nimble, skillful enough to stay ahead, to be entertaining so his didacticism doesn't set up resistances. Auden was that intelligent and skillful and he publicly regretted it. Here, in this room, I'm trying to teach you to be private poets because that's what I am and I'm limited to teaching what I know. As a private poet, your job is to be honest and to try not to be too boring. However, if you must choose between being eclectic and various or being repetitious and boring, be repetitious and boring. Most good poets are, if read very long at one sitting.

If you are a private poet, then your vocabulary is limited by your obsessions. It doesn't bother me that the word "stone" appears more than thirty times in my third book, or that "wind" and "gray" appear over and over in my poems to the disdain of some reviewers. If I didn't use them that often I'd be lying about my feelings, and I consider that unforgivable. In fact, most poets write the same poem over and over. Wallace Stevens was honest enough not to try to hide it. Frost's statement that he tried to make every poem as different as possible from the last one is a way of saying that he knew it couldn't be.

So you are after those words you can own and ways of putting them in phrases and lines that are yours by right of obsessive musical deed. You are trying to find and develop a way of writing that will be yours and will, as Stafford puts it, generate things to say. Your triggering subjects are those that ignite your need for words. When you are honest to your feelings, that triggering town chooses you. Your words used your way will generate your meanings. Your obsessions lead you to your vocabulary. Your way of writing locates, even creates, your inner life. The relation of you to your language gains power. The relation of you to the triggering subject weakens. . . .

LUCILLE CLIFTON

Lucille Clifton (1936–) was born in Depew, New York, matriculated at Howard University, transferred to Fredonia State Teachers College (now SUNY Fredonia), and began work as an actor. Her poems came to the attention of Robert Hayden, who entered them in the YM-YWHA Discovery Contest, which she won in 1969. She is now Distinguished Professor of the Humanities at St. Mary's College in Maryland. The widow of Fred Clifton, she is the mother of five grown children. Clifton is known for her spare, deceptively simple poems, which are testimony to African American working-class urban life. Her concern for family, racial history, and womanhood marks her work in prose as well as poetry; *Generations: A Memoir* is a matrilinear slave narrative, which traces her family from its African roots in 1830 to the present. Her great-great-grandmother Caroline was kidnapped from Dahomey and brought to this country as a slave. Caroline's daughter bears the dubious distinction of having been the first African American woman lynch victim. Clifton's tenth collection, *Blessing the Boats; Poems 1988–2000,* which won the National Book Award, brings together poems that reflect her ethnic pride and her feminist principles, as well as works of lyrical mysticism, where Old Testament stories and the Hindu goddess of creativity meld and overlap. She is also the author of a distinguished collection of children's books, beginning with *Some Days in the Life of Everett Anderson* (1970). Everett Anderson figures in nine books; he remains a boy of six or seven, though his environment expands, Christmas comes and goes, and he copes with his father's death. Clifton has garnered many awards, including a Lannan Literary Award, two fellowships from the National Endowment for the Arts, the Shelley Memorial Award, and an Emmy from the American Academy of Television Arts and Sciences.

The poem reprinted here from *Quilting: Poems 1987–1990,* for all its deliberate minimalism and break from Eurocentric convention, tackles the inexpressible: where poems come from. It takes a sly, deliberate stance that announces Clifton's separatist and womanist position. She wants it known that she is not one of the academy.

"when i stand around among poets . . ."

1

when i stand around among poets
i am embarrassed mostly,
their long white heads,
the great bulge in their pants,

their certainties.

i don't know how to do
what i do in the way
that i do it. it happens
despite me and i pretend

to deserve it.

but i don't know how to do it.
only sometimes when
something is singing
i listen and so far

i hear.

2

when i stand around
among poets, sometimes
i hear a single music
in us, one note
dancing us through the
singular moving world.

WISLAWA SZYMBORSKA

Born in western Poland (1923–), Szymborska has lived in the medieval city of Krakow since 1931. During the German occupation of Poland, she attended illegal classes and worked for a railroad company to avoid deportation to a labor camp in Germany. After the war she studied Polish literature and sociology at the Jagiellonian University and later worked on a Krakow literary magazine as poetry editor and columnist and helped to initiate the Polish Writers' Association. Her first two books of poems, subjected to Communist censorship, were written in the socialist-realist mode, and she has since repudiated them. In a 1957 poem, "Calling out to Yeti," she criticized Stalin's regime and likened Stalin to the Abominable Snowman.

Szymborska, deeply political and tartly witty, is a very well-known, popular poet in Poland. Her poem "Nothing Twice" provided lyrics for Polish rock star Cora, and "Love at First Sight" inspired Krzysztof Kieslowski's film *Red*. Deliberately accessible and readable, she has been compared to Emily Dickinson and Elizabeth Bishop. Her subjects are often modest: ants, grasshoppers, the onion, and clouds, for example, which she combines with bits of knowledge from natural history, Shakespeare, the history of painting or philosophy. A handful of her poems, such as "Starvation Camp Near Jaslo," concentrate directly on the atrocities of modern Polish history. As another Polish Nobel Prize winner, Czeslaw Milosz has said, Szymborska "writes in the place of the generation of poets who made their debut during the war and did not survive." Often her poems concern the difficulty of telling the truth and the necessity of avoiding partial truths and official evasions. And inspiration, she says, is born from a continuous "I don't know."

Syzmborska, who has been married twice and widowed since the early 1990s, lives very quietly. She has published sixteen collections of poetry and received many literary awards, culminating in the Nobel Prize for Literature in 1996. She is one of very few women writers to receive this honor. Her acceptance speech is included here.

The Poet and the World, Nobel Lecture, 1996

They say that the first sentence in any speech is always the hardest. Well, that one's behind me, anyway. But I have a feeling that the sentences to come—the third, the sixth, the tenth, and so on, up to the final line—will be just as hard, since I'm supposed to talk about poetry. I've said very little on the subject—next to nothing, in fact. And whenever I have said anything, I've always had the sneaking suspicion that I'm not very good at it. This is why my lecture will be rather short. All imperfection is easier to tolerate if served up in small doses.

Contemporary poets are skeptical and suspicious even, or perhaps especially, about themselves. They publicly confess to being poets only reluctantly, as if they were a little ashamed of it. But in our clamorous times it's much easier to acknowledge your faults, at least if they're attractively packaged, than to recognize your own merits, since these are hidden deeper and you never quite believe in them yourself . . . When filling in questionnaires or chatting with strangers, that is, when they can't avoid revealing their profession, poets prefer to use the general term "writer" or replace "poet" with the name of whatever job they do in addition to writing. Bureaucrats and bus passengers respond with a touch of incredulity and alarm when they discover that they're dealing with a poet. I suppose philosophers may meet with a similar reaction. Still, they are in a better position, since as often as not they can embellish their calling with some kind of scholarly title. Professor of philosophy—now that sounds much more respectable.

But there are no professors of poetry. This would mean, after all, that poetry is an occupation requiring specialized study, regular examinations, theoretical articles with bibliographies and footnotes attached, and, finally, ceremoniously conferred diplomas. And this would mean, in turn, that it's not enough to cover pages with even the most exquisite poems in order to become a poet. The crucial element is some slip of paper bearing an official stamp. Let us recall that the pride of Russian poetry, the future Nobel Laureate Joseph Brodsky was once sentenced to internal exile precisely on such grounds. They called him "a parasite," because he lacked official certification granting him the right to be a poet . . .

Several years ago, I had the honor and the pleasure of meeting Brodsky in person. And I noticed that, of all the poets I've known, he was the only one who enjoyed calling himself a poet. He pronounced the word without inhibitions.

Just the opposite—he spoke it with defiant freedom. It seems to me that this must have been because he recalled the brutal humiliations that he experienced in his youth.

In more fortunate countries, where human dignity isn't assaulted so readily, poets yearn, of course, to be published, read, and understood, but they do little, if anything, to set themselves above the common herd and the daily grind. And yet it wasn't so long ago, in this century's first decades, that poets strove to shock us with their extravagant dress and eccentric behavior. But all this was merely for the sake of public display. The moment always came when poets had to close the doors behind them, strip off their mantles, fripperies, and other poetic paraphernalia, and confront—silently, patiently awaiting their own selves—the still white sheet of paper. For finally this is what really counts.

It's not accidental that film biographies of great scientists and artists are produced in droves. The more ambitious directors seek to reproduce convincingly the creative process that led to important scientific discoveries or the emergence of a masterpiece. And one can depict certain kinds of scientific labor with some success. Laboratories, sundry instruments, elaborate machinery brought to life: such scenes may hold the audience's interest for a while. And those moments of uncertainty—will the experiment, conducted for the thousandth time with some tiny modification, finally yield the desired result?—can be quite dramatic. Films about painters can be spectacular, as they go about recreating every stage of a famous painting's evolution, from the first penciled line to the final brushstroke. Music swells in films about composers: the first bars of the melody that rings in the musician's ears finally emerge as a mature work in symphonic form. Of course this is all quite naive and doesn't explain the strange mental state popularly known as inspiration, but at least there's something to look at and listen to.

But poets are the worst. Their work is hopelessly unphotogenic. Someone sits at a table or lies on a sofa while staring motionless at a wall or ceiling. Once in a while this person writes down seven lines, only to cross out one of them fifteen minutes later, and then another hour passes, during which nothing happens . . . Who could stand to watch this kind of thing?

I've mentioned inspiration. Contemporary poets answer evasively when asked what it is, and if it actually exists. It's not that they've never known the blessing of this inner impulse. It's just not easy to explain to someone else what you don't understand yourself.

When I'm asked about this on occasion, I hedge the question too. But my answer is this: inspiration is not the exclusive privilege of poets or artists generally. There is, has been, will always be a certain group of people whom inspiration visits. It's made up of all those who've consciously chosen their calling and do their job with love and imagination. It may include doctors, teachers, gardeners—I could list a hundred more professions. Their work becomes one continuous adventure as long as they manage to keep discovering new challenges in it. Difficulties and setbacks never quell their curiosity. A swarm of new questions emerges from every problem that they solve. Whatever inspiration is, it's born from a continuous "I don't know."

There aren't many such people. Most of the earth's inhabitants work to get by. They work because they have to. They didn't pick this or that kind of job out of passion; the circumstances of their lives did the choosing for them. Loveless work, boring work, work valued only because others haven't got even that much, however loveless or boring— this is one of the harshest human miseries. And there's no sign that coming centuries will produce any changes for the better as far as this goes.

And so, though I deny poets their monopoly on inspiration, I still place them in a select group of Fortune's darlings.

At this point, though, certain doubts may arise in my audience. All sorts of torturers, dictators, fanatics, and demagogues struggling for power with a few loudly shouted slogans also enjoy their jobs, and they, too, perform their duties with inventive fervor. Well, yes, but they "know." They know, and whatever they know is enough for them once and for all. They don't want to find out about anything else, since that might diminish their argument's force. And any knowledge that doesn't lead to new questions quickly dies out: it fails to maintain the temperature required for sustaining life. In the most extreme cases, cases well known from ancient and modern history, it even poses a lethal threat to society.

This is why I value that little phrase "I don't know" so highly. It's small, but it flies on mighty wings. It expands our lives to include the spaces within us as well as those outer expanses in which our tiny Earth hangs suspended. If Isaac Newton had never said to himself, "I don't know," the apples in his little orchard might have dropped to the ground like hailstones and at best he would have stooped to pick them up and gobble them with gusto. Had my compatriot Marie Sklodowska-Curie never said to herself "I don't know," she probably would have wound up teaching chemistry at some private high school for young ladies from good families, and would have ended her days performing this otherwise perfectly respectable job. But she kept on saying "I don't know," and these words led her, not just once but twice, to Stockholm, where restless, questing spirits are occasionally rewarded with the Nobel Prize.

Poets, if they're genuine, must also keep repeating "I don't know." Each poem marks an effort to answer this statement, but as soon as the final period hits the page, the poet begins to hesitate, starts to realize that this particular answer was pure makeshift, absolutely inadequate to boot. So the poets keep on trying, and sooner or later the consecutive results of their self-dissatisfaction are clipped together with a giant paperclip by literary historians and called their "oeuvre" . . .

I sometimes dream of situations that can't possibly come true. I audaciously imagine, for example, that I get a chance to chat with the Ecclesiastes, the author of that moving lament on the vanity of all human endeavors. I would bow very deeply before him, because he is, after all, one of the greatest poets, for me at least. That done, I would grab his hand. "'There's nothing new under the sun': that's what you wrote, Ecclesiastes. But you yourself were born new under the sun. And the poem you created is also new under the sun, since no one wrote it down before you. And all your readers are also new under the sun, since those who lived before you couldn't read your poem. And that cypress that you're sitting under hasn't been growing since the dawn of time. It came into being by way of another cypress similar to yours, but not exactly the same. And Ecclesiastes, I'd also like to ask you what new thing under the sun you're planning to work on now? A further supplement to the thoughts that you've already expressed? Or maybe you're tempted to contradict some of them now? In your earlier work you mentioned joy—so what if it's fleeting? So maybe your new-under-the-sun poem will be about joy? Have you taken notes yet, do you have drafts? I doubt that you'll say, 'I've written everything down, I've got nothing left to add.' There's no poet in the world who can say this, least of all a great poet like yourself."

The world—whatever we might think when we're terrified by its vastness and our own impotence or embittered by its indifference to individual suffering, of people, animals, and perhaps even plants, for why are we so sure that plants feel no pain; whatever we might think of its expanses pierced by the rays of stars surrounded by planets we've just begun to discover, planets already dead? still dead? we just don't know; whatever we might think of this measureless theater to which we've got reserved tickets, but tickets whose life span is laughably short, bounded as it is by two arbitrary dates; whatever else we might think of this world—it is astonishing.

But "astonishing" is an epithet concealing a logical trap. We're astonished, after all, by things that deviate from some well-known and universally acknowledged norm, from an obviousness we've grown accustomed to. Now the point is, there is no such obvious world. Our astonishment exists per se and isn't based on a comparison with something else.

Granted, in daily speech, where we don't stop to consider every word, we all use phrases such as "the ordinary world," "ordinary life," "the ordinary course of events." . . . But in the language of poetry, where every word is weighed, nothing is usual or normal. Not a single stone and not a single cloud above it. Not a single day and not a single night after it. And above all, not a single existence, not anyone's existence in this world.

It looks as though poets will always have their work cut out for them.

PABLO NERUDA

Pablo Neruda (1904–73) was born Neftalí Ricardo Reyes Basoalto in southern Chile. His father worked for the railroad as a train conductor and crew foreman. After his mother's death when he was three, his father married Trinidad Candia Malverde, a woman Neruda later called "the tutelary angel of my childhood." The family moved south to Temuco, a richly forested, humid region that provided the powerful natural images appearing repeatedly in Neruda's poems. The local Temuco newspapers published his first poetic efforts. By the age of ten he knew he was a poet and described the coming of that knowledge: "Poetry arrived / in search of me. I don't know, I don't know where / it came from, from winter or a river? / I don't know how or when. . . ." He studied in Santiago, but left the institute at twenty to devote himself to his writing. Because his family did not approve of his occupation, he published under the nom de plume Pablo Neruda, which he took as his legal name in 1946. The name itself is thought to be a gesture of solidarity with the Czech revolutionary Jan Neruda.

Neruda's writing includes many styles and forms and a vast number of subjects. Although he began writing when Modernism in Chile was in its death throes, its influence appears in his early work. He moved toward Realism and Surrealism almost immediately. As a lifelong Marxist, he wanted his poetry "useful and usable / like metal and cereal," a poetry that worked as communication and as social action. Neruda was also a career diplomat, in the Latin American tradition of awarding diplomatic posts to artists. He was assigned to Colombo, Singapore, Rangoon, Mexico, and much later, France. As Chilean consul in Buenos Aires in 1933, he developed a friendship with the Spanish poet, Federico García Lorca. During the Spanish civil war, Neruda chronicled events, which included the execution of Lorca, from the front in *Espana en el corazon* (1937). Because of his sympathy for the Loyalist cause, he was recalled from Madrid. Returning to Europe on his own, he helped to settle refugees from the war in the United States. He served in the Chilean senate and joined the Communist Party in 1943. When the government declared communism illegal, he was expelled from the senate. In hiding he wrote *Canto General* (1950). Throughout his life, political activities and his prolific writing of poetry seemed naturally and remarkably integrated.

His awards include the International Peace Prize, the Lenin Peace Prize and the Stalin Peace Prize, as well as the 1971 Nobel Prize for Literature.

Neruda's poems have been translated worldwide and have had wide impact. In the United States, poets of the 1970s and 1980s such as Robert Bly and W. S. Merwin studied his work and, under its influence, developed the idea of the deep image. Neruda is considered the greatest South American poet since Reuben Dario and one of the most influential poets of the twentieth century.

from Towards the Splendid City, Nobel Lecture, 1971

My speech is going to be a long journey, a trip that I have taken through regions that are distant and antipodean, but not for that reason any less similar to the landscape and the solitude in Scandinavia. I refer to the way in which my country stretches down to the extreme South. So remote are we Chileans that our boundaries almost touch the South Pole, recalling the geography of Sweden, whose head reaches the snowy northern region of this planet.

Down there on those vast expanses in my native country, where I was taken by events which have already fallen into oblivion, one has to cross, and I was compelled to cross, the Andes to find the frontier of my country with Argentina. Great forests make these inaccessible areas like a tunnel through which our journey was secret and forbidden, with only the faintest signs to show us the way. There were no tracks and no paths, and I and my four companions, riding on horseback, pressed forward on our tortuous way, avoiding the obstacles set by huge trees, impassable rivers, immense cliffs and desolate expanses of snow. . . .

Ladies and Gentlemen,

I did not learn from books any recipe for writing a poem, and I, in my turn, will avoid giving any advice on mode or style which might give the new poets even a drop of supposed insight. When I am recounting in this speech something about past events, when reliving on this occasion a never-forgotten occurrence, in this place which is so different from what that was, it is because in the course of my life I have always found somewhere the necessary support, the formula which had been waiting for me not in order to be petrified in my words but in order to explain me to myself.

During this long journey I found the necessary components for the making of the poem. There I received contributions from the earth and from the soul. And I believe that poetry is an action, ephemeral or solemn, in which there enter as equal partners solitude and solidarity, emotion and action, the nearness to oneself, the nearness to mankind and to the secret manifestations of nature. And no less strongly I think that all this is sustained—man and his shadow, man and his conduct, man and his poetry—by an ever-wider sense of community, by an effort which will for ever bring together the reality and the dreams in us because it is precisely in this way that poetry unites and mingles them. And therefore I say that I do not know, after so many years, whether the lessons I learned when I crossed a daunting river, when I danced around the skull of an ox, when I bathed my body in the cleansing water from the topmost heights—I do not know whether these lessons welled forth from me in order to be imparted to many others or whether it was all a message which was sent to me by others as a demand or an accusation. I do not know whether I experienced this or created it, I do not know whether it was truth or poetry, something passing or permanent, the poems I experienced in this hour, the experiences which I later put into verse.

From all this, my friends, there arises an insight which the poet must learn through other people. There is no insurmountable solitude. All paths lead to the same goal: to convey to others what we are. And we must pass through solitude and difficulty, isolation and silence in order to reach forth to the enchanted place where we can dance our clumsy dance and sing our sorrowful song—but in this dance or in this song there are fulfilled the most ancient rites of our conscience in the awareness of being human and of believing in a common destiny.

The truth is that even if some or many consider me to be a sectarian, barred from taking a place at the common table of friendship and responsibility, I do not wish to defend myself, for I believe that neither accusation nor defence is among the tasks of the poet. When all is said, there is no individual poet who administers poetry, and if a poet sets himself up to accuse his fellows or if some other poet wastes his life in defending himself against reasonable or unreasonable charges, it is my conviction that only vanity can so mislead us. I consider the enemies of poetry to be found not among those who practise poetry or guard it but in mere lack of agreement in the poet. For this reason no poet has any considerable enemy other than his own incapacity to make himself understood by the most forgotten and exploited of his contemporaries, and this applies to all epochs and in all countries.

The poet is not a "little god." No, he is not a "little god." He is not picked out by a mystical destiny in preference to those who follow other crafts and professions. I have often maintained that the best poet is he who prepares our daily bread: the nearest baker who does not imagine himself to be a god. He does his majestic and unpretentious work of kneading the dough, consigning it to the oven, baking it in golden colours and handing us our daily bread as a duty of fellowship. And, if the poet succeeds in achieving this simple consciousness, this too will be transformed into an element in an immense activity, in a simple or complicated structure which constitutes the building of a community, the changing of the conditions which surround mankind, the handing over of mankind's products: bread, truth, wine, dreams. If the poet joins this never-completed struggle to extend to the hands of each and all his part of his undertaking, his effort and his tenderness to the daily work of all people, then the poet must take part, the poet will take part, in the sweat, in the bread, in the wine, in the whole dream of humanity. Only in this indispensable way of being ordinary people shall we give back to poetry the mighty breadth which has been pared away from it little by little in every epoch, just as we ourselves have been whittled down in every epoch. . . .

It is today exactly one hundred years since an unhappy and brilliant poet, the most awesome of all despairing souls, wrote down this prophecy: "A l'aurore, armés d'une ardente patience, nous entrerons aux splendides Villes." "In the dawn, armed with a burning patience, we shall enter the splendid Cities."

I believe in this prophecy of Rimbaud, the Visionary. I come from a dark region, from a land separated from all others by the steep contours of its geography. I was the most forlorn of poets and my poetry was provincial, oppressed and rainy. But always I had put my trust in man. I never lost hope. It is perhaps because of this that I have reached as far as I now have with my poetry and also with my banner.

Lastly, I wish to say to the people of good will, to the workers, the poets, that the whole future has been expressed in this line by Rimbaud: only with a *burning patience* can we conquer the splendid City which will give light, justice and dignity to all mankind.

In this way the song will not have been sung in vain.

THERESA HAK KYUNG CHA

Theresa Hak Kyung Cha was born in Korea in 1951. Her family moved to California in 1964. Fluent in French, English, and Korean, Cha earned four degrees in comparative literature and art from University of California at Berkeley and did postgraduate work in film theory in Paris with major theorists Christian Metz and Thierry Kuntzel. In addition to writing, her works include performance art, ceramics, textiles, artist's books, stamp and mail art, video, and the poetry/film installation Exilée. Her best-known work, the experimental autobiographical *Dictée,* was published in 1982. A few days later, Cha was raped and murdered by a serial rapist in New York City. *Dictée* is widely studied in poetry, art history, women's studies, and ethnic studies courses. "The Dream of the Audience," an exhibit of Cha's works, opened in 2001 and toured in the United States, Korea, and Europe.

Dictée is a pastiche of images, documents, historical fragments, meditation, and handwritten drafts divided into nine parts structured around the Greek Muses. Exploring the identity labeled "Korean-American" within the context of the fragmented and tormented history of Korea, the book involves stories of the suffering of several women: the Korean revolutionary Yu Guan Soon, Demeter and Persephone, Joan of Arc, Cha's mother, and Cha herself. *Dictée* explores issues of ethnicity, gender, and identity, dislocation and the fragmentation of memory; as Cha describes her own work, "the main body of my work is with language before it is born on the tip of the tongue."

DISEUSE

She mimicks the speaking. That might resemble speech. (Anything at all.) Bared noise, groan, bits torn from words. Since she hesitates to measure the accuracy, she resorts to mimicking gestures with the mouth. The entire lower lip would lift upwards then sink back to its original place. She would then gather both lips and protrude them in a pout taking in the breath that might utter some thing. (One thing. Just one.) But the breath falls away. With a slight tilting of her head backwards, she would gather the strength in her shoulders and remain in this position.

It murmurs inside. It murmurs. Inside is the pain of speech the pain to say. Larger still. Greater than is the pain not to say. To not say. Says nothing against the pain to speak. It festers inside. The wound, liquid, dust. Must break. Must void.

From the back of her neck she releases her shoulders free. She swallows once more. (Once more. One more time would do.) In preparation. It augments. To such a pitch. Endless drone, refueling itself. Autonomous. Self-generating. Swallows with last efforts last wills against the pain that wishes it to speak.

She allows others. In place of her. Admits others to make full. Make swarm. All barren cavities to make swollen. The others each occupying her. Tumorous layers, expel all excesses until in all cavities she is flesh.

She allows herself caught in their threading, anonymously in their thick motion in the weight of their utterance. When the amplification stops there might be an echo. She might make the attempt then. The echo part. At the pause. When the pause has already soon begun and has rested there still. She waits inside the pause. Inside her. Now. This very moment. Now. She takes rapidly the air, in gulfs, in preparation for the distances to come. The pause ends. The voice wraps another layer. Thicker now even. From the waiting. The wait from pain to say. To not to. Say.

She would take on their punctuation. She waits to service this. Theirs. Punctuation. She would become, herself, demarcations. Absorb it. Spill it. Seize upon the punctuation. Last air. Give her. Her. The relay. Voice. Assign. Hand it. Deliver it. Deliver.

She relays the others. Recitation. Evocation. Offering. Provocation. The begging. Before her. Before them.

Now the weight begins from the uppermost back of her head, pressing downward. It stretches evenly, the entire skull expanding tightly all sides toward the front of her head. She gasps from its pressure, its contracting motion.

Inside her voids. It does not contain further. Rising from the empty below, pebble lumps of gas. Moisture. Begin to flood her. Dissolving her. Slow, slowed to deliberation. Slow and thick.

The above traces from her head moving downward closing her eyes, in the same motion, slower parting her mouth open together with her jaw and throat which the above falls falling just to the end not stopping there but turning her inside out in the same motion, shifting complete the whole weight to elevate upward.

Begins imperceptibly, near-perceptible. (Just once. Just one time and it will take.) She takes. She takes the pause. Slowly. From the thick. The thickness. From weighted motion upwards. Slowed. To deliberation even when it passed upward through her mouth again. The delivery. She takes it. Slow. The invoking. All the time now. All the time there is. Always. And all times. The pause. Uttering. Hers now. Hers bare. The utter.

From the original

JANE HIRSHFIELD

Jane Hirshfield (1953–) was born in New York City. A diary kept when she was ten years old reveals that her interests and passions have changed little since that time: reading and writing, animals, plants, and questions of metaphysics and love. Hirshfield was educated at Princeton University, where she studied creative writing and literature in translation. Between 1974 and 1982 she practiced Zen full time, including three years of monastic practice, and received lay ordination in Soto Zen in 1979. She published her first book of poetry, *Alaya*, in 1982, followed by *Of Gravity & Angels* (1988), *The October Palace* (1994), *The Lives of the Heart* (1997), and *Given Sugar, Given Salt* (2001), a finalist for the 2001 National Book Critics Circle Award and winner of the Bay Area Book Reviewers Award. Hirshfield has received numerous other honors including Guggenheim and Rockefeller fellowships and the Poetry Center Book Award.

In the Canadian magazine *Brick: A Literary Journal,* Hirshfield wrote in answer to the question, "What would you have been if you hadn't been a writer?" "I imagine I'd have ended up either a translator of classical Japanese poetry or a Zen priest, had poem-making not been there as the central magnet. Further afield, maybe a horse trainer? I've already been a cook in a vegetarian restaurant, a substitute teacher in the public schools of Fresno, a driver of a Ford double-trailered lumber-hauling truck, and an editor of non-fiction books—but such things are common enough for poets along the path."

Hirshfield is also the author of a book of essays, *Nine Gates: Entering the Mind of Poetry* (1997), and editor and co-translator of two collections of poetry by women writers of the past. Featured in two Bill Moyers PBS poetry specials, she has taught at the University of California, Berkeley, the University of San Francisco, Bennington College's MFA Writing Seminars and has been a visiting poet at many universities around the country. She has lived in the San Francisco Bay Area since 1974. In the selection here from *Nine Gates: Entering the Mind of Poetry,* Hirshfield discusses poetry as "language put into the forms of remembrance . . . the progenitor of all the technologies of memory to come."

Poetry as a Vessel of Remembrance

The story of poetry has many beginnings. . . .

In Mnemosyne's time, memory was not yet imagined as a book or a storage room into which one could look. It was a being who spoke, and the way she spoke was in shapeliness, in verse. When poetry came later to be housed in the material realm of symbol and ink, how and why it was used changed, many of its means changed—but the fundamental sound of Mnemosyne's speech continued to permeate its nature, as does some echo, however faint, of her absolutely central place in human life.

To see how the requirements of memorability created poetry, we need first to imagine the nature of language and knowledge in a purely oral world. As a number of scholars have pointed out, before literacy, sound, not sight, is the sense-realm in which words exist. Perhaps the most striking difference between these two senses is their differing relationships to time. The visual world holds still through time—an oak tree or rock seen yesterday will remain to be seen tomorrow. Or if what we look at moves, we can follow that movement, or at least trust that the thing we have seen could still be found; one of the early, hard-earned lessons of infancy is that what goes out of sight does not cease to exist. Similarly, the written word—language placed into the realm of sight—remains stable over time, staying faithfully, reliably, in its place. Set down in a book, on a shelf, it can be readily returned to hand and mind when needed. . . .

Repetition lies also at the heart of other linguistic devices we associate with poetry's beauty and sensual pleasure. The parallel structures and balanced sentence patterns seen especially in classical Chinese poetry; the alliteration found in the earliest English-language poems; assonance; the thought-patterns of the sonnet or the word-patterns of such rhetorical figures as chiasmus; lists, especially those using anaphora, in which each part begins with the same word—all serve to lead the mind with accuracy from one word to the next. They do this by helping to shape where a thought is going by the recall of where it has been. Consider the literal meaning of this synonym for the act of memory—"recall," to voice again. Repetition embracing variation is the thread of the cloth Mnemosyne wears. . . .

The mind of oral memory dwells always in a physical body. Neither emotion nor ideas have yet been abstracted; they live instead in the form of gods and goddesses whose angers, desires, moralities, and jealousies affect human behavior in the form of furious storms, biting gadflies, and irresistibly beautiful singing. Such physical descriptions let us enter a story vividly, as if from within. We do not only receive a powerfully described world in our minds, we occupy it—sleeping in the cradle of its rocky harbors, eating of its honey cakes sprinkled with dark seeds of poppy.

In a culture that likes to think it is founded on the powers of logical, rational mind, the term "imaginary" has taken on overtones of the trivial or the frivolous. Yet the imagination was oral mind's earliest tool for conceiving of the abstract at all, by binding ideas into physical, visual form. Grief at the very existence of death becomes the image of Achilles' two immortal horses lowering their dusty heads to weep over the body of Patroclus. The concept of life's ceaseless abundance, difficult as well as joyous, is carved by Homer and the craftsman-god Hephaestus onto Achilles' shield of war: A bridal procession unfolds near a marketplace argument over the blood-price of a murdered man; ploughmen drink flagons of wine as they pause in their labors; lions tear into the slaughtered body of an ox, oblivious of the nearby baying of dogs; acrobats and courting couples flank the blood-drenched figure of Death, busy harvesting her pick of young men from amid a battle. And all is ultimately enclosed by the great river that bounds the edge of the shield—water circling the realm of what can be seen and heard and touched, beyond which oral consciousness could not go.

These life-holding devices of Mnemosyne, story and physical embodiment, can still be found in the familiar precept given new writers: "Show, don't tell." Now, as twenty-eight hundred years ago, a poet's task is to cast a convincing spell, to create in the mind of another a lasting and particular vision of human experience, whether as sweeping as Homer's or as tightly focused as a single fragment by Sappho. A poem's task is to seduce—its readers or listeners must find in it something irresistible, something to which they want to surrender. The power of beautiful sound and structured language is one such lure; the power of vivid imagining is another; and a third is the human curiosity called forth by story, which lingers not only in poems that are obvious narratives but also in the way good poems root themselves in specificity of situation and event. In any good lyric poem—even one as brief as a haiku—a tiny narrative exists: there is a moment of transformation. Something happens, to writer, to reader, over its course. . . .

PART 2

Making

Jabberwocky

'Twas brillig, and the slithy toves
    Did gyre and gimble in the wabe:
All mimsy were the borogoves,
    And the mome raths outgrabe.

"Beware the Jabberwock, my son!
    The jaws that bite, the claws that catch!
Beware the Jubjub bird, and shun
    The frumious Bandersnatch!"

He took his vorpal sword in hand:
    Long time the manxome foe he sought—
So rested he by the Tumtum tree,
    And stood awhile in thought

And, as in uffish thought he stood,
    The Jabberwock, with eyes of flame,
Came whiffling through the tulgey wood,
    And burbled as it came!

One, two! One, two! And through and through
    The vorpal blade went snicker-snack!
He left it dead, and with its head
    He went galumphing back.

"And hast thou slain the Jabberwock?
    Come to my arms, my beamish boy!

O frabjous day! Callooh! Callay!"
He chortled in his joy.

'Twas brillig, and the slithy toves
Did gyre and gimble in the wabe:
All mimsy were the borogoves,
And the mome raths outgrabe.

Carroll then proceeds to interpret the words as follows:

BRYLLYG (derived from the verb to Bryl or Broil), 'the time of broiling dinner, i.e. the close of the afternoon.'

SLYTHY (compounded of slimy and lithe). 'Smooth and active.'

TOVE. A species of Badger. They had smooth white hair, long hind legs, and short horns like a stag: lived chiefly on cheese.

GYRE, verb (derived from Gyaour or Giaour, 'a dog'). To scratch like a dog.

GYMBLE (whence gimblet). 'To screw out holes in anything.'

WABE (derived from the verb to swab or soak). 'The side of a hill' (from its being *soaked* by the rain).

MIMSY (whence mimserable and miserable). 'Unhappy.'

BOROGOVE. An extinct kind of Parrot. They had no wings, beaks turned up, and made their nests under sundials: lived on veal.

MOME (hence SOLEMOME, SOLEMONE, and SOLEMN). 'Grave.'

RATH. A species of land turtle. Head erect: mouth like a shark: forelegs curved out so that the animal walked on its knees: smooth green body: lived on swallows and oysters.

OUTGRABE, past tense of the verb to OUTGRIBE. (It is connected with old verb to GRIKE, or SHRIKE, from which are derived 'shriek' and 'creak'). 'Squeaked.'

Hence the literal English of the passage is: 'It was evening, and the smooth active badgers were scratching and boring holes in the hill-side; all unhappy were the parrots; and the grave turtles squeaked out.'

There were probably sundials on the top of the hill, and the 'borogoves' were afraid that their nests would be undermined. The hill was probably full of the nests of 'raths,' which ran out, squeaking with feare, on hearing the 'toves' scratching outside. This is an obscure but yet deeply-affecting, relic of ancient Poetry.

Making

Chaucer opens his tragedy *Troilus and Criseyde* with an invocation to Clio, Muse of History. But before the first stanza is over, he has revealed his real preoccupation: his decision to write in English rather than Latin, and the fear that in doing so he is endangering the permanence of his contribution to literature. This glimpse into the self-consciousness of a long-ago poet about his artistic choices reminds us that technical issues are among poets' perennial concerns. All the essays in this section concern the poet's medium: words, the constant with which poets must contend in each poem they write, no matter how different the theme, style, or audience may be. No wonder various poets have been obsessed by every possible aspect of words and have held conflicting positions on just about all of them.

As language changes and poets adjust to the new verbal ecology, issues of diction surface and resurface. Several centuries after Chaucer's daring choice to abandon Latin diction, poets like Alexander Pope maintained a deep sense of poetic decorum, an insistence on appropriately allusive Latinate language modeled on the ancients. This aesthetic, in turn, pushed Wordsworth and Coleridge to a departure almost as radical as Chaucer's, when they discarded "poetic" diction in their effort to write only in the common language of the early nineteenth century. In the multicultural and multilinguistic contemporary world, poets are especially aware of the power of diction, as when Harryette Mullen revels in her ability to blend phrases from Portuguese, Yoruba, and the black vernacular of oral tradition into her poems.

Poets' words, sometimes in spite of themselves, align language into configurations that imply a reality beyond words, as personal pronoun shades into lyric voice which shades into poetic persona which shades into identity. Anne Finch defends herself for publishing poems during an era when it was considered unladylike to write by comparing herself to the more socially acceptable women whose vanities are indulged by eighteenth-century culture. Langston Hughes seeks to build an African American lyric voice distinct from the expectations of the surrounding white world. Aware that the "lyric I" can be a dangerous illusion, Annie

Finch posits a new kind of poetic self, open to postmodern ideas of the decentered subject within a syntactically coherent language.

Like the lyric self, the image is a key area of poetics where words can imply a reality beyond words. Ever since Ezra Pound's dicta of Imagism, heavily influenced by his readings in Chinese poetics, were published in 1913, imagery has been a focus of much discussion by poets. Pound himself, however, abandoned Imagism for Vorticism, which stressed energy, the quality he believed the Imagists lacked. For Marianne Moore, on the other hand, "excess is the common substitute for energy." Moore argues that "precision is a thing of the imagination." She sees precision in terms of metaphor, which stands at the heart of the image. Eliot's "objective correlative," defined in his essay on Hamlet, has become the byword for image, the essential ingredient. The image is literal; the symbol occurs when associations accrue to it. For Yeats, the power of a symbolic image goes beyond itself, as sounds, colors, and forms "call down among us certain disembodied powers." Images are far from symbols for Yusef Komunyakaa, who writes movingly about serving an apprenticeship in carpentry with both his father and grandfather and who finds his voice in the rhythm of actual rasping and scraping. Frank O'Hara, a cult figure of the late fifties, anchors his poems to the streets, restaurants, and skyscrapers of New York. His manifesto in praise of Personism declares that the poet must wrest the poem away from the page and transform it into an intimate exchange.

In contrast to poets who want to use words to communicate in the clearest way possible, there has long been a lineage of poets committed to what George Moore called "pure poetry": poems that use words for their physical qualities more than for their meanings. Hart Crane uses the details of the real world only "as a springboard" and then gives the poem its head, allowing it to take its own direction. Lewis Carroll's "Jabberwocky" emphasizes the extent to which words can be separated from clear reference and still do their poetic work. The reader can still understand the thrust of the story without a glossary of terms. As Martin Gardner points out, speculating on Carroll's playfulness with language, "In one sense words are our masters, or communication would be impossible. In another we are the masters; otherwise there could be no poetry."

The arrangements of words into repeating patterns, or poetic form, has long been one of the most contentious areas of discussion about poetics. The history of form is full of continuities (the heroic couplet was written continuously for five hundred years), breaks (the unprecedented early-twentieth-century break with meter) and rebirths (the sonnet was abandoned for two hundred years and has since enjoyed an amazing renaissance). Poets' views on form inevitably reflect the aesthetic pressures of their own era. At the height of the Renaissance, Ben Jonson gives us a tongue-in-cheek attack on the rigidity of rhyme and meter in a poem that conforms to both, and Samuel Daniel declares that rhyme gives poets wings that carry them "to a far happier flight." Only a generation later, however, Milton makes the decision to discard rhyme and writes *Paradise Lost* in blank verse for its gravitas.

Historically, the choice between formal and free verse is often vexed to the point of outrage. William Carlos Williams cries death to iambic pentameter. Louise Bogan declares that particular poetic forms may be exhausted, but never the impulse toward form, which is deeply embedded in the human psyche. Other poets of the period, however, connect the use of form in poetry to a wish for control in the social sphere and claim that those who resort to conventional constraints fear the violent energy of true poetry. Both views of the forms of poetry and their various attendant music spark energetic debates to this day. Charles Olson bluntly rejects the inherited line and stanza to focus on the process of composition, on the transfer of energy from poet to page as one perception rapidly succeeds another. From this juncture, it is an easy leap to contemporary poet Heather McHugh's perception that the line breaks up a made object and disrupts our normal way of reading.

T. S. Eliot once quipped that the main reason poets write criticism is to justify their own practice, and the poetics of form are no exception. Milton's preface defending the blank verse of *Paradise Lost* and Coleridge's preface announcing the new meter he used to write "Christabel" have contemporary descendants in the poets who are committed to the making of new forms, from Fanny Howe, who proposes a three-dimensional poem, to Richard Kostelanetz, a pioneer in the creation of radically formed poems. On the other hand, Edna St. Vincent Millay's Petrarchan sonnet in defense of that form—"I will put Chaos into fourteen lines / And keep him there" leads us to Rafael Campo, a contemporary bilingual physician, who says that only the sonnet "mirrors what I discover in my patients' occupying of their physical bodies."

Marilyn Nelson resolves such questions into a harmonious vision of tradition as an ongoing and communal process: we receive a common literary gene pool and we add "our shared understanding of encoded meanings, the history of our words." Nelson is a shapeshifter who believes that as a contemporary African American woman she participates in, enjoys, and contributes to the literary tradition, which she calls "the living O.E.D." As we acknowledge our common ground, the boundaries between cultures erode and poetry "enables us to think and sing along with many other minds."

With so many technical issues at hand, is it worth wondering, as Roethke and Auden do, what constitutes the ideal technical education for a poet? Auden's "daydream College for Bards" argues for some delicious practicalities, such as tending a garden and caring for domestic animals as well as learning ancient languages and memorizing thousands of lines of poetry in those languages. Such formidable tasks will turn away all but the stout-hearted. Roethke is hard-headed in another direction. Imitate the masters, he counsels: "In a time when the romantic notion of the inspired poet still has considerable credence, true 'imitation' takes a certain courage."

And why not? Edgar Allan Poe, famous for "The Raven," describes his composition as proceeding in sequence "with the precision and rigid consequence of a mathematical problem." Yet, working in this way, he narrowed down the choices for his refrain line to the single hypnotic word that has made this poem a popular classic. The study of poetics shows again and again how the most technical concerns conjoin with the most powerful of poetries. Gerard Manley Hopkins' preface to his *Collected Poems* offers a truly bewildering array of invented technical terms: *running rhythm, sprung rhythm, rocking feet.* Despite the didacticism of this brief introduction, Hopkins's poems are among the most passionate, musical, and life-giving that have been handed down to us. Whitman's wild free verse runs in deep triple rhythms, and the loose structures of the Psalms, also often used as an example of "free verse," are built on a powerful binary skeleton of two halves per line. The arts thrive on technical skill and those voluntary constraints that are the stuff of "shop talk." In spite of the mystique of the Muse, why should poetry be any different? After all, "spontaneous" inspiration is most likely to descend after great efforts have been made in another direction, as when Robert Frost suddenly channeled all the words to "Stopping By Woods on a Snowy Evening" in a single rush after a long night of labor on an entirely different poem.

CALLIMACHUS

Callimachus was born in 280 b.c. in Africa, in Cyrene, in present-day Libya. He was educated in Athens, taught at Eleusina, and was then employed by Ptolemy II as chief librarian for the Library of Alexandria, a position he held for twenty years. He is renowned in library history for his catalog of the Alexandrian Library, *Pinakes,* which consisted of critical and biographical information about the books in the library and their authors. This catalog is regarded as the first book of literary criticism. Callimachus also wrote other works in prose but was best known as a poet and is said to have written more than eight hundred poems, of which only six hymns, several epigrams, and fragments of some other poems survive. His greatest work was the *Aetia,* a collection of ancient legends. Other longer poems of which fragments remain are *The Lock of Berenice, Hecale,* and *Iambi.*

Callimachus's poetry is notable for brevity, polish, wit, learning, and inventiveness in form. His work had a considerable influence on later Greek and Roman poets, especially Catullus. Callimachus is famous for a literary quarrel with Apollonius of Rhodes over whether well-crafted short poems were superior to long poems. Apollonius's *Argonautica* was a continuous epic poem imitating Homeric language and style. Callimachus's poetic program, as set out in his preface to the *Aetia,* below, argues for short over long poetry and a discontinuous, informal style rather than continuous, high-flown epic. Like many literary arguments, however, this one is more complex than it seems; there are many correspondences between Apollonius's and Callimachus's poetry including similar subject matter, an ironic tone, and much learned allusion, and the *Argonautica* has a narrator who subverts epic poetry and parodies Homeric forms by applying them to non-heroes.

from Prologue to The Aetia

The malignant gnomes who write reviews in Rhodes
are muttering about my poetry again—
tone-deaf ignoramuses out of touch with the Muse—

because I have not consummated a continuous epic
    of thousands of lines on heroes and lords
but turn out minor texts as if I were a child
    although my decades of years are substantial.
To which brood of cirrhotic adepts
    I, Callimachus, thus:

A few distichs in the pan outweigh *Deméter's Cornucopia*,
    and Mimnermos is sweet for a few subtle lines,
not that fat *Lady* poem. Let "cranes fly south to Egypt"
    when they lust for pygmy blood,
and "the Masságetai arch arrows long distance"
    to a lodge in a Mede,
but nightingales are honey-pale
    and small poems are sweet.
So evaporate, Green-Eyed Monsters,
or learn to judge poems by the critic's art
    instead of by the parasang,
and don't snoop around here for a poem that rumbles:
    not I but Zeus owns the thunder.

When I first put a tablet on my knees, the Wolf-God
    Apollo appeared and said:
"Fatten your animal for sacrifice, poet,
    but keep your muse slender." And
"follow trails unrutted by wagons,
don't drive your chariot down public highways,
    but keep to the back roads though the going is narrow.
We are the poets for those who love
    the cricket's high chirping, not the noise of the jackass."
A long-eared bray for others, for me delicate wings,
    dewsip in old age and bright air for food,

mortality dropping from me like Sicily shifting
    its triangular mass from Enkélados's chest.
No nemesis here:
    the Muses do not desert the gray heads
of those on whose childhood
    their glance once brightened.

GEOFFREY CHAUCER

We know only the facts about Geoffrey Chaucer's life (1343–1400) that were recorded in official documents. His father was a wine merchant, but nothing is known of Chaucer himself until, in his teens, he became a page in the household of the Duke of Clarence. Although there are no records of formal education, he was said to have read everything available, at a time when only 5 percent of the population of England was literate. He grew up speaking French and wrote his first poems in that language but worked as a courtier and a civil servant all his life, never as a professional writer. He did not become a member of a literary circle until the 1380s. He married a lady-in-waiting to Edward III's queen, not happily, according to rumor, and had three children. Traveling to the continent on diplomatic missions, he learned Italian and may have met Petrarch, though critics disagree on this point. He worked for many years as comptroller of customs on furs, skins, and hides for the port of London and later as Clerk of the King's Works.

Chaucer's writing is divided into three periods. In the first, his work is based on French models. *The Book of the Duchess* is his first important work. In his second period, called Italian, he wrote works modelled on Dante and Boccaccio. The best-known work of this time is *Troilus and Criseyde*, based on Boccaccio's *Filostrato* and considered one of the greatest love poems in the English language. In this work he perfected rhyme royal, a stanza of seven lines. *The Canterbury Tales*, seventeen thousand lines long, is the great work of Chaucer's last period, although left unfinished at the time of his death. Resembling Boccaccio's *Decameron* in its structure, it is famous for the rich cross section of fourteenth-century life it presents. The pilgrims traveling together to Canterbury include a parson, a miller, a reeve (a minor official), a cook, a man of law, a merchant, a squire, a prioress, a physician, the famous Wife of Bath and others, for a total of thirty well-developed characters who tell their tales in a variety of literary forms. *The Canterbury Tales*, the first major secular work published by Caxton, is also the first attempt to form vernacular English into a poetic language.

In Chaucer's time the common people spoke English, the aristocracy French, and those children who went to school were taught in French. The Parliament used French although some legal matters were still recorded in Latin. But the status of English, the language of the conquered, was changing and the language became more respectable during Chaucer's lifetime. Using actual speech as the basis of his style, as Chaucer does throughout the *Tales,* led to the acceptance of English as a language suitable to literature. Nevertheless, this passage shows Chaucer's insecurity about the daring choice to write in English rather than Latin. He realizes from experience how much language can change "with-inne a thousand yeer," and, knowing that the fate of his poetry depends, in large part, on the fate of the language in which it is written, he asks the blessing of Clio, Muse of History, on his poem.

from Book Two, Troilus and Criseyde

1.

Out of these blake wawes for to sayle,
O wind, O wind, the weder ginneth clere;
For in this see the boot hath swich travayle,
Of my conning, that unnethe I it stere:
This see clepe I the tempestous matere
Of desespeyr that Troilus was inne:
But now of hope the calendes biginne.

2.

O lady myn, that called art Cleo,
Thou be my speed fro this forth, and my muse,
To ryme wel this book til I have do;
Me nedeth here noon other art to use,
For-why to every lovere I me excuse,
That of no sentement I this endyte,
But out of Latin in my tonge it wryte.

3.

Wherfore I nil have neither thank ne blame
Of al this werk, but prey yow mekely,
Disblameth me if any word be lame,
For as myn auctor seyde, so seye I.
Eek though I speke of love unfelingly,
No wondre is, for it no-thing of newe is;
A blind man can nat juggen wel in hewis.

4.

Ye knowe eek, that in forme of speche is chaunge
With-inne a thousand yeer, and wordes tho
That hadden prys, now wonder nyce and straunge
Us thinketh hem; and yet they spake hem so,
And spedde as wel in love as men now do;
Eek for to winnen love in sondry ages,
In sondry londes, sondry been usages.

5.

And for-thy if it happe in any wyse,
That here be any lovere in this place
That herkneth, as the storie wol devyse,
How Troilus cam to his lady grace,
And thenketh, "so nolde I nat love purchace,"
Or wondreth on his speche or his doinge,
I noot; but it is me no wonderinge; . . .

BASHŌ

Matsuo Bashō (1644–93) was born in a small town thirty miles from Kyoto, but information about his early years is scant. His father may have been a low-ranking samurai and a farmer. Bashō himself began his career, perhaps as a page, in the service of a relative of a feudal lord. He and his master became close companions who experimented with verse together. After his friend died suddenly, Bashō left home for five years. He may have been devastated by grief, or he may have feared a diminished role under a new master. Other accounts speculate that he left because of illicit love affairs. Eventually, Bashō appeared in Kyoto as a poet and teacher specializing in haiku, the seventeen-syllable form of which he is the acknowledged master.

A practitioner of Zen who later became a lay monk, Bashō incorporated Zen beliefs about the self into his writing theory and practice. He stressed the need to identify with the object written about and minimize the role of the self. One of his disciples wrote, "The Master said: 'Learn about a pine tree from a pine tree, and about a bamboo stalk from a bamboo stalk.'" The writer should enter the object "sharing its delicate life and feelings." By the time he was thirty-four, Bashō had made a reputation as a poet and gathered a group of talented disciples. He organized and judged haiku contests, writing commentaries on the poems. Around 1680 his students built a small house in Edo for him and planted a banana (basho) tree next to it. The hut was originally called the Bashō hut and Bashō took his nom de plume from it.

But Bashō never stayed long in one place. A wanderer for much of his life, he found that travel stimulated his creative energy. At least three times he sold his belongings, left his home, embarking on long walks around the country. Many of his poems describe the places and people he encountered or record moments of his journeys. He chronicled his travels in the prose journals *Journal of a Weather-Beaten Skeleton* and *The Records of a Travel-Worn Satchel*. At forty-five, after Bashō sold his home and traveled north, he wrote *Narrow Road to the Far North,* considered his masterpiece. But as he grew older he sought solitude and silence. Bashō contributed a mystical dimension to haiku, which had been a form of light verse, and expressed the largest themes in simple natural images. As the reprinted conversation with his student shows, he stressed fidelity to nature, frankness about human experience and precision in language.

from Kyorai's Conversations with Bashō

Yuku haru wo	The departing spring
Omi no hito to	With the men of Omi
Oshimikeru	Have I lamented.
	BASHŌ

The Master said, "Shōhaku criticized this poem on the grounds that I might just as well have said 'Tamba' instead of 'Ōmi' or 'departing year' instead of 'departing spring.' How does this criticism strike you?" Kyorai replied, "Shōhaku's criticism misses the mark entirely. What could be more natural than to regret the passing of the spring, when the waters of the Lake of Ōmi are veiled so enchantingly in mist? Besides, it is especially fitting a poem for one who lives by the lake to have written." The Master said, "Yes, the poets of old loved spring in this province almost as much as the capital." Kyorai, deeply struck by these words, continued. "If you were in Ōmi at the close of the year, why should you regret its passing? Or, if you were in Tamba at the end of the spring, you would not be likely to have such a feeling. What truth there is in the feelings of a man who has genuinely been stirred by some sight of Nature!" The Master said, "Kyorai, you are a person with whom I can talk about poetry." He was very pleased.

Kogarishni ni	Will the two-day moon
Futsuka no tsuki no	Be blown from the sky
Fukichiru ka	By the winter wind?
	KAKEI

Kogarashi no	Kept by the winter wind
Chi ni mo otosanu	From falling to earth—
Shigure ka na	The drizzling rain.
	KYORAI

Kyorai said, "I feel that Kakei's verse is far superior to mine. By asking if it will be 'blown from the sky' he makes his mention of the two-day moon all the more clever." Bashō answered, "Kakei's verse is built around the words 'two-day moon.' Take away the 'two-day moon' and there is nothing left to the poem. It is not apparent on what you based your poem. It is good all around."

Kiyotaki ya	Clear cascades!
Nami ni chiri naki	In the immaculate waves
Natsu no tsuki	The summer moon.
	BASHŌ

. . . Yamu Kari no	A sick wild duck
Yosamu ni ochite	Falling in the evening cold—
Tabine ka na	These traveler's lodgings!
	BASHŌ

Ama no ya wa	The fisherman's hut
Koebi ni majiru	Mixed with little shrimps
Itodo ka na	Some crickets!
	BASHŌ

When we were compiling *The Monkey's Cloak* we were asked to choose one of these two poems for inclusion. Boncho said, "The verse about the sick wild duck is good, but the other about the crickets mixing with the little shrimps has a freshness that makes it truly outstanding." Kyorai said, "The verse about the shrimps is unusual, but had I thought of the scene in the fisherman's hut I could have written it myself. The one about the wild duck, on the other hand, is so noble in tone, so subtly perceptive, that I wonder how anyone could have conceived it." After some discussion we finally asked permission to include both verses. The Master said, laughing, "You seem to have argued yourself into thinking that a sick duck and a little shrimp have about equal value."

Iwahana ya	The tips of the crags—
Koko ni mo hitori	Here too is someone,
Tsuki no kyaku	Guest of the moon.
	KYORAI

Kyorai said, "Shadō thinks that the last line should be 'monkey of the moon' but I think that 'guest' is better." The Master said, "How can he suggest such a word as 'monkey'? What had you in mind when you wrote the poem?" Kyorai answered, "One night, when I was walking in the mountains by the light of the harvest moon, composing poetry as I went along, I noticed another poet standing by the crags." The Master said, "How much more interesting a poem it would be if by the lines 'here too is someone, guest of the moon' you meant yourself. You must be the subject of this verse."

Shimokyō was a very quiet district of Kyoto.

Shimokyō ya	Shimokyō!
Yuki tsumu ue no	On the piled-up snow
Yo no ame	The night rain.
	BONCHO

This verse at first lacked an opening line, and everyone from the Master downward tried to think of one. At length the Master settled on the above line. Boncho said yes to it, but still didn't seem satisfied. The Master said, "Boncho, why don't you think of a better opening line? If you do, I'll never write another haiku!" Kyorai said, "Anyone can see how good a line it is, but it's not so easy to appreciate that no other line would do. If members of some other school of poetry heard what you said, they would think that you were ridiculously self-assured, and they would make up any number of opening lines. But the ones that they considered to be good would seem laughably bad to us." . . .

BEN JONSON

Ben Jonson (1572–1637) was born into a tragic setting; his Protestant father had died, and his impoverished mother had married a bricklayer to provide support for her and the baby. Jonson was educated at Westminster School where he became the disciple of William Camden, the great classical scholar of the age. Unable to afford university, he was apprenticed as a bricklayer but left the trade, joined the army, and fought in Flanders, where he killed a man in hand-to-hand combat. In 1592, he returned to London to work for Philip Henslowe as an actor in his company and then as a playwright. His first success, *Every Man in his Humour* (1598), in which Shakespeare acted, popularized the comedy of humors which satirizes the mores of the Elizabethan age. He married Anne Lewis in 1594; their first son, born two years later, was stricken by the plague at the age of seven. Jonson wrote a brief but very powerful elegy for him in which he called the boy his "best piece of poetry." Jonson's pugnacity led him into a duel with another actor, whom he killed. He was sent to prison, his property was confiscated, and he narrowly escaped a death sentence by pleading benefit of clergy, a special exemption. He went to prison once again when he produced a play that referred to Scottish royalty in an unflattering light, causing the new king, James I, to take offense.

Jonson's career as a playwright burgeoned with the production of *Volpone* in 1605. He was appointed Poet Laureate in 1616, awarded an honorary master's degree by Oxford in 1619, and, surrounded by young poets and playwrights who called themselves "the tribe of Ben," he held forth for most nights in the Apollo Room of the Devil Tavern. The Cavalier poets, including Herrick, Lovelace, and others, were an outgrowth of this group. In "A Fit of Rhyme Against Rhyme," Jonson, a poet devoted to rhyme, uses ironic humor to join an ongoing debate of the Renaissance: was rhyme, sometimes considered an inferior invention of the "barbaric" Middle Ages, appropriately dignified for English poetry? (See Milton's preface to *Paradise Lost* in this book.) Jonson continued to write until he suffered a debilitating stroke in 1626. He was buried in Westminster Abbey under a stone on which was later engraved "O rare Ben Jonson!"

A Fit of Rhyme Against Rhyme

Rhyme, the rack of finest wits,
That expresseth but by fits
   True Conceipt,
Spoiling Senses of their Treasure,
Cozening Judgement with a measure,
   But false weight;
Wresting words, from their true calling,
Propping Verse for feare of falling
   To the ground;
Joynting Syllables, drowning Letters,
Fastning Voweles as with fetters
   They were bound!
Soone as lazie thou wert knowne,
All good Poëtrie hence was flowne,
   And Art banished.
For a thousand yeares together,
All *Parnassus'* Green did wither,
   And wit vanished.
Pegasus did flie away,
At the Wells no Muse did stay,
   But bewailed
So to see the Fountaine drie,
And *Apollo's* Musique die,
   All light failed!
Starveling rimes did fill the Stage,
Not a Poët in an Age,
   Worth crowning;
Not a work deserving baies,
Not a lyne deserving praise,
   Pallas frowning.
Greeke was free from Rime's infection,

Happy Greeke by this protection,
    Was not spoyled.
Whilst the Latin, Queene of Tongues,
Is not yet free from rimes wrongs,
    But rests foiled.
Scarce the Hill againe doth flourish,
Scarce the world a Wit doth nourish
    To restore
Phoebus to his Crowne againe;
And the Muses to their braine:
    As before.
Vulgar languages that want
Words, and sweetnesse, and be scant
    Of true measure,
Tyran Rime hath so abusëd,
That they long since have refusëd
    Other ceasure.
He that first invented thee,
May his joynts tormented be,
    Cramp'd for ever.
Still may Syllabes jarre with time,
Still may reason warre with rime,
    Resting never.
May his Sense, when it would meet
The cold tumor in his feet,
    Grow unsounder.
And his Title be long foole,
That in rearing such a Schoole,
    Was the founder.

SAMUEL DANIEL

Samuel Daniel (1562–1619) was born in Somersetshire, England, the son of a music teacher. He attended Oxford University and then worked as a tutor to Shakespeare's friend and patron William Herbert. He met the influential poet Mary, Countess of Pembroke, traveled in Italy, and translated Italian poetry. In 1603 he wrote an occasional poem on the accession of James I and was then given a job at court as inspector of the Children of the Queen's Revels (a company of boy actors). He held that position for the rest of his life and became a successful court poet, writing poetry for public occasions and dramatic entertainments for the court. In 1604 Queen Anne commissioned a masque from him, *The Vision of the Twelve Goddesses,* and took part in the performance. As a court poet, Daniel was not free to offend the throne. After writing his tragedy *Philotas,* which was thought to represent the Earl of Essex's 1600 rebellion in a sympathetic light, he published an "Apology" and regained royal favor. In his later years, he lived quietly on a farm in Somerset.

Daniel continually revised his works, aiming for a style characterized by clarity and restraint. The nineteenth-century English romantic poets greatly admired his purity of diction, and he has been characterized, because of his serious and stately manner, as the Matthew Arnold of his age. He is known chiefly for his first book *Delia* (1592), a collection of sonnets which was praised by Edmund Spenser in *Colin Clouts Come Home Againe.* He also published *The Complaint of Rosamund* and *Musophilus* as well as two tragedies, a historical epic called *The Civil Wars between the Two Houses of Lancaster and York* and the *History of England* in prose. When Daniel wrote his *A Defense of Rhyme* (1603), some poets had been engaged for the previous fifty years in an impossible attempt to import the classical system of quantitative meter, based on vowel quantity, into English poetry. Thomas Campion was among those who believed that, like everything classical, classical meter was more civilized and refined than the Germanic-English system of meter based on accent. Since classical poetry didn't rhyme, Campion argued in his 1602 *Observations in the Art of English Poesie* that rhyme was "vulgar and unartificial," (i.e., inartistic). In this reply to Campion, Daniel defends native English poetic traditions, using historical precedent as an argument.

from A Defense of Rhyme

. . . And indeed I have wished that there were not that multiplicity of rhymes as is used by many in sonnets, which yet we see in some so happily to succeed, and hath been so far from hindering their inventions, as it hath begot conceit beyond expectation, and comparable to the best inventions of the world. For sure in an eminent spirit, whom nature hath fitted for that mystery, rhyme is no impediment to his conceit, but rather gives him wings to mount, and carries him, not out of his course, but as it were beyond his power, to a far happier flight. All excellencies being sold us at the hard price of labor, it follows, where we bestow most thereof we buy the best success; and rhyme, being far more laborious than loose measures (whatsoever is objected), must needs, meeting with wit and industry, breed greater and worthier effects in our language. So that if our labours have wrought out a manumission from bondage and that we go at liberty, notwithstanding these ties, we are no longer the slaves of rhyme, but we make it a most excellent instrument to serve us. Nor is this certain limit observed in sonnets, any tyrannical bounding of the conceit, but rather a reducing it in *girum* [into a circuit] and a just form, neither too long for the shortest project, nor too short for the longest, being but only employed for a present passion. For the body of our imagination, being as unformed *Chaos* without fashion, without day, if by the divine power of the spirit it be wrought into an orb of order and form, is it not more pleasing to nature, that desires a certainty and comports not with that which is infinite, to have these closes rather than not to know where to end or how far to go, especially seeing our passions are often without measure? . . .

JOHN MILTON

Milton's life (1608–74), like the period of English history through which he lived, was divided into three parts: the Great Rebellion, the Commonwealth, and the Restoration. Milton was born in London to a father who was a prosperous lawyer and a successful composer and had been disinherited by his Roman Catholic family when he turned Protestant. Milton Sr. had the money to see that John, who showed early promise, was well educated. John attended St. Paul's School and Christ's College, Cambridge, where he wrote poetry in Latin, Italian, and English. He earned an MA as well as BA degrees, which usually were stepping stones to ordination in the Church of England. But, abandoning that plan because of his growing differences with the church, John retreated to his parents' country house where he studied for six years, writing "L'Allegro," "Il Penseroso" (1632), "Comus," (1634), and "Lycidas" (1637) and reading nearly everything written in European languages.

When sectarian tensions increased in England, Milton returned, taking the side of Parliament against the assertion of monarchical rights by Charles I and writing numerous pamphlets on the subject. He married Mary Powell in 1642, but she retreated to her Royalist parents' home one month later. Three years later she returned to Milton with a number of relatives in tow. In the same year, Milton's *Poems* was published.

For the next twenty years, Milton was engrossed in the political and religious issues of the time. Concerned with the Puritan cause, he wrote a series of pamphlets on such issues as church reform, divorce—the right to which he supported—and government and constitutional reforms. Also, in a pamphlet supporting regicide, he included a justification for the execution of Charles by the parliamentarians. When Oliver Cromwell acceded to power, Milton was appointed foreign secretary, reading and responding to letters in a variety of languages. When his sight began to fail—he may have had glaucoma—he continued his work with the help of aides.

Milton married twice more after the death of his first wife, Mary Powell, in childbirth. His second wife, Katherine Woodcock, died two years after marriage, also in childbirth. His third wife, Elizabeth Minshull, whom he married in 1662, was twenty-four; he was fifty-five. The marriages were unhappy; he did not find the true marriage of mind as well as body that he had argued for in his famous essay, "The Doctrine and Discipline of Divorce." However, during his brief second marriage, Milton began to work on *Paradise Lost* and hired Andrew Marvell as a secretary. After the restoration of Charles II in 1660, Milton was arrested as a defender of the Commonwealth. As such, he was in potential danger of the penalties of disembowelment, death, and dismemberment exacted against seventeenth-century traitors and carried out against those who signed the king's death warrant. But Milton was soon released, thanks to influential friends and to the king's desire to make the gesture of sparing the elderly, blind poet. For the rest of his life, Milton remained a relatively poor man. The Great Fire of London and the plague delayed the publication of *Paradise Lost* until 1667, when it was very well received. *Paradise Regained* and *Samson Agonistes* were published in 1671, three years before Milton's death.

Paradise Lost was reprinted in the year of Milton's death. Milton had reorganized the poem from ten books into twelve, following the model of classical epic poems such as the *Iliad* and the *Aeneid*. Purportedly because readers complained that they missed the heroic couplets they were used to, he added the following preface defending his use of blank verse. This famous preface criticizes the "modern bondage of Riming" in contrast with the great example of ancient unrhymed epic poetry and stresses the importance of enjambment in blank verse.

from Introduction to Paradise Lost

> . . . *I too transported by the Mode offend,*
> *And while I meant to Praise thee must Commend.*
> *Thy Verse created like thy Theme sublime,*
> *In Number, Weight, and Measure, needs not Rime.*
>
> A. M. [ANDREW MARVELL]

THE PRINTER TO THE READER

Courteous Reader, There was no Argument at first intended to the Book, but for the satisfaction of many that have desired it, I have procured it, and withal a reason of that which stumbled many others, why the Poem Rimes not.

THE VERSE

The measure is *English* Heroic Verse without Rime, as that of *Homer* in *Greek*, and of *Virgil* in *Latin*; Rime being no necessary Adjunct or true Ornament of Poem or good Verse, in longer Works especially, but the Invention of a barbarous Age, to set off wretched matter and lame Meter; grac't indeed since by the use of some famous modern Poets, carried away by Custom, but much to their own vexation, hindrance, and constraint to express many things otherwise, and for the most part worse than else they would have exprest them. Not without cause therefore some both *Italian* and *Spanish* Poets of prime note have rejected Rime both in longer and shorter Works, as have also long since our best *English* Tragedies, as a thing of itself, to all judicious ears, trivial and of no true musical delight; which consists only in apt Numbers, fit quantity of Syllables, and the sense variously drawn out from one Verse into another, not in the jingling sound of like endings, a fault avoided by the learned Ancients both in Poetry and all good Oratory. This neglect then of Rime so little is to be taken for a defect, though it may seem so perhaps to vulgar Readers, that it rather is to be esteem'd an example set, the first in *English*, of ancient liberty recover'd to Heroic Poem from the troublesome and modern bondage of Riming.

ANNE FINCH

Anne Finch (1661–1720) was born Anne Kingsmill in Kent, England. Orphaned at three, she was raised by her grandmother until she was eleven, then by her stepfather. Since the family had progressive views about education for women, Finch received some formal schooling. She studied the classics, French, Italian, history, poetry and drama. In 1682, she went to St. James Palace as a maid of honor. The court was known as the "Court of Wits," and she enjoyed its intellectual stimulation in spite of the frequent misogyny. Seeing the hostile treatment given to Anne Killigrew for publishing her poems, Anne Kingsmill kept her own early poems secret but began to write satirical poetry criticizing sexist social expectations.

At the court she met Heneage Finch, and in 1684 they began a long and very happy marriage. Heneage supported Anne's writing and wrote out a manuscript folio of her poems because her handwriting was hard to read. In 1688 the couple moved to the country to escape fines and imprisonment because of their Royalist loyalties; nevertheless, Heneage was arrested. Finch's poems from this time reflect her depression; "The Spleen," a poem about depression published as an anonymous song, was to be her most popular poem during her life. In 1710–11, they moved back to London, and Finch was there encouraged to publish by Alexander Pope and others. In 1713 *Miscellany Poems, on Several Occasions* appeared, the fifth collection of poems by a woman ever published in English. It included eighty-six poems and a play. In 1715, after political troubles and legal and financial battles brought on by the Finches' unexpected inheritance of the titles of earl and countess, Finch became severely ill, and her last poems are spiritual in orientation. She died in London on August 5, 1720, leaving a body of work valued for its intelligence, directness and humor. "The Appology" is a defiant and playful justification of her decision to publish in spite of the patriarchal Augustan climate that made her so hesitant.

The Appology

'Tis true I write and tell me by what Rule
I am alone forbid to play the fool
To follow through the Groves a wand'ring Muse
And fain'd Idea's for my pleasures chuse
Why shou'd it in my Pen be held a fault
Whilst Mira paints her face, to paint a thought
Whilst Lamia to the manly Bumper flys
And borrow'd Spiritts sparkle in her Eyes
Why shou'd itt be in me a thing so vain
To heat with Poetry my colder Brain
But I write ill and there-fore shou'd forbear
Does Flavia cease now at her fortieth year
In ev'ry Place to lett that face be seen
Which all the Town rejected at fifteen
Each Woman has her weaknesse; mind [sic] indeed
Is to write tho' hoplesse to succeed
Nor to the Men is this so easy found
Ev'n in most Works with which the Witts abound
(So weak are all since our first breach with Heav'n)
Ther's lesse to be Applauded then forgiven.

ALEXANDER POPE

Alexander Pope (1688–1744) was born in London, an only child of Roman Catholic parents. His father retired from his business as a linen draper after the birth, perhaps because of the intense anti-Catholicism of the time that banned Catholics from living within ten miles of London. Pope was tutored at home by a priest and then enrolled in two Catholic schools, but he was largely self-educated; as a Catholic he was not allowed to attend a university. He learned to read Latin, Greek, French, and Italian as a child and later claimed that he began very early to write poetry: "I lisp'd in numbers, for the numbers came" ("numbers" was a term for meter at that time). In 1705, when the family had moved to Windsor Forest, Pope contracted a tubercular infection of the spine. It left him frail, humpbacked, in frequent pain, and never to grow more than four and a half feet tall.

Eventually Pope moved to London and in 1711 published *An Essay on Criticism,* which brought him to the attention of prominent writers. The same year, he wrote and published the first version of his satirical mock-epic about a stolen piece of hair, *The Rape of the Lock.* Pope emulated the Roman poets Horace and Virgil and translated the *Iliad* and *Odyssey* into English couplets. His translations sold well, and he became the first author in English history to live entirely on income from literary publication. His many other works include the meditative *Essay on Man* and a savage satire of his literary contemporaries, *The Dunciad.* In 1718 he moved with his widowed mother to Twickenham, where he built a notorious grotto walled with shells and pieces of mirror. He died in 1744, leaving us such familiar quotations as "a little learning is a dangerous thing." His impact on eighteenth-century English literature was such that the period is often called "the age of Pope." With the growth of Romanticism his poetry was increasingly seen as outdated, and it was not until the 1930s that a serious attempt was made to rediscover his work.

Pope's poetry is written in heroic couplets, each couplet a complete and self-contained unit using devices such as logical parallelism or logical crossing to link the two lines. In keeping with the eighteenth-century ideal of a rational, balanced poetry which would balance the mind and emotions, each line is exactly ten syllables, with any extra syllables elided. While Pope is here demonstrating his own metrical subtlety by mocking poets who feel the need to make sound crudely echo sense, in fact this passage has become a textbook example of how meter can add to a poem's meaning: pyrrhics speed up a line, spondees slow it down, and so on.

from An Essay on Criticism

'Tis hard to say, if greater Want of Skill
Appear in *Writing* or in *Judging* ill;
But, of the two, less dang'rous is th' Offence,
To tire our *Patience*, than mis-lead our *Sense*. . . .

    Yet if we look more closely we shall find
    Most have the *Seeds* of Judgment in their Mind;
Nature affords at least a *glimm'ring Light*;
The lines, tho' touch'd but faintly, are drawn right. . . .

    Some have at first for *Wits*, then *Poets* past,
Turn'd *Criticks* next, and prov's plain *Fools* at last;
Some neither can for *Wits* nor *Criticks* pass,
As heavy Mules are neither *Horse* nor *Ass*. . . .

    First follow NATURE, and your Judgment frame
By her just Standard, which is still the same:
Unerring Nature, still divinely bright,
One *clear, unchang'd* and *Universal* Light,
Life, Force and Beauty, must to all impart.
At once the *Source*, and *End*, and *Test* of Art. . . .

    You then whose Judgment the right Course wou'd steer,
Know well each ANCIENT's proper *Character*,
His *Fable, Subject, Scope* in ev'ry Page,
Religion, Country, Genius of his *Age*:
Without all these at once before your Eyes,

You may *Confound*, but never *Criticize*.
Be *Homer's* Works your *Study*, and *Delight*,
Read them by Day, and meditate by Night,
Thence form your Judgment, thence your Notions bring
And trace the Muses *upward* to their *Spring*;
Still with *it Self compar'd*, his *Text* peruse;
And let your *Comment* be the *Mantuan Muse*. . . .

Musick resembles *Poetry*, in each
Are *nameless Graces* which no Methods teach,
And which a *Master-Hand* alone can reach. . . .

    A *little Learning* is a dang'rous Thing;
Drink deep, or taste not the *Pierian* Spring:
Then *shallow Draughts* intoxicate the Brain,
And drinking *largely* sobers us again.

Be not the *first* by whom the *New* are try'd,
Nor yet the *last* to lay the *Old* aside.
    But most by *Numbers* judge a Poet's Song,
And *smooth* or *rough*, with such, is *right* or *wrong*;
In the bright *Muse* tho' thousand *Charms* conspire,
Her *voice* is all these tuneful Fools admire,
Who haunt *Parnassus* but to please their Ear,
Not mend their Minds; as some to *Church* repair,
Not for the *Doctrine*, but the *Musick* there.
These *Equal Syllables* alone require,
Tho' oft the Ear the *open Vowels* tire,
While *Expletives* their feeble Aid *do* join. . . .

A *needless Alexandrine* ends the Song,
That like a wounded Snake, drags its slow length along. . . .

True ease in *Writing* comes from *Art*, not Chance
As those move easiest who have learn'd to Dance.
'Tis not enough no Harshness gives Offence,
The *Sound* must seem an *Eccho* to the *Sense*. . . .

Good-Nature and *Good-Sense* must ever join;
To Err is *Human*; to Forgive, *Divine*. . . .

WILLIAM WORDSWORTH

William Wordsworth (1770–1850) was born in the village of Cockermouth, Cumberland, one of five children. His mother died when he was eight and his father five years later. In 1778 he was sent to Hawkshead Grammar School, near Windermere, where his interest in poetry began. He attended St. John's College, Cambridge, but not a very motivated student, left briefly for a tour of Switzerland and Italy. He returned to graduate and left again for a walking tour of France, where the democratic ideals associated with the early stages of the Revolution impressed him and influenced his later writing deeply. He also had an affair with a French woman, Annette Vallon, who was both Catholic and Royalist, and fathered a daughter, Caroline. He returned to England before the execution of Louis XVI, very much under the influence of Rousseau and his English disciple, William Godwin.

In 1794 he was reunited with his sister Dorothy—the siblings had been separated early. She was his friend, his main support, and house-keeper and lived with him, and later with his family, until the end of her life. They settled in Somersetshire, near Samuel Taylor Coleridge, who became Wordsworth's constant companion and the friend with whom he regularly discussed poetry. Together they published *Lyrical Ballads* (1798), a collection which broke with current neo-classical ideals and was condemned by some as bad poetry and by others as "revolution-ary," or atheistic or pagan. The small volume included different types of poems, Coleridge famously writing those of supernatural or romantic interest and Wordsworth those concerning everyday events, characters, and incidents "such as will be found in every village and its vicinity where there is a meditative and feeling mind to seek after them." Thus Coleridge wrote "The Ancient Mariner," Wordsworth "Goody Blake" and "Simon Lee." In a second edition, Wordsworth added a preface (excerpted here) articulating the poetic ideas which reflected the ideals of democracy, nature worship and simple, clear diction. Wordsworth's greatest work may be *The Prelude,* a long poem, much-revised and not published until after his death in 1850, tracking the spiritual life and development of the poet.

After the rise of Napoleon, Wordsworth's attitude toward France changed, although he traveled there to meet his daughter when she was nine and to provide money for her education. On his return to England he courted and married Mary Hutchinson, an old friend; they had five children. Wordsworth accepted a small government job and gradually rejected his early radical positions. He succeeded his friend Robert Southey as poet laureate, but by then the great days of his writing were over. Later poets such as Byron bemoaned Wordsworth's transformation from young rebel to placid conservative: Wordsworth's great work, which defined the spirit of Romanticism, had all been accomplished in a twenty-five year span. The poet lived peacefully in the Lake Country until the end of his long life.

from Preface to Lyrical Ballads

The principal object, then, proposed in these Poems was to choose incidents and situations from common life, and to relate or describe them, throughout, as far as possible, in a selection of language really used by men, and, at the same time, to throw over them a certain colouring of imagination, whereby ordinary things should be presented to the mind in an unusual aspect; and further, and above all, to make these incidents and situations interesting by tracing in them, truly though not ostentatiously, the primary laws of our nature; chiefly, as far as regards the manner in which we associate ideas in a state of excitement. Humble and rustic life was generally chosen, because in that condition, the essential passions of the heart find a better soil in which they can attain their maturity, are less under restraint, and speak a plainer and more emphatic language. . . .

The language, too, of these men has been adopted (purified indeed from what appear to be its real defects, from all lasting and rational causes of dislike or disgust) because such men hourly communicate with the best objects from which the best part of language is originally derived; and because, from their rank in society and the sameness and narrow circle of their intercourse, being less under the influence of social vanity, they convey their feelings and notions in simple and unelaborated expressions. . . .

The reader will find that personifications of abstract ideas rarely occur in these volumes, and are utterly rejected, as an ordinary device to elevate the style, and raise it above prose. My purpose was to imitate, and, as far as possible, to adopt the very language of men; and assuredly such personifications do not make any natural or regular part of that language. . . .

Aristotle, I have been told, has said that poetry is the most philosophic of all writing: it is so: its object is truth, not individual and local, but general, and operative; not standing upon external testimony, but carried alive into the heart by passion; truth which is its own testimony, which gives competence and confidence to the tribunal to which it appeals, and receives them from the same tribunal. Poetry is the image of man and nature. . . .

I have said that poetry is the spontaneous overflow of powerful feelings; it takes its origin from emotion recollected in tranquility: the emotion is contemplated till, by a species of re-action, the tranquility gradually disappears, and an emotion, kindred to that which was before the subject of contemplation, is gradually produced, and does itself actually exist in the mind. . . . Now the music of harmonious metrical language, the sense of difficulty overcome, and the blind association of pleasure which has been previously received from works of rhyme or meter of the same or similar construction, an indistinct perception renewed of language closely resembling that of real life, and yet, in the circumstance of meter, differing from it so widely—all these imperceptibly make up a complex feeling of delight, which is of the most important use in tempering the painful feeling always found intermingled with powerful descriptions of the deeper passions. . . .

SAMUEL TAYLOR COLERIDGE
(headnote in Part 1)

from Biographia Literaria

CHAPTER XIV

Occasion of the Lyrical Ballads, and the objects originally proposed—Preface to the second edition—The ensuing controversy, its causes and acrimony—Philosophic definitions of a poem and poetry with scholia.

During the first year that Mr. Wordsworth and I were neighbors, our conversations turned frequently on the two cardinal points of poetry, the power of exciting the sympathy of the reader by a faithful adherence to the truth of nature, and the power of giving the interest of novelty by the modifying colors of imagination. The sudden charm, which accidents of light and shade, which moon-light or sun-set diffused over a known and familiar landscape, appeared to represent the practicability of combining both. These are the poetry of nature. The thought suggested itself (to which of us I do not recollect) that a series of poems might be composed of two sorts. In the one, the incidents and agents were to be, in part at least, supernatural; and the excellence aimed at was to consist in the interesting of the affections by the dramatic truth of such emotions, as would naturally accompany such situations, supposing them real. And real in *this* sense they have been to every human being who, from whatever source of delusion, has at any time believed himself under supernatural agency. For the second class, subjects were to be chosen from ordinary life; the characters and incidents were to be such, as will be found in every village and its vicinity, where there is a meditative and feeling mind to seek after them, or to notice them, when they present themselves.

In this idea originated the plan of the "Lyrical Ballads"; in which it was agreed, that my endeavours should be directed to persons and characters supernatural, or at least romantic; yet so as to transfer from our inward nature a human interest and a semblance of truth sufficient to procure for these shadows of imagination that willing suspension of disbelief for the moment, which constitutes poetic faith. Mr. Wordsworth, on the other hand, was to propose to himself as his object, to give the charm of novelty to things of every day, and to excite a feeling analogous to the supernatural, by awakening the mind's attention from the lethargy of custom, and directing it to the loveliness and the wonders of the world before us; an inexhaustible treasure, but for which, in consequence of the film of familiarity and selfish solicitude we have eyes, yet see not, ears that hear not, and hearts that neither feel nor understand.

With this view I wrote "The Ancient Mariner," and was preparing among other poems, "The Dark Ladie," and the "Christabel," in which I should have more nearly realized my ideal, than I had done in my first attempt. But Mr. Wordsworth's industry had proved so much more successful, and the number of his poems so much greater, that my compositions, instead of forming a balance, appeared rather an interpolation of heterogeneous matter. Mr. Wordsworth added two or three poems written in his own character, in the impassioned, lofty, and sustained diction, which is characteristic of his genius. In this form the "Lyrical Ballads" were published; and were presented by him, as an *experiment,* whether subjects, which from their nature rejected the usual ornaments and extra-colloquial style of poems in general, might not be so managed in the language of ordinary life as to produce the pleasurable interest, which it is the peculiar business of poetry to impart. To the second edition he added a preface of considerable length; in which, notwithstanding some passages of apparently a contrary import, he was understood to contend for the extension of this style to poetry of all kinds, and to reject as vicious and indefensible all phrases and forms of style that were not included in what he (unfortunately, I think, adopting an equivocal expression) called the language of *real* life. From this preface, prefixed to poems in which it was impossible to deny the presence of original genius, however mistaken its direction might be deemed, arose the whole long-continued controversy. For from the conjunction of perceived power with supposed heresy I explain the inveteracy and in some instances, I grieve to say, the acrimonious passions, with which the controversy has been conducted by the assailants.

Had Mr. Wordsworth's poems been the silly, the childish things, which they were for a long time described as being; had they been really distinguished from the compositions of other poets merely by meanness of language and inanity of thought; had they indeed contained nothing more than what is found in the parodies and pretended imitations of them; they must have sunk at once, a dead weight, into the slough of oblivion, and have dragged the preface along with them. But year after year increased the number of Mr. Wordsworth's admirers. They were found too not in the lower classes of the reading public, but chiefly among young men of strong sensibility and meditative minds; and their admiration (inflamed perhaps in some degree by opposition) was distinguished by its intensity, I might almost say, by its *religious* fervor. . . .

EDGAR ALLAN POE

Edgar Poe (1808–49) was born in Boston; his parents were touring actors, but his father was given to alcoholic binges and abandoned his wife and three children when Edgar was only two. His mother took them all to Richmond, Virginia, where she died only a few months later. He was separated from his siblings and taken in by a childless couple, John and Frances Allan, from whom he acquired his middle name. For several years, Poe attended school in England where his "stepfather"— he was never legally adopted—conducted his business, and he was said to be a fine scholar.

In 1820, Allan and his wife and Edgar returned to Richmond. Once again, Poe did very well at school and excelled in athletics. Relentlessly teased by his classmates as the son of actors (acting was considered a disreputable profession), he became something of a loner. In 1826, an unstable and gifted Poe entered the University of Virginia, where he incurred unpayable gambling debts in an effort to keep up with the high lifestyle; to escape, he joined the U. S. Army the following year under a false name. In 1830, Poe entered West Point, only to be courtmartialled and dismissed one year later. However, he had already published (at his own expense) his first book, *Tamerlane and Other Poems* (1827). In 1831 *Poems,* in which "To Helen" and "Israfel" appeared, was published. Five years later, Poe married his thirteen-year-old cousin Virginia Clemm, and they remained together until her death from tuberculosis in 1847.

Despite his drinking problem, Poe went on to edit several popular literary magazines of his time and to create such murder stories told from the perspective of the murderer as "The Tell-tale Heart" and "The Cask of Amontillado." "His Murders in the Rue Morgue," the first modern detective story, was published in *Graham's Magazine.* He began to write poetry again in 1845, after moving to Fordham, New York. "The Raven" was warmly received. It was followed by "Ulalume" and, in the last year of his life, "Annabel Lee."

Although best known for his macabre stories, Poe was a gifted poet. His poems almost without exception deal with bereaved lovers and visions of another world, and though their strong rhymes and rhythms earned Poe the condescending name of "jingle-master" from Ezra Pound, poems such as "The Raven" and "The Bells" have long been immensely popular and still resonate with readers today.

At the peak of his career, Poe was a sought-after lecturer on American poetry and addressed overflow crowds as he expatiated on his theory of poetics. The excerpt below is from his "The Philosophy of Composition." Unfortunately, Poe was unable to renounce alcohol or gambling. He died, drunk and impoverished, in Baltimore in 1849.

from The Philosophy of Composition

. . . Most writers—poets in especial—prefer having it understood that they compose by a species of fine frenzy—an ecstatic intuition— and would positively shudder at letting the public take a peep behind the scenes, at the elaborate and vacillating crudities of thought—at the true purposes seized only at the last moment—at the innumerable glimpses of idea that arrived not at the maturity of full view. . . .

For my part, I have neither sympathy with the repugnance alluded to, nor, at any time, the least difficulty in recalling to mind the progressive steps of any of my compositions, and, since the interest of an analysis or reconstruction, such as I have considered a *desideratum,* is quite independent of any real or fancied interest in the thing analysed, it will not be regarded as a breach of decorum on my part to show the *modus operandi* by which some one of my own works was put together. I select "The Raven" as most generally known. It is my design to render it manifest that no one point in its composition is referable either to accident or intuition—that the work proceeded step by step, to its completion, with the precision and rigid consequence of a mathematical problem. . . .

The initial consideration was that of extent. . . .

What we term a long poem is, in fact, merely a succession of brief ones—that is to say, of brief poetical effects. It is needless to demonstrate that a poem is such only inasmuch as it intensely excites, by elevating the soul; and all intense excitements are, through a psychal necessity, brief. For this reason, at least, one-half of the "Paradise Lost" is essentially prose. . . .

. . . [T]he extent of a poem may be made to bear mathematical relation to its merit . . . to the degree of the true poetical effect which it is capable of inducing; for it is clear that the brevity must be in direct ratio of the intensity of the intended effect. . . .

Holding in view these considerations . . . I reached at once what I conceived the proper *length* for my intended poem—a length of about one hundred lines. It is, in fact, a hundred and eight. . . .

. . . [T]hroughout the construction, I kept steadily in view the design of rendering the work *universally* appreciable . . . [T]he point upon which I have repeatedly insisted, and which, with the poetical, stands not in the slightest need of demonstration—the point, I mean, [is] that Beauty is the sole legitimate province of the poem. . . . That pleasure which is at once the most intense, the most elevating, and the most pure is, I believe, found in the contemplation of the beautiful. When indeed, men speak of Beauty, they mean, precisely, not a quality, as supposed, but an effect—they refer, in short, just to that intense and pure elevation of soul—*not* of intellect, or of heart—upon which I have commented, and which is experienced in consequence of contemplating the "beautiful." Now I designate Beauty as the province of the poem, merely because it is an obvious rule of Art that effects should be made to spring from direct causes—that objects should be attained through means best adapted for their attainment—no one as yet having been weak enough to deny that the peculiar elevation alluded to is *most readily* attained in the poem. . . .

Regarding, then, Beauty as my province, my next question referred to the *tone* of its highest manifestation—and all experience has shown that this tone is one of *sadness.* Beauty of whatever kind, in its supreme development, invariably excites the most sensitive soul to tears. Melancholy is thus the most legitimate of all the poetical tones.

The length, the province, and the tone, being thus determined, I betook myself to ordinary deduction, with the view of obtaining some artistic piquancy which might serve me as a key-note in the construction of the poem—some pivot upon which the whole structure might turn. . . . I did not fail to perceive immediately that no one had been so universally employed as that of the *refrain.* . . . As commonly used, the refrain, or burden, not only is limited to lyric verse, but depends for its impression upon the force of monotone—both in sound and thought. The pleasure is deduced solely from the sense of identity—of repetition . . . I determined to produce continuously novel effects, by the variation of the *application of the refrain*—the *refrain* itself remaining, for the most part, unvaried. . . .

Having made up my mind to a *refrain,* the division of the poem into stanzas was of course a corollary, the *refrain* forming the close to each stanza. That such a close, to have force, must be sonorous and susceptible of protracted emphasis, admitted no doubt, and these considerations inevitably led me to the long *o* as the most sonorous vowel in connection with *r* as the most producible consonant.

The sound of the refrain being thus determined, it became necessary to select a word embodying this sound. . . . In such a search it would have been absolutely impossible to overlook the word "Nevermore." In fact it was the very first which presented itself. . . .

I had now gone so far as the conception of the Raven, the bird of ill-omen, monotonously repeating the one word "Nevermore" at the conclusion of each stanza. . . . Now, . . . I asked myself—"Of all melancholy topics, what, according to the *universal* understanding of mankind, is the *most* melancholy?" Death, was the obvious reply. "And when," I said, "is this most melancholy of topics most poetical?" . . . "When it most closely allies itself to *Beauty:* the death then of a beautiful woman is unquestionably the most poetical topic in the world, and equally is it beyond doubt that the lips best suited for such topic are those of a bereaved lover."

I now had to combine the two ideas of a lover lamenting his deceased mistress and a Raven continuously repeating the word "Nevermore." . . . I had to combine these . . . imagining the Raven employing the word in answer to the queries of the lover. . . . I saw that I could make the first query a commonplace one, the second less so, the third still less, and so on until the lover . . . is at length excited to superstition, and wildly propounds queries of a far different character . . . half in superstition and half in that species of despair which delights in self-torture. . . .

Here then the poem may be said to have had its beginning—at the end where all works of art should begin. . . .

GERARD MANLEY HOPKINS

Gerard Manley Hopkins (1844–89) was born to prosperous middle-class parents in London, educated at the Highgate School with a solid background in classics, and entered Balliol College at Oxford, already well known as an adolescent poet. He continued to write poetry even as he was being caught up in the fervor of conversions from the Anglican Church to Catholicism that swept England at that time. In 1866 he was received into the Catholic Church; of his parents' replies to his letter announcing his conversion, he wrote the theologian, later cardinal, Newman "their answers are terrible: I cannot read them twice." Two years later, Hopkins became a Jesuit and not only abandoned his poetry but burned all of it. (Luckily, Robert Bridges, his patient advocate and friend, saved copies of much of Hopkins's work.)

The rigorous discipline of the Jesuit order emphasizing strict obedience attracted Hopkins, a depressive with a strong ascetic, if not masochistic, streak. Because his mental and physical health was always precarious, he was often not permitted to take part in various church fasts, to his disappointment. He was first sent to Liverpool to work in the slums, then posted to London, then Oxford.

In 1875, when Hopkins was encouraged by his superior to memorialize the sinking of the Deutschland with five German nuns aboard, he wrote "The Wreck of the Deutschland." A difficult poem with its powerful rhythms, it was not published in his lifetime, but served as the wellspring to many of his finest poems. "God's Grandeur," "The Starlight Night" and "Spring," written in 1877, demonstrate his preoccupation with what he called *inscape* and *instress,* the God-given unique quality of an object or a landscape, and the intrinsic power stemming from God that sustains it. "The Windhover" is perhaps the best example of these qualities as well as of sprung rhythm, the subject of the essay that accompanies this note.

Other sonnets, "I wake and feel the fell of dark, not day," and the three that follow, "came like inspirations unbidden and against my will," he wrote Bridges. "'Carrion Comfort,'" he said, "is written in blood." In the last few years of his life, Hopkins sank into a depression from which he never recovered. He died in Dublin from typhoid fever. In 1918, his collected poems appeared, with an introduction by Bridges, who saved this remarkable poet from obscurity. The preface below ascribes extremely complicated theories to his rhythmic practices.

from **Preface to Poems**

The poems in this book are written some in Running Rhythm, the common rhythm in English use, some in Sprung Rhythm, and some in a mixture of the two. And those in the common rhythm are some counterpointed and some not.

Common English rhythm, called Running Rhythm above, is measured by feet of either two or three syllables and (putting aside the imperfect feet at the beginning and end of lines and also some unusual measures, in which feet seem to be paired together and double or composite feet to arise) never more or less.

Every foot has one principal stress or accent, and this or the syllable it falls on may be called the Stress of the foot and the other part, the one or two unaccented syllables, the Slack. Feet (and the rhythms made out of them) in which the stress comes first are called the Falling Feet and Falling Rhythms, feet and rhythm in which the slack comes first are called Rising Feet and Rhythms, and if the stress is between two slacks there will be Rocking Feet and Rhythms. These distinctions are real and true to nature; but for purposes of scanning it is a great convenience to follow the example of music and take the stress always first, as the accent or the chief accent always comes first in a musical bar. If this is done there will be in common English verse only two possible feet—the so-called accentual Trochee and Dactyl, and correspondingly only two possible uniform rhythms, the so-called Trochaic and Dactylic. But they may be mixed and then what the Greeks called a Logaoedic Rhythm arises. These are the facts and according to these the scanning of ordinary regularly-written English verse is very simple indeed and to bring in other principles is here unnecessary. . . .

Sprung Rhythm, as used in this book, is measured by feet of from one to four syllables, regularly, and for particular effects any number of weak or slack syllables may be used. It has one stress, which falls on the only syllable, if there is only one, or, if there are more, then scanning as above, on the first, and so gives rise to four sorts of feet, a monosyllable and the so-called accentual Trochee, Dactyl, and the First Paeon. And there will be four corresponding natural rhythms; but nominally the feet are mixed and any one may follow any other. And hence Sprung Rhythm differs from Running Rhythm in having or being only one nominal rhythm, a mixed or "logaoedic" one, instead of three, but on the other hand in having twice the flexibility of foot, so that any two stresses may either follow one another running or be divided by one, two, or three slack syllables. But strict Sprung Rhythm cannot be counterpointed. In Sprung Rhythm, as in logaoedic rhythm generally, the feet are assumed to be equally long or strong and their seeming inequality is made up by pause or stressing.

Remark also that it is natural in Sprung Rhythm for the lines to be *rove over,* that is for the scanning of each line immediately to take up that of the one before, so that if the first has one or more syllables at its end the other must have so many the less at its beginning; and in fact the scanning runs on without break from the beginning, say, of a stanza to the end and all the stanza is one long strain, though written in lines asunder.

Two licences are natural to Sprung Rhythm. The one is rests, as in music . . . The other is *hangers* or *outrides,* that is one, two, or three slack syllables added to a foot and not counting in the nominal scanning. They are so called because they seem to hang below the line or ride forward or backward from it in another dimension than the line itself, according to a principle needless to explain here. These outriding half feet or hangers are marked by a loop underneath them, and plenty of them will be found.

The other marks are easily understood, namely accents, where the reader might be in doubt which syllable should have the stress; slurs, that is loops *over* syllables, to tie them together into the time of one; little loops at the end of a line to shew that the rhyme goes on to the first letter of the next line; what in music are called pauses, to shew that the syllable should be dwelt on; and twirls to mark reversed or counterpointed rhythm.

Note on the nature and history of Sprung Rhythm—Sprung Rhythm is the most natural of things. For (1) it is the rhythm of common speech and of written prose, when rhythm is perceived in them. (2) It is the rhythm of all but the most monotonously regular music, so that in the words of choruses and refrains and in songs written closely to music it arises. (3) It is found in nursery rhymes, weather saws, and so on; because, however these may have been once made in running rhythm, the terminations having dropped off by the change of language, the stresses come together and so the rhythm is sprung. (4) It arises in common verse when reversed or counterpointed, for the same reason. . . .

PAUL VALÉRY

Paul Valéry (1871–1945), was born of Italian parents in a village on the French Mediterranean. Under the influence of Poe, Mallarmé, and the Symbolists, he started writing poetry at age thirteen. After finishing law studies, he moved to Paris and began to publish his poems. But in 1892, after a frustrating failed love affair, he gave up poetry as too emotional. Seeking to cultivate a "universalist" mind like that of Leonardo da Vinci, he meditated for several hours each morning, recording his voluminous observations about science, language, art, and consciousness in a series of sixty-one notebooks, which were published after his death. Every day for fifty years he had written in them in the hours between "lamp and dawn," as he put it. During this time he published a study of da Vinci and wrote his first stories about the overly intellectual Monsieur Teste. In 1900 Valery married Jeannie Gobillard, niece of the prominent painter Berthe Morisot. For twenty-two years he was employed as a private secretary, which gave him time to focus on his scientific studies and raise their three children.

In 1912, André Gide persuaded him to begin writing poetry again. He spent five years writing *The Young Fate* (1917) and published a book of revised early poems in 1920, followed by *Charmes* (1922), which brought him fame as a poet. But Valéry remained ambivalent about poetry, reluctant to give it status equal to that of math and science. "Poetry," he wrote, "has never been a goal for me—more an instrument, an exercise, and its character derives from this—an artifice—product of will." Valéry's continuing obsession was his search for an understanding of the mind's operations.

Valéry spent his later years as a public intellectual, giving lectures and writing essays on the important topics of the day. He was known for his wit and for aphorisms such as "The trouble with our times is that the future is not what it used to be," and "God made everything out of nothing, but the nothingness shows through." About poetry he said: "A poem is never finished, only abandoned." He remained fascinated by science and knew most of the great scientists of his time, including Einstein and Farraday, while continuing to publish poetry, essays, and humorous stories about Teste, as well as attempting plays and an opera.

In 1925 he was elected to the Académie Française and was later employed as "Professor of Poetry," a position created especially for him, by the Collège de France. He died of heart trouble in 1945, shortly after the Allies liberated France and was honored with a state funeral attended by thousands. He is buried in his birthplace by the sea, Sète, under a stone carved with two lines from his poem "The Cemetery by the Sea": "After a thought, O then what recompense / A long gaze at the gods' serenity!"

from Remarks on Poetry

Speech is a complex thing; it is a combination of properties at once linked in fact and independent by nature and function. A discourse may be logical and full of sense, but without rhythm or measure; it may be agreeable to the ear, and completely absurd or meaningless; it may be clear and useless, vague and delightful. . . . But to grasp its strange multiplicity, it is enough to enumerate all the sciences created to deal with this diversity, each to exploit one of its elements. One may study a text in many independent ways, for it falls successively under the jurisdiction of phonetics, semantics, syntax, logic, and rhetoric—not forgetting metrics and etymology.

Here, then, is the poet at grips with this shifting and adulterated matter, forced to speculate by turns on the sound and the meaning, on the musical phrase, and again on various intellectual conditions such as logic, grammar, the poem's subject, figures, ornaments of all kinds— not to mention conventional rules. Consider what effort is implied in the undertaking to finish satisfactorily a discourse in which so many requirements must be miraculously satisfied at the same time!

Here begin the uncertain and painstaking operations of the literary art. But this art presents two aspects; there are two great methods which, at their extremes, are opposed, but which, however, meet and are linked by a host of intermediate degrees. There is *prose* and there is *verse*. Between them are all the mixtures of the two, but it is in their extreme forms that I will consider them today. One might illustrate this opposition of extremes by a slight exaggeration: one might say that the bounds of language are, on the one side, *music* and, on the other, *algebra*.

*   *   *

I shall have recourse to a comparison I have often used in order to make what I have to say on this subject easier to grasp. One day when I was speaking of all this in a foreign city, and had used the same comparison, one of my listeners sent me a remarkable quotation, which made me see that the idea was not a new one. Or rather it was new only to me.

Here is the quotation. It is an extract from a letter from Racan to Chapelain, in which Racan tells us that Malherbe likened prose to walking and poetry to dancing—as I am about to do:

> Give what name you please [said Racan] to my prose—gallant, simple, sprightly. I am resolved to hold to the precepts of my first master, Malherbe, and never to strive after number or cadence in my periods nor for any other ornament than the clarity that may express my thoughts. This good man compared prose to ordinary walking and poetry to dancing and used to say that in the things we are obliged to do we may tolerate some carelessness, but in those we do from vanity it is ridiculous to be no more than mediocre. The lame and gouty cannot help walking, but nothing compels them to dance a waltz or a cinquepace.

The comparison that Racan attributes to Malherbe, and which I for my part had easily perceived, is a direct one. I will show you how productive it is. It can be extensively developed in astonishing detail. It is perhaps something more than a surface likeness.

Walking, like prose, always has a definite object. It is an act directed *toward* some object that we aim to reach. The actual circumstances—the nature of the object, my need, the impulse of my desire, the state of my body and of the ground—regulate the rhythm of walking, prescribe its direction, speed, and termination. All the properties of walking derive from these instantaneous conditions, which combine *in a novel way* each time, so that no two movements of this kind are identical, and each time there is special creation, which is each time abolished and as it were absorbed in the completed act.

Dancing is quite different. It is, of course, a system of acts, but acts whose end is in themselves. It goes nowhere. Or if it pursues anything it is only an ideal object, a state, a delight, the phantom of a flower, or some transport out of oneself, an extreme of life, a summit, a supreme point of being. . . . But however diffferent it may be from utilitarian movement, this essential yet infinitely simple observation must be noted: *that it uses the same limbs, the same organs, bones, muscles, and nerves as walking does.*

It is exactly the same with poetry, which uses the same words, the same forms, the same tones as prose.

*   *   *

Prose and poetry are distinguished, therefore, by the difference between certain laws or momentary conventions of movement and function, applied to identical elements and mechanisms. This is why one must be careful not to think about poetry in the way one thinks about prose. What is true of the one has often no meaning when one seeks it in the other. And for this reason (to give an example), it is at once easy to justify the use of inversions; for these alterations of the customary and, in some ways, elementary order of words in French have been criticized at various periods, very superficially in my opinion, for reasons that come down to this unacceptable formula: poetry is prose.

Let us go a little further with our comparison, which can bear extension. A man is walking. He moves from one place to another, following a path that is always the path of least action. Note here that poetry would be impossible if its were confined to the rule of the straight line. One is taught: "Say it is raining if you mean that it is raining!" But a poet's object is not and never can be to tell us that it is raining. We do not need a poet to persuade us to take our umbrella. Think what would become of Ronsard and Hugo, what would become of the rhythm, images, and consonances of the finest verses in the world once you subjected poetry to the system of "Say it is raining!" It is only by clumsily confusing genres and occasions that one can blame a poet for his indirect expressions and complex forms. One fails to see that poetry implies a decision to change the function of language.

I return to the man walking. When this man has completed his movement, when he has reached the place, the book, the fruit, the object he desired, this possession immediately annuls his whole act, the effect consumes the cause, the end absorbs the means, and whatever the modalities of his act and steps, only the result remains. Once the lame or gouty, of whom Malherbe spoke, have painfully reached the armchair at which they were aiming, they are no less seated than the most alert man, who might reach the chair with a quick and light step. It is just the same with the use of prose. Language I have used, which has expressed my aim, my wish, my command, my opinion, my question, or my answer, language that has fulfilled its office, vanishes once it has *arrived*. I sent it forth to perish, to be irrrevocably transformed in you, and I shall know I am *understood* by the remarkable fact that my discourse no longer exists. It is entirely and definitively replaced by its meaning, or at least by a certain meaning, that is, by the images, impulses, reactions, or acts of the person to whom one speaks; in a work, by an inner modification or reorganization of that person. But if someone has not understood, he preserves and repeats the words. The experiment is simple. . . .

If poetry really affects someone, it is not by dividing him in his nature, by communicating to him illusions of a fancied and purely mental life. It does not impose on him a false reality that demands the docility of the mind and hence the absence of the body. Poetry must extend over the whole being; it stimulates the muscular organization by its rhythms, it frees or unleashes the verbal faculties, ennobling their whole action, or regulates our depths, for poetry aims to arouse or reproduce the unity and harmony of the living person, an extraordinary unity that shows itself when a man is possessed by an intense feeling that leaves none of his powers disengaged. . . .

WILLIAM CARLOS WILLIAMS

William Carlos Williams (1883–1963) was born into a middleclass family in Rutherford, New Jersey, and in a sense never left there. He began writing poetry while in high school, struggled over the decision, which he ultimately made, to attend medical school to fulfill his father's wishes, but managed to balance his two careers as physician and writer during his long and productive life. After acquiring his medical degree from the University of Pennsylvania and an advanced degree in pediatrics from the University of Leipzig, he practiced obstetrics and pediatrics in Rutherford, married his longtime sweetheart Florence Herman, and eventually became head pediatrician of the General Hospital in the nearby working-class city of Paterson.

While in medical school, he met Ezra Pound and H.D., who became his close friends. He began to publish poems and stories in literary magazines, and his poems appeared on a regular basis in Pound's and Amy Lowell's Imagist poetry collections. Although he met many of that era's outstanding literary figures—Marianne Moore, Wallace Stevens, Mina Loy—Williams was restless. Prolific as poet, novelist, essayist, even playwright, he continued to seek a truly American poetic idiom, one that reflected the everyday life of the common people he saw around him in his medical practice. He experimented with lineation, with a triadic stanza, and with a relaxed colloquialism that has been compared to Whitman's. Although his popularity grew slowly during the twenties and thirties when he published a broad experimental range of prose and poems, he resented the powerful Europeanized influence Eliot had on American poetry and came to detest the fascistic views expressed by Pound. But it wasn't until 1946, with the publication of *Paterson I,* that Williams found his voice. He is the doctor-persona named Paterson of the book-length poem. He lives in industrialized Paterson, he observes without judging the lives of his townspeople in a free-form poetry and prose poem that is distinctively idiomatic and open. The book was well received by the critics and Williams immediately pursued the second volume of his epic.

In 1950, *Selected Poems* and *Paterson III* won the National Book Award. Three years later, he shared the Bollingen Prize with Archibald MacLeish but did not receive the appointment as Consultant in Poetry to the Library of Congress that he had hoped for because of his supposed links to communism. However, in the fifties and sixties, following his reading tour of the West Coast, Williams's work began to attract the attention of Allen Ginsberg and the Beats, who were influenced by his direct, nonsymbolic images and encouraged by his willingness to exchange ideas with them. Two collections of his late poems appeared, *The Desert Music* in 1954, and *Journey to Love* in 1955, the latter containing his love poem to his wife, "To Asphodel." Despite a series of debilitating strokes, Williams continued writing until his death in 1963. He was awarded the Pulitzer Prize posthumously that same year.

The Poem as a Field of Action

TALK GIVEN AT THE UNIVERSITY OF WASHINGTON, 1948

Let's begin by quoting Mr. Auden—(from *The Orators*):
"Need I remind you that you're no longer living in ancient Egypt?"
I'm going to say one thing to you—for a week! And I hope to God when I'm through that I've succeeded in making you understand me. It concerns the poem as a field of action, at what pitch the battle is today and what may come of it.

As Freud says bitterly in the first chapter of his *The Interpretation of Dreams,* speaking of the early opposition to his theory: (the aversion of scientific men to learning something new) we shall learn that it is a characteristic quite as pronounced in literature—where the old the will *copy* "the new"—but the tiresome repetition of this "new," now twenty years old, disfigures every journal: I said a field of action. I can see why so many wish rather, avoiding thought, to return to the classic front of orthodox acceptance. As Anatole France put it in Freud's time, *"Les savants ne sont pas curieux."*

It is next to impossible to bring over the quantitative Greek and Latin text into our language. But does anyone ever ask *why* a Latin line in translation tends to break in half in our language? *Why* it cannot be maintained in its character, its quantitative character as against our accented verse? Have all the equivalents been exhausted or even tried? I doubt it.

I offer you then an initiation, what seems and what is actually only a half-baked proposal—since I cannot follow it with proofs or even *final* examples—but I do it with at least my eyes open—for what I myself may get out of it by presenting it as well as I can for you.

I propose sweeping changes from top to bottom of the poetic structure. I said structure. So now you are beginning to get the drift of my theme. I say we are *through* with the iambic pentameter as presently conceived, at least for dramatic verse; through with the measured quatrain, the staid concatenations of sounds in the usual stanza, the sonnet. More has been done than you think about this though not yet been specifically named for what it is. I believe something can be said. Perhaps all that I can do here is to call attention to it; a revolution in the conception of the poetic foot—pointing out the evidence of something that has been going on for a long time. . . .

But it might at this time be a good thing to take up first what is spoken of as free verse.

How can we accept Einstein's theory of relativity, affecting our very conception of the heavens about us of which poets write so much, without incorporating its essential fact—the relativity of measurements—into our own category of activity: the poem. Do we think we stand outside the universe? Or that the Church of England does? Relativity applies to everything, like love, if it applies to anything in the world.

What, by this approach I am trying to sketch, what we are trying to do is not only to disengage the elements of a measure but to seek (what we believe is there) a new measure or a new way of measuring that will be commensurate with the social, economic world in which we are living as contrasted with the past. It is in many ways a different world from the past calling for a different measure.

According to this conception there is no such thing as "free verse" and so I insist. Imagism was not structural: that was the reason for its disappearance. . . .

I wish I could enlist Auden in an attack, a basic attack upon the whole realm of structure in the poem. I have tried but without success so far. I think that's what he came here looking for, I think he has failed to find it (it may be constitutional with him). I think we have disappointed him. Perhaps he has disappointed himself. I am sure the attack must be concentrated on the *rigidity of the poetic foot.*

This began as a basic criticism of Auden's poems—as a reason for his coming to America, and has at least served me as an illustration for the *theory* upon which I am speaking.

Look at his poems with this in view—his very skill seems to defeat him. It need not continue to do so in my opinion.

Mr. Eliot, meanwhile, has written his *Quartets.* He is a very subtle creator—who knows how to squeeze the last ounce of force out of his material. He has done a good job here though when he speaks of developing a new manner of writing, new manners following new manners only to be spent as soon as that particular piece of writing has been accomplished—I do not think he quite knows what he is about.

But in spite of everything and completely discounting his subject matter, his *genre,* Eliot's experiments in the *Quartets* though limited, show him to be more American in the sense I seek than, sad to relate, Auden, with his English ears and the best will in the world, will ever be able to be. . . .

Now we come to the question of the origin of our discoveries. Where else can what we are seeking arise from but speech? From speech, from American speech as distinct from English speech, or presumably so, if what I say above is correct. In any case (since we have no body of poems comparable to the English) from what we *hear* in America. Not, that is, from a study of the classics, not even the American "Classics"—the *dead* classics which—may I remind you, we have *never heard* as living speech. No one has or can *hear* them as they were written any more than we can *hear* Greek today.

I say this once again to emphasize what I have often said—that we here must *listen* to the language for the discoveries we hope to make. This is not the same as the hierarchic or tapeworm mode of making additions to the total poetic body: the mode of the schools. This will come up again elsewhere.

That being so, what I have presumed but not proven, concerning Auden's work, can we not say that there are many more *hints* toward literary composition in the American language than in English—where they are inhibited by classicism and "good taste." (Note the French word tête, its derivation from "pot.") I'd put it much stronger, but let's not be diverted at this point, there are too many more important things pressing for attention.

In the first place, we have to say, following H. L. Mencken's *The American Language,* which American language? Since Mencken pointed out that the American student (the *formative* years—very important) is bilingual, he speaks English in the classroom but his own tongue outside of it.

We mean, then, American—the language Mr. Eliot and Mr. Pound carried to Europe *in their ears*—willy-nilly—when they left here for their adventures and which presumably Mr. Auden came here to find—perhaps too late. A language full of those hints toward newness of which I have been speaking. I am not interested in the history but these things offer a point worth making, a rich opportunity for development lies before us at this point.

I said "hints toward composition." This does not mean realism in the language. What it does mean, I think, is ways of managing the language, new ways. Primarily it means to me opportunity to expand the structure, the basis, the actual making of the poem. . . .

EZRA POUND

Born in Hailey, Idaho, Ezra Pound (1885–1972) grew up in Pennsylvania, spent two years at the University of Pennsylvania and completed his degree at Hamilton College. After a brief teaching stint, he traveled to Spain, Italy, and England, where he met his hero, W. B. Yeats. Between 1908 and 1911 he published six collections of poems, all influenced by his love of early Italian and Provençal poetry. In 1912, Pound became the spokesman for the Imagist movement which advocated free verse, economy in language, and emphasis on images, all apparent in his brief lyric "In a Station of the Metro" which reads: "In a station of the Metro / faces on a wet, black bough."

Acquainted with many visual artists in London, Pound was influenced by post-Cubist art in the next poetic program he championed, Vorticism. He also turned Chinese and Japanese poems, translated literally by the scholar Ernest Fenollosa, into delicate lyrics in the volume *Cathay*. Pound benefited from Fenollosa's ideas about the Chinese ideogram, finding there some of Modernism's prominent characteristics: the use of allusion and quotation; clarity and precision; the inclusion of narrative fragments; and the absence of traditional rhyme and meter. Pound became a major figure in the art world before World War I and actively advanced the careers of such writers as Yeats, Frost, William Carlos Williams, Marianne Moore, H.D., Hemingway, and especially T. S. Eliot. Through major cuts, he transformed Eliot's poem *The Wasteland* into the work we have now.

In 1914 Pound married Dorothy Shakespear and became the London editor of *The Little Review*. After a stay in Paris, Pound settled in Rapallo, Italy, in 1924 where he immersed himself in writing *The Cantos* and studying economic theory. He believed that the Social Credit theory of Major H. C. Douglas was a way to control the evils of capitalism. He also believed that the dictator Mussolini, whom he supported, could be persuaded to enact Douglas's theories. Pounds's main target was usury, which he soon began to connect with the Jews. From 1941 to 1943 Pound broadcast 120 vitriolic, anti-Semitic editorials over Radio Rome. A sample from two of them are these lines: "You let in the Jew and the Jew rotted your empire. . . . Your Jews have ruined your home manufacturers . . . it might be a good thing to hang Roosevelt and a few hundred yidds. . . ." In 1945

Pound was arrested for treason by partisans and turned over to U.S. troops. Found mentally unfit to stand trial, he was acquitted, but committed to a hospital in Washington, D.C., where he remained until 1958. During the years of Pound's incarceration, the jury of the Bollingen-Library of Congress Award overlooked his support of the Fascists and awarded him the prize for *The Pisan Cantos*. Many of his fellow poets also lobbied for his release, and in 1958 Pound returned to Italy where he died fourteen years later. Pound remains a controversial figure. His work is uneven, often marred by bizarre opinions, prosiness, and didacticism. At the same time, he is acknowledged for the new energy he brought to poetry and for his generosity to other writers, as well as for his best writing. Poetry in the twentieth century would have been different without him.

A Few Don'ts by an Imagiste

An "Image" is that which presents an intellectual and emotional complex in an instant of time. I use the term "complex" rather in the technical sense employed by the newer psychologists, such as Hart, though we might not agree absolutely in our application.

It is the presentation of such a "complex" instantaneously which gives that sense of sudden liberation; that sense of freedom from time limits and space limits; that sense of sudden growth, which we experience in the presence of the greatest works of art.

It is better to present one Image in a lifetime than to produce voluminous works.

All this, however, some may consider open to debate. The immediate necessity is to tabulate A LIST OF DON'TS for those beginning to write verses. But I can not put all of them into Mosaic negative.

To begin with, consider the three rules recorded by Mr. Flint, not as dogma—never consider anything as dogma—but as the result of long contemplation, which, even if it is some one else's contemplation, may be worth consideration.

Pay no attention to the criticism of men who have never themselves written a notable work. Consider the discrepancies between the actual writing of the Greek poets and dramatists, and the theories of the Graeco-Roman grammarians, concocted to explain their metres.

LANGUAGE

Use no superfluous word, no adjective which does not reveal something.

Don't use such an expression as "dim lands *of peace.*" It dulls the image. It mixes an abstraction with the concrete. It comes from the writer's not realizing that the natural object is always the *adequate* symbol.

Go in fear of abstractions. Don't retell in mediocre verse what has already been done in good prose. Don't think any intelligent person is going to be deceived when you try to shirk all the difficulties of the unspeakably difficult art of good prose by chopping your composition into line lengths.

What the expert is tired of today the public will be tired of tomorrow.

Don't imagine that the art of poetry is any simpler than the art of music, or that you can please the expert before you have spent at least as much effort on the art of verse as the average piano teacher spends of the art of music.

Be influenced by as many great artists as you can, but have the decency either to acknowledge the debt outright , or to try to conceal it.

Don't allow "influence" to mean merely that you mop up the particular decorative vocabulary of some one or two poets whom you happen to admire. A Turkish war correspondent was recently caught red-handed babbling in his dispatches of "dove-gray" hills, or else it was "pearl-pale," I can not remember.

Use either no ornament or good ornament.

RHYTHM AND RHYME

Let the candidate fill his mind with the finest cadences he can discover, preferably in a foreign language so that the meaning of the words may be less likely to divert his attention from the movement; e.g., Saxon charms, Hebridean Folk Songs, the verse of Dante, and the lyrics of Shakespeare—if he can dissociate the vocabulary from the cadence. Let him dissect the lyrics of Goethe coldly into their component sound values, syllables long and short, stressed and unstressed, into vowels and consonants.

It is not necessary that a poem should rely on its music, but if it does rely on its music that music must be such as will delight the expert.

Let the neophyte know assonance and alliteration, rhyme immediate and delayed, simple and polyphonic, as a musician would expect to know harmony and counterpoint and all the minutiae of his craft. No time is too great to give to these matters or to any one of them, even if the artist seldom have need of them.

Don't imagine that a thing will "go" in verse just because it's too dull to go in prose.

Don't be "viewy"—leave that to the writers of pretty little philosophic essays. Don't be descriptive; remember that the painter can describe a landscape much better than you can, and that he has to know a deal more about it.

When Shakespeare talks of the "Dawn in russet mantle clad" he presents something which the painter does not present. There is in this line of his nothing that one can call description; he presents.

Consider the way of the scientists rather than the way of an advertising agent for a new soap.

The scientist does not expect to be acclaimed as a great scientist until he has *discovered* something. He begins by learning what has been discovered already. He goes from that point onward. He does not bank on being a charming fellow personally. He does not expect his friends to applaud the results of his freshman class work. Freshmen in poetry are unfortunately not confined to a definite and recognizable class room. They are "all over the shop." Is it any wonder "the public is indifferent to poetry?"

Don't chop your stuff into separate *iambs*. Don't make each line stop dead at the end, and then begin every next line with a heave. Let the beginning of the next line catch the rise of the rhythm wave, unless you want a definite longish pause.

In short, behave as a musician, a good musician, when dealing with that phase of your art which has exact parallels in music. The same laws govern, and you are bound by no others.

Naturally, your rhythmic structure should not destroy the shape of your words, or their natural sound, or their meaning. It is improbable that, at the start, you will be able to get a rhythm-structure strong enough to affect them very much, though you may fall a victim to all sorts of false stopping due to line ends and caesurae.

The musician can rely on pitch and the volume of the orchestra.

You can not. The term harmony is misapplied to poetry; it refers to simultaneous sounds of different pitch. There is, however, in the best verse a sort of residue of sound which remains in the ear of the hearer and acts more or less as an organ-base. A rhyme must have in it some slight element of surprise if it is to give pleasure; it need not be bizarre or curious, but it must be well used if used at all.

Vide further Vildrac and Duhamel's notes on rhyme in "*Technique Poétique.*"

That part of your poetry which strikes upon the imaginative *eye* of the reader will lose nothing by translation to a foreign tongue; that which appeals to the ear can reach only those who take it in the original.

Consider the definiteness of Dante's presentation, as compared with Milton's rhetoric. Read as much of Wordsworth as does not seem too unutterably dull.

If you want the gist of the matter go to Sappho, Catullus, Villon, Heine when he is in the vein, Gautier when he is not too frigid; or, if you have not the tongues, seek out the leisurely Chaucer. Good prose will do you no harm, and there is good discipline to be had by trying to write it.

Translation is likewise good training, if you find that your original matter "wobbles" when you try to rewrite it. The meaning of the poem to be translated can not "wobble."

If you are using a symmetrical form, don't put in what you want to say and then fill up the remaining vacuums with slush.

Don't mess up the perception of one sense by trying to define it in terms of another. This is usually only the result of being too lazy to find the exact word. To this clause there are possibly exceptions.

The first three simple proscriptions will throw out nine-tenths of all the bad poetry now accepted as standard and classic; and will prevent you from many a crime of production.

". . . *Mais d'abord il faut être un poète,*" as MM. Duhamel and Vildrac have said at the end of their little book, "*Notes sur la Technique Poétique*"; but in an American one takes that at least for granted, otherwise why does one get born upon that august continent!

MARIANNE MOORE

Marianne Moore (1887–1972) was born in Kirkwood, Missouri, and grew up with her brother and mother in the home of her maternal grand-father, a minister there. Moore's parents separated before she was born, after her father suffered a nervous breakdown; as a consequence, she never met him. Late in her life, however, she expressed interest in exploring that side of the family and entered into correspondence with some of her paternal cousins. Moore and her brother and mother moved to Carlisle, Pennsylvania, in 1896. In 1909 she graduated from Byrn Mawr College, where H.D. had been one of her classmates. Her college years were a period of literary apprenticeship; she knew by this time that she wanted to be a writer. Toward this end, she was advised to acquire skill on the keyboard and attended Carlisle Commercial College to learn typing. Because the family was cool to the prospect of Moore's moving away, she took a position teaching school at the Carlisle Indian School.

In 1918, the little nuclear family moved to New York City and Moore soon became a librarian at the New York Public Library. She began to meet and correspond with other writers, among them Wallace Stevens, William Carlos Williams, E. E. Cummings, and younger writers such as Louise Bogan and W. H. Auden. As her career enlarged, beginning with her editorship of *The Dial* from 1925 to 1929, her correspondence with these poets as well as with many others gaining prominence around her is significant not only historically but for the way it defines her and her role in the literary community. Marianne Moore's prodigious correspondence—letters to her immediate family alone run to more than thirteen thousand items—provide the interested reader with an intimate portrait of her quirky, satiric, and often self-mocking style. (See *The Selected Letters of Marianne Moore*, 1997.) Marianne Moore's honors include the Bollingen Prize, the National Book Award, and the Pulitzer Prize. A modernist, she frequently incorporated in her poems quotations from items that piqued her interest, fitting bits together like an intricate mosaic. Many of her poems are written in syllabics. She was particularly taken with oddities of the animal kingdom and much of her imagery is evoked by the natural world. To a *New York Herald Tribune* interviewer in 1951, she said, "I am fond of animals and take inordinate interest in mongooses, squirrels, crows, elephants." Further, when asked about her writing habits, she disclosed, "When I have finished a thing it is, so far as I know, the last thing I shall write; but if taken unaware by what charms or stirs me up, I may write again."

The Complete Poems of Marianne Moore (1967) contains her eleven previous collections, including what are perhaps the two best known: *What Are Years?* and *O To Be a Dragon.* The selection included here amplifies her poetic avowal that art expresses human need: "is feeling, modified by the writer's moral and technical insights."

But this headnote would not be complete without mention of Moore's love of and loyalty to baseball, particularly to the then Brooklyn Dodgers, whose home games she attended and her admiration of the boxer Muhammad Ali, for whom she wrote the liner notes to his declamatory record, *I Am the Greatest!*

from Feeling and Precision

Feeling at its deepest—as we all have reason to know—tends to be inarticulate. If it does manage to be articulate, it is likely to seem over-condensed, so that the author is resisted as being enigmatic or disobliging or arrogant.

One of New York's more painstaking magazines asked me, at the suggestion of a contributor, to analyze my sentence structure, and my instinctive reply might have seemed dictatorial: you don't devise a rhythm, the rhythm is the person, and the sentence but a radiograph of personality. The following principles, however, are aids to composition by which I try, myself, to be guided: if a long sentence with dependent clauses seems obscure, one can break it into shorter units by imagining into what phrases it would fall as conversation; in the second place, expanded explanation tends to spoil the lion's leap—an awkwardness which is surely brought home to one in conversation; and in the third place, we must be as clear as our natural reticence allows us to be. . . .

When writing with maximum impact, the writer seems under compulsion to set down an unbearable accuracy; and in connection with precision as we see it in metaphor, I think of Gerard Hopkins and his description of the dark center in the eye of a peacock feather as "the colour of the grape where the flag is turned back"; also his saying about some lambs he had seen frolicking in a field, "It was as though it was the ground that tossed them"; at all events, precision is a thing of the imagination; and it is a matter of diction, of diction that is virile because galvanized against inertia. . . .

When we think we don't like art it is because it is artificial art. "Mere technical display," as Plato says, "is a beastly noise"—in contrast with art, which is "a spiritual magnetism" or "fascination" or "conjuring of the soul."

Voltaire objected to those who said in enigmas what others had said naturally, and we agree; yet we must have the courage of our peculiarities. . . .

We call climax a device, but is it not the natural result of strong feeling? It is, moreover, a pyramid that can rest either on its point or on its base, witty anticlimax being one of Ludwig Bemelmans' best enticements, as when he says of the twelve little girls, in his story *Madeline*:

> They smiled at the good
> and frowned at the bad
> and sometimes they were very sad.

Intentional anticlimax as a department of surprise is a subject by itself; indeed, an art, "bearing," as Longinus says, "the stamp of vehement emotion like a ship before a veering wind," both as content and as sound; but especially as sound, in the use of which the poet becomes a kind of hypnotist—recalling Kenneth Burke's statement that "the hypnotist has a way out and a way in."

Concealed rhyme and the interiorized climax usually please me better than the open rhyme and the insisted-on climax. . . .

With regard to unwarinesses that defeat precision, excess is the common substitute for energy. We have it in our semi-academic, too conscious adverbs—awfully, terribly, frightfully, infinitely, tremendously; in the word "stunning," the phrase "knows his Aristotle," or his Picasso, or whatever it may be; whereas we have a contrastingly energetic usefulness in John Crowe Ransom's term "particularistic," where he says T. S. Eliot "is the most particularistic critic that English poetry and English criticism have met with." Similarly with Dr. Johnson's "encomiastick," in the statement that Dryden's account of Shakespeare "may stand as a perpetual model of encomiastick criticism." . . .

And unmistakably Ezra Pound's instinct against preciosity is part of his instinct for precision and accounts for his "freedom of motion" in saying what he has to say "like a bolt from a catapult"—not that the catapult is to us invariably a messenger of comfort. . . .

Professor Maritain, when lecturing on scholasticism and immortality, spoke of those suffering in concentration camps, "unseen by any star, unheard by any ear," and the almost terrifying solicitude with which he spoke made one know that belief is stronger even than the struggle to survive. And what he said so unconsciously was poetry. So art is but an expression of our needs; is feeling, modified by the writer's moral and technical insights.

WILLIAM BUTLER YEATS

William Butler Yeats (1865–1939), poet, playwright, politician, and winner of the Nobel Prize in Literature (1923), was born in Dublin, Ireland. His father, a lawyer turned portrait painter, took the family to London when Yeats was an infant. They moved back to Dublin in 1881 where he studied painting but soon found that poetry had the greater appeal. Yeats was also attracted to esoteric cults and supernatural systems, an interest he clung to throughout his life. He became active in the Celtic revival, a movement that encouraged the celebration of the Irish national heritage rather than the Victorian English cultural influences that were dominant at that time. In 1889 Yeats met the woman he adored, the Irish revolutionary Maud Gonne, an actress of great beauty. In 1903 she married another man, but her influence on Yeats was profound and lasting. "No Second Troy," one of his most famous poems, is said to have been written when he lost her to Major MacBride. (Not until 1917 did Yeats take a wife, George Hyde-Lees, half his age, who with her talent for automatic writing reignited his interest in the occult.) His continuing involvement in Irish political life is reflected in his poetry, where it takes the form of an ever-growing pessimism over the state of politics, not only in his native land but throughout Europe. Although he affirmed the aims of the Irish nationalist movement, he deplored the bigotry that colored it, and his poetry of the period is full of lamentation and sorrow. (For examples, see "Easter, 1916" and "The Wild Swans at Coole.") T. S. Eliot, Ezra Pound, and possibly Wallace Stevens as well must be seen as influential in Yeats's growing conservatism, but not in his ongoing use of form.

Yeats's attraction to folk literature was evident in his early work, a publication of Irish fairy tales. In 1897 he met Lady Gregory, who joined him in establishing the Irish Literary Theatre (later, the Abbey Theatre); he became its first director and wrote several plays for performance there. *Cathleen ni Houlihan* (1902), based on the exploits of an early Irish heroine, is his most famous. The theater also produced plays by John Millington Synge and Sean O'Casey; Synge's *Playboy of the Western World* set off a riot. Its satirical humor and strong language portraying Irish peasant life offended the Irish upper class. Yeats's later plays, first inspired by Ezra Pound's adaptations of Japanese Noh plays, employed music, dance, and masks. While the Nobel Prize was awarded to him as a playwright, it is his poetry for which he is rightfully famous. He died in 1939.

from A General Introduction for My Work

I. THE FIRST PRINCIPLE

A poet writes always of his personal life, in his finest work out of its tragedy, whatever it be, remorse, lost love, or mere loneliness; he never speaks directly as to someone at the breakfast table, there is always a phantasmagoria. Dante and Milton had mythologies, Shakespeare and the characters of English history or of traditional romance; even when the poet seems most himself, when he is Raleigh and gives potentates the lie, or Shelley "a nerve o'er which do creep / the else unfelt oppressions of this earth," or Byron when "the soul wears out the breast" as "the sword outwears its sheath," he is never the bundle of accident and incoherence that sits down to breakfast; he has been reborn as an idea, something intended, complete. A novelist might describe his accidence, his incoherence, he must not; he is more type than man, more passion than type. He is Lear, Romeo, Oedipus, Tiresias; he has stepped out of a play, and even the woman he loves is Rosalind, Cleopatra, never The Dark Lady. He is part of his own phantasmagoria and we adore him because nature has grown intelligible, and by so doing a part of our creative power. "When mind is lost in the light of the Self," says the Prashna Upanishad, "it dreams no more; still in the body it is lost in happiness." "A wise man seeks in Self," says the Chandogya Upanishad, "those that are alive and those that are dead and gets what the world cannot give." The world knows nothing because it has made nothing, we know everything because we have made everything. . . .

III. STYLE AND ATTITUDE

Style is almost unconscious. I know what I have tried to do, little what I have done. Contemporary lyric poems, even those that moved me—*The Stream's Secret, Dolores*—seemed too long, but an Irish preference for a swift current might be mere indolence, yet Burns may have felt the same when he read Thomson and Cowper. The English mind is meditative, rich, deliberate; it may remember the Thames valley. I planned to write short lyrics or poetic drama where every speech would be short and concentrated, knit by dramatic tension, and I did so with more confidence because young English poets were at that time writing out of emotion at the moment of crisis, though their old slow-moving meditation returned almost at once. Then, and in this English poetry has followed my lead, I tried to make the language of poetry coincide with that of passionate, normal speech. I wanted to write in whatever language comes most naturally when we soliloquise, as I do all day long, upon the events of our own lives or of any life where we can see ourselves for the moment. I sometimes compare myself with the mad old slum women I hear denouncing and remembering; "How dare you," I heard one say of some imaginary suitor, "and you without health or a home!" If I spoke my thoughts aloud they might be as angry and as wild. It was a long time before I had made a language to my liking; I began to make it when I discovered some twenty years ago that I must seek, not as Wordsworth thought, words in common use, but a powerful and passionate syntax, and a complete coincidence between period and stanza. Because I need a passionate syntax for passionate subject-matter I compel myself to accept those traditional metres that have developed with the language. Ezra Pound, Turner, Lawrence wrote admirable free verse, I could not. I would lose myself, become joyless like those mad old women. The translators of the Bible, Sir Thomas Browne, certain translators from the Greek when translators still bothered about rhythm, created a form midway between prose and verse that seems natural to impersonal meditation; but all that is personal soon rots; it must be packed in ice or salt. Once when I was in delirium from pneumonia I dictated a letter to George Moore telling him to eat salt because it was a symbol of eternity; the delirium passed, I had no memory of that letter, but I must have meant what I now mean. If I wrote of personal love or sorrow in free verse, or in any rhythm that left it unchanged, amid all its accidence, I would be full of self-contempt because of my egotism and indiscretion, and foresee the boredom of my reader. I must choose a traditional stanza, even what I alter must seem traditional. I commit my emotion to shepherds, herdsmen, camel-drivers, learned men, Milton's or Shelley's Platonist, that tower Palmer drew. Talk to me of originality and I will turn on you with rage. I am a crowd, I am a lonely man, I am nothing. Ancient salt is best packing. The heroes of Shakespeare convey to us through their looks, or through the metaphorical patterns of their speech, the sudden enlargement of their vision, their ecstasy at the approach of death: "She should have died hereafter," "Of many thousand kisses, the poor last," "Absent thee from felicity awhile." They have become God or Mother Goddess, the pelican, "My baby at my breast," but all must be cold; no actress has ever sobbed when she played Cleopatra, even the shallow brain of a producer has never thought of such a thing. The supernatural is present, cold winds blow across our hands, upon our faces, the thermometer falls, and because of that cold we are hated by journalists and groundlings. There may be in this or that detail painful tragedy, but in the whole work none. I have heard Lady Gregory say, rejecting some play in the modern manner sent to the Abbey Theatre, "Tragedy must be a joy to the man who dies." Nor is it any different with lyrics, songs, narrative poems; neither scholars nor the populace have sung or read anything generation after generation because of its pain. The maid of honour whose tragedy they sing must be lifted out of history with timeless pattern, she is one of the four Maries, the rhythm is old and familiar, imagination must dance, must be carried beyond feeling into the aboriginal ice. Is ice the correct word? I once boasted, copying the phrase from a letter of my father's, that I would write a poem "cold and passionate as the dawn."

When I wrote in blank verse I was dissatisfied; my vaguely medi-aeval *Countess Cathleen* fitted the measure, but our Heroic Age went better, or so I fancied, in the ballad metre of *The Green Helmet*. There was something in what I felt about Deirdre, about Cuchulain, that rejected the Renaissance and its characteristic metres, and this was a principal reason why I created in dance plays the form that varies blank verse with lyric metres. When I speak blank verse and analyse my feelings, I stand at a moment of history when instinct, its traditional songs and dances, its general agreement, is of the past. I have been cast up out of the whale's belly though I still remember the sound and sway that came from beyond its ribs, and, like the Queen in Paul Fort's ballad, I smell of the fish of the sea. The contrapuntal structure of the verse, to employ a term adopted by Robert Bridges, combines the past and present. If I repeat the first line of *Paradise Lost* so as to emphasise its five feet I am among the folk singers—"Of mán's first dísobédience ánd the frúit," but if I speak it as I should I cross it with another emphasis, that of passionate prose— "Of mán's fírst disobédience and the frúit," or "Of mán's fírst disobedi-ence and the frúit"; the folk song is still there but a ghostly voice, an unvariable possibility, an unconscious norm. What moves me and my hearer is a vivid speech that has no laws except that it must not exorcise the ghostly voice. I am awake and asleep, at my moment of revelation, self-possessed in self-surrender; there is no rhyme, no echo of the beaten drum, the dancing foot, that would overset my balance. When I was a boy I wrote a poem upon dancing that had one good line: "They snatch with their hands at the sleep of the skies." If I sat down and thought for a year I would discover that but for certain syllabic limitations, a rejection or acceptance of certain elisions, I must wake or sleep.

The Countess Cathleen could speak a blank verse which I had loosened, almost put out of joint, for her need, because I thought of her as mediaeval and thereby connected her with the general European movement. For Deirdre and Cuchulain and all the other figures of Irish legend are still in the whale's belly. . . .

HART CRANE

Harold Hart Crane (1899–1932) was born in Garrettsville, Ohio, and began writing poetry as a teenager. He never attended college but read brilliantly on his own, especially Marlowe, Donne, Shakespeare, and Rimbaud. His father, a candy maker whose products included Lifesavers candy, did not support his writing. His mother was more sympathetic, and he took Hart, her maiden name, as his first name when he moved to New York to make a career in literature. Alcoholism and poverty, instability and loneliness plagued Crane in New York. Conflict between his identities as a poet and as a gay man troubled him deeply, and he wrote numerous unpublished poems that attempt to make sense of his experience. Driven to a series of brief affairs, he wrote his magnificent sequence "Voyages" after his longest involvement, with the ship's purser, Emil Opffer.

A rhapsodic, very musical poet, Crane combined traditional meter with highly compressed language and a Whitmanian vision of American greatness, expressed especially in his book-length poem *The Bridge*. His major work with epic ambitions to encompass American history and mythology, it takes the Brooklyn Bridge as a symbol of a glorious modern future grounded in technology. In the letter to Harriet Monroe printed here, Crane defends his poem "At Melville's Tomb," describing what he called the "logic of metaphor" that unfolds, through connotations of words, underneath the surface of a poem's language.

In 1926 Crane published his first collection, *White Buildings;* the publication of *The Bridge* in 1930 was enthusiastically received. In 1931 he won a Guggenheim Fellowship and used it to live in Mexico. On the steamship back to New York, dissipated, broke, and with few friends to return to, Crane committed suicide at the age of thirty-three by jumping from the deck.

from To Harriet Monroe, Editor of Poetry: A Magazine of Verse

Your good nature and manifest interest in writing me about the obscurities apparent in my Melville poem certainly prompt a wish to clarify my intentions in that poem as much as possible. But I realize that my explanations will not be very convincing. For a paraphrase is generally a poor substitute for any organized conception that one has fancied he has put into the more essentialized form of the poem itself.

At any rate, and though I imagine us to have considerable differences of opinion regarding the relationship of poetic metaphor to ordinary logic (I judge this from the angle of approach you use toward portions of the poem), I hope my answers will not be taken as a defense of merely certain faulty lines. I am really much more interested in certain theories of metaphor and technique involved generally in poetics, than I am concerned in vindicating any particular perpetrations of my own.

My poem may well be elliptical and actually obscure in the ordering of its content, but in your criticism of this very possible deficiency you have stated your objections in terms that allow me, at least for the moment, the privilege of claiming your ideas and ideals as theoretically, at least, quite outside the issues of my own aspirations. To put it more plainly, as a poet I may very possibly be more interested in the so-called illogical impingements of the connotations of words on the consciousness (and their combinations and interplay in metaphor on this basis) than I am interested in the preservation of their logically rigid significations at the cost of limiting my subject matter and perceptions involved in the poem.

This may sound as though I merely fancied juggling words and images until I found something novel, or esoteric; but the process is much more predetermined and objectified than that. The nuances of feeling and observation in a poem may well call for certain liberties which you claim the poet has no right to take. I am simply making the claim that the poet does have that authority, and that to deny it is to limit the scope of the medium so considerably as to outlaw some of the richest genius of the past.

This argument over the dynamics of metaphor promises as active a future as has been evinced in the past. Partaking so extensively as it does of the issues involved in the propriety or non-propriety of certain attitudes toward subject matter, etc., it enters the critical distinctions usually made between "romantic," "classic" as an organic factor. It is a problem that would require many pages to state adequately—merely from my own limited standpoint on the issues. Even this limited statement may prove onerous reading, and I hope you will pardon me if my own interest in the matter carries me to the point of presumption. . . .

You ask me how a <u>portent</u> can possibly be wound in a <u>shell</u>. Without attempting to answer this for the moment, I ask you how Blake could possibly say that, "a <u>sigh</u> is a <u>sword</u> of an Angel King." You ask me how <u>compass</u>, <u>quadrant</u> and <u>sextant</u> "<u>contrive</u>" tides. I ask you how Eliot can possibly believe that "Every street <u>lamp</u> that I pass <u>beats</u> like a fatalistic <u>drum</u>!" Both of my metaphors may fall down completely. I'm not defending their actual value in themselves; but your criticism of them in each case was leveled at an illogicality of relationship between symbols, which similar fault you must have either overlooked in case you have ever admired the Blake and Eliot lines, or have there condoned them on account of some more ultimate convictions pressed on you by the impact of the poem in their entirety.

It all comes to the recognition that emotional dynamics are not to be confused with any absolute order of rationalized definitions; ergo, in poetry the <u>rationale</u> of metaphor belongs to another order of experience than science, and is not to be limited by a scientific, and arbitrary code of relationships either in verbal inflections or concepts. . . .

Not to rant on forever, I'll beg your indulgence and come at once to the explanations you requested on the Melville poem:

"The dice of drowned men's bones he saw bequeath
An embassy."

Dice bequeath an embassy, in the first place, by being ground (in this connection only, of course) in little cubes from the bones of drowned men by the action of the sea, and are finally thrown up on the sand, having "numbers" but no identification. These being the bones of dead men who never completed their voyage, it seems legitimate to refer to them as the only surviving evidence of certain messages undelivered, mute evidence of certain things, experiences that the dead mariners might have had to deliver. Dice as a symbol of chance and circumstance is also implied.

"The calyx of death's bounty giving back," etc.

This calyx refers in a double ironic sense both to a cornucopia and the vortex made by a sinking vessel. As soon as the water has closed over a ship this whirlpool sends up broken spars, wreckage, etc., which can be alluded to as <u>livid hieroglyphs</u>, making a <u>scattered chapter</u> so far as any complete record of the recent ship and her crew is concerned. In fact, about as much definite knowledge might come from all this as any-one might gain from the roar of his own veins, which is easily heard (haven't you ever done it?) by holding a shell close to one's ear.

"Frosted eyes lift altars."

Refers simply to a conviction that a man, not knowing perhaps a definite god yet being endowed with a reverence for deity—such a man naturally postulates a deity somehow, and the altar of that deity by the very <u>action</u> of the eyes <u>lifted</u> in searching.

"Compass, quadrant and sextant contrive no farther tides."

Hasn't it often occurred that instruments originally invented for record and computation have inadvertently so extended the concepts of the entity they were invented to measure (concepts of space, etc.) in the mind and imagination that employed them, that they may metaphori-cally be said to have extended the original boundaries of the entity meas-ured? This little bit of "relativity" ought not to be discredited in poetry now that scientists are proceeding to measure the universe on principles of pure <u>ratio</u>, quite as metaphorical, so far as previous standards of sci-entific methods extended, as some of the axioms in Job. . . .

WALLACE STEVENS

Wallace Stevens (1879–1955) grew up in Reading, Pennsylvania, graduated from public high school, and left for Harvard in 1897. His father was a schoolteacher, an attorney, and an occasional poet who encouraged Stevens's ambitions and advised him in a letter to "paint truth but not always in drab clothes." Like his father, Stevens devised a life that included both practical and imaginative work. Stevens kept these realms separate; he observed their interactions, though he also wrote that "the imaginative world is the only real world after all." After attending Harvard for three years and publishing in the *Harvard Advocate* and the *Harvard Monthly,* he left to try newspaper reporting. Then he took his father's advice and entered New York Law School, graduated, and passed the bar. But not succeeding in his law practice, he joined the Hartford Accident and Insurance Company and moved with his wife, Elsie Moll, to Hartford, Connecticut, where they lived until their deaths. The couple had one daughter, Holly Bight, born in 1924.

Stevens wrote almost in isolation, remote from the poetry world throughout most of his career. The people he worked with had no idea about the second life he pursued in the evening, on weekends, and during the summer when his wife was in the country. He kept his distance from the poetic controversies of the 20s and 30s, masquerading as a businessman while writing some of the most experimental poetry of his time. Analogously, he lived a quiet, middle-class life while incorporating, in his writing, flamboyant sensuous experience and riotous, colorful language. A few reminiscences by astute observers reveal that despite his business suits and reserved behavior, Stevens enjoyed the pleasures of cinnamon buns, gorgeous antiques, the humid air of Florida, and the beauty of Greta Garbo.

He published his first book, *Harmonium,* in 1923, the year before his daughter's birth and then, fully engrossed in family and business, ceased writing for six years. After becoming a vice president of the Hartford Company in 1934, he resumed writing with fervor. *Ideas of Order* appeared in 1935, *Owl's Clover* in 1936, *The Man with the Blue Guitar* in 1937, *Parts of a World* (1942), *Transport to Summer* (1947), and *Auroras of Autumn* (1950). He began to give occasional readings and lectures at various colleges, which became the basis for *The Necessary Angel* (1951). Always interested in the theory of poetry, Stevens engages the questions of American poetry that Emerson and Whitman had tackled: What is the role of poetry, or of the imagination, in relation to the external world we term "real"? His response is that we cannot live without the "supreme fictions" that art provides, that art helps us survive modern life, that it enables us to perceive order in chaos, that it helps us to live. Despite these lofty aims, it is impossible to overlook the flair, humor, self-mockery, the dazzling play with language, and the intense sensuous pleasures of Stevens's poems. He received the Bollingen Prize in 1950 and the National Book Award and the Pulitzer Prize in 1955.

from The Noble Rider and the Sound of Words

4

. . . Suppose we try, now, to construct the figure of a poet, a possible poet. He cannot be a charioteer [a reference to Plato's *Phaedrus*] traversing vacant space, however ethereal. He must have lived all of the last two thousand years, and longer, and he must have instructed himself, as best he could, as he went along. He will have thought that Virgil, Dante, Shakespeare, Milton placed themselves in remote lands and in remote ages; that their men and women were the dead—and not the dead lying in the earth, but the dead still living in their remote lands and in their remote ages, and living in the earth or under it, or in the heavens —and he will wonder at those huge imaginations, in which what is remote becomes near, and what is dead lives with an intensity beyond any experience of life. He will consider that although he has himself witnessed, during the long period of his life, a general transition to reality, his own measure as a poet, in spite of all the passions of all the lovers of the truth, is the measure of his power to abstract himself, and to withdraw with him into his abstraction the reality on which the lovers of truth insist. He must be able to abstract himself and also to abstract reality, which he does by placing it in his imagination. He knows perfectly that he cannot be too noble a rider, that he cannot rise up loftily in helmet and armor on a horse of imposing bronze. He will think again of Milton and of what was said about him: that "the necessity of writing for one's living blunts the appreciation of writing when it bears the mark of perfection. Its quality disconcerts our hasty writers; they are ready to condemn it as preciosity and affectation. And if to them the musical and creative powers of words convey little pleasure, how out of date and irrelevant they must find the . . . music of Milton's verse." Don Quixote will make it imperative for him to make a choice, to come to a decision regarding the imagination and reality; and he will find that it is not a choice of one over the other and not a decision that divides them, but something subtler, a recognition that here, too, as between these poles, the universal interdependence exists, and hence his choice and his decision must be that they are equal and inseparable. To take a single instance: When Horatio says,

> Now cracks a noble heart. Good night, sweet prince,
> And flight of angels sing thee to thy rest!

are not the imagination and reality equal and inseparable? . . .

5

. . . I am interested in the nature of poetry and I have stated its nature, from one of the many points of view from which it is possible to state it. It is an interdependence of the imagination and reality as equals. This is not a definition, since it is incomplete. But it states the nature of poetry. Then I am interested in the role of the poet and this is paramount. In this area of my subject I might be expected to speak of the social, that is to say sociological or political, obligation of the poet. He has none. That he must be contemporaneous is as old as Longinus and I dare say older. But that he is contemporaneous is almost inevitable. How contemporaneous in the direct sense in which being contemporaneous is intended were the four great poets of whom I spoke a moment ago? I do not think that the poet owes any more as a social obligation than he owes as a moral obligation, and if there is anything concerning poetry about which people agree it is that the role of the poet is not to be found in morals. I cannot say what that wide agreement amounts to because the agreement (in which I do not join) that the poet is under a social obligation is equally wide. Reality is life and life is society and the imagination and reality; that is to say, the imagination and society are inseparable. That is pre-eminently true in the case of the poetic drama. The poetic drama needs a terrible genius before it is anything more than a literary relic. Besides the theater has forgotten that it could ever be terrible. It is not one of the instruments of fate, decidedly. Yes: the all-commanding subject-matter of poetry is life, the never-ceasing source. But it is not a social obligation. One does not love and go back to one's ancient mother as social obligation. One goes back out of a suasion not to be denied. Unquestionably if a social movement moved one deeply enough, its moving poems would follow. No politician can command the imagination, directing it to do this or that. Stalin might grind his teeth the whole of a Russian winter and yet all the poets in the Soviets might remain silent the following spring. He might excite their imaginations by something he said or did. He would not command them. He is singularly free from the "cult of pomp," which is the comic side of the European disaster; and that means as much as anything to us. The truth is that the social obligation so closely urged is a phase of the pressure of reality which a poet (in the absence of dramatic poets) is bound to resist or evade today. Dante in Purgatory and Paradise was still the voice of the Middle Ages but not through fulfilling any social obligation. Since that is the role most frequently urged, if that role is eliminated, and if a possible poet is left facing life without any categorical exactions upon him, what then? What is his function? Certainly it is not to lead people out of the confusion in which they find themselves. Nor is it, I think, to comfort them while they follow their readers to and fro. I think that his function is to make his imagination theirs and that he fulfills himself only as he sees his imagination become the light in the minds of others. His role, in short, is to help people to live their lives. Time and time again it has been said that he may not address himself to an élite. I think he may. There is not a poet whom we prize living today that does not address himself to an élite. The poet will continue to do this: to address himself to an élite even in a classless society, unless, perhaps, this exposes him to imprisonment or exile. In that event he is likely not to address himself to anyone at all. He may, like Shostakovich, content himself with pretence. He will, nevertheless, still be addressing himself to an élite, for all poets address themselves to someone and it is of the essence of that instinct, and it seems to amount to an instinct, that it should be to an élite, not to a drab but to woman with the hair of a pythoness, not to a chamber of commerce but to a gallery of one's own, if there are enough of one's own to fill a gallery. And that élite, if it responds, not out of complaisance, but because the poet has quickened it, because he has educed from it that for which it was searching in itself and in the life around it and which it had not yet quite found, will thereafter do for the poet what he cannot do for himself, that is to say, receive his poetry.

I repeat that his role is to help people to live their lives. He has had immensely to do with giving life whatever savor it possesses. He has had to do with whatever the imagination and the senses have made of the world. He has, in fact, had to do with life except as the intellect has had to do with it and, as to that, no one is needed to tell us that poetry and philosophy are akin. I want to repeat for two reasons a number of observations made by Charles Mauron. The first reason is that these observations tell us what it is that a poet does to help people to live their lives and the second is that they prepare the way for a word concerning escapism. They are: that the artist transforms us into epicures; that he has to discover the possible work of art in the real world, then to extract it, when he does not himself compose it entirely; that he is *un amoreux perpétuel* of the world that he contemplates and thereby enriches; that art sets out to express the human soul; and finally that everything like a firm grasp of reality is eliminated from the aesthetic field. With these aphorisms in mind, how is it possible to condemn escapism? The poetic process is psychologically an escapist process. The chatter about escapism is, to my way of thinking, merely common cant. My own remarks about resisting or evading the pressure of reality mean escapism, if analyzed. Escapism has a pejorative sense, which it cannot be supposed that I include in the sense in which I use the word. The pejorative sense applies where the poet is not attached to reality, where the imagination does not adhere to reality, which, for my part, I regard as fundamental. If we go back to the collection of solid, static objects extended in space, which Dr. Joad posited, and if we say that the space is blank space, nowhere, without color, and the objects, though solid, have no shadows and, though static, exert a mournful power, and, without elaborating this complete poverty, if suddenly we hear a different and familiar description of the place:

> *This City now doth, like a garment, wear*
> *The beauty of the morning, silent bare,*
> *Ships, towers, domes, theatres, and temples lie*
> *Open unto the fields, and to the sky;*

All bright and glittering in the smokeless air;

if we have this experience, we know how poets help people to live their lives. This illustration must serve for all the rest. There is, in fact, a world of poetry indistinguishable from the world in which we live, or, I ought to say, no doubt, from the world in which we shall come to live, since what makes the poet the potent figure that he is, or was, or ought to be, is that he creates the world to which we turn incessantly and without knowing it and that he gives to life the supreme fictions without which we are unable to conceive of it.

And what about the sound of words? What about nobility, of which the fortunes were to be a kind of test of the value of the poet? I do not know of anything that will appear to have suffered more from the passage of time than the music of poetry and that has suffered less. The deepening need for words to express our thoughts and feelings which, we are sure, are all the truth that we shall ever experience, having no illusions, makes us listen to words when we hear them, loving them and feeling them, makes us search the sound of them, for a finality, a perfection, an unalterable vibration, which it is only within the power of the acutest poet to give them. Those of us who may have been thinking of the path of poetry, those who understand that words are thoughts and not only our own thoughts but the thoughts of men and women ignorant of what it is that they are thinking, must be conscious of this: that, above everything else, poetry is words; and that words, above everything else, are, in poetry, sounds. . . .

ROBERT FROST

America's most popular poet, Robert Frost (1874–1963), was born in San Francisco but relocated to Lawrence, Massachusetts, with his mother and sister on the death of his father at the age of thirty-six from tuberculosis. While his widowed mother took up her former teaching career in Salem, New Hampshire, young Frost, a fifth-grade student, played baseball, trapped animals, and, it is safe to assume, swung on birch trees. Thanks to his mother's enthusiasm for reading aloud to her children from Emerson, Wordsworth, and others, Robert became an omnivorous reader of poetry and prose.

In high school he studied Greek and Latin, became a top scholar, and published poems in the high school *Bulletin*. He also played football and fell in love with Elinor White in his senior year. They were co-valedictorians in 1892. After a stormy period of restlessness and what he perceived as unrequited love, Frost, who had dropped out of Dartmouth, settled down as a teacher. In 1895, he and Elinor were married. Nine months later their first child, Elliott, was born. More difficulties ensued; Frost entered Harvard but dropped out two years later.

The threat of tuberculosis always imminent persuaded Frost to give up the role of teacher and take up poultry farming. Elliott, then three, died only two months later from a form of chicken cholera. With their fourteen-month-old daughter Lesley, the Frosts moved to a farm in Derry, New Hampshire; here Frost farmed by day and wrote by night. Many of the poems that make up his first three books—*A Boy's Will*, *North of Boston*, and *Mountain Interval*—were written here. But with four children under the age of seven, money was short and Frost took a teaching post at Pinkerton Academy, where he was very well liked. Nevertheless, after five years he resigned.

In 1912 the couple sailed to Glasgow, then settled outside London. Frost's most productive and successful period of creativity led to the long dialogue-narrative poems to be found in *North of Boston*. He met Ezra Pound, who reviewed his first two books favorably, and came to know such English writers as Robert Bridges, Wilfred Gibson, and Edward Thomas. Strongly appreciative reviews followed, but the onset of World War I drove the Frosts to return to the United States. Frost bought a farm in Franconia, New Hampshire, and was then invited to teach at Amherst

College. He was one of the first poets to begin "barding around," as he put it, to "say" his poems aloud to audiences, with comments and general reflections. Frost's fourth book, *New Hampshire,* garnered the first of his four Pulitzer Prizes in 1924. Honors thereafter were showered on him: his *Collected Poems* (1930) won a second Pulitzer. But during this decade, disasters accumulated.

His youngest daughter died from puerperal fever after giving birth to her first child; in 1938, Frost's wife Elinor died suddenly of a heart attack; his son Carol committed suicide in 1940; and his daughter Irma had to be placed in a mental hospital. Frost resigned from teaching, sold the Amherst house, and returned to the farm. The director of the Bread Loaf Conference invited Frost to speak and the director's wife, Kathleen Morrison, became Frost's secretary-manager and intimate companion.

The last fourteen years of his life included not only the awarding of forty-four honorary degrees and government tributes, but far more important to the poet, the growing mature perceptions of his work by major literary figures of the time, ranging from Randall Jarrell to Lionel Trilling.

from Conversations on the Craft of Poetry with Cleanth Brooks and Robert Penn Warren

WARREN: Mr. Frost, I once heard you say that for a poem to stick it must have a dramatic accent.

FROST: If it doesn't, it will not stay in anybody's head. It won't be *catchy* [. . .]

Catchiness has a lot to do with it, all of it, all the way up from the ballads you hear on the street to the lines in Shakespeare that stay with you without your trying to remember them. I just say catchy. They stick on you like burrs thrown on you in holiday foolery. You don't have to try to remember them. It's from the way they're said, you know, an archness or something.

WARREN: Well, I'm sure you're right about the dramatic quality being the basic quality of good poetry. That would bring up the relation of meter and rhythm to the dramatic moment-by-moment—in a poem, wouldn't it?

FROST: That's right.

WARREN: I'd like to hear you say it in your way, how meter enters into this picture—the dramatic quality.

FROST: The meter seems to be the basis of—the waves and the beat of the heart seems to be basic in all making of poetry in all languages—some sort of meter.

WARREN: The strain of the rhythm against the meter. Is that itself just a dramatic fact that permeates a poem?

FROST: From those two things rises what we call this tune that's different from the tune of the other kind of music. It's a music of itself. And when people say that this will easily turn into—be set to music, I think it's bad writing. It ought to fight being set to music if it's got expression in it.

BROOKS: Yes, there's something resistant and unique in it; you can't just turn it into something else. This is to overstate the matter, but I do want to get it clear, if I can for myself: Would you say that even though the meter is based on the human pulse or some kind of basic rhythm in our natures, still for the poet it's something to be played over against—it's something to be fought with, to be tussled with? It's not directly expressive—ta-DA, ta-DA, ta-DA, ta-DA, ta-DA.

FROST: No, it's doggerel when you do that. You see, and how you save it from doggerel is having enough dramatic meaning in it for the other thing to break the doggerel. And it mustn't break *with* it.

   I said years ago that it reminds me of a donkey and a donkey cart; for some of the time the cart is on the tugs and some of the time on the hold-backs. You see it's that way all the time. The one's doing that and the other—the one's holding the thing back and the other's pushing it forward—and so on, back and forward. . . . I puzzled over it many years and tried to make people see what I meant. They use the word "rhythm" about a lot of free verse; and gee, what's the good of the rhythm unless it is on something that trips it—that it ruffles? You know, it's got to ruffle the meter.

BROOKS: Isn't this the fault of—to name the name of a man who did write some very fine poems, I think: Vachel Lindsay depends too much on just the doggerel—the stamp of the . . .

FROST: Singsong, yes. And you know when he had something else, he thought he ought to put a note about it in the margin. Did you notice that?

BROOKS: Yes, to tell you how to read it.

FROST: "Say this in a golden tone," he says. You ought not to have to say that in the margin.

BROOKS: No, no. It's built in.

FROST: That ought to be in the meaning. This is why you have to have a meaning, 'cause you don't know what to do with anything if you don't have a meaning. It makes you act up; you've got to act up. "What sayest thou, old barrelful of lies?" Chaucer says. What d'you say, "old barrelful of lies"? And you can hear it talk just the same today—and all of it. That's why it exists. It's beautiful, anywhere you look into Chaucer:

> Since I from love escaped am so fat,
> I never think to have been in his prison lean;
> Since I am free, I count him not a bean.

This is Chaucer talking too. It's just the same now. I hear the country people talking, England and here, with these same ways of acting up. Put it that way—call it "acting up."

You act up when you talk. Some do more than others. Some little children do: some just seem to be rather straight line, but some switch their whole body when they talk—switch their skirts. *Expressiveness* comes over them. Words aren't enough.

And of course all before words came the expressiveness—groans and murmurs and things like that emerging into words. And some few of these linger, like "um-hnm" and "unh-unh" and "mmm" and all our groans. By myself sometimes I groan at something already done that I'd like to avert.

WARREN: From a groan to a sonnet's a straight line.

FROST: Yes, that's right.

WARREN: You are distinguishing, then, the meaning in the most limited sense from the over-all, felt meaning of the whole thing. Is that it?

FROST: That's your whole guide, the over-all meaning.

WARREN: That's your guide and your end product.

FROST: Yes, your end product. And also, you know, one of the funny
things is that this mood you're writing in foretells the end product. See, it begins sort of that way and a way of talking that
foretells the end product. There's a logic of that sort of thing.

Somebody said to be a master writer you don't have to wait for
your moods. That'd be like Browning as he got older. You get to
be a virtuoso, and you aren't a poet any more. He'd lost his
moods somewhere. He'd got to be a master. We don't want to
be masters.

WARREN: In other words you don't want even to be master—is that
right?—of the particular poem. Before you start you're moving
from mood to the exploration of the mood, is that it?

BROOKS: Poem is a discovery. . . .

FROST: Yes, that's right. You're on a little voyage of discovery. And
there's a logic in it. You're going to come out somewhere with
great certainty. And you can tell whether you've lost it on the
way. And you throw the poem away—if you lose it.

WARREN: Yes.

FROST: Down the years, looking back over it all. And you see, a good
many who think they're writing free verse are really writing old-
fashioned iambic. A good deal of Whitman's like that, and a lot
of Masters is like that: he just never got away from blank verse—
the sound of blank verse.

And so there are places where this thing takes place that I'm
talking about—there's both the meter and the expressiveness on
it and so we get a poem.

Ezra Pound used to say that you've got to get all the meter out
of it—extirpate the meter. If you do, maybe you've got true free
verse, and I don't want any of it!

WARREN: Well, you can go at it another way: I guess it's Winters
who said that behind all good free verse—I may be misinterpret-
ing him, but I think that's what he says—behind all good free
verse there's a shadow of formal verse.

FROST: That's right. And if we hadn't had the years of formal verse,
this stuff wouldn't be any good, you know. The shadow is there;
that's what gives it any charm it has. You see, I'm hard on free
verse a little—too hard, I know.

BROOKS: Would you be hard, Mr. Frost, also, on the business of the beatniks and chanting poetry to jazz? Is that letting too much of music—of the wrong side of music come in?

FROST: Yes, absolutely. Death! Hang 'em all!

This fellow that's going to talk with me (A. P. Herbert from London) tomorrow, they've told me what his prejudices are, you know, to see if they couldn't rouse me to say something to him. He's in favor of hanging delinquent children. That's the funniest prejudice. And he'd be in favor of exterminating the free-verse writers, I'm pretty sure. I'm not as bad as that.

Let's put it this way that prose and verse are alike in having high poetic possibilities of ideas, and free verse is anywhere you want to be between those two things, prose and verse. I like to say, guardedly, that I could define poetry this way: It is that which is lost out of both prose and verse in translation. That means something in the way the words are curved and all that— the way the words are taken, the way you take the words.

WARREN: The best-order notion: the old Coleridgean best-order notion.

FROST: Yes, I'm pretty extreme about it.

You know, I've given offense by saying that I'd as soon write free verse as play tennis with the net down. I want something there—the other thing—something to hold and something for me to put a strain on; and I'd be lost in the air with just cutting loose—unless I'm in my other mood of making it prose right out, you know, and I don't write much of that. But that's another thing [. . .]

BROOKS: Speaking of tune, Yeats said that he started a poem with a little tune in his head.

FROST: Yeats said a good many things, and I've talked with him about that. He said that nothing he hated more than having his poems set to music. It stole the show. It wasn't the tune he heard in his ear. And what this other thing is. . . . If he meant a tune, it doesn't seem to go with that, does it?

Burns without any doubt had old music—old songs—in his head that he wrote from. But I don't think that of Yeats; I don't know what he meant by that. But if he meant a tune. . . . I have a tune, but it's a tune of the blend of these two things. Something rises—it's neither one of these things. It's neither the meter nor the rhythm; it's a tune arising from the stress on those—same as your fingers on the strings, you know. The twang!

WARREN: The twang.

FROST: The twang of one on the other. And I don't know what he meant. I think he must have meant what we mean: from a result of something beginning to rise from it right away when you're playing one on the other; that's what he carried. There must be a oneness as you're doing it. You aren't putting two things together—laying them together. It isn't synthetic like that; no.

BROOKS: No, it's growing a plant, not building a wall.

WARREN: Growing in terms of this dominating mood—is that right?—that you referred to as a germ of the poem?

FROST: Yes.

WARREN: The tune is the mood groping for its logic, is that it? Something like that?

FROST: That's right; that's right, yes. I'm glad that we feel that way together. Yes, you know that, when I begin a poem I don't know—I don't want a poem that I can tell was written toward a good ending—one sentence, you know. That's trickery. You've got to be the happy discoverer of your ends.

BROOKS: That's a very fine way of phrasing it, "the happy discoverer of your end." Because otherwise it is contrived. You can see it coming a mile off.

FROST: A mile away.

I've often said that another definition of poetry is dawn—that it's something dawning on you while you're writing it. It comes off if it really dawns when the light comes at the end. And the feeling of dawn—the freshness of dawn—that you didn't think this all out and write it in prose first and then translate it into verse. That's abhorrent! [. . .]

One of the things that I notice with myself is that I can't make certain word sounds go together, sometimes; they won't say. This has got something to do with the way one vowel runs into another, the way one syllable runs into another. And then I never know—I don't like to reason about that too much. I don't understand it, but I've changed lines because there was something about them that my ear refused. And I suppose it has something to do with the vowels and consonants.

You know what I've thought sometimes: that the mouth and throat are like this, that it's certain sounds are here, and you can't go right from this one to that one; you've got to go like this. The mouth's got to be doing that inside. I don't know.

But gee, you know, I don't want any science of it. It's got to be—not trial and error. You don't correct it if you're going well—if you're felicitous—if you're having a happy day.

Well, we've come a good way. And it's fun. I don't often sit with somebody to talk about it this way. Sometimes from the platform I say some of these things, you know. And I used to do it more than I do it now. I had a notion I had to tell the public how to read lines. Then I decided no; that's in them anyway. They all had Mother Goose and everything. Don't you see that you throw them back on their Mother Goose? . . .

JULIA ALVAREZ

Julia Alvarez (1950–) was raised in the Dominican Republic in a large, extended family replete with aunts, uncles, grandparents, dozens of cousins, and a host of maids, who cooked, housekept, and looked after the children.

When she was ten, her family immigrated to the United States seeking political refuge. Alvarez attended Connecticut College and graduated summa cum laude from Middlebury College in 1971. She earned her MA in creative writing at Syracuse University in 1975 and wrote her first book of poems, *Homecoming,* while teaching at the University of Vermont eight years later. As Alvarez explains in her memoir, *Something to Declare,* her yearning to become a writer was in conflict with her Old World, strict Catholic upbringing that allowed only for the traditional female roles of wife and mother. In her poem, "By Accident," Alvarez muses, "Sometimes I think I became the woman / I am by accident." She married twice, and divorced, scandalous failures in her culture's estimation, which only later she came to realize inadvertently freed her from traditional expectations. No longer able to be the romantic heroine and angel of the house, she was able to follow what she considers her truer calling: "this love did prove the truest, after all" ("Did I Redeem Myself?").

Alvarez relates that while writing at the writers' colony Yaddo, she was so intimidated by the sound of typewriters from the rooms around her that she instead followed the noise of a vacuum in the hallway, ending up in an inspiring conversation with cooks in the kitchen: "[M]y voice would not be found up in a tower, in those upper reaches or important places, but down in the kitchen among the women who first taught me about service, about passion, about singing as if my life depended on it." She married Bill Eichner, a doctor from Nebraska with two teenage daughters, in 1989. They live in Vermont, where she teaches at Middlebury College as a writer-in-residence, having given up her full-time job a few years after earning tenure, in order to spend more time on her writing.

Alvarez has published twelve books including novels, poetry, essays, and children's books. Her novel, *How the García Girls Lost Their Accents,* (1991) was an international bestseller and won a PEN Oakland/Josephine Miles Award and a notable book designation with the American Library

Association and the *New York Times*. Her poetry, for the most part formal-ist, is largely autobiographical and very accessible. Kathrine Varnes has written, "Julia Alvarez's poetic voice comes across as both plain-spoken and cagey, an appropriate choice for negotiating borders, be they personal, national, lingual or prosodic." In this essay, Alvarez establishes her iden-tity as a poet who uses the disciplines of housework to propel her into tra-ditional forms.

Housekeeping Cages

Sometimes people ask me why I wrote a series of poems about housekeeping if I'm a feminist. Don't I want women to be liberated from the oppressive roles they were condemned to live? I don't see housekeeping that way. They were the crafts we women had, sewing, embroidering, cooking, spinning, sweeping, even the lowly dusting. And like Dylan Thomas said, we sang in our chains like the sea. Isn't it already thinking from the point of view of the oppressor to say to ourselves, what we did was nothing?

You use what you have, you learn to work the structure to create what you need. I don't feel that writing in traditional forms is giving up power, going over to the enemy. The word belongs to no one, the houses built of words belong to no one. We have to take them back from those who think they own them.

Sometimes I get in a mood. I tell myself I am taken over. I am writ-ing under somebody else's thumb and tongue. See, English was not my first language. It was, in fact, a colonizing language to my Spanish Caribbean. But then Spanish was also a colonizer's language; after all, Spain colonized Quisqueya. There's no getting free. We are always writ-ing in a form imposed on us. But then, I'm Scheherezade in the Sultan's room. I use structures to survive and triumph! To say what's important to me as a woman and as a Latina.

I think of form as territory that has been colonized, but that you can free. See, I feel subversive in formal verse. A voice is going to inhabit that form that was barred from entering it before! That's what I tried in the "33" poems, to use my woman's voice in a sonnet as I would use it sitting in the kitchen with a close friend, talking womanstuff. In school, I was always trying to inhabit those forms as the male writers had. To pitch my voice to "Of man's first disobedience, and the fruit . . ." If it didn't hit the key of "Sing in me, Muse, and through me tell the story," how could it be important poetry? The only kind?

While I was in graduate school some of the women in the program started a Women's Writing Collective in Syracuse. We were musing each other into unknown writing territory. One woman advised me to listen to my own voice, deep inside, and put that down on paper. But what I heard when I listened were voices that said things like "Don't put so much salt on the lettuce, you'll wilt the salad!" I'd never heard that in a poem. So how could it be poetry? Then, with the "33" sonnet sequence, I said, I'm going to go in there and I'm going to sound like myself. I took on the whole caboodle. I was going into form, sonnets no less. Wow.

What I wanted from the sonnet was the tradition that it offered as well as the structure. The sonnet tradition was one in which women were caged in golden cages of beloved, in perfumed gas chambers of stereotype. I wanted to go in that heavily mined and male labyrinth with the string of my own voice. I wanted to explore it and explode it too. I call my sonnets free verse sonnets. They have ten syllables per line, and the lines are in a loose iambic pentameter. But they are heavily enjambed and the rhymes are often slant-rhymes, and the rhyme scheme is peculiar to each sonnet. One friend read them and said, "I didn't know they were sonnets. They sounded like you talking!"

By learning to work the sonnet structure and yet remaining true to my own voice, I made myself at home in that form. When I was done with it, it was a totally different form from the one I learned in school. I have used other traditional forms. In my poem about sweeping, since you sweep with the broom and you dance—it's a coupling—I used rhyming couplets. I wrote a poem of advice mothers give to their daughters in a villanelle, because it's such a nagging form. But mostly the sonnet is the form I've worked with. It's the classic form in which we women were trapped, love objects, and I was trapped inside that voice and paradigm, and I wanted to work my way out of it.

My idea of traditional forms is that as women much of our heritage is trapped in them. But the cage can turn into a house if you housekeep it the right way. You housekeep it by working the words just so.

STANLEY KUNITZ

Stanley Kunitz (1905–) was born in Worcester, Massachusetts, the son of Lithuanian immigrants. His father committed suicide before Kunitz was born, a catastrophe that appears in his poems, "The Portrait," "Father and Son," and others. He attended Classical High and went on to Harvard University where he graduated summa cum laude, received the Garrison Medal for poetry, and an MA degree. Rejected for a teaching position on grounds that Harvard students would not be comfortable being taught English literature by a Jew, he returned to Worcester where he covered the Sacco and Vanzetti trial for the *Worcester Telegram*. In 1927 he moved to New York. There, he edited the *Wilson Library Bulletin* and helped to compile major biographical dictionaries of English and American authors.

Kunitz's first book, *Intellectual Things,* appeared in 1930. His second collection, *Passport to War,* was published fourteen years later. He served in the military during World War II, was awarded a Guggenheim fellowship, and then accepted a teaching position at Bennington College, the first of several academic jobs which included Yale, Princeton, Rutgers, and ultimately Columbia University, where he mentored many young poets in the graduate writing program.

As a translator, Kunitz crafted acclaimed English versions of Akhmatova, Yevtushenko, Mandelstam, and others. He edited *The Essential Blake, Poems of John Keats,* and, from 1969 to 1977, the Yale Series of Younger Poets. He served as Consultant in Poetry to the Library of Congress before that position was renamed Poet Laureate of the United States, and again as laureate in 2000. Kunitz was a founder of the Fine Arts Work Center in Provincetown, where he has maintained a home and fabled garden for many summers. He was the first president of Poets House in New York City, where he lives the rest of the year. From 1957 until her death in 2004, Kunitz was married to the painter and poet, Elise Asher. In 1958, his *Selected Poems* was awarded a Pulitzer Prize; in 1995, *Passing Through: The Later Poems, New and Selected,* received the National Book Award. The list of his laurels is lengthy, including an award from the National Institute of Arts and Letters and the Bollingen Prize for poetry. The National Endowment for the Arts honored him in 1984 with a Senior Fellowship, taking note of his generosity to younger writers.

His poems have been translated into several languages including Japanese, French, Swedish, Hebrew, and Arabic.

from Table Talk,
A Paris Review Interview with Chris Busa

INTERVIEWER: One of your poems—"The Science of the Night"— has a passage: "We are not souls but systems, and we move in clouds of our unknowing." Is that a direct reference to the text by the medieval religious mystic?

KUNITZ: Yes. *The Cloud of Unknowing*—haunting phrase. But, sure, I think that what we strive for is to move from the world of our immediate knowing, our limited range of information, into the unknown. My poems don't come easy—I have to fight for them. In my struggle I have the sense of swimming underwater toward some kind of light and open air that will be saving. Redemption is a theme that concerns me. We have to learn how to live with our frailties. The best people I know are inadequate and unashamed.

INTERVIEWER: Can you say something about how you manage to find "the language that saves"?

KUNITZ: The poem in the head is always perfect. Resistance starts when you try to convert it into language. Language itself is a kind of resistance to the pure flow of self. The solution is to become one's language. You cannot write a poem until you hit upon its rhythm. That rhythm not only belongs to the subject matter, it belongs to your interior world, and the moment they hook up there's a quantum leap of energy. You can ride on that rhythm, it will carry you somewhere strange. The next morning you look at the page and wonder how it all happened. You have to triumph over all your diurnal glibness and cheapness and defensiveness.

INTERVIEWER: One of my ideas about your poetry is that there are two voices, arguing with each other. One is the varied voice of personality, the other the voice that speaks in the context of a dramatic situation. The other is an internal voice, the voice that's rhythm. It governs a poem's movement the way the waves govern the movement of a boat—seldom do the two want to go in the same direction.

KUNITZ: The struggle is between incantation and sense. There's always a song lying under the surface of these poems. It's an incantation that wants to take over—it really doesn't need a language—all it needs is sounds. The sense has to struggle to assert itself, to mount the rhythm and become inseparable from it.

INTERVIEWER: Would you say that rhythm is feeling, in and of itself?

KUNITZ: Rhythm to me, I suppose, is essentially what Hopkins called the taste of self. I taste myself as rhythm.

INTERVIEWER: How wide a variety of rhythms do you feel?

KUNITZ: The psyche has one central rhythm—capable, of course, of variations, as in music. You must seek your central rhythm in order to find out who you are.

INTERVIEWER: So you would agree you could say about music that Bach's central rhythm is devotional and Mozart's is gay, sunny, and exuberant. How would you define your own rhythm in these terms?

KUNITZ: Mine, I think, is essentially dark and grieving—elegiac. Sometimes I counterpoint it, but the ground melody is what I mostly hear.

INTERVIEWER: With respect to rhythm, could you discuss your term "functional stressing"?

KUNITZ: Functional stressing is simply my way of coping with the problem of writing a musical line that isn't dependent on the convention of alternating slack and stressed syllables. What I usually hear these days is a line with three strong stresses in it—that's my basic measure. I don't make a point of counting stresses—the process is largely unconscious, determined by my ear. A line can have any number of syllables, and sometimes it will add or eliminate a stress. Rhythm depends on a degree of regularity, but the imagination requires an illusion of freedom. The system of stresses is the organizing principle of a poem. I tend to dwell on long vowels and to play them against the consonants; and I love to modulate the flow of a poem, to change the pace, so that it quickens and then slows, becomes alternately fluid and clotted. The language of a poem must do more than convey experience: it must embody it. . . .

INTERVIEWER: What is the source for the imagery of depreciation toward the end of this poem ["Open the Gates"] such as the "cardboard doorway"?

KUNITZ: I see a movie set, furnished with memories like studio props. Doorways figure largely throughout the poem—entrances into my past, into the woods, into truth itself. I had recently gone back to Worcester to receive an honorary degree from Clark University and had asked to be taken to the scenes of my childhood. The nettled field had changed into a housing development, the path into the woods had become an express highway, and the woods themselves were gone. That's where the poem began, with the thought that reality itself is dissolving all around us.

INTERVIEWER: You indicate that with images pasted together like a collage?

KUNITZ: A montage, I would say.

INTERVIEWER: Can you say something about the arrangement of the lines for this poem?

KUNITZ: I started working with flush margins, and had difficulty achieving any sort of linear tension. Furthermore, I found the look of the page uninteresting, that long poem with all those short lines. I didn't develop a triadic sense until I began tinkering with the lines, as I often do at the beginning of a poem, trying to find the formal structure. The moment I hit on the tercets, the poem began to move.

INTERVIEWER: I am impressed by your capacity to break the tone abruptly or to shift the voice in a poem. Sometimes it is only for a line, but these outbreaks seem to have an idiosyncratic dramatic function.

KUNITZ: It's something I may have learned from working with dramatic monologues. In an extended passage I sense the need for an interruption of the speech-flow, another kind of voice breaking into the poem and altering its course. I recall one occasion when I was hunting for a phrase to do just that, so that I could push the poem one step further, beyond its natural climax. My

inability to achieve the right tone infuriated me. I must have
tried thirty different versions, none of which worked. I was
ready to beat my head on the wall when I heard myself saying,
"Let be! Let be!" and there it was, simple and perfect—I had my
line. If you have a dialectical mind like mine and if a poem of
yours is moving more or less compulsively towards its destina-
tion, you feel the need of a pistol shot to stop the action, so that
it may resume on another track, in a different mood or tempo.
One of the reasons I write poems is that they make revelation
possible. I sometimes think I ought to spend the rest of my life
writing a single poem whose action reaches an epiphany only at
the point of exhaustion, in the combustion of the whole life,
and continues and renews, until it blows away like a puff of
milkweed. Anybody who remains a poet throughout a lifetime,
who is still a poet let us say at sixty, has a terrible will to survive.
He has already died a million times and at a certain age he faces
this imperative need to be reborn. All the phenomena of his life,
all the memories, all the stuff that makes him feel himself, is
rematerialized and reblended. He's capable of perpetuation, he
turns up again in new shapes. Any poem he writes could be a
hundred poems. He could take a poem written at twenty or
thirty and re-experience it and come out again with something
absolutely different and probably richer. He can't excuse himself
by saying he has written everything he has to write. That's a
damn lie. He's swamped with material, it's overwhelming.

INTERVIEWER: What are your thoughts on the way you end
a poem?

KUNITZ: I think of a beginning, a middle, and an end. I don't believe
in open form. A poem may be open, but then it doesn't have
form. Merely to stop a poem is not to end it. I don't want to suggest that I believe in neat little resolutions. To put a logical cap
on a poem is to suffocate its original impulse. Just as the truly
great piece of architecture moves beyond itself into its environment, into the landscape and the sky, so the kind of poetic closure that interests me bleeds out of its ending into the whole
universe of feeling and thought. I like an ending that's both a
door and a window.

INTERVIEWER: Your poems are packed; they have a weight. To me,
it is a question of scale.

KUNITZ: Thanks. I've heard the opposite reaction, that my poems are too heavy. One critic wrote quite recently that my poems sounded as though they had been translated from the Hungarian. I don't know why, but somehow that made me feel quite light-hearted.

INTERVIEWER: Most of your poems are written in a high style.

KUNITZ: That used to be truer than it is today. I've tried to squeeze the water out of my poems.

INTERVIEWER: Mostly in your earlier poetry you have a stylistic habit of animating abstractions by hinging them to metaphors, as in the "bone of mercy" or the "lintel of my brain."

KUNITZ: There's some confusion about this type of prepositional construction. When it has weak specification, when it incorporates a loose abstraction, it is a stylistic vice, and I've grown increasingly wary of it. I resist phrases like "stars of glory." But when I say "the broad lintel of his brain," I am perceiving the brain as a house. The brain is not, in this usage, an abstraction. It's just as real as the lintel. Pound was the first, I think, to define this particular stylistic vice, and modern criticism has blindly followed suit, without bothering to make the necessary discriminations. In any event, I don't accept arbitrary rules about poetry. . . .

T. S. ELIOT
(headnote in Part 1)

from Hamlet and His Problems

... The only way of expressing emotion in the form of art is by finding an "objective correlative"; in other words, a set of objects, a situation, a chain of events which shall be the formula of that *particular* emotion; such that when the external facts, which must terminate in sensory experience, are given, the emotion is immediately evoked. If you examine any of Shakespeare's most successful tragedies, you will find this exact equivalence; you will find that the state of mind of Lady Macbeth walking in her sleep has been communicated to you by a skilful accumulation of imagined sensory impressions; the words of Macbeth on hearing of his wife's death strike us as if, given the sequence of events, these words were automatically released by the last event in the series. The artistic "inevitability" lies in this complete adequacy of the external to the emotion. ...

W. H. AUDEN

Wystan Hugh Auden (1907–73) was born in North Yorkshire, Great Britain, the third son of a highly regarded physician, and educated at Christ Church College, Oxford, where he took a disappointing third in English. But these were seminal years for the young poet. He became one of a group of leftist writers which included Louis MacNiece, Stephen Spender, and Christopher Isherwood. During his postgraduate year in Germany in 1928–29 he witnessed the rise of Nazism; in 1935 he married Thomas Mann's daughter Erika Mann so that she could acquire a British passport and leave Germany. The following year he traveled to Iceland with poet Louis MacNiece. His reputation as a leftist intellectual was enhanced by his 1937 visit to Spain where he worked briefly broadcasting propaganda for the Republican government. Auden collaborated with Christopher Isherwood on the play *On the Frontier;* the two traveled to China in 1938, and Auden returned by way of the United States, which he crossed by train. At this time he made his final decision to move to America, teaching at various schools and universities from 1939 to 1953, among them Swarthmore, the University of Michigan, Mt. Holyoke, Barnard, and Bennington.

He met the then nineteen-year-old Chester Kallman in 1939, and the two lived together for the next twenty years. In 1946 Auden became an American citizen. His vast range of friendships, in addition to his fellow poets, included Reinhold and Ursula Niebuhr, Oliver Sacks, Hannah Arendt, and Anne Fremantle. Religion was a frequent topic; to Ursula Niebuhr Auden declared himself "[l]iturgically . . . Anglo-Catholic though not too spiky, I hope. As for forms of church organization, I don't know what to think."

Auden's output was prodigious, including opera librettos for Stravinsky's *The Rake's Progress,* Mozart's *Don Giovanni,* Britten's *Paul Bunyan,* three plays with Christopher Isherwood, and lectures on Shakespeare as well as numerous collections of his own poetry. His vivacity and wit and his abiding interest in, and the broad intellect he brought to bear on, the culture and politics of his day suffused his poetry with a rare combination of humor and passion. His technical virtuosity in a variety of metrical forms is outstanding in such volumes as *The Double Man* (1941) and the Pulitzer Prize–winning *The Age of Anxiety* (1947). Later books, *The Shield of Achilles* (1955) and *About the House* (1965), display his often playful, sometimes irreverent short poems. But he is best remembered for his political antiwar sentiments, lyrically expressed in "The Unknown Citizen" and "September 1, 1939." In 1972 Auden left New York for a cottage in Oxford provided by Christ Church. He died shortly after giving a poetry reading in his beloved Vienna in 1973.

from Writing

. . . A poet has to woo, not only his own Muse but also Dame Philology, and, for the beginner, the latter is the more important. As a rule, the sign that a beginner has a genuine original talent is that he is more interested in playing with words than in saying something original; his attitude is that of the old lady, quoted by E. M. Forster—"How can I know what I think till I see what I say?" It is only later, when he has wooed and won Dame Philology, that he can give his entire devotion to his Muse.

Rhymes, meters, stanza forms, etc., are like servants. If the master is fair enough to win their affection and firm enough to command their respect, the result is an orderly happy household. If he is too tyrannical, they give notice; if he lacks authority, they become slovenly, impertinent, drunk and dishonest.

The poet who writes "free" verse is like Robinson Crusoe on his desert island: he must do all his cooking, laundry and darning for himself. In a few exceptional cases, this manly independence produces something original and impressive, but more often the result is squalor—dirty sheets on the unmade bed and empty bottles on the unswept floor.

There are some poets, Kipling for example, whose relation to language reminds one of a drill sergeant: the words are taught to wash behind their ears, stand properly at attention and execute complicated maneuvers, but at the cost of never being allowed to think for themselves. There are others, Swinburne, for example, who remind one more of Svengali: under their hypnotic suggestion, an extraordinary performance is put on, not by raw recruits, but by feeble-minded schoolchildren.

Due to the Curse of Babel, poetry is the most provincial of the arts, but today, when civilization is becoming monotonously the same all the world over, one feels inclined to regard this as a blessing rather than a curse: in poetry, at least, there cannot be an "International Style."

My language is the universal whore whom I have to make into a virgin. *(KARL KRAUS.)* It is both the glory and the shame of poetry that its medium is not its private property, that a poet cannot invent his words and that words are products, not of nature, but of a human society which uses them for a thousand different purposes. In modern societies where language is continually being debased and reduced to nonspeech, the poet is in constant danger of having his ear corrupted, a danger to which the painter and the composer, whose media are their private property, are not exposed. On the other hand, he is more protected than they from another modern peril, that of solipsist subjectivity; however esoteric a poem may be, the fact that all its words have meanings which can be looked up in a dictionary makes it testify to the existence of other people. Even the language of *Finnegans Wake* was not created by Joyce *ex nihilo;* a purely private verbal world is not possible. . . .

from The Virgin & The Dynamo

. . . Every poet, consciously or unconsciously, holds the following absolute presuppositions, as the dogmas of his art:

> 1) A historical world exists, a world of unique events and unique persons, related by analogy, not identity. The number of events and analogical relations is potentially infinite. The existence of such a world is a good, and every addition to the number of events, persons and relations is an additional good.

> 2) The historical world is a fallen world, i.e., though it is good that it exists, the way in which it exists is evil, being full of unfreedom and disorder.

> 3) The historical world is a redeemable world. The unfreedom and disorder of the past can be reconciled in the future.

It follows from the first presupposition that the poet's activity in creating a poem is analogous to God's activity in creating man after his own image. It is not an imitation, for were it so, the poet would be able to create like God *ex nihilo;* instead, he requires pre-existing occasions of feeling and a preexisting language out of which to create. It is analogous in that the poet creates not necessarily according to a law of nature but voluntarily according to provocation.

It is untrue, strictly speaking, to say that a poet should not write poems unless he must; strictly speaking it can only be said that he should not write them unless he can. The phrase is sound in practice, because only in those who can and when they can is the motive genuinely compulsive.

In those who profess a desire to write poetry, yet exhibit an incapacity to do so, it is often the case that their desire is not for creation but for self-perpetuation, that they refuse to accept their own mortality, just as there are parents who desire children, not as new persons analogous to themselves, but to prolong their own existence in time. The sterility of this substitution of identity for analogy is expressed in the myth of Narcissus. When the poet speaks, as he sometimes does, of achieving immortality through his poem, he does not mean that he hopes, like Faust, to live forever, but that he hopes to rise from the dead. In poetry as in other matters the law holds good that he who would save his life must lose it; unless the poet sacrifices his feelings completely to the poem so that they are no longer his but the poem's, he fails.

It follows from the second presupposition, that a poem is a witness to man's knowledge of evil as well as good. It is not the duty of a witness to pass moral judgment on the evidence he has to give, but to give it clearly and accurately; the only crime of which a witness can be guilty is perjury. When we say that poetry is beyond good and evil, we simply mean that a poet can no more change the facts of what he has felt than, in the natural order, parents can change the inherited physical characteristics which they pass on to their children. The judgment good-or-evil applies only to the intentional movements of the will. Of our feelings in a given situation which are the joint product of our intention and the response to the external factors in that situation it can only be said that, given an intention and the response, they are appropriate or inappropriate. Of a recollected feeling it cannot be said that it is appropriate or inappropriate because the historical situation in which it arose no longer exists.

Every poem, therefore, is an attempt to present an analogy to that paradisal state in which Freedom and Law, System and Order are united in harmony. Every good poem is very nearly a Utopia. Again, an analogy, not an imitation; the harmony is possible and verbal only.

It follows from the third presupposition that a poem is beautiful or ugly to the degree that it succeeds or fails in reconciling contradictory feelings in an order of mutual propriety. Every beautiful poem presents an analogy to the forgiveness of sins; an analogy, not an imitation, because it is not evil intentions which are repented of and pardoned but contradictory feelings which the poet surrenders to the poem in which they are reconciled.

The effect of beauty, therefore, is good to the degree that, through its analogies, the goodness of created existence, the historical fall into unfreedom and disorder, and the possibility of regaining paradise through repentance and forgiveness are recognized. Its effect is evil to the degree that beauty is taken, not as analogous to, but identical with goodness, so that the artist regards himself or is regarded by others as God, the pleasure of beauty taken for the joy of Paradise, and the conclusion drawn that, since all is well in the work of art, all is well in history. But all is not well there.

from The Poet & The City

In my daydream College for Bards, the curriculum would be as follows:

> 1) In addition to English, at least one ancient language, probably Greek or Hebrew, and two modern languages would be required.
>
> 2) Thousands of lines of poetry in these languages would be learned by heart.
>
> 3) The library would contain no books of literary criticism, and the only critical exercise required of students would be the writing of parodies.
>
> 4) Courses in prosody, rhetoric and comparative philology would be required of all students, and every student would have to select three courses out of courses in mathematics, natural history, geology, meteorology, archaeology, mythology, liturgics, cooking.
>
> 5) Every student would be required to look after a domestic animal and cultivate a garden plot. . . .

ELIZABETH BISHOP

Elizabeth Bishop (1911–1979) was born in Worcester, Massachusetts. Her father died when she was an infant. When she was five years old, her mother was committed to a psychiatric sanatorium and never saw her child again. Elizabeth lived happily in Nova Scotia with her mother's family for a few years, but was then uprooted by her paternal grandparents, who took her back to Worcester to achieve a proper education in private schools. It was a difficult and unhappy time for her, and she suffered from extended periods of ill health, which plagued her the rest of her life. Nevertheless, she was an excellent scholar and went on to Vassar College where, with her classmates Mary McCarthy and Eleanor Clark, Bishop started a literary magazine. The Vassar librarian helped arrange a meeting with Marianne Moore and they became lifelong friends. In 1946, Moore wrote a recommendation for Bishop's first book, *North and South,* which then won the Houghton Mifflin Prize. Robert Lowell reviewed it; he and Bishop enjoyed a lasting friendship. In 1950, she was the Consultant in Poetry to the Library of Congress. The following year she embarked on the trip she had dreamed of, to travel around Cape Horn, but en route was brought low by an allergic reaction. She was nursed back to health by Lota de Macedo Soares, with whom she fell in love. They lived together in Brazil for the next fifteen years. Bishop's second book, *Poems: North and South—A Cold Spring,* was awarded the Pulitzer Prize in 1956. *Questions of Travel* (1965), her third book, addresses memories of her childhood and reflections on the geography and landscape of Brazil.

In 1966, Bishop came to the states to teach at the University of Washington, but then returned to Rio after two semesters, hoping to re-establish her life with Soares. Both women were suffering from depression and both were hospitalized for a time. Bishop flew to New York in 1967 with the understanding that Soares would follow in time. She did so, against her doctor's wishes, only to take her own life the next day. It was a terrible loss for Bishop, but she did not stop writing poems. Her *Complete Poems* won the National Book Award in 1970, and in the fall of that year she accepted a four-year teaching position at Harvard. She later taught at New York University and at MIT. Bishop's final collection, *Geography III,* won the Book Critic's Circle Award in 1977 and underscored her status as a major poet. Her work continues to receive well-deserved critical attention and acclaim. Her villanelle, "One Art," and her sestina, simply titled "Sestina," are acknowledged as models of their forms. The letter reprinted here, addressed to John Frederick Nims, editor of the *Harper Anthology of Poetry*, was written on the day of her death in Boston, Massachusetts, in 1979.

On Footnotes (To John Frederick Nims)

437 Lewis Wharf
Boston, Massachusetts
October 6, 1979

. . . I'm going to take issue with you—rather violently—about the idea of footnotes. With one or two exceptions (I'll mention them later) I don't think there should be ANY footnotes. You say the book is for college students, and I think anyone who gets as far as college should be able to use a dictionary. If a poem catches a student's interest at all, he or she should damned well be able to look up an unfamiliar word in the dictionary. (I know they don't—or most of them don't—but they should be made to, somehow. The [historically] earlier poems you are using of course may require some help—but mine certainly don't!) "Isinglass" is in the dictionary; so is "gunnel" (see "gunwale"); so is "thwarts" [these three words occur in "The Fish"].

One of my few exceptions is the ESSO-Exxon note to "Filling Station," because I'm not sure how long ago now that happened, but a good many years. Also, I'd let students figure out—in fact, I TELL them [in the poem]—the cans are arranged to say so-so-so, etc., so I don't think *that* has to be explained. However—most of them might well not know that so-so-so was—perhaps still is in some places—the phrase people use to calm and soothe horses. All flower names can be looked up, certainly —some students even SEE flowers still, although I know only too well that TV has weakened the sense of reality so that very few students see anything the way it is in real life.

In "The Moose" I'd prefer to have you use just the first sentence of the note—on page 1226. (!) I don't think page 1227 needs any notes at all, nor does 1228. Please leave all that out! (A Japanese anthology quoted another poem in which I mentioned the Port of Santos—and that footnote said, "Port—a dark red wine." Also—the Norton Anthology is full of such stupid remarks—they locate St. John's [Newfoundland] in the Caribbean somewhere, and so on & so on.) "Macadam" is in the dictionary. And—a lot of the poem is about "childhood recollections"—I almost say it in so many words. If they can't figure that out, they shouldn't be in college—THERE!

You can see what a nasty teacher I must be—but I do think students get lazier and lazier & expect to have everything done *for* them. (When I suggest buying a small paperback, almost the whole class whines, "Where can I find it?") My best example of this sort of thing is what one rather bright Harvard honors student told me. She told her roommate or a friend—who had obviously taken my verse-writing course—that she was doing her paper with me, and the friend said, "Oh don't work with *her*! It's awful! She wants you to look words up in the dictionary! It isn't *creative* at all!" In other words, it is better *not* to know what you're writing or reading. Perhaps my class at M.I.T. has embittered me—but so did N.Y.U. and some of the Harvard classes—although there have been good students and a few wonderful ones from time to time. But they mostly seem to think that poetry—to read or to write—is a snap—one just has to *feel*—and not for very long, either. Well, I could go on and on—but I won't! Two or three years ago I was talking away about "The Quaker Graveyard" and when I asked a question the whole class responded in chorus with what I discovered (I was using my own book) were the footnotes from the Norton anthology—some right, in that case, but again some wrong. We finally all got to laughing—but that was an unusually bright class.

Of course I am writing this just about my own inclusions—and "The Moose" may well be too long. And of course there are many [historically] early poems I can see the necessity for notes for. If "The Moose" is too long, I'd suggest another from *Geography III*—any you like. I do hope I haven't offended you now—but I think the teaching of literature now is deplorable—and if you can get students to *reading,* you will have done a noble work. Affectionately . . .

LANGSTON HUGHES

Langston Hughes (1902–67), poet, novelist, columnist, and playwright, was born in Joplin, Missouri. His parents divorced when he was a small child, and he was raised by his grandmother until, at thirteen, he rejoined his mother and her second husband in Cleveland, Ohio. Jobs were hard to find and they moved often seeking work. During his rootless adolescence in many towns in the Midwest, Hughes absorbed the music of the blues and spirituals, elements he would subsequently weave into his poetry. After graduating from high school with the designation of class poet, Hughes spent a year in Mexico with his father. On the long train ride back, he wrote one of his most acclaimed poems, "The Negro Speaks of Rivers," which was first published in the NAACP's magazine, *Crisis*. Hughes's father agreed to pay his son's tuition at Columbia University provided he would major in engineering, but Langston soon dropped out to pursue his own dream, that of a professional writer. In 1923 he boarded a freighter bound for Senegal, Nigeria, and other African ports, then on to Italy and France. In 1924 he moved to Harlem, just in time to become part of the Harlem Renaissance, an upsurge of creativity in all of the arts celebrating racial pride. Here he met W. E. B. Du Bois, Countee Cullen, Zora Neale Hurston, and others. In 1926 he published the first of his many poetry collections, *The Weary Blues*, attended Lincoln University, the first all-black college in the United States, and published a second volume, *Fine Clothes to the Jew*, in 1927. By now he had become a celebrity in Harlem, but his use of dialect and his focus on the working-class struggle offended many middle-class readers who, as he put it in his powerful essay, "The Negro Artist and the Racial Mountain," first published in *The Nation* in 1926 and excerpted here, "would surrender racial pride in the name of false integration."

In his extensive career Hughes published thirty-five volumes of poetry, novels, essays, and plays. He went to the Soviet Union in 1932 and as a columnist for the *Chicago Defender* described his travels. Nineteen thirty-seven found him in Spain reporting on the civil war there. When World War II broke out, Hughes managed to escape conscription, but he wrote jingles for the sale of war bonds and encouraged blacks to support the war effort despite the segregation that prevailed in the military. His output was prodigious, including librettos for operas, children's books, short stories, translations from Spanish poets, and plays. In the '30s and '40s he founded theater groups for blacks in Los Angeles, Chicago and Harlem. In the '50s he was attacked by Senator Joseph McCarthy but escaped blacklisting.

Many of his contemporaries were embittered by his political fence-straddling. In the last decade of his life, Hughes wrote at a frenzied pace. He continued to publish works about his invented character, Jesse B. Semple, known as Simple, a streetwise Harlemite whose extended auto-biography stretched from the '20s to the final volume in 1965. Overall, he published 16 volumes of poetry. In 1961 he was invited to join the National Institute of Arts and Letters.

from The Negro Artist and the Racial Mountain

One of the most promising of the young Negro poets said to me once, "I want to be a poet—not a Negro poet," meaning, I believe, "I want to write like a white poet"; meaning subconsciously, "I would like to be a white poet"; meaning behind that, "I would like to be white." And I was sorry the young man said that, for no great poet has ever been afraid of being himself. And I doubted then that, with his desire to run away spir-itually from his race, this boy would ever be a great poet. But this is the mountain standing in the way of any true Negro art in America—this urge within the race toward whiteness. . . .

Most of my own poems are racial in theme and treatment, derived from the life I know. In many of them I try to grasp and hold some of the meanings and rhythms of jazz. I am as sincere as I know how to be in these poems and yet after every reading I answer questions like these from my own people: Do you think Negroes should always write about Negroes? I wish you wouldn't read some of your poems to white folks. How do you find anything interesting in a place like a cabaret? Why do you write about black people? You aren't black. What makes you do so many jazz poems?

But jazz to me is one of the inherent expressions of Negro life in America; the eternal tom-tom beating in the Negro soul—the tom-tom of revolt against weariness in a white world, a world of subway trains, and work, work, work; the tom-tom of joy and laughter, and pain swallowed in a smile. Yet the Philadelphia clubwoman is ashamed to say that her race created it and she does not like me to write about it. The old sub-conscious "white is best" runs through her mind. Years of study under white teachers, a lifetime of white books, pictures, and papers, and white manners, morals, and Puritan standards make her dislike the Spirituals. And now she turns up her nose at jazz and all its manifestations—likewise almost everything else distinctly racial. . . . She wants the artist to flatter her, to make the white world believe that all Negroes are as smug and as near white in soul as she wants to be. But, to my mind, it is the duty of the younger Negro artist, if he accepts any duties at all from outsiders, to change through the force of his art that old whispering "I want to be white," hidden in the aspirations of his people, to "Why should I want to be white? I am a Negro and beautiful"?

So I am ashamed for the black poet who says, "I want to be a poet, not a Negro poet." . . .

Let the blare of Negro jazz bands and the bellowing voice of Bessie Smith singing the Blues penetrate the closed ears of the colored near-intellectuals until they listen and perhaps understand. . . . We younger Negro artists who create now intend to express our individual dark-skinned selves without fear or shame. If white people are pleased we are glad. If they are not, it doesn't matter. We know we are beautiful. And ugly too. The tom-tom cries and the tom-tom laughs. If colored people are pleased we are glad. If they are not, their displeasure doesn't matter either. We build our temples for tomorrow, strong as we know how, and we stand on top of the mountain, free within ourselves.

FRANK O'HARA

Although his life was cut short by a sand-buggy accident, Frank O'Hara (1926–66) left a decisive mark on American poetry. The only son of strict Irish-Catholic parents in Massachusetts, he studied piano at the New England Conservatory for three years and seemed destined for a musical career. But World War II drove him to enlist in the navy after his high-school graduation, and he served in the South Pacific on a destroyer until 1946. He went to Harvard on the GI Bill, majored in music, studied with John Ciardi, and began publishing poems in the college literary magazine with the encouragement of fellow student John Ashbery. He changed his major to English and thanks to Ciardi's recommendation won a fellowship to the University of Michigan, where he won the Hopwood Award for a collection of poems and a verse play in 1951.

New York City was O'Hara's next stop. Once the Hopwood prize money was exhausted, he found the ideal job working at the front desk of the Museum of Modern Art. But no one would have guessed that he would rise from desk clerk to curator. Between selling postcards he wrote breezy poems and visited with his art buddies, Ashbery, Kenneth Koch, Larry Rivers, and others. Here, his homosexuality was accepted. He began writing reviews for *Art News* and soon became an editorial associate. Although poetry was his life's blood, he cavalierly wrote and failed to keep copies of his work. Many of his major poems were passed from hand to hand among his friends, who saved them for publication. Larry Rivers did two drawings that accompany thirteen poems in O'Hara's *A City Winter and Other Poems;* later, the two were to collaborate on a series of lithographs, poems done directly on stone. O'Hara had to write backward so his work would be readable in the finished lithograph. When Donald Allen included fifteen of his poems in *The New American Poetry: 1945–1960,* O'Hara's position in the New York School of poets was secure. Identifying with artists of the abstract expressionist movement—Willem de Kooning, Franz Kline, Jackson Pollock, Jasper Johns—O'Hara became a champion of the avant-garde of his time. Only two more books, *Lunch Poems* and *Love Poems* were published during his lifetime. In 1972 his *Collected Poems,* with an introduction by Ashbery, won the National Book Award posthumously. The casual language in these poems with their lyric street scenes, eroticisms and elegies is seen by some as providing a bridge to the language poetics of the 1980s and '90s. The prose piece published here has the same jazzy, impromptu, colloquial, down-at-the-heels but elegant style that marks his poetry.

Personism: A Manifesto

Everything is in the poems, but at the risk of sounding like the poor wealthy man's Allen Ginsberg I will write to you because I just heard that one of my fellow poets thinks that a poem of mine that can't be got at one reading is because I was confused too. Now, come on. I don't believe in god, so I don't have to make elaborately sounded structures. I hate Vachel Lindsay, always have, I don't even like rhythm, assonance, all that stuff. You just go on your nerve. If someone's chasing you down the street with a knife you just run, you don't turn around and shout, "Give it up! I was a track star for Mineola Prep."

That's for the writing poems part. As for their reception, suppose you're in love and someone's mistreating *(mal aimé)* you, you don't say, "Hey, you can't hurt me this way, I care!" you just let all the different bodies fall where they may, and they always do after a few months. But that's not why you fell in love in the first place, just to hang onto life, so you have to take your chances and try to avoid being logical. Pain always produces logic, which is very bad for you.

I'm not saying that I don't have practically the most lofty ideas of anyone writing today, but what difference does that make? They're just ideas. The only good thing about it is that when I get lofty enough I've stopped thinking and that's when refreshment arrives.

But how can you really care if anybody gets it, or gets what it means, or if it improves them. Improves them for what? For death? Why hurry them along? Too many poets act like a middle-aged mother trying to get her kids to eat too much cooked meat, and potatoes with drippings (tears). I don't give a damn whether they eat or not. Forced feeding leads to excessive thinness (effete). Nobody should experience anything they don't need to, if they don't need poetry bully for them, I like the movies too. And after all, only Whitman and Crane and Williams, of the American poets are better than the movies. As for measure and other technical apparatus, that's just common sense: if you're going to buy a pair of pants you want them to be tight enough so everyone will want to go to bed with you. There's nothing metaphysical about it. Unless, of course, you flatter yourself into thinking that what you're experiencing is "yearning."

Abstraction in poetry, which Allen [Ginsberg] recently commented on in *It Is,* is intriguing. I think it appears mostly in the minute particulars where decision is necessary. Abstraction (in poetry, not in painting) involves personal removal by the poet. For instance, the decision involved in the choice between "the nostalgia *of* the infinite" and "the nostalgia *for* the infinite" defines an attitude towards degree of abstraction. The nostalgia *of* the infinite representing the greater degree of abstraction, removal, and negative capability (as in Keats and Mallarmé). Personism, a movement which I recently founded and which nobody knows about, interests me a great deal, being so totally opposed to this kind of abstract removal that it is verging on a true abstraction for the first time, really, in the history of poetry. Personism is to Wallace Stevens what *la poésie pure* was to Béranger. Personism has nothing to do with philosophy, it's all art. It does not have to do with personality or intimacy, far from it! But to give you a vague idea, one of its minimal aspects is to address itself to one person (other than the poet himself), thus evoking overtones of love without destroying love's life-giving vulgarity, and sustaining the poet's feelings towards the poem while preventing love from distracting him into feeling about the person. That's part of Personism. It was founded by me after lunch with LeRoi Jones on August 27, 1959, a day in which I was in love with someone (not Roi, by the way, a blond). I went back to work and wrote a poem for this person. While I was writing it I was realizing that if I wanted to I could use the telephone instead of writing the poem, and so Personism was born. It's a very exciting movement which will undoubtedly have lots of adherents. It puts the poem squarely between the poet and the person, Lucky Pierre style, and the poem is correspondingly gratified. The poem is at last between two persons instead of two pages. In all modesty, I confess that it may be the death of literature as we know it. While I have certain regrets, I am still glad I got there before Alain Robbe-Grillet did. Poetry being quicker and surer than prose, it is only just that poetry finish literature off. For a time people thought that Artaud was going to accomplish this, but actually, for all their magnificence, his polemical writings are not more outside literature than Bear Mountain is outside New York State. His relation is no more astounding than Dubuffet's to painting.

What can we expect of Personism? (This is getting good isn't it?) Everything, but we won't get it. It is too new, too vital a movement to promise anything. But it, like Africa, is on the way. The recent propagandists for technique on the one hand, and for content on the other, had better watch out.

September 3, 1959

CESARE PAVESE

Cesare Pavese (1908–50) was the youngest of five children in a lower middle-class family from rural San Stefano Belbo, southwest of Turin, Italy. After his father died, the family moved to a suburb of Turin where he attended high school and the university, graduating with a thesis on Walt Whitman. He then worked for a publisher, translating Melville's *Moby Dick* and Sherwood Anderson's *Dark Laughter*. As editor of the journal *La Cultura*, he wrote essays on contemporary writers such as Dos Passos, Gertrude Stein, Faulkner, and James Joyce, posthumously collected in *American Literature: Essays and Opinions*.

His *Dialogues with Leuco* represents a desire to return to classical myths as an attempt to transcend time, and is structured as a series of conversations between mythic figures who discuss a number of philosophical, artistic, and ethical issues (as Pavese himself loved to do in several bars and coffee shops around Turin). A founding editor of the publishing house Einaudi, Pavese helped foster an appreciation for American literature in Italy. Always a voracious reader, his letters are filled with references to books, many of which he heavily annotated, often, as with the scene of the knight Rinaldo about to rescue a maiden in *Orlando Furioso*, passages that he felt related to hopes for his own life. The isolated landscape of vineyards and small towns also heavily influenced his writing. In *The Moon and the Bonfires*, perhaps his greatest novel, the protagonist attempts to return to the hills after World War II and finds, like Pavese himself, that the past is profoundly past: the result is the nostalgic melancholy that pervades his best work.

In 1935 Pavese was arrested and imprisoned for political reasons related to his work, an event he draws on for his novel *The Political Prisoner*. During a year in prison in Calabria, he completed his best-known volume of poems, *Lavorare Stanca*, usually translated as *Hard Labor* and later, two volumes based on his prison experiences. Although called up by the army in 1940, he was dismissed because of a serious asthmatic condition. At the end of the war, he joined the Italian Communist Party and wrote for a party newspaper.

Having identified his essential self as a writer, and identified the writer with the lover in his journals, ironically titled *The Art of Living*, he was understandably prone to depression. Severely jilted in the summer of 1950 by an American actress, he committed suicide in August, in Turin in the Hotel Roma, his favorite hotel, shortly after being awarded the Strega Prize for *La Bella Estate.*

from Postscript II:
Notes on Certain Unwritten Poems

. . . The new group, my future poems, could of course be structured along autobiographical lines, which would mean narrative in the realistic sense of the word. For the time being, I have excluded this possibility. . . .

The winter of 1935–1936 was for me an acutely critical time. A long period of optimism and self-confidence was beginning to break down, and I was trying to rethink my attitude toward my profession from scratch. My reflections were committed to my diary and gradually turned into a lengthy examination of my entire life which, combined with subsequent anxieties (1937–1939), finally convinced me to try my hand at short stories and novels. Now and then I wrote a poem; in the winter of 1937–1938, during an effective return to the conditions of 1934, the year of *Hard Labor,* I wrote several. But I became more and more convinced that my real field was prose and that these poems were in fact an "afterglow." Then, in 1939, I wrote no poetry at all. In early 1940, when I once again returned to poetry, it was to ask whether these unassigned poems belonged to *Hard Labor* or indicated a new departure.

The fact is that, when I picked up the book and adjusted the order so as to include several poems deleted by the censors in 1935, the later poems fell naturally into place and seemed to form a whole. Practically speaking, then, I had the answer to my question, but the fact remains that the direction of these unassigned later poems gave me clear hopes of writing a whole new group. . . .

The truth of the matter is that during those years of personal crisis (1937–1939), my artistic purpose expressed itself, not so much in these new poems as in the reflections I was making in my diary at the same time—reflections which finally suffocated the poetry. Since periods of poetic activity usually end with critical awareness, and since my diary constantly stressed the *problem* of my poetry, a crisis—a crisis of renewal— was clearly in the offing. Put it this way. In the actual work of writing *Hard*

Labor I had succeeded in defining what I was doing, and when I recently went back to the book and rearranged it, I discovered that it had a formal structure (an idea which in 1934 struck me as ludicrous). And this very discovery shows that I intended to go beyond *Hard Labor*, to strike out in a new direction. By the very act of examining the poetics involved in the poems I had written after 1936, by my discovery that they were compatible with the rest of *Hard Labor*, I indicated my desire to work out a new poetics and suggested the direction it might take. Why, then, those constant, fragmentary critical inquiries which occupied me for three long years? . . .

I finished with the [earlier] techniques by demonstrating a need for new rhythms and new forms (and a few meager efforts to achieve them). My criticism has fallen, as it should, with special severity on my idea of the image. My ambitious definition of 1934—that the image was identical with the plot of the story—was shown to be false or at least inadequate. More recently, I have created real figures by rooting them in their background by means of internal metaphors, but this metaphor itself has never been the subject of the story for the simple reason that the subject was a character or a real landscape. It is no accident, after all, that I saw that the only possible unity of *Hard Labor* was a real human adventure. As is the *canzoniere* as a whole, so is the individual poem.

Let me say it clearly: tomorrow's adventure, my future poetry, must have different reasons, different motives.

This future collection, this new *canzoniere,* will clarify itself only when it has been written—by which time I will be obliged to repudiate it. . . .

LOUISE BOGAN

Louise Bogan (1897–1970) was born in Livermore Falls, Maine, where her father was a paper mill superintendent. After attending the rigorous Girls' Latin School in Boston, she spent one year at Boston University. Bogan largely educated herself as a writer, reading poetry and training herself in meter as she developed the compressed, tightly structured lyric style that would mark her work throughout her life. After two marriages that did not last, she moved with her young daughter in 1919 to New York City to become a freelance writer. William Carlos Williams, Marianne Moore, and Edmund Wilson were part of her circle; Wilson became her mentor. Eventually Bogan became poetry reviewer for the *New Yorker* and held the position for thirty-eight years. Her books of poetic criticism include *Achievement in American Poetry* (1951) and *A Poets' Alphabet* (1970).

Although Bogan's *Collected Poems* won a Bollingen Prize in 1955, she often felt invisible in the literary world. Isolated by her gender and her struggle with depression, Bogan was a courageously individual writer who wrote about female-centered themes during an era when her friend and student Theodore Roethke could declare in a positive review of her poetry (1961) that a "typical" female poet is always "running between the boudoir and the altar, stamping a tiny foot against God." Publishing her first book *Body of This Death* in 1922, a year after T. S. Eliot's hugely influential *The Waste Land* with its associative free verse, Bogan also remained committed to formal poetry at a time when that was a very unpopular position. Other books of poetry include *Dark Summer* (1929) and *The Sleeping Fury* (1937). She was famous for unstinting revisions and almost impossibly high standards, relentless in her quest for the pure and well-made poem. The poem "The Daemon" depicts her muse as a demanding monster.

Two years before her death, she published the third and final version of her collected poems, *The Blue Estuaries: Poems 1923–1968,* which she had winnowed down to only 103 poems. Feminist interest led to the posthumous publication of her autobiographical pieces, *Journey around My Room.* A Pulitzer Prize–winning biography of her life, *Louise Bogan: A Portrait,* written by Elizabeth Frank, appeared in 1985. The following essay comes out of Bogan's very personal struggle to remain a formal poet and her deep love for the demands and riches of form.

from The Pleasures of Formal Poetry

Before I try to analyze out certain basic virtues of formal poetry, I should like to state, and to analyze, certain modern objections to form. The first objection to form that rises in our minds is that form binds. The second objection to the use of form in modern poetry is that poetic form has become exhausted.

....

The main tendency in poetry since Baudelaire, Rimbaud, and Whitman would seem to be bound up with efforts to free poetry from formal restrictions. This tendency has been central, but it has never been, as a matter of fact, steady. Baudelaire, whom we now name the great ancestor of modern poetry, wrote in a form that was so strict that it was often Racinian. Rimbaud, who smashed the French Alexandrine and wrote the first French *vers libre,* was continually going back to form; he wrote exquisitely balanced sonnets and, even in the late *Saison en enfer,* the most delicate and evanescent sort of formal lyric. Mallarmé, of course, was a tremendous formalist up to and including *Un Coup de dés,* for in this late and seemingly experimental work Mallarmé (according to Thibaudet) "wished to produce a visual and typographic aesthetic, built on the difference between the kinds of type, the largeness of the white spaces between, the dimension of the lines—[on] the entire architecture of the page." The subtlety of the language and of the inner rhymes and echoes in this poem certainly bring it over to the side of form. Mallarmé is adding another "formality" to verse.

This alternate and gradual loosening and tightening of form continues, through Laforgue, who could write in the most precise "lightverse" style, through Pound, Apollinaire, and Eliot. As a matter of fact, as we look back on "modern" poetry as a whole, we find as much experimentation *in* form as out of it.

One cannot deny, however, that certain set forms in the verse of all European languages now seem to the modern poet either pedantic or trivial. Certain formal verse patterns, therefore, seem to have been exhausted. Certain modern poets cannot function, for example, in the sonnet form. Others cannot function in any form which has regular stress, or which is pointed up by any sort of rhyme. It is interesting to remember in what way, and for what reasons, this exhaustion came about. For the dislike of form, in many young writers, amounts to actual fear and revulsion. The matter of form as opposed to non-form or free form sometimes slips over from the field of aesthetics into the moral plane. Nowadays young poets avoid form as they would avoid some stupid or reprehensible action.

The exhaustion of formal poetry goes back to a complex of reasons, and some of these reasons are closely meshed in with the history of morals in the nineteenth century. In France, at the height of the French Romantic movement, poets (notably Victor Hugo) began to load their form with fantastic emotion and with cloying music. The middle-class revolution in taste was bound closely in with all this; as well as patriotic fervor, political conviction, and so on. In France, however, an anti-Romantic reaction occurred early, in 1857, the year of publication of *Les Fleurs du Mal* and *Madame Bovary* to be exact. So that it was quite natural for Verlaine, years later, to demand that poets wring the neck of rhetoric, even while he made, as the same time, poetry into pure music. In England, poetry was taken over bodily by the middle-class assumptions, and there was no adequate facing up to the situation by any major poet known in the Victorian era. (Hopkins was not published until 1916.) And the more that serious poets became absorbed into the society which surrounded them, the more complicated and unfitting forms they devised. Poetry was *used:* as a means of consolation, to bolster up flagging spirits, to cheer on, to cheer up; to create optimism where optimism was cheaply applied or out of place; to back up middle-class social ideas as well as certain philosophical ideals concerning human perfectibility. And a split occurred between "serious" and "light" verse. The quick and varied meters and the witty rhymes which Byron had devised as carriers for satire were siphoned off from the main stream of serious poetry. Within serious poetry, poets like Tennyson, meanwhile, doggedly experimented with unsuitable (to English) meters, in order to give some show of variety to their repetitive and tiresome subject matter. These experiments reached a dead end in Robert Bridges'—a true upholder of Victorian tradition—experiments with quantitative verse. These experiments were dead because the breath of life did not exist in the poets themselves or in the material with which they were attempting to deal.

"Light verse" took up the entire satiric burden, and lost caste because of its involvement with *opéra bouffe* (as used by William Gilbert in combination with Arthur Sullivan's music); or because of its (to the Victorian mind) even sillier relationship to the nonsense rhymes of Lewis Carroll and Edward Lear. These are the two limits to which poets in English pushed form: dull imitation of Greek and Roman poetry on the one hand, and gay and complicated satirical "patter songs" and nonsense verse on the other. Both limits are unusable, in modern poetry. But the best nineteenth-century poets soon realized that a reunion of these two streams was not only important but imperative. For complicated rhythmic patterns and light and limber and dancing rhythms have existed in serious poetry since the Greeks. When Gilbert Murray wishes to give an example of a rhythmic pattern used in Greek comedy, he is forced to quote a Gilbert stanza. It is a breach in culture when such rhythmic effects are lost; and French poets realized this fact before English ones did. Rimbaud goes back to folk song; Laforgue goes back to "light verse," whenever they sensed some tone of emotion which demanded these meters; neither was too proud or too inflexible not to make use of any meter that successfully carried his thought and feeling.

It is still the task of modern poets to bridge the division between serious and light forms; to refresh the drooping and weary rhythms of serious poetry with the varied, crisp, and fresh qualities of light verse. In English Pound and Eliot have performed miracles of deflation and revivification. Auden, as well, has worked to break down artificial barriers of form and tone, between the lively and the grave subject and treatment.

What is formal poetry? It is poetry written in form. And what is *form?* The elements of form, so far as poetry is concerned, are meter and rhyme. Are these elements merely mold and ornaments that have been impressed upon poetry from without? Are they indeed restrictions which bind and fetter language and the thought and emotion behind, under, within language in a repressive way? Are they arbitrary rules which have lost all validity since they have been broken to good purpose by "experimental poets," ancient and modern? Does the breaking up of form, or its total elimination, always result in an increase of power and of effect; and is any return to form a sort of relinquishment of freedom, or retreat to old fogeyism?

Let us examine meter. Meter is rhythm. In the words of the Scots professor who, in the nineteenth century, edited, with a preface, Walker's eighteenth-century *Rhyming Dictionary:* "A little consideration will lead to the conclusion, that verse, in most languages, differs from prose in the *return* of a certain number of syllables that have a peculiar relation to one another as *accented* and *unaccented,* or as long and short. It is universally felt that a degree of *pleasure* arises from this definite arrangement, and the origin of that pleasure is to be traced back to the sense of time with which men are generally endowed." (You will remember Yeats saying of himself, "I have the poet's exact time-sense.") Now, when I asked a group of students, recently, to name some definite bodily rhythm which might illustrate mankind's sense of time, and with which a definite pleasure might be said to be connected, they could think only of the dance. This answer is interesting, because it shows how many rhythmic habits and rhythmic effects have become rare either as observed phenomena, or as direct experience, with the advent of the machine. Students in a former century would think immediately, I believe, of the rhythmic principles underlying the actions which the Scottish professor at once brings forward as examples. "It is the principle which regulates," he goes on to say, "the step of a man or the stroke of an oar; and hence the pleasure we experience in beholding the regular step of a company of soldiers in their march, and the simultaneous sweep of the oars of a well-manned boat." Marching as a sort of everyday ritual—as seen in the changing of a guard, in a religious procession, or in a funeral cortege—is now a fairly rare sight; and so is the spectacle of rowers in "a well-manned boat." The Scotch professor then illustrates his point by the *time,* as distinguished from the tune, in music, but I do not want to bring rhythm in music (or in language) into the discussion at this point. I want to keep on emphasizing the pleasure to be found in bodily rhythm as such. What else formerly went to rhythm? We think of certain tasks, the rhythm of which has become set. Sowing, reaping, threshing, washing clothes, rowing, and even milking cows go to rhythm. The variety of rhythm in sea shanties depends upon the variety of tasks on board a sailing ship, with the doing of which a sailor was confronted. Hauling up sail or pulling it down, coiling rope, pulling and pushing and climbing and lifting, all went to different rhythms; and these rhythms are preserved for us, fast or slow, smooth or rough, in sailors' songs.

How far back can we push this sense of time? It appears everywhere in the most primitive culture. It certainly springs from the fact that a living man has rhythm built into him, as it were. His heart beats. He has a pulse. A pulse of some sort exists in all living creatures—in plants as well, I think scientists have proved—and man shares with the animals not only a pulse but an attendant rhythm: his breathing.

So we see man, long before he has much of a "mind," celebrating and extending and enjoying the rhythms of his heartbeat and of his breath. He is still at the point, let us say, where he performs these extensions without speech, or with the most rudimentary form of speech. Even without speech, a great many rhythmic effects can be produced by a human being. He can clap his hands rhythmically and he can stamp his feet rhythmically. Here is the beginning of the dance, of ritual, of drama. Then artifacts began to increase the pleasure of rhythm. The first aids and abettors of human rhythm were undoubtedly percussion instruments. A beaten hollow log must have been a great aid. The clicking together of the chestnut shells from which castanets take their name was another.

Eliot has said that poetry goes back to a savage beating a tom-tom in a jungle. That is, it goes back to reiterative beat. The Greeks have no god of the drum, no muse of the drum, it is true. The Muses, when we first hear of them, are three only: one of study, one of memory, and one of song. But Greek poetry, when we first come upon it, is a highly sophisticated and complex affair: the fruit of centuries of trial and error, of matching rhythm to language and language to rhythm, of a complicated and civilized relationship between dance and song. When we come upon the epics of Homer, written in the infinitely resonant and infinitely variable dactylic hexameter; or, later, when we read the no less fixed yet no less variable Sapphics or Alcaics of the Greek lyric, we have passed far beyond a Stone Age. Man has become a worker in metals; the cymbal and the bell have been added to the castanet and the drum; man is now a musician as well as a dancer.

One Greek word combines dance and song, the word *molpe;* and the word constantly applied to the *effect* of all good singing and harping (for the lyre was the purely Greek instrument, since the wind instrument, the *aulos,* was always considered of Asiatic origin) was *himeroeis,* meaning "not merely beautiful, but possessing that sort of beauty which makes the heart yearn." "*Himeros*" and *rhythmos*—longing and rhythm—are the two special elements which the voice finds strengthened in the movement of the body. *Metron* means measurement; and the things measured are the *feet* or *steps* on which the words of the song move. For the words had to dance with the dancers . . ."

Why are Greek rhythms now unusable? Why does the Greek hexameter, which managed to pass over into Latin poetry, remain forever outside any feasible use in English? The chief reason is that both Greek and Latin, being inflected languages, are nearer to each other than either of them can ever be to English. "A highly inflected language," Gilbert Murray says in his valuable study *The Classical Tradition in Poetry*, "must have each syllable clearly spoken, because each syllable up to the last may seriously alter the meaning. This is perhaps the reason why, in Latin and Greek pronunciation, *quantity* was the chief variable; while modern uninflected languages have fallen back more and more on the easy careless method of stress." (And we should remember here that certain rhythmic effects in modern poetry do indeed stem from Greek rhythms. Gerard Manley Hopkins was saturated in Greek. He was one of Jowett's brilliant young men at Balliol, and many of the effects in Hopkins which we think of as triumphs of "modern" compression are actually models of Greek compression, transformed into English verse by the hands of a master.)

I want to quote, at this point—before I quote some incisive remarks by Eliot on the limits of freedom in verse—another passage from Gilbert Murray, a passage concerned with the inner meaning of the Greek term *molpe*. Murray says:

> Love, Strife and Death and that which is beyond Death; an atmosphere formed by the worship of Nature and the enchantment of Memory; a combination of dance and song like the sweep of a great singing bird; all working toward an ecstasy or a transcending of personality, a "standing outside" of the prison of the material present, to be merged in some life that is the object of adoration or desire: these seem to be the subjects, and this the spirit and setting of that primitive MOLPE which is the foundation of ancient classical poetry. The tradition, if there is a tradition, rises there.

And this tradition, let us remember, goes back to *rhythm*, the effect of which attracted the adjective *himeroeis*: "not merely beautiful, but possessing that sort of beauty which makes the heart yearn."

*   *   *

Here, perhaps, I should make a few remarks on that other element of formal poetry as we know it today: rhyme. Rhyme becomes necessary in poetry as rhythm weakens. The Greeks of the great period scorned rhyme; and so did Latin writers, although certain internal rhymes can be detected in Ovid and later Latin versifiers. Rhyme has probably always been present in folk song and folk poetry (we know how pleased children are when they strike upon two words that rhyme); but high formal art for a long time dismissed and ignored it. But as rhythm began to break down, and when what we now think of as "monkish Latin" began to appear, rhyme appears as well. As soon as the ordinary speech of the people— the so-called "vulgar tongues"—began to build up a body of formal literature, rhyme became usual. The Provencal poets elaborated and extended the use of rhyme to a remarkable degree; so that by the time Dante began to write in Italian, his native vulgar tongue—having had as his master the Provencal poet Arnaut Daniel—he had at his disposal a great variety of rhymed forms, the sonnet among them; and Dante used the sonnet and, later, *terza rima* as a *rhymed* carrier of his long poem, *The Divine Comedy.* "Greek and Latin could do without rhyme because they had clear meters. Rhyme is needed to mark clearly the end of the line, and to provide the ear with fixed resting places. Without such divisions the metrical form would become dull and obscure. The hearer would not be sure where one line ended and the other began; he might not even be sure whether he was listening to prose or to verse. It is worth noticing that Latin took to rhyme when it had begun to lose the sense of quantity. Chinese insists on rhyme because it has no meter." This is still Murray, who says a little farther on: "The renewed popularity of rhyme in the time of Dryden followed upon an increasing looseness of the treatment of blank verse by the later Jacobean dramatists, and was part of a general reaction toward severity of form."

Every language seems to seek its own large meter—its own dramatic carrier, capable of long breaths, capable of bearing weights, capable of projecting maximum emotional power and yet allowing for delicate variation, capable of assuming various speeds, and capable of letting through intricacy of thought and sharpness of wit; a meter suited to the syntax and the rhythm of any given language, to the preponderance within that language of actual vowels and consonantal sounds. The vulgar tongues have more light vowels and fewer massive clusters of consonants than the classical languages. A spoken language, from Dante on, seems to fall most naturally into an iambic line of one length or another. English poetry has for a long time been based on the iamb—a short followed by a long beat—an unaccented syllable followed by an accented one; and the classic and large carrier of English poetry has for centuries been the iambic pentameter or five-beat line (sometimes with an additional syllable at the end, as in "To be or not to be, that is the question"): blank verse.

Now, it was a tremendous task to smash the Alexandrine, as Rimbaud smashed it, when it had been recently charged with music and feelings by the Romantics. To smash iambic pentameter has not been such a tremendous task; for, all during the nineteenth century, as we have seen, the line was becoming more and more feeble, since no strong talent had taken hold of it and filled it with refreshing power. (Browning's innovations were not strong enough.) The line continued to dwindle, and when it was finally smashed, it was already at its last gasp, as it were. Now, a dominant formal meter cannot become absolutely enfeebled if the common language which surrounds it continues to feed it. If the common, everyday language itself changes, the dominant meter must also change. If the accent shifts in the common tongue, then the accent in the dominant meter must shift, too.

Certain Victorian poets sensed this shift—Browning particularly—and in Bridges and in Swinburne, the iambic beat is broken by the introduction of trochaic, dactylic, anapestic, and spondaic feet. These innovations went back, in part, to Milton, who, in his later works, had introduced a consistent trochaic variation; and to Coleridge, who counted *only* the accented syllables in a line. It was the introduction of a sense of rhythms foreign to classical English, in three English-speaking "foreigners," that finally broke the iambic hold. These poets—William Butler Yeats, Ezra Pound, and T. S. Eliot—by their experiments changed the iambic line so that it again became flexible and vigorous. The trochaic foot—a long followed by a short—had become dominant in ordinary speech. It has also become dominant in the formal poetry of our day.

How far can this mingling of meters go? Soon we come upon a mingling of meters—in sections of Pound's *Cantos,* for example—that is nearer the beat of prose than of verse: that *is* prose. Prose has its own rhythm, certainly. But is not something lost to us, being, as we are, rhythmic creatures, in the disappearance of many "rich and exquisite" poetic meters? Free verse is valuable only when it continues to broaden and enrich, and it becomes as hampering as any rigid meter when it rules out *any* return to form.

"It seems to be almost a necessity in good verse that the ear should subconsciously expect a certain pattern, and have its hope, alternately or varyingly, suspended and fulfilled." There speaks the student of classical meters. But we hear very much the same dictum in Eliot's remark that "the ghost of some simple meter should lurk behind the arras in even the 'freest' verse; to advance menacingly as we doze, and withdraw as we rouse." A failure in any discoverable beat is a failure in tension.

Eliot himself, one of the greatest English metrists, has made other remarks on modern versification. He says, for example, "that no *vers* is *libre* for the man who wants to do a good job."

....

"Verse as speech" and "verse as song": these are the two attitudes toward formal poetry—or rather in formal poetry—that die out first, and perennially need to be renewed. Formal poetry should continually remain in contact with the speech and the life around it, but this it does not do; and this division is made easier by the fact that poetry has for centuries been encased—one might say almost embalmed—in print. The technique becomes rigidified, and poets begin to write by the rules that scholars have deduced from this or that poetic canon. Poets become frightened of emotion and of the Sublime (young poets today, I have found, are particularly terrified of the Sublime; they want no part of it!). In this situation, we have the keepers of the canon, and we have the breakers of the canon. Let us listen to Eliot again, as he fruitfully defines originality:

[Here Bogan quotes at length again from Eliot's essay on vers libre, in which he remarks that "True originality is merely development" of the tradition.]

Eliot then says that spurious originality usually gives the public a greater shock than true originality; and ends by stating that Pound's originality is genuine in that his versification is a logical development of the verse of his English predecessors.

The technical tradition, then, runs on unbroken. We now know more of the linkages which connect any art to human function, and this

knowledge should make us take more pleasure, rather than less, in *form*.
I again quote Gilbert Murray:

> ....
>
> Poetry tries to convey truth concerning those subjects about which
> we care most and know least [. . .]. Fierce mysteries were the sub-
> jects with which the Greek MOLPE [defined by Murray as "a com-
> bination of dance and song like the sweep of a great singing bird"]
> was concerned—Love, Strife, Death and that which is beyond
> Death.

We still celebrate these subjects and face these mysteries, and formal art—art in which the great tradition is still alive and by which it still
functions—is as modern as this moment, and as ancient as the farthest
antiquity. This is the formal art fragments of which we should not only
as readers "shore against our ruins," but keep as a directing influence in
whatever we manage to build—to create.

(1953)

ROBERT HASS

Robert Hass (1941–) was born in San Francisco and educated at a Catholic school in San Rafael, Marin County. In his teens he was drawn to the expanding poetry network in and around San Francisco, the work of Gary Snyder; Allen Ginsberg, Ferlinghetti and the Beats; the burgeoning of East Asian literature and the influence of Kenneth Rexroth. In 1962, while a student at St. Mary's College in Moraga, California, he married Earlene Leif. From 1967 to 1971 Hass taught at SUNY Buffalo, in his own words "a place as romantic to me as Paris," where his colleagues included Robert Creeley, John Barth, and the young John Coetzee. The couple had three children while Hass worked on his MA and his PhD at Stanford University. From 1971 to 1989 he taught at St. Mary's; he then joined the faculty at the University of California at Berkeley.

Hass's first book, *Field Guide,* was chosen by Stanley Kunitz as the winner of the Yale Series of Younger Poets competition in 1973. It was followed by *Praise* (1979), which won the William Carlos Williams Award; *Human Wishes* (1989); and *Sun Under Wood* (1996), winner of the National Book Critics Circle Award in poetry. His poems tackle subjects that range from domestic love poems to political violence. Birds, fish, sea otters, berries, Polish immigrants, and shifts in the weather are all captured in his verse. In addition, his collection of essays on poetry, *Twentieth Century Pleasures: Prose on Poetry,* from which this excerpt is taken, won the National Book Critics Circle Award in criticism in 1984. Hass served as Poet Laureate of the United States from 1995 to 1997. He has also co-translated from the Polish eight collections of poems by Czeslaw Milosz.

While Hass was Poet Laureate, he traveled extensively to promote literacy, and urged civic groups and corporations to understand the links among literacy, environmental literacy, and the health of communities. He encouraged high-school English teachers to bring their individual sensibilities to poetry rather than requiring students to search for "the one true meaning." As a lifelong Californian, he is a passionate spokesperson for ecological awareness. At present, Hass lives in Berkeley with his second wife, the poet Brenda Hillman, whom he married in 1995.

from Listening and Making

. . . Repetition makes us feel secure and variation makes us feel free. What these experiences must touch in us is the rhythm of our own individuation. It's easy enough to observe in small children the force of these pulls between the security of infancy and the freedom of their own separateness. When my oldest child was two or so, we used to take walks. He had a zen carpenter's feeling for distance, running ahead of me in an abandoned waddle, coming to an abrupt stop when he felt he had come to the edge of some magical zone of protection which my presence generated, and then gazing back at me over his shoulder with a look of droll glee. He knew he was right out there on the edge—the distance seemed to be about eleven or twelve squares of sidewalk. Sometimes he would take one more step, then another, looking back each time, and if I uttered a warning sound he would collapse in hilarity which seemed to be a celebration of his own daring. I was listening at the same time to Miles Davis, to how far he was willing to move away from the melody, to the way the feeling intensified the further away from it he got, as if he were trying to describe what it is like to get out there so far into the wandering hunger for the next note that it seemed at the same time exultant and explosively lonely and probably impossible to come back ever. I was also reading Theodore Roethke, the long poems with their manic inward-driven nursery-rhyme rhythms:

> The shape of a rat?
> It's bigger than that.
> It's sleek as an otter
> With wide webby toes.
> Just under the water
> It usually goes.

And it made me feel that there was not, in this, much difference between child and grown-up, between my son's impulses and the tidal pulls of adult life, the desire for merger, union, loss of self and the desire for freedom, surprise, singularity. I think it is probably the coming together of our pattern-discerning alertness with this pull between polarities in our psychic life that determines our feelings about rhythm.

It is important that we both want a rapt symbiotic state and don't want it; that we want solitariness and self-sufficiency and don't want it. Rhythmic repetition initiates a sense of order. The feeling of magic comes from the way it puts us in touch with the promise of a deep sympathetic power in things: heartbeat, sunrise, summer solstice. This can be hypnotically peaceful; it can also be terrifying, to come so near self-abandonment and loss of autonomy, to whatever in ourselves wants to stay there in that sound, rocking and weeping, comforted. In the same way, freedom from pattern offers us at first an openness, a field of identity, room to move; and it contains the threat of chaos, rudderlessness, vacuity. Safety and magic on one side, freedom and movement on the other; their reverse faces are claustrophobia and obsession or agoraphobia and vertigo. They are the powers we move among, listening to a rhythm, as the soul in the bardo state moves among the heavens and the hells, and they are what makes the relation between repetition and variation in art dialectical and generative.

An example, from a metrical poem:

> A slumber did my spirit seal,
> I had no human fears;
> She seemed a thing who could not feel
> The touch of earthly years.
>
> No motion has she now, no force.
> She neither hears nor sees,
> Rolled round in earth's diurnal course
> With rocks and stones and trees.

In this poem of grief at the death of a young girl, Wordsworth brings us in the last lines to a small, majestic, orderly music in which we feel reconciled to the way the child has entered the natural universe. Like a cradle rocking, bringing us to rest. At least that is how I read the poem for a long time, until someone pointed out to me the randomness of the last sequence: rocks, stones, trees. What is the difference between a rock and a stone? Who knows? What difference could it make? Rocks and stones. She has passed into brute matter, into the huge, mute spaces that terrified Pascal. For a while, with all the bad habits of education, I wondered which was the correct interpretation. I've come to see that the poem is so memorable and haunting because the two readings and feelings are equally present, married there, and it is the expressive power of rhythm that makes this possible.

First we hear: an order is insisted upon by the meter; then we listen, for that order is questioned immediately by the arrangement of the stanzas. Four beats in the first line, an insistent order; three beats in the second line, the same order but lighter, easier to live with. Four beats in the third line: the heavier order enters again, intensified slightly by the almost audible extra stress of "not feel." Three beats again in the fourth line, a lightening. The fifth line is interesting because the pause seems to promise an alteration in the pattern, to give us three beats, the lighter order, but no, after the pause we get two heavy stresses, "no force"; it almost says: were you wondering if "not feel" was two stresses? "Not feel" is two stresses. It is like a musical theme; we have begun to hear not just a play between three- and four-stress phrases, but a secondary drama of the four stresses tending toward a heavier and menacing five. In the sixth line we return to the three-stress pattern. In the seventh line the five stresses appear in full force, made large and dizzy by the long vowel sounds. They say, in effect, that from a human point of view an insistent order is equivalent to a chaos, and they are at the same time wondering, wonderful. In the last line we return to three stresses, the bearable rhythm, but we have already been made to hear the menace in the idea of order, so that last phrase, deliberate and random at once, leaves us with a deep and lingering uneasiness.

To speak of a sense of closure brings us to the third phase of rhythmic experience. Many things in the world have rhythms and many kinds of creatures seem to be moved by them but only human beings complete them. This last phase, the bringing of rhythmic interplay to a resolution, is the particular provenance of man as a maker. A rhythm is not a rhythmic form; in theory, at least, a rhythmic sequence, like some poetry readings, can go on forever, the only limits being the attention of the auditor and the endurance of the performer. Meter is that kind of sequence. The flow of blank verse suggests no natural stopping place of itself and most of the other metrical shapes, sonnets and the various stanzaic forms, are defined by their rhyme schemes. Daydream and hypnotic rhythm have it in common that their natural form is exhaustion. The resolution of rhythmic play, not just the coming down on one side or the other but the articulation of what ending feels like, is active making.

Think of the words you might want to use. *End:* to die. *Finish:* to be done with. *Conclude:* obligation over. *Complete:* to fulfill. *Consummate: really* to fulfill. *Close, terminate, arrive, leave off, release.* There are many senses of ending and they are drawn from our different experiences of it. There are rhythmic forms in nature—the day, a season, the life of a blossom. In human life, orgasm, the sentences in which we speak, falling asleep, the completion of tasks, the deaths we all see and the one death each of us must imagine. Many of our senses of ending are conventional—imagine the sound of a door opening: anticipation; of a door closing: finality. There are many possibilities of ending. In that way, each work of art is a three-line haiku. You go, I go—and the artist must provide the third line.

What hovers behind all this, I would guess, is a wish. Formally, the completion of a pattern imitates the satisfaction of a desire, a consummation, which is why orgasm is a preferred metaphor of conclusion. And because the material of poetry is language, it seems inevitable that an ending would also imitate the experience of insight. And because it is an ending, it will be death-obsessed. Sexual pleasure is a merging, a voluntary abandonment of the self; insight is a freeing, the central experience of our own originality. We don't know what death is. The wish behind the human play of artistic form is to know how these three are related: probably it is the hope that they are, or can be, the same thing. And there is another element to be added here, which belongs to the riddles of completion. When the poet or reader listens through to the moment of resolution, it is over. The poet has not created until the thing is gone from his hands.

It's possible that what humans want from works of art are shapes of time in which the sense of coming to an end is also, as it very seldom is in the rest of life, a resolution. Hence the art formula common to television comedy and Wagner and the Shakespearean sonnet: tension, release; tension, release; tension, more tension, release. There is a large and familiar repertoire of formal techniques which produce this effect. It is probably a definition of a rigidifying art-practice that it has more answers than it has questions. In the early twentieth century, painting got rid of perspective, music of tonality, poetry of meter and rhyme so that they could tell what ending felt like again, and give it again the feel of making. It is this feeling of the made thing, of craft and of an event in time, that gives the poem—and the world—the feeling of historicity, of having been made by men, and therefore in movement, alive to our touch and to the possibility of change which the familiarity of convention is always deadening. The task is to listen to ourselves and make endings true enough to experience that they eliminate the ground for the old senses of completion or renew them.

So, there are three phases of the experience of rhythm: hearing it, developing it, bringing it to form. And real listening, like deep play, engages us in the issues of our lives. . . .

EDNA ST. VINCENT MILLAY

Edna St. Vincent Millay (1892–1950) was named St. Vincent after the New York City hospital where her uncle's life was saved shortly before she was born. She grew up in Rockland, Maine, the oldest of three daughters raised in near-poverty by their self-sufficient mother Cora. On the strength of Millay's poem "Renascence," which won fourth prize in *The Lyric Year* (1912) and was commended by Louis Untermeyer and noted in *The New York Times Book Review,* she won a scholarship to Vassar. She was a brilliant student, but her college career became a scandalous legend: she smoked, drank, cut classes at will, failed to attend compulsory chapel, and left college from time to time without permission. Still, she published her first book *Renascence and Other Poems* in 1917, the year of her graduation, and wrote *The Lamp and the Bell,* her first verse play, for the Vassar drama department. A drama about love between women, it was published in 1921.

Shortly after graduation, Vincent, as she was known to her friends, took a small apartment in Greenwich Village with her sister Norma. Although surrounded by leftist intellectuals who wrote for *The Masses* and later *The Liberator,* Millay never took part in any political or social movement. She wrote her most famous sonnets during her three-year tenure in the Village while conducting a series of perfervid love affairs that fed the poetry. An early member of the Provincetown Players, she became friends with Edmund Wilson, Witter Bynner, Susan Glaspell, and Floyd Dell. She wrote and directed her antiwar chamber verse drama, *Aria da Capo,* at the Provincetown Playhouse in 1919; it went on to become a resounding success across the country. *A Few Figs from Thistles,* her second book of poems (1920), created a small firestorm for its descriptions of female sexuality and avowed feminist stance. *The Harp Weaver and Other Poems* (1923) won the Pulitzer Prize; she was the first woman to receive this award.

That same year, Millay married Eugen Boissevain, the wealthy Dutch widower of the suffragist leader Inez Milholland. He took on the roles of father, lover, and manager of her career, accompanying her to all subsequent public appearances. Their twenty-six-year marriage was open, both enjoying numerous extramarital rendezvous. Boissevain died in 1949 and Millay lived only one year longer. From 1923 to her death,

Millay lived with her husband in Austerlitz, New York, at their farmhouse at Steepletop, now a National Historic Landmark and home for the Millay Colony for the Arts.

Millay infused traditional poetic forms such as the ballad and sonnet with a fervent contemporary spirit. Edmund Wilson deemed her the best writer of sonnets in English since Shakespeare, and her sonnets written in the twenties and thirties have earned a lasting place as exemplars of both the Elizabethan and Petrarchan models. In the Petrarchan sonnet included here, Millay self-consciously reverses the convention, dating since Petrarch himself, of men using the sonnet to write about or address women. She turns the genders inside out and uses her sonnet as a vehicle in which to control, trap, and finally "make good" the fierce male energy of Chaos. Many of her other sonnets and lyrics center on love; its anguish and rewards are one of her prime subjects. She is also remembered for her political poem, "Justice Denied in Massachusetts," about the Italian anarchists, Sacco and Vanzetti, the cobbler and fish peddler who were executed on August 23, 1927, for allegedly murdering a paymaster and guard at a shoe factory.

In later years Millay applied her art to the Allied war effort and other social causes. However, her patriotic propaganda poems were attacked by the critics and her reputation plummeted. In 1976 her work was omitted from *The New Oxford Book of American Verse*. She has only recently been readmitted to the canon, as evidenced by the republications of her early work.

"I will put Chaos into fourteen lines"

I will put Chaos into fourteen lines
And keep him there; and let him thence escape
If he be lucky; let him twist, and ape
Flood, fire and demon—his adroit designs
Will strain to nothing in the strict confines
Of this sweet Order, where, in pious rape,
I hold his essence and amorphous shape,
Till he with Order mingles and combines.
Past are the hours, the years, of our duress,
His arrogance, our awful servitude:
I have him. He is nothing more nor less
Than something simple not yet understood;
I shall not even force him to confess;
Or answer. I will only make him good.

THEODORE ROETHKE

Theodore Roethke (1908–63) grew up in Saginaw, Michigan, where his parents and uncle owned a local greenhouse. His father's death from cancer in 1923 profoundly marked his adolescence, but he went on to graduate magna cum laude from the University of Michigan and enrolled in a graduate program at Harvard where Robert Hillyer mentored him. Roethke took a teaching position at Lafayette College from 1931 to 1935; here it was his good fortune to meet Rolfe Humphries, and through Humphries, Louise Bogan and Stanley Kunitz, who became his supporters and colleagues.

While teaching at Michigan State University in 1935, Roethke experienced the first of what were to be recurring episodes of incapacitating depressions. He learned to utilize these periods for psychic growth, "to reach a new level of reality." Although his first book, *Open House,* was not published until 1941, his reputation as poet and teacher was already solidly established with publications in prestigious journals. The following year, he delivered the Morris Gray lectures at Harvard. Subsequently, he taught at Bennington College, Pennsylvania State, and finally, at the University of Washington, where he numbered among his students Carolyn Kizer, David Wagoner, and James Wright. In 1948 he published what many critics consider his pivotal book, *The Lost Son,* which opens with fourteen lyrics of the greenhouse. These place the child in a primal world which Roethke described as "both heaven and hell," where the boundaries between inner and outer realities dissolve and the natural world becomes the landscape of the psyche. Several books were to follow. *The Waking* received the Pulitzer Prize in 1954 and marked Roethke's return to formalist verse; the title poem is his famous villanelle. He continued to explore themes from early childhood, associative encounters with the unconscious, erotic sensuality, and personal confession in his later work. Reviewing *Words for the Wind* (1959), Delmore Schwartz wrote, "These poems appear, at first glance, to be subliminal outcries, the voices of roots, stones, leaves, logs, small birds. . . . Roethke uses a variety of devices, with the utmost cunning and craft, to bring the unconsciousness to the surface of articulate expression." Roethke's awards included a Fulbright grant, the Bollingen Prize, and the National Book Award. He suffered a fatal heart attack in 1963.

from How to Write Like Somebody Else

. . . Imitation, conscious imitation, is one of the great methods, perhaps *the* method of learning to write. The ancients, the Elizabethans, knew this, profited by it, and were not disturbed. As a son of Ben, Herrick more than once rewrote Jonson, who, in turn, drew heavily on the classics. And so on. The poems are not less good for this: the final triumph is what the language does, not what the poet can do, or display. The poet's ultimate loyalty—the phrase belongs to Stanley Kunitz—is to the poem. The language itself is a compound, or, to change the figure, a bitch. The paradoxical thing, as R. P. Blackmur said of some of the young in the thirties, is that the most original poets are the most imitative. The remark is profound: if a writer has something to say, it will come through. The very fact he has the support of a tradition, or an older writer, will enable him to be more himself—or more than himself.

In a time when the romantic notion of the inspired poet still has considerable credence, true "imitation" takes a certain courage. One dares to stand up to a great style, to compete with papa. In my own case, I should like to think I have over-acknowledged, in one way or another, my debt to Yeats. One simple device provides, I believe, an important technical difference: in the pentameter, I end-stop almost every line—a thing more usual when the resources of the language were more limited. This is not necessarily a virtue—indeed, from many points of view, a limitation. But it is part of an effort, however clumsy, to bring the language back to bare, hard, even terrible statement. All this Yeats himself, a bowerbird if there ever was one, would have understood, and, possibly, approved.

from Some Remarks on Rhythm

What do *I* Like? Listen:

> *Hinx, minx, the old witch winks!*
> *The fat begins to fry!*
> *There's nobody home but Jumping Joan,*
> *And father, and mother, and I.*

Now what makes that "catchy," to use Mr. Frost's word? For one thing: the rhythm. Five stresses out of a possible six in the first line, though maybe "old" doesn't take quite as strong a stress as the others. And three— keep noticing that magic number—internal rhymes, *hinx, minx, winks.* And notice too the apparent mysteriousness of the action: something happens right away—the old witch winks and she sets events into motion. The fat begins to fry, literally and symbolically. She commands—no old fool witch this one. Notice that the second line, "The fat begins to fry," is absolutely regular metrically. It's all iambs, a thing that often occurs when previous lines are sprung or heavily counterpointed. The author doesn't want to get too far from his base, from his ground beat. The third line varies again with an anapest and variations in the "o" and "u" sounds. "There's nobody home but Jumping Joan." Then the last line—anapest lengthening the line out to satisfy the ear, "And father, and mother, and I." Sometimes we are inclined to feel that Mother Goose, or the traditional kind of thing, is almost infallible as memorable speech—the phrase is Auden's. But this is by no means so. There is another version that goes,

> Hink, mink, the old witch stinks,
> The fat begins to fry:
> Nobody's home but Jumping Joan,
> Jumping Joan and I.

Well, the whole situation has obviously altered, for the better perhaps from the standpoint of the speaker at least. But in his excitement he has produced a much inferior poem.

First, deleting the "x"'s takes some of the force away from the three rhyming words—"Hinx, minx, the old witch winks,"—the triad. What's more, he has become tiresomely naturalistic. "The old witch stinks"— hardly a fresh piece of observation. *Stinks* is a splendid old word, but here it is a bore. It is a prerogative of old witches to stink: part of their stock and trade as it were, and nobody mentions it. Take the change from *minx,* which means of course a pert little vixen of a girl, and carries with it overtones of tenderness; or, further back, a wanton, a roaring girl. And the mink—a wonderful little predatory animal with a characteristic odor. But if we keep *that* in mind, the line becomes an olfactory horror. It's some fusty little cave these two have in the absence of father and mother. And *their* absence takes away the real drama from the situation. It's a roll in the hay, and nothing more.

Allow me another I love:

> *I.N. spells IN.*
> *I was in my kitchen*
> *Doin' a bit of stitching.*
> *Old Father Nimble*
> *Came and took my thimble*
> *I got a great big stone,*
> *Hit him on the belly-bone.*
> *O.U.T. spells OUT.*

Here we see how light "i" and short "i" and feminine endings can make for speed, rhythmical quickness, and velocity, and then, with the words following the action, that truly awesome and portentous line with its spondees, "I gŏt a great bíg stóne . . ."; and then the sudden speed-up in the action—the triumphant release from a frustration, I suppose the Freudians would say—"Hit him on the belly-bone. / O.U.T. spells out.

Take another, a single line, which is always a test:

> *Great A, little a, bounding B.*

There are three shifts of pace—it's a triad again, lovely alliteration, the long full vowels combined.

Names themselves can be a love—and half the poem:

> *Julius Caesar Pompey Green*
> *Wore a jacket of velveteen.*

What's my point by these little examples? It's this: that, while our genius in the language may be essentially iambic, particularly in the formal lyric, much of memorable or passionate speech is strongly stressed, irregular, even "sprung," if you will. Now we see that the name itself, the direct address, makes for the memorable, for rhythmical interest; often it makes for implied dialogue. Take the ridiculous:

> *Oh father dear, do ships at sea*
> *Have legs way down below?*

Of course they do, you goosey you,
Or else how could they go?

But you may protest, these are the rhythms of children, of folk material, strongly stressed—memorable perhaps, but do they appear in poetry today? The answer is yes, certainly in some poems. . . .

CHARLES OLSON

Charles Olson (1910–70) was born in Worcester, Massachusetts, the son of a postman. He earned his BA and MA at Wesleyan College, then taught at Clark University for two years before completing the course work for a PhD in American civilization at Harvard. He received a Guggenheim Fellowship when he was twenty-nine and wrote an eccentric, non-academic study of Melville's *Moby Dick* entitled *Call Me Ishmael.* Instead of pursuing the academic career he had trained for, Olson turned to Depression-era politics. He worked for the ACLU and, during World War II, served as assistant chief of foreign language of the Office of War Information. Although a promising political career in the Roosevelt administration was available, Olson left the political world and chose to write.

In 1950 he published "Projective Verse," a groundbreaking essay important to poets of the generation after Pound and William Carlos Williams. It recommends "open" verse, in which a poem is defined as "energy transferred from where the poet got it . . . by way of the poem itself, all the way over to the reader." In addition, syntax should be shaped by sound, not sense, and sense conveyed by rapid movement from one perception to another rather than by rational argument. The way the words are placed on the page—the "composition by field"—should direct the reader how to read the lines. *In Cold Hell, in Thicket* (1953), in particular demonstrates Olson's application of his poetic theories.

Olson became the energizing force in a group of poets writing in the 1950s, including Robert Duncan, Denise Levertov, and Robert Creeley, as well as a guru for many enthusiastic followers. This reputation came from his years as director of Black Mountain College, which was known for its large share of avant-garde artists (Merce Cunningham in dance, John Cage in music, and Robert Rauschenberg and Franz Kline in painting). During his years at Black Mountain, Olson traveled to the Yucatan to study Mayan culture. He was interested in how to break through layers of culture to find the intimate concealed connections between humans and nature of which Western culture has deprived us. *The Mayan Letters* (1953) collects letters written to Robert Creeley from Mexico on mythology, anthropology, language, and history. In his own poetry, Olson had a similar goal: to dig down past convention to the hidden unconscious. In *The Maximus*

Poems, a lifelong poetic project also begun in letters, Olson searched for the spirit of Gloucester, Massachusetts, the fishing village where he grew up. By studying the effects of the town on his central character, Maximus, he hoped to find "the primal features of those founders who lie buried in us." Olson lived in Gloucester in his last years and entered wholeheartedly into the life of the community, arguing local issues and writing frequent letters to the newspaper. He disapproved of "epicene poets—poets who do not enter the society." In 1995, the town of Gloucester held a festival in honor of Charles Olson at which Robert Creeley, Hettie Jones, and others from his poetry life came together with townspeople (attendance was about fifty-fifty) to celebrate his many contributions to poetry and the town.

from Projective Verse

(projectile   (percussive   (prospective
vs.
The NON-Projective

(or what a French critic calls "closed" verse, that verse which print bred and which is pretty much what we have had, in English & American, and have still got, despite the work of Pound & Williams:

it led Keats, already a hundred years ago, to see it (Wordsworth's, Milton's) in the light of "the Egotistical Sublime"; and it persists, at this latter day, as what you might call the private-soul-at-any-public wall)

Verse, now, 1950, if it is to go ahead, if it is to be of *essential* use, must, I take it, catch up and put into itself certain laws and possibilities of the breath, of the breathing of the man who writes as well as of his listenings. (The revolution of the ear, 1910, the trochee's heave, asks it of the younger poets.)

I want to do two things: first, try to show what projective or OPEN verse is, what it involves, in its act of composition, how, in distinction from the non-projective, it is accomplished; and II, suggest a few ideas about what stance toward reality brings such verse into being, what that stance does, both to the poet and to his reader. (The stance involves, for example, a change beyond, and larger than, the technical, and may, the way things look, lead to new poetics and to new concepts from which some sort of drama, say, or of epic, perhaps may emerge.)

First, some simplicities that a man learns, if he works in OPEN, or what can also be called COMPOSITION BY FIELD, as opposed to inherited line, stanza, over-all form, what is the "old" base of the non-projective.

(a) the *kinetics* of the thing. A poem is energy transferred from where the poet got it (he will have some several causations), by way of the poem itself to, all the way over to, the reader. Okay. Then the poem itself must, at all points, be a high energy-construct and, at all points, an energy-discharge. So: how is the poet to accomplish same energy, how is he, what is the process by which a poet gets in, at all points energy at least the equivalent of the energy which propelled him in the first place, yet an energy which is peculiar to verse alone and which will be, obviously, also different from the energy which the reader, because he is a third term, will take away?

This is the problem which any poet who departs from closed form is specially confronted by. And it involves a whole series of new recognitions. From the moment he ventures into FIELD COMPOSITION— puts himself in the open—he can go by no track other than the one the poem under hand declares, for itself. Thus he has to behave, and be, instant by instant, aware of some several forces just now beginning to be examined. (It is much more, for example, this push, than simply such a one as Pound put, so wisely, to get us started: "the musical phrase," go by it, boys, rather than by, the metronome.)

(2) is the *principle,* the law which presides conspicuously over such composition, and, when obeyed, is the reason why a projective poem can come into being. It is this: FORM IS NEVER MORE THAN AN EXTENSION OF CONTENT. (Or so it got phrased by one, R. Creeley, and it makes absolute sense to me, with this possible corollary, that right form, in any given poem, is the only and exclusively possible extension of content under hand.) There it is, brothers, sitting there, for USE.

Now (3) the *process* of the thing, how the principle can be made so to shape the energies that the form is accomplished. And I think it can be boiled down to one statement (first pounded into my head by Edward Dahlberg): ONE PERCEPTION MUST IMMEDIATELY AND DIRECTLY

LEAD TO A FURTHER PERCEPTION. It means exactly what it says, is a matter of, at *all* points (even I should say, of our management of daily reality as of the daily work) get on with it, keep moving, keep in, speed, the nerves, their speed, the perceptions, theirs, the acts, the split second acts, the whole business, keep it moving as fast as you can, citizen. And if you also set up as a poet, USE USE USE the process at all points, in any given poem always, always one perception must must must MOVE, INSTANTER, ON ANOTHER!

So there we are, fast, there's the dogma. And its excuse, its usableness, in practice. Which get us, it ought to get us, inside the machinery, now, 1950, of how projective verse is made.

If I hammer, if I recall in, and keep calling in, the breath, the breathing as distinguished from the hearing, it is for cause, it is to insist upon a part that breath plays in verse which has not (due, I think, to the smothering of the power of the line by too set a concept of foot) has not been sufficiently observed or practiced, but which has to be if verse is to advance to its proper force and place in the day, now, and ahead. I take it that PROJECTIVE VERSE teaches, is, this lesson, that that verse will only do in which a poet manages to register both the acquisitions of his ear *and* the pressures of his breath.

Let's start from the smallest particle of all, the syllable. It is the king and pin of versification, what rules and holds together the lines, the larger forms, of a poem. I would suggest that verse here and in England dropped this secret from the late Elizabethans to Ezra Pound, lost it, in the sweetness of meter and rime, in a honey-head. (The syllable is one way to distinguish the original success of blank verse, and its falling off, with Milton.)

It is by their syllables that words juxtapose in beauty, by these particles of sound as clearly as by the sense of the words which they compose. In any given instance, because there is a choice of words, the choice, if a man is in there, will be, spontaneously, the obedience of his ear to the syllables. The fineness, and the practice, lie here, at the minimum and source of speech.

> O western wynd, when wilt thou blow
> And the small rain down shall rain

> O Christ that my love were in my arms
> And I in my bed again

It would do no harm, as an act of correction to both prose and verse as now written, if both rime and meter, and, in the quantity words, both sense and sound, were less in the forefront of the mind than the syllable, if the syllable, that fine creature were more allowed to lead the harmony on. With this warning, to those who would try: to step back here to this place of the elements and minims of language is to engage speech where it is least careless—and least logical. Listening for the syllables must be so constant and so scrupulous, the exaction must be so complete, that the assurance of the ear is purchased at the highest—40 hours a day—price. For from the root out, from all over the place, the syllable comes, the figures of, the dance:

> "Is" comes from the Aryan root, *as*, to breathe. The English "not" equals the Sanscrit *na*, which may come from the root *na*, to be lost, to perish. "Be" is from *bhu*, to grow.

I say the syllable, king, and that it is spontaneous, this way: the ear, the ear which has collected, which has listened, the ear, which is so close to the mind that it is the mind's, that it has the mind's speed . . .

it is close, another way: the mind is brother to this sister and is, because it is so close, is the drying force, the incest, the sharpener . . .

it is from the union of the mind and the ear that the syllable is born.

But the syllable is only the first child of the incest of verse (always, that Egyptian thing, it produces twins!). The other child is the LINE. And together, these two, the syllable *and* the line, they make a poem, they make that thing, the—what shall we call it, the Boss of all, the "Single Intelligence." And the line comes (I swear it) from the breath, from the breathing of the man who writes, at the moment that he writes, and thus is, it is here that, the daily work, the WORK, gets in, for only he, the man who writes, can declare, at every moment, the line its metric and its ending—where its breathing, shall come to, termination.

The trouble with most work, to my taking, since the breaking away from traditional lines and stanzas, and from such wholes as, say Chaucer's *Troilus* or S's *Lear*, is: contemporary workers go lazy RIGHT HERE WHERE THE LINE IS BORN.

Let me put it baldly. The two halves are:

    the HEAD, by way of the EAR, to the SYLLABLE
    the HEART, by way of the BREATH, to the LINE

And the joker? That is in the 1st half of the proposition that, in composing, one lets-it-rip; and that it is in the 2nd half, surprise, it is the LINE that's the baby that gets, as the poem is getting made, the attention, the control, that it is right here, in the line, that the shaping takes place, each moment of the going. . . .

II

. . . From the moment the projective purpose of the act of verse is recognized, the content does—it will—change. If the beginning and the end is breath, voice in its largest sense, then the material of verse shifts. It has to. It starts with the composer. The dimension of his line itself changes, not to speak of the change in his conceiving, of the matter he will turn to, of the scale in which he imagines that matter's use. I myself would pose the difference by a physical image. It is no accident that Pound and Williams both were involved variously in a movement which got called "objectivism." But that word was then used in some sort of a necessary quarrel, I take it, with "subjectivism." It is now too late to be bothered with the latter. It has excellently done itself to death, even though we are all caught in its dying. What seems to me a more valid formulation for present use is "objectism," a word to be taken to stand for the kind of relation of man to experience which a poet might state as the necessity of a line or a work to be as wood is, to be as clean as wood is as it issues from the hand of nature, to be shaped as wood can be when a man has had his hand to it. Objectism is the getting rid of the lyrical interference of the individual as ego, of the "subject" and his soul, that peculiar presumption by which western man has interposed himself between what he is as a creature of nature (with certain instructions to carry out) and those other creations of nature which we may, with no derogation, call objects. For a man is himself an object, whatever he may take to be his advantages, the more likely to recognize himself as such the greater his advantages, particularly at that moment that he achieves an humilitas sufficient to make him of use.

It comes to this: the use of a man, by himself and thus by others, lies in how he conceives his relation to nature, that force to which he owes his somewhat small existence. If he sprawl, he shall find little to sing but himself, and shall sing, nature has such paradoxical ways, by way of artificial forms outside himself. But if he stays inside himself, if he is contained within his nature as he is participant in the larger force, he will be able to listen, and his hearing through himself will give him secrets objects share. And by an inverse law his shapes will make their own way. It is in this sense that the projective act, which is the artist's act in the larger field of objects, leads to dimensions larger than the man. For a man's problem, the moment he takes speech up in all its fullness, is to give his work his seriousness, a seriousness sufficient to cause the thing he makes to try to take its place alongside the things of nature. This is not easy. Nature works from reverence, even in her destructions (species go down with a crash). But breath is man's special qualification as animal. Sound is a dimension he has extended. Language is one of his proudest acts. And when a poet rests in these as they are in himself (in his physiology, if you like, but the life in him, for all that) then he, if he chooses to speak from these roots, works in that area where nature has given him size, projective size. . . .

ROBERT DUNCAN

Born in Oakland, California, Robert Duncan (1919–88) was adopted by Theosophists after his mother's death in childbirth. Raised in the mysterious religion founded in the nineteenth century by Madame Blavatsky, Duncan took from Theosophy a lifelong fascination with the occult. An accident when he was three left him with double vision, which came to represent in his poetry the duality of the physical and spiritual worlds.

Encouraged by a high-school teacher, Duncan began to write poetry, which earned him a scholarship to the University of California at Berkeley in 1936. Two years later he moved to New York, where he was active in the emerging arts movements and helped to found the *Experimental Review*, which published Anaïs Nin, Kenneth Patchen, Laurence Durrell, and others. He was drafted into the army in 1941, but after a month in boot camp he declared his homosexuality and was discharged.

After a brief marriage in 1943, Duncan returned to San Francisco where he entered into the lively poetry scene including Kenneth Rexroth, Jack Spicer, and others. In 1947 he met Charles Olson, who invited him to teach at the nascent Black Mountain College he had founded in North Carolina. There, Duncan wrote his first mature collection, *The Opening of the Field* (1960). Olson's theory of projective verse involving the use of open forms and the line ordered by the poet's breath was the base line from which Duncan constructed his collage theory, seeing the poem as a compositional field. He worked to create poems of a purely organic form, utilizing complex repetitions and intentionally archaic diction.

Two further collections, *Roots and Branches* (1964) and *Bending the Bow* (1968) established Duncan as a major poet. In 1961 he won the Harriet Monroe Memorial Prize. A Guggenheim fellowship followed in 1963, Poetry Magazine's Levinson Award in 1964, and a series of National Endowment for the Arts fellowships thereafter. After a long struggle with kidney disease and dialysis, he died in San Francisco in 1988.

from Ideas on the Meaning of Form

. . . Form to the mind obsessed by convention, is significant in so far as it shows control. What has nor rime nor reason is a bogie that must be dismissed from the horizons of the mind. It is a matter of rules and conformities, taste, rationalization, and sense. Beyond, as beyond in the newly crowded Paris or London of the Age of Reason, lies the stink of shit and pestilence. Wherever the feeling of control is lost, the feeling of form is lost. . . .

. . . The tension, the reality of the verse, depends upon its being sufficiently haunted by the thought of its energy as a violence and the thought of its form as repose for the poet to take her stance. . . .

Fact and reason are creations of man's genius to secure a point of view protected against a vision of life where information and intelligence invade us, where what we know shapes us and we become creatures, not rulers, of what is. Where, more, we are part of the creative process, not its goal. It was against such intolerable realizations that these men took thought. The rationalist gardener's art is his control over nature, and beauty is conceived as the imposed order visible in the pruned hedgerow and the ultimate tree compelled into geometric globe or pyramid that gives certainty of effect.

The poet's art was one of control over the common speech, forcing natural metaphor from all hint of meaningful experience or intuition of the universe and maintaining it as a form of speech, and disciplining syntax and line away from the energies of the language itself into balanced phrases, regular meters and heroic couplets. . . .

But my point here is that the minuet, the game of tennis, the heroic couplet, the concept of form as the imposing of rules and establishing of regularities, the theories of civilization, race, and progress, the performances in sciences and arts to rationalize the universe, to secure balance and class—all these are a tribal magic against a real threat of upset and things not keeping their place. . . .

DAVID LEHMAN

David Lehman (1948–) was born and grew up in New York City. He graduated from Columbia University and went to Cambridge University on a Kellett Fellowship. Lehman wrote a dissertation on the prose poem earning a Columbia PhD in 1978 while teaching at Hamilton College. A postdoctoral fellowship year at Cornell in 1980 convinced him that "theory" had hijacked literary studies and that he'd be better off outside academe. He set himself up as a freelance writer, reviewed books regularly for *Newsweek* and other publications, and eventually became a vice president of the National Book Critics Circle.

An Alternative to Speech, a first book of poems, came out in 1986 from Princeton University Press. In 1988 he launched *The Best American Poetry* and has served ever since as the series editor of this annual anthology. For two years beginning in 1996 he wrote a poem every day as an experiment. One hundred and fifty of these daily poems were gathered in *The Daily Mirror* (2000). He maintained the practice, and a second "journal in poetry," *The Evening Sun* (2002), chronicled the turn of the century. His nonfiction books include *Signs of the Times: Deconstruction and the Fall of Paul de Man* (1991) and *The Last Avant-Garde: The Making of the New York School of Poets* (1998). He edited *Great American Prose Poems: From Poe to the Present* (2003). With Star Black, Lehman initiated the celebrated KGB Bar Monday Night Poetry series in New York's East Village in February 1997. Black and Lehman hosted more than 180 poetry evenings by the time they stepped down in May 2003. At Donald Hall's suggestion, Lehman succeeded Hall as general editor of the University of Michigan Press's *Poets on Poetry Series* in 1994. Lehman now teaches in the graduate writing programs at Bennington College and the New School University. He lives in New York City and spends as much time as he can manage in Ithaca, New York.

from The Prose Poem: An Alternative to Verse

. . . What is a prose poem? The best short definition is almost tautological. The prose poem is a poem written in prose rather than verse. On the page it can look like a paragraph or fragmented short story, but it acts like a poem. It works in sentences rather than lines. With the one exception of the line-break, it can make use of all the strategies and tactics of poetry. Just as free verse did away with meter and rhyme, the prose poem does away with the line as the unit of composition. It uses the means of prose toward the ends of poetry.

The prose poem is, you might say, poetry that disguises its true nature. In the prose poem the poet can appropriate such unlikely models as the newspaper article, the memo, the list, the parable, the speech, the dialogue. It is a form that sets store by its use of the demotic, its willingness to locate the sources of poetry defiantly far from the spring on Mount Helicon sacred to the muses. It is an insistently modern form. Some would argue further that it is, or was, an inherently subversive one. Marguerite Murphy's A *Tradition of Subversion* (1992) contends that an adversarial streak characterizes the genre. Others are drawn to the allegorical formula that would align the prose poem with "working-class discourse" undermining the lyric structures of the upper bourgeoisie. Many examples and precedents elude or combat this facile notion, and commentators have begun to stress the inclusiveness of the genre and not its putatively subversive properties. While it sometimes seems that the only generalization you can safely make about the prose poem is that it resists generalization, certain terms recur in essays and critical discussions. The prose poem is a *hybrid* form, an *anomaly* if not a *paradox* or *oxymoron*. It offers the enchantment of *escape* whether from the invisible chains of the superego, or from the oppressive reign of the alexandrine line, from which Charles Baudelaire broke vehemently in his *Petits Poèmes en prose* (1862), which inaugurated the genre in France. Sooner or later in the discussion it will be said that the prose poem, born in rebellion against *tradition,* has itself become a tradition. It will be noted approvingly that the prose poem *blurs boundaries.* "My own formal literary education had not accorded much regard to what in English are referred to as 'prose poems,' and I am not at all sure what the genre is supposed to entail," W. S. Merwin wrote in a 1994 reprinting of *The Miner's Pale Children* (1970). "I recalled what I thought were precedents—fragments, essays, journal entries, instructions and lists, oral tales, fables. What I was hoping for as I went was akin to what made a poem seem complete. But it was prose that I was writing, and I was pleased when the pieces raised questions about the boundary between prose and poetry, and where we think it runs."

The words *poetry* and *prose* seem to be natural antagonists. The French Renaissance poet Pierre Ronsard said they were "mortal enemies." Matthew Arnold, thinking to damn the poets Dryden and Pope, called them "classics of our prose." Oscar Wilde subtly refined the insult: "Meredith is a prose Browning, and so is Browning. He used poetry as a medium for writing in prose." In these examples, it is *prose* that has the negative charge, but the opposite can sometimes be true. Not every poet accused of writing *poetic prose* today will feel complimented, though to Baudelaire in Paris in 1862 it represented an ideal. No doubt *poetry* and *prose* will continue to exist in an antithetical relationship if only because they, and *poetry* in particular, are not neutrally descriptive but have an evaluative meaning. This complicates any discussion of the prose poem and assures that it will probably always retain its oxymoronic status. Nevertheless, there is a way to cut to the quick. As soon as you admit the possibility that verse is an adjunct of poetry and not an indispensable quality, the prose poem ceases to be a contradiction in terms. *Verse* and *prose* are the real antonyms, and the salient difference between them is that verse occurs in lines of a certain length determined by the poet whereas prose continues to the end of the page. In Richard Howard's formulation, verse reverses—the reader turns at the end of the line—while prose proceeds. The form of a prose poem is not an absence of form. It is just that the sentence and the paragraph must act the part of the line and the stanza, and there are fewer rules and governing traditions to observe, or different ones, because the prose poem has a relatively short history and has enjoyed outsider status for most of that time. Writing a prose poem can therefore seem like accepting a dare to be unconventional. It is a form that invites the practitioner to re-invent it. . . .

Certainly the prose poem in the United States today is not as predictably unpredictable as it may once have seemed, in part because it has loosened its ties to the French tradition. There is a renewed sense that the home-made American prose poem is a thing that could not exist without the idea of America preceding it. This is not entirely a new story. In a 1957 prologue to his early *Kora in Hell: Improvisation,* William Carlos Williams took pains to distinguish the book from "the typically French prose poem," whose "pace was not my own"—despite the debt, evident in the title, to Rimbaud's *Season in Hell*. The question "what is American about the American prose poem" remains second to "what is American about American poetry," a topic that can be debated and discussed endlessly without any prospect of a resolution. . . .

In prose the poet gives up the meaning-making powers of the linebreak. The poet in prose must use the structure of the sentence itself, or the way one sentence modifies the next, to generate the surplus meaning that helps separate poetry in prose from ordinary writing.

Writing in prose you give up much, but you gain in relaxation, in the possibilities of humor and incongruity, in narrative compression, and in the feeling of escape or release from tradition or expectation. The prose poem can feel like a holiday from the rigors of verse, as is sometimes the case in Shakespeare's plays. In *Hamlet,* for example, prose can serve the purposes of the "antic disposition" the prince affects to make people think he is mad. In *Much Ado About Nothing,* on the other hand, prose stands for plain sense, verse for hyperbole, ornament; Benedick is an inept rhymester, but his love for Beatrice and hers for him has a chance to endure because it is founded not on the fantastical language of romantic courtship but on the sallies and scorn of prose wit. The prose poem can have this anti-poetical, down-to-earth quality, can stand as a corrective to the excesses to which verse is susceptible. . . .

There is a moment in Frank O'Hara's poem "Why I Am Not a Painter" when the poet—urbane, bohemian buddy of avant-garde painters that he is—exultantly says of his latest poetic effort: "It is even in / prose, I am a real poet." There is an ambiguity here that readers may not notice at first. If the excerpt were shortened to "even in prose, I am a real poet," it would mean "I am a real poet even when I write prose," and *prose* would be counted not a virtue but a defect. But of course we read the line to mean, "It is even in prose, [and therefore] I am a real poet"—the act of writing a prose poem certifies me as an authentic 100% avant-garde American poet (though at this moment I happen to be writing in verse). While we shouldn't overlook the characteristically ironic spin O'Hara gave to his words, they retain their element of truth and their larger element of ambiguity, and their bravado is exactly what readers should have in mind as they prepare to encounter the American prose poem in all its glorious variety.

FANNY HOWE

Fanny Howe (1940–) was born in Buffalo, New York, at the onset of World War II. While her father was overseas, her mother brought her and her sister Susan to Cambridge, Massachusetts, to live. This way they were near their paternal family; their mother's family was in Ireland and therefore inaccessible until after the war. They lived in an apartment until their father returned and then they moved into a house not far from Harvard Square. The third child, another daughter, Helen, was born in 1949.

Their father was a professor of constitutional law and admiralty and a civil-rights activist who also acted as a legal counselor to a few people accused by then-senator Joseph McCarthy of being communists. Their mother founded the Poets Theater in Cambridge, using her own experience in the Abbey and Gate theaters in Dublin as a model. The extraordinary difference between one parent and the other was a source of rebellion and mental activity for Fanny Howe, who followed her father's interests but lived by her mother's artistic outsider ethic.

Fanny Howe went to Stanford at seventeen, dropped out, married, divorced, and began a kind of uprooted existence that could not be shaken, even after giving birth to three children in four years during her second marriage. Neither of her sisters nor she graduated from college or followed a conventional academic or professional path. They had no inheritance except for the lively bookish environment in which they grew.

Fanny Howe wrote pulp novels to make a living when she was in her twenties, and at the same time wrote stories, novels, and poetry that made no money. She lived in and around Boston, moving constantly, and began teaching at an adjunct level that lasted for many years. She first published with Houghton Mifflin—*Eggs,* a book of poems, and *Forty Whacks,* stories—and then became increasingly eccentric in her style and moved over to small press publications where she remained until the University of California Press published three of her books, *Selected Poems, Gone,* and *The Wedding Dress.*

In her interview with Daniel Kane she talks about her relationship to her work, which is fundamentally non-iconic, itinerant, impersonal, and often reverberates with the feeling expressed by an Inuit saying: "We do not believe. We fear."

from an Interview with Daniel Kane

DK: Individual poems in your recent *Selected Poems* are untitled, though you do have titles for groups of poems. This makes me think of your work as "serial poetry." How would you define a serial poem in your own terms? And, what does a poem gain by lacking a title?

FH: The term "serial poem" has always seemed artificial to me, although I know what you mean by it. The fact is, I don't even like "modernism" or "material text" or any term that tries to surround an action that is simultaneously trying to be free. So this leads directly to my problem with titles, because (to me) they put a lid on the loneliness of the poem. And they influence the way it is read. Freedom at any cost! . . .

DK: I found the poems represented under the title *Q* particularly moving and interesting. They strike me as a narrative of travel— from one physical location to another, from one political aware- ness to another, and from one emotional condition to another. Did you write this series during a particularly peripatetic period in your life?

FH: *Q* was written in an intense period of uprootedness that was a more exaggerated version of the one I had experienced for twenty years, and longer. I don't know what's wrong with me, but I can't get settled. It is deeply unpleasant, especially because my family isn't traveling with me anymore. *Q* was part of the two-year period I spent working in London, seven years ago. I had to travel by train, constantly, as part of the job, and stay in dismal B & B's in the outskirts of small cities. Trains made me happy by contrast, and even now I feel most at rest in motion.

DK: In the poem from *Q* that begins "Creation was the end that pre- ceded meaning," you write:

> Rain streamed on evergreen and ferns
> in a larger darkness
> than anyone could witness
>
> A boy emerged from a cocoon
> crying I have no right to be here!

I'm interested in the lack of punctuation in your poems. The openendedness such a lack evokes seems particularly suited to the travel narrative.

FH: I think for me poems are sentences, which may be why they are getting shorter. I love a complete sentence, and all that it contains in the way of balance and aspiration. I love prose sentences. But a whole poem of mine is a sentence composed of sound-lines (bars), each line being the equivalent of a complex word. Each sound-line floats in tandem with the next one. Each one is a word. The group of sound-lines or words forms a sort of sentence which is a poem.

A few words create together one word, and that word is on a line, and the next line consists of another long word made up of words. Then the poem is composed of both many and few words. The lines themselves demonstrate their separateness and, at the same time, the gravitational pull in relation to each other.

Prose only differs to the extent that the lines jump on each other, left to right, instead of falling down from an upwards position. The jumping to the side saves paper (time and space), but it also indicates another thought process—one with a goal. It's the difference between taking a walk and sitting still. Prose has just as much poetry in it as a poem does. It's just in a rush to get somewhere and bears more guilt, always trying to justify itself. . . .

ALICE FULTON

Alice Fulton (1952–) was born and raised in Troy, New York. Her father, John R. Fulton, owned Lansingburgh's historic Phoenix Hotel; her Irish-Catholic mother, Mary Callahan, was a nurse and homemaker. Her two older sisters left for college when Fulton was about eight years old, and she had the solitary upbringing of an only child, finding company in books, music, and art. Today, she and her husband, the artist Hank De Leo, live in Ithaca where she is the Ann S. Bowers Professor of English at Cornell University. Her honors include MacArthur, Guggenheim, and Ingram Merrill fellowships, as well as the 2002 Bobbitt Award from the Library of Congress. Fulton's poetics belong to no easily categorized school; she is regarded as one of the most original English language poets writing today.

As she was completing her MFA degree at Cornell University, Fulton's first book, *Dance Script with Electric Ballerina*, was chosen by W. D. Snodgrass for the 1982 Associated Writing Programs Award. In his introduction, Snodgrass notes that Pound "identifies three ways the language of poetry is charged or energized: melopoeia, phanopoeia, and logopoeia 'the dance of the intellect among words.'" Snodgrass reads Fulton's debut as a rare example of logopoeia and writes that "we are always engaged by the sense of linguistic virtuosity, a constant delight in language textures, the ever-shifting shock and jolt of an electric surface."

Fulton's second volume, *Palladium* (1986), chosen by Mark Strand for the National Poetry Series Prize, extended the exploration of surface as well as substance. Her boldly experimental *Powers of Congress* (1990) was the first poetry collection to explore such visual possibilities as flush-right alignment and hand-written marginalia. Writing of this book in *Poetry*, David Baker noted "No one matches her ability to perform a kind of marginal sneak attack, a slipping-in of subject, substance, sound—to insinuate the unknown into the known, to fracture, fuse, repair."

In the past decade, Fulton has countered notions of "the natural" with a postmodern poetics that defies convention and admits artifice. Her books *Sensual Math* (1995) and *Felt* (2001) opened a new "fractal" space, in which the poem plane shifts between richly musical and transparent passages, between the poem as voice and the poem as construct.

Informed by feminism, philosophy, science, religion, and popular culture, Fulton's poetry often manages to be funny while engaging with the most heartbreaking aspects of being. Her essay collection, *Feeling as a Foreign Language: The Good Strangeness of Poetry,* calls for a subversive "poetry of inconvenient knowledge" that will resist the cultural and political status quo and take a "passional" stand against cruelty and injustice. When asked about the influence of her mentor, A. R. Ammons, she remarked that "Like Dickinson, Archie showed me the beauty and necessity of the marginal, the peripheral." Fulton's "maximalist" aesthetic is one of inclusiveness and generosity, and her classic 1986 essay provides insight into what Ammons deemed "the great integrative force" of her poetics.

from Of Formal, Free, and Fractal Verse: Singing the Body Electric

. . . In the largest terms, the search for a style is a search for a language that does justice to our knowledge of how the world works . . .

Perhaps popular literature and culture have made people aware of . . . theories, such as the view that reality consists of a steadily increasing number of parallel universes; that consciousness creates reality; or that the world is twofold, consisting of potentials and actualities. Heisenberg's uncertainty principle, which forbids accurate knowledge of a quantum particle's position and momentum, is certainly well known. A truly engaged and contemporary poetry must reflect this knowledge. As a body of literature it might synthesize such disparate theories into a comprehensive metaphor for the way the world appears to us today. Or it may be that synthesis and unity are fundamentally premodern concepts. In this case, a fragmentary, diffuse literature is the perfect expression of our world knowledge. In a sense, our search for a language mirrors science's search for a quantum reality. . . .

The mathematician Benoit Mandebrot observed that "25 or 30 years ago, science looked at things that were regular and smooth." In contrast, he became intrigued by what are called chaotic phenomena: the occurrence of earthquakes; the way our neurons fire when we search our memories; patterns of vegetation in a swamp; price jumps in the stock market; turbulence in the weather; the distribution of galaxies; and the flooding of the Nile. . . . He found that certain chaotic structures (including the preceding list) contained a deep logic or pattern. In 1975, he coined the word *fractals* (from the Latin *fractus,* meaning "irregular or fragmented") to describe such configurations. (Pound's injunction to "break the pentameter" is nicely implicit in the term.)

To put it simply, each part of a fractal form replicates the form of the entire structure. Increasing detail is revealed with increasing magnification, and each smaller part looks like the entire structure, turned around or tilted a bit. This isn't true of the classical Euclidean forms of line, planes, and spheres. For example, when a segment of a circle is subjected to increasing magnification it looks increasingly like a straight line rather than a series of circles. But a fractal form has a substructure (we might say a subtext) that goes on indefinitely, without reposing into ordinary curves. The bark patterns on oak, mud cracks in a dry riverbed, a broccoli spear—these are examples of fractal forms: irregular structures containing just enough regularity so that they can be described. Such forms are, at least to my perception, quite pleasing. Like free verse, they zig and zag, spurt and dawdle, while retaining an infinite complexity of detail. (In contrast, formal verse travels at a regular pace and is less dynamic, less potentially volatile.) The fascination of these intricate forms ("the fascination of what's difficult" you might say) indicates that we don't need an obvious or regular pattern to satisfy our aesthetic or psychological needs. Nonobjective art, which often reflects the fractal patterns of nature, makes the same point. In fact, asymmetrical or turbulent composition may be the essence of twentieth-century aesthetics.

There are two kinds of fractals: geometric and random. The geometric type repeats an identical pattern at various scales. As a corollary, imagine a poem structured on the concept of the oxymoron. The linkage of opposites on the smallest scale might appear in antonymic word usage; on a larger scale in one stanza's ability to oppose or reverse the form and content of another; and at the grandest scale in the poem's overall form becoming a paradoxical or self-reflexive contradiction of content. Thus far, the poem could be a sonnet or an ode. After all, ordered forms about chaos were rather popular in the eighteenth century. But let's suppose that the poem's rhythm is also oxymoronic: that a smooth, regular line is purposefully followed by a rambunctious or jagged utterance. If repeated throughout, this juxtaposition would constitute the poem's metrical form.

Random fractals, to consider another possibility, introduce some elements of chance. In the composition of poetry, this could be as simple a factor as opening a book at random and using the metrical pattern happened upon as a contributing factor in the verse. . . .

Since free verse has become a misnomer, perhaps we could use the irregular yet beautifully structured forms of nature as analogues and call the poetry of irregular form *fractal verse*. Its aesthetic might derive from the structural limitations of self-similar fractal form. I offer the following as a tentative exploration of fractal precepts: Any line when examined closely (or magnified) will reveal itself to be as richly detailed as was the larger poem from which it was taken; the poem will contain an infinite regression of details, a nesting of pattern within pattern (an endless imbedding of the shape into itself, recalling Tennyson's idea of the inner infinity); digression, interruption, fragmentation and lack of continuity will be regarded as formal functions rather than lapses into formlessness; all directions of motion and rhythm will be equally probably (isotropy); the past positions of motion, or the preceding metrical pattern, will not necessarily affect the poem's future evolution (independence).

HEATHER McHUGH

Heather McHugh (1948–) was born in San Diego to Canadian parents. She received her BA from Harvard University in 1970, her MA from the University of Denver two years later. A peripatetic teacher, she is Milliman Distinguished Writer-in-Residence at the University of Washington, and on the summer faculty of the MFA program at Warren Wilson College in North Carolina.

Her six books of poems have received considerable critical attention: *Hinge and Sign* was a finalist for the National Book Award and won the Pollock/Harvard Book Review prize in 1994. Her most recent book, *Eyeshot,* was a finalist for the Pulitzer Prize. *The Father of the Predicaments,* which appeared in 1999, is often jazzy, playful, even sarcastic, yet the title poem about the dying and death of a dear friend is suffused with humility and love. McHugh's poems reflect a spunky, vigorous sensibility. They are full of good humor and puns, word games and flashbacks, dialect, dialogue, wisecracks, praise and remembrance. One critic labels her "a post-modern metaphysician, descending from John Donne via Jacques Derrida." In the preface to *Hinge and Sign* she describes herself as "the world's shyest child" who never spoke in school but went home directly to her room to write. "If I could keep from words," she says, "I would."

With her husband Nikolai Popov, she translated Paul Celan (*Glottal Stop: 101 Poems by Paul Celan*) in 2000. In that same year, her translation of Euripides' *Cyclops* appeared. *Broken English: Poetry and Partiality* (1993), contains essays on Rilke, Valéry, Celan, Gertrude Stein, Emily Dickinson, archaic Greek poets, and the Yoruba poets of western Nigeria, as well as a chapter considering the definite and indefinite grammatical articles. Completed but not yet in print is a collection of essays, in her own words "emphasizing chiastic and intertransitive exchanges in artistic encounter, taking for their occasion the anatomical drawings of Vesalius, numbers and nakedness in the poems of the English Renaissance, and works of various poets."

In the piece excerpted here, we get a tantalizing glimpse of McHugh's humor and extraordinary talents.

from Moving Means, Meaning Moves

This essay first took form as a lecture given in Bergen, Norway . . .
I was there for one academic quarter, without the benefit of any knowledge of Norwegian, and it reminded me of the general truth that poets
bear a naive or estranged relation to language. For example, it kept striking me as concretely evocative that the word for *speak* was *snakker*:
"Snakker du engelsk?" smacked of "Do you eat the English?" (not the
fast food of choice, in America). And every time I saw that perfectly
innocent Norwegian phrase meaning "Very good," I was subject to a
sudden sense of titillating oxymoron: the Norwegian reads *bare bra* and
cannot help packing, in an American eye, considerable wallop. This is
the curse of a poetic or naive relation to language: you don't know
where it's going but you're very susceptible to traveling whatever road
it takes you down.

At every corner store in Bergen was a large sign saying, "SPILL
HER"; in fact this turned out to mean something rather less mythic, and
more mundane, than my persistent mental image of great vessels of
Norwegian womanhood, brimming over and ready to be tipped. For
Americans, the phrase is "fill 'er up." . . .

A poet is materially engaged in estranging language, all the time—
her own language must become strange to her. The motion of a poem
(in Norwegian "motion" is *fart*) is, in some essential way, an estranging
motion. A poem means to move you, but in unexpected directions. I fall
into spatial metaphors, perhaps because I think a poem is a *passage* in a
more literal sense than a prose piece is. By this I mean that a lineated
lyric draws a reader's attention, by design, more to immediate spatial
and structural relations—to the course the reader travels from departure to arrival point, the pattern of curves en route. In prose the margin's arbitrarily placed; you're not supposed to notice it. Not so in
poems. In poems, the convention of continuance is always being queried
by poetic structure: a lineated poem is constantly ending. A sentence
can have many line breaks in it, and each line break significantly recon-
ceives not only the status of the sentence, but the status of the narrative the sentence stands for. Line breaks willfully remind us of the
wordlessness that surrounds and shapes the verbal passage; one could

even say (if one wished to sabotage a fashionable critical locution) that in poetry the margin isn't marginalized.

Indeed, the margin's of the essence—it's an absence that makes its presence felt at every turn. As every student knows, the root of the word *verse* lies in the Latin for "turning." As every student also knows, the Greek root of *poetry (poesis)* means "making"; but a lineated poem is a making full of breakings. A poem is, in other words, not only *in words:* it is a structure of internal resistances, and it's no accident that paradoxes arise at the very premises of its act. This is, I think, the most fundamental sense of Whitman's saying, "Do I contradict myself? Very well, I contradict myself," and Keats's insistence on negative capability. A constant unsettling in the grounds of the poetic, an obsessive literalness about approaching the edge, forcing each line of thought to walk the plank, again and again, to a provisional end where it must hang, for a moment, at the edge of wordlessness—these features of the lyric definitively undermine the constitutional groundwork of narration. We are creatures of habit; given a blank we can't help trying to fill it in along lines of customary seeing or saying. But the best poetic lines undermine those habits, break the pre- off the -dictable, unsettle the suburbs of your routine sentiments, and rattle the tracks of your trains of thought. . . .

RICHARD KOSTELANETZ

Richard Kostelanetz (1940–)was born in New York City. A writer, artist, critic, and editor, he received a BA from Brown University and an MA from Columbia University and studied at King's College, London. He has served as guest artist at a variety of institutions and lectured widely. In 1971, employing a radically formalist approach, Kostelanetz produced the novel *In the Beginning,* which consists of the alphabet, in single- and double-letter combinations, unfolding over thirty pages. Most of his other literary work also challenges the reader in unconventional ways and is often printed in limited editions at small presses. His "visual poetry" consists of arrangements of words on a page, using such devices as linking language and sequence, punning, alliteration, parallelism, constructivism, and minimalism. He has also worked with language in film, including one with six different soundtracks about the great Jewish cemetery of Berlin; book-art books, prints, and photo linens that have been exhibited around the world; audiotapes, videotapes, and holograms. Texts of his were incorporated into the traveling exhibition Identities initiated by the Media Lab at MIT in 2001. *The Old Poetries and the New* (1981) and *The New Poetries and Some Olds* (1990) are collections of his essays exclusively about poetry.

Kostelanetz has also published books of general literary criticism, cultural history, alternative autobiography, experimental prose, fiction, and essays on music and the visual arts, in addition to anthologies of poetry and criticism. His most theoretical literary book is *An ABC of Contemporary Reading* (1995). The summa of his critical enterprise is his *Dictionary of the Avant-Gardes* (1991; 2nd ed., 2000). Kostelanetz's nonfiction work *The End of Intelligent Writing: Literary Politics in America* (1974) charged the New York literary and publishing establishment with inhibiting the publishing and promotion of works by innovative younger authors. After nearly three decades residing in Manhattan's SoHo, which he recalls in a memoir (2003), and a decade before that in the East Village, he has relocated to a building he calls Wordship 2 in the Rockaways, New York City's outpost on the Atlantic, where he keeps his books and art in a library one hundred feet long. He has said, "disliking personal categories, I rarely speak of myself as a poet. Rather, 'poetry' is one of several things I do as a writer/artist." In these notes, he emphasizes the importance of poetry "revealing properties of words previously hidden," and implies a definition of poetry as that which "can't be classified as anything else."

from More WordWorks

One difference between experimental writing and commercial poetry is that the former is primarily concerned with discoveries within language; the latter is generally read (and praised) for its sociology, psychology, politics, archetypes, journalism, author's exotic background, or other ephemera. This distinction between experimental and commercial, developed by me decades ago, is still valuable.

The measure of poetic innovation is the development of an invention that is generally dismissed before it is widely imitated.

The principal subject of my poems is qualities indigenous to words themselves; everything else should be shunted aside as something else.

One motive behind visual enhancements is revealing properties of words previously hidden.

Learning from visual arts, I want to create after-images that are remembered apart from my name.

Should my poems be considered "light," because they certainly aren't heavy? I call them poems because they can't be classified as anything else.

Whereas traditional poetry accepts familiar limitations, innovative poetry explores possibilities within unfamiliar constraints.

One measure of maturity in poetry should be the achievement of a personal, instantly identifiable verbal style; the measure of stylistic signature is the creation of poems that could appear in a multi-person compilation without the poet's name adjacent to his text.

Among the secondary virtues of my poems is the elimination of all first-person pronouns and their variations. Lacking commentary on my personal experience, they eschew the most convenient source of thematic weight.

Form comes first; content follows, as the notion of any "organic" relation between the two usually means that form is subordinate to content.

One reason why certain poets adopt extreme subjects is seducing an audience's interest, but art as its truest and best has nothing to do with seduction.

Because art is created by and for the mind, it can scarcely rival life, let alone journalism, at stimulating emotions.

The greatest vulgarity of recent poetry writing has been letting Personality take the place of form in defining an individual work, such displacements depending upon conventional, transparent styles to succeed. In forcing attention to form, experimental work allies with traditional esthetics.

Because my poems are superficially "unacceptable" to most poetry editors, I take pride in noting that in Len Fulton's canvassing of poetry editors I currently get the fifth highest number of enthusiastic votes when they are asked to select a favorite five.

If the mark of poetry is linguistic distinction, the business of personality is publicity. One virtue I claim for my poetry is that it cannot be declaimed before an audience. If obscurity and excessive difficulty within traditional forms are vices typical of pretentious poetry, clarity and simplicity in poetry should be the equivalents of plain speaking in prose.

HARRYETTE MULLEN

Harryette Romell Mullen (1953–) was born in Florence, Alabama, grew up in Fort Worth, Texas, and is named after both her grandmothers. Her parents, both only children, had met at a historically black college in Alabama. Although they had divorced by the time she was four years old, her mother, an elementary-school teacher, encouraged Mullen and her younger sister to write letters to their father, a Chicago social worker. That early correspondence was the origin of a lifelong writing practice. Mullen's grandfather, a Baptist minister, was another early influence, poring over books as he wrote his Sunday sermons and reading Mother Goose rhymes to his granddaughters. Mullen's mother established the habit of regular visits to the public library and kept her daughters well supplied with reading, writing, and art materials. Her maternal grandmother, a federal worker, taught her to type.

Although she was expected to become a doctor, Mullen preferred to study literature, earning degrees from University of Texas, Austin and University of California, Santa Cruz. She has worked in the Texas Artists in Schools program and taught at Cornell University. She currently teaches African American literature, American poetry, and creative writing at UCLA. She is author of a book of criticism, *Freeing the Soul: Race, Subjectivity, and Difference in Slave Narratives* (1999) and five books of poems: *Tree Tall Woman* (1981), *Trimmings* (1991), *S*PeRM**K*T* (1992), *Muse & Drudge* (1995), and *Sleeping with the Dictionary* (2002), which was a finalist for the National Book Critics Circle Award and the *Los Angeles Times* Book Prize. Since her second book, Mullens's poetic method, as the title *S*PeRM**K*T* (a variation on the word "supermarket") suggests, has involved fracture and fragmentation. Her work is an unusual blend of accessible oral poetic traditions, sometimes using very regular rhymed quatrains, with nonlinear syntax and the play of different linguistic frameworks. In the interview excerpt below, Mullen discusses her poetic method, including the juxtaposition of various languages in her poetry.

from A Conversation with Harryette Mullen

HM: . . .The essentializing of black English as the natural way that black people are supposed to speak is problematic for me. Of course, I enjoy using different linguistic registers and I enjoy throwing Spanish words into my poems, you know, and I think that the variety of languages and dialects makes life more interesting. Standardization for its own sake is boring. We like to taste the different flavors, and that's something delicious about literature. You know, Langston Hughes' poem "Motto": "I play it cool and dig all jive / and that's the reason I'm alive. / My motto as I live and learn / is to dig and be dug in return." And the more people you can talk to and understand, the richer your life and experience can be, potentially. But also we learn these languages and these dialects and these ways of presenting ourselves in an atmosphere of coercion. There's the coercion of the school and workplace telling us: "You must speak this way or you will not be employable." Then there's the coercion of the streets: "You can't hang with us if you talk too proper." And on both sides there's coercion. So that's something to bear in mind when we're talking about language, that there is violence, there is pressure, there is force involved in making people conform to a particular way of speaking, writing and so forth.

FG: . . . I mean, when did you recognize that you had this fascination and obsession with playfulness [of language]? . . . Did that come very early on, before you identified yourself as a poet, so to speak, or did they come together? How did that relationship with language take place?

HM: I think that very much in one way comes from the tradition of the community because we were *always* spouting poetry. You know when I think about the way that I remember the black community that I grew up in, it was mainly organized into experiences at church, experiences at school, maybe some kind of yard and playground experiences, and then what happened at home. At school and at church we were always called on to memorize and recite poems—a whole lot of Langston Hughes and James Weldon Johnson and Paul Lawrence Dunbar especially. Those were *the* three that everybody could quote something from, and there were occasions when we had to perform.

You were expected to get up there and say your piece. And then
there was all the rhyming on the playground, in jump-rope,
circle games, and the rhythmic hand-clapping games. I mean
all of the games that we played were—at least that the girls
played—were very *verbal* games that involved rhyming along
with some sort of physical activity, you know, show your motion
and jump-rope and "Little Sally Walker" and all of that. And
then we had, in the interplay between the girls and the boys,
and what the boys did with one another—riddles and jokes, the
dozens, capping, signifying, verbal duels—you know, when
people begin to be pre-adolescent there's all the pseudo-
courtship, the formulaic exchanges that people have. The boy
says, "What's cookin' good lookin'?" and the girl says, "Ain't
nothin' cookin' but the beans in the pot, and they wouldn't be if
the water wasn't hot" [laughter]. That was in the repertoire and
then, every now and then someone would invent a new rhyme,
and that would be incorporated into the collective repertoire.
That was the sort of environment that we were all growing up
in, and we may have had similar experiences.

FG: Right. Now I find it interesting that you say that given that—
I'm thinking here both in terms of your work as a critic, and the
interviews that I've read with you, and the conversations that
we've had where you challenge the notion of a black literary
tradition based only in a oral vernacular tradition.

HM: Right.

FG: So, do you want to talk a little bit about that challenge? I mean,
because you immediately went to the vernacular oral tradition.

HM: Mm-hm. It's *there*. I want to claim the oral as much as the written tradition. That vernacular tradition is important, of course,
but it's important not to lose sight of our tradition of writing
and literature. Yes, Dunbar, Hughes and James Weldon Johnson
were working with a vernacular tradition in their poetry, but it
was written, and we had access to it through *books*. In my family,
books were important, just as public speaking, and the ability to
communicate face to face were important. I think the playful
aspect of my work is certainly connected to that vernacular tradition, and some of that tradition I know only from books or
media—just like you usually won't hear traditional black spirituals in black churches today. As a child, I knew the spirituals only

because of records, movies, and the occasional recital by one of the black opera singers. We might have sung "Swing Low, Sweet Chariot" in the chorus at school, and we'd have to learn it with sheet music. It was part of the oral tradition at one time, but now it exists only because someone cared enough to write it down. And writing something down changes it. Turning something into a poem changes it. Langston Hughes didn't write blues poems that were exactly like the traditional blues. He did something else to them. He was, in a way, digesting the blues tradition and synthesizing it with other traditions in order to create this poetry. And Dunbar didn't write down exactly the way people spoke dialect, in fact Dunbar was a standard English speaker. Growing up in Ohio and being the one black student in his class, the class poet, you *know* he spoke standard English. We tend to overlook all those poems he wrote in standard English and traditional verse. So, there's the balance between the two and, you know, a speakerly text may also be a very writerly text. . . .

LYN HEJINIAN

Lyn Hejinian (1941–) is a poet, essayist, and translator, born six months before the bombing of Pearl Harbor at the Alameda (California) Naval Base hospital. She grew up in the San Francisco Bay area in a middle-class family, both sides of which came to California in the 1840s. Both her parents were interested in modernist literature and art. Her mother was an amateur violinist and her father, who worked as an academic administrator, was an accomplished painter. Hejinian went to public schools through eighth grade, then to private high school and Radcliffe College/Harvard University. In 1976 Hejinian became editor of Tuumba Press, and from 1981 to 1999 she was the co-editor (with Barrett Watten) of *Poetics Journal*. She has traveled and lectured extensively in Russia as well as in Europe, and published two books of translations of contemporary Russian poet Arkadii Dragomoshchenko. Translations of her own work have been published in Denmark, France, Spain, Japan, Italy, Russia, Sweden, China, and Finland. She is married to musician-composer Larry Ochs and lives in Berkeley, where she is a professor in the English department at the University of California, Berkeley. In the fall of 2000, she was elected the sixty-sixth Fellow of the Academy of American Poets.

Hejinian's best-known book is the influential book-length prose poem *My Life*, which she first published in 1978, at the age of thirty-seven. The first edition is in thirty-seven sections of thirty-seven sentences each. At forty-five, she revised the book into forty-five sections of forty-five sentences each. Though *My Life* is clearly autobiographical, it uses the objects of life as occasions for internal meditation and consistently disrupts conventional syntax and meaning in order to engage the reader in a deeper, freeing awareness of language. Other works such as *Writing Is an Aid to Memory* (1978) and *The Cell* (1992) are less linguistically and poetically accessible. Hejinian's writing is philosophical and principally concerned with the ways that the self affects knowledge. Her many other books include *Leningrad* (written in collaboration with Michael Davidson, Ron Silliman, and Barrett Watten), *The Cold of Poetry*, and *Sight*, written in collaboration with Leslie Scalapino, as well as *A Border Comedy, Slowly*, and *The Beginner*. Her collection of essays *The Language of Inquiry* appeared in 2000. She has been involved in collaborative projects with painters, musicians, and filmmakers and has won numerous awards for her work. In the essay below, Hejinian rejects traditional roles of author, reader, and text in favor of an open-ended reading process that frees the elements of language from conventional roles.

from The Rejection of Closure

. . . What . . . is the fundamental necessity for openness? Or, rather, what is there in language itself that compels and implements the rejection of closure? . . .

Even words in storage, in the dictionary, seem frenetic with activity, as each individual entry attracts to itself other words as definition, example, and amplification. Thus, to open the dictionary at random, mastoid attracts nipple-like, temporal, bone, ear, and behind. Then turning to temporal we find that the definition includes time, space, life, world, transitory, and near the temples, but, significantly, not mastoid. . . .

In the gap between what one wants to say (or what one perceives there is to say) and what one can say (what is sayable), words provide for a collaboration and a desertion. We delight in our sensuous involvement with the materials of language, we long to join words to the world —to close the gap between ourselves and things, and we suffer from doubt and anxiety as to our capacity to do so because of the limits of language itself.

Yet the very incapacity of language to match the world allows it to do service as a medium of differentiation. The undifferentiated is one mass, the differentiated is multiple. The (unimaginable) complete text, the text that contains everything, would be in fact a closed text. It would be insufferable.

For me, a central activity of poetic language is formal. In being formal, in making form distinct, it opens—makes variousness and multiplicity and possibility articulate and clear. While failing in the attempt to match the world, we discover structure, distinction, the integrity and separateness of things.

RAFAEL CAMPO

Rafael Campo (1964–) was born in Dover, New Jersey, the son of a Cuban immigrant father and an Italian American mother. After graduating from Amherst College, he attended Harvard Medical School. Poet, physician, and translator, he is now on the faculty of Harvard Medical School and the Beth Israel Deaconess Medical Center, where his practice in internal medicine serves Latinos and people with AIDS. He is the author of four collections of poems: *The Other Man Was Me,* his first, won the 1993 National Poetry Series Award. *What the Body Told* won a Lambda Literary Award, and *Diva* was a finalist for the National Book Critics Circle Award.

He is, he tells us, in a long poem titled "In the Cuban Way" (from *Diva*) "compelled to sing in rhyme." But AIDS has been Campo's inspiration and nemesis, allowing him as physician a level of empathic communication with dying patients while as a human being he must still confront the ravages of the disease he cannot cure. In "The Changing Face of AIDS" (*Diva*) he provides the reader with an epidemiology of the disease. He examines the role of the press and the professors; he limns the multicultural melting pot to be found on Boston's "Center Street": "the art / of Africa, a lesbian cafe, / the Cuban-Puerto Rican mini-mart." Campo has also translated Federico García Lorca's homoerotic cycle *Sonetos del Amor Oscuro,* an homage to the Spanish poet's status as artist. In Campo's fourth collection, *Landscape with Human Figure,* he candidly explores his identity as a doctor and Cuban American gay man. The hybrid inner voice that he hears and articulates is a musical mix of Spanish and English.

Conscious of his disparate roots and the varied sources of his muse, Campo displays his technical mastery of form in the sonnet, villanelle, sestina, and pantoum—a dazzling array that nevertheless does not intimidate but rather confirms the role of poetry in our complex world. The essay that follows expresses the visceral pleasure this poet takes in conforming to, yet pressing against, the rules of the sonnet.

from Of the Sonnet and Paradoxical Beauties:
an interview with Joyce Wilson

. . . The reasons for my affinity to the sonnet are manifold. First, the sonnet has always stood at the imagined intersection of the romance languages and English (given its history)—as a bilingual writer, I've always longed for ways to make English sound somehow like Spanish, to re-create the musicality of my first language in my adopted tongue. Second, I find the erotics of the form terribly compelling—as a gay writer, I relish the paradox of claiming this traditional medium of the love song as my own, playing by the rules and yet crossing boundaries, and thus demonstrating that the rhythms and pleasures of lovemaking truly are universal. Lastly, I would say of the sonnet that no other way of writing poetry so completely mirrors what I discover in my patients occupying of their physical bodies—the undercurrent of iambs in the beating heart and breathing lungs, the gorgeousness of rhyme akin to dressing up the body in layers of clothes, the replication of the same patterns across centuries a kind of literary genetics.

. . . I don't think of what I'm doing as really "subverting" form—but in the tradition of Shakespeare or Donne, and in our era, Marilyn Hacker and Julia Alvarez, instead challenging the form to make room for a diversity of experiences and resonating voices. I love the idea of pressing against the walls of the narrow room of the sonnet form until my (intellectual) muscles ache, and I take great pleasure at the same time in obeying the rules that the form absolutely requires. I find that the friction creates a kind of heat that courses through the poems that result.

YUSEF KOMUNYAKAA

Yusef Komunyakaa (1947–) was born in Bogalusa, Louisiana, the oldest of six children. Contrary to popular assumptions, he is not a Muslim; his grandfather brought his unusual surname from Trinidad. Growing up as an African American in the '50s in a typical paper mill town in the South with its active Ku Klux Klan, Komunyakaa learned to cope with exclusion and racism by daydreaming his way, as he put it, "in far-off mental landscapes." He served in Vietnam as war correspondent of the military newspaper *Southern Cross* and was awarded the Bronze Star.

In 2001, Wesleyan University Press published *Pleasure Dome: New and Collected Poems*, which followed *Talking Dirty to the Gods* (2000) and *Thieves of Paradise* (1998), both finalists for the National Book Critics Circle Award, and *Neon Vernacular: New & Selected Poems 1977–1989*, for which he received the Pulitzer Prize and the Kingsley Tufts Poetry Award. *Dien Cai Dau* (1988), which means "crazy" in Vietnamese, published fourteen years after his tour of duty in Vietnam, tapped into the reservoir of his experiences there. The *Village Voice* wrote that "[the] poems grapple with the numbing violence of the war and with the frustrations of black soldiers in predominantly white platoons." Komunyakaa said that these images began to pour out as he stood on a ladder renovating his house in New Orleans. The essay reprinted here focuses on his carpentry skills and the rhythms of the hammer. He also published four earlier books of poems as well as a prose collection titled *Blues Notes: Essays, Interviews & Commentaries*.

Komunyakaa's highly original idiom is surrealistic, jazz-inspired, and often autobiographical. The music of Otis Redding and John Coltrane, Charlie Mingus and Thelonius Monk provides the backdrop for his twin emotions of despair and hope. In an interview he gave in 1990 (*Callaloo*), he said, "There's a sameness about American poetry. . . . It represents a poetry of the moment, a poetry of evasion, and I have problems with this. I believe poetry has always been political, long before poets had to deal with the page and white space." Komunyakaa was elected a chancellor of the Academy of American Poets in 1999. He is a professor in the Council of the Humanities and Creative Writing Program at Princeton University.

from Control Is the Mainspring

In spring of 1984 I found myself writing about my experiences and observations in Vietnam during 1969–70. The first three poems were "Somewhere near Phu Bai," "Starlight Scope Myopia," and "Missing in Action"; these poems seemed to have merely gushed out of me, and they surfaced with imagery that dredged up so much unpleasant psychic debris. All the guilt and anger coalesced into a confused stockpile of unresolved conflict. These poems were prompted by a need; they had fought to get out. I hadn't forgotten a single thread of evidence against myself.

However, I needed to slow down the pace of these volatile images since they were coming forth at such a panic-ridden haste. Something was happening to me, and I was afraid. I had purposefully evaded Vietnam-related literature and had seen only one "Vietnam War" movie, *Apocalypse Now,* about five years earlier in the pseudo-safety of southern California's Newport Beach. I remember leaving the movie house enraged—enraged at myself. But here I was in New Orleans, with the weight of the Old South pulsating underneath a thin facade, and I was readying myself to renovate an old house, 818 Piety Street, in the Bywater district. The ugly scars of history were all around me, and it became even more grotesque when moments of severe beauty showed through. Beneath the chipped and cracked horsehair plaster, the hundred-year-old oak slats looked new, untouched by mildew and ravages of poverty.

Those old houses have twelve- and fourteen-foot ceilings. The humid New Orleans summer had begun edging in, and I wanted to get the hard, high work finished first, where the stifling heat collected. I put a pad of paper and pen on a table in the next room. This had a purpose. The images were coming so fast that, whenever I made a trek down the ladder, each line had to be worth its weight in sweat. That spring and summer I must've discarded thousands of images, ones that just a few months earlier I would've given up a thumb for. I learned that the body and the mind are indeed connected: good writing is physical and men-tal. I welcomed the knowledge of this because I am from a working-class people who believe that physical labor is sacred and spiritual.

My great-grandfather Melvin had been a carpenter; so was my father, and they both taught me the value of tools—saws, hammers, chisels, files, rulers, etc. It all dealt with conciseness and precision. It eliminated guesswork. One has to know his tools, so he doesn't work against himself. Tools make the job easier. More accuracy.

At this time I started rereading some of the Negritude poets such as Aimé Césaire, Nicolas Guillen, Réné Depestre, Léopold Sédar Senghor, and Jacques Rabenmananjara. I was also coming closer to the imagistic narrative: a poem moved by images and the inherent music in language. I wrote during the day and read at night.

Perched on the top rung of the ladder, each step down served as a kind of metrical device—made me plan each word and syllable. In the background, at the other end of the house, in the kitchen, jazz pulsed underneath the whole day. Sometimes I worked twelve to twenty hours. I realized that language is man's first music, and, consequently, I began to approach the poem with this in mind. Again, I was hungry for the essence and magic of language, of how it connects the poet to listener, elated that it all centers around communication. I believe that the apprenticeship I served with my father and great-grandfather years earlier guided my hand as I wrote poetry that spring and summer in the Crescent City. The rhythm of my breath and work was the metronome dividing the words I committed to paper, as I used rasps and sandpaper to scrape the wood back to its earlier symmetry and perfection.

MARILYN NELSON

Marilyn Nelson (1946–) was born in Cleveland, Ohio, to Melvin M. Nelson, an Air Force officer and Tuskegee Airman, and Johnnie Mitchell Nelson, a teacher. Brought up on Air Force bases around the country, Nelson earned a BA from the University of California, Davis, a master's from the University of Pennsylvania (1970), and a PhD from the University of Minnesota (1979). Her books include *Carver: A Life in Poems* (2001), which won the Flora Stieglitz Straus Award and was a finalist for the National Book award, a Newbery Honor book, and a Coretta Scott King Honor book; *The Fields of Praise: New and Selected Poems* (1997), which was a finalist for the 1998 Lenore Marshall Poetry Prize, the 1997 National Book Award, and the PEN Winship Award; *Magnificat*, (1994); and *Fortune's Bones: The Manumission Requiem* (1994). *The Homeplace* (1990) won the 1992 Annisfield-Wolf Award and was a finalist for the 1991 National Book Award. She has also published two collections of verse for children: *The Cat Walked through the Casserole and Other Poems for Children* (with Pamela Espeland, 1984) and Halfdan Rasmussen's *Hundreds of Hens and Other Poems for Children* (1982), which she translated from Danish with Pamela Espeland. Her honors include two creative writing fellowships from the National Endowment for the Arts, a Fulbright Teaching Fellowship, the 1990 Connecticut Arts Award, and a Guggenheim Fellowship. From 1978 until 2002 she taught at the University of Connecticut, Storrs, from which she retired as professor of English in order to take a senior position at the University of Delaware. In 2004 she returned to the University of Connecticut to teach half-time and to direct Soul Mountain Retreat, a small writer's colony.

Nelson's poetry ranges from low to high diction, from artless free verse to finely wrought sonnets. Her virtuoso crowns of sonnets, "Thus Far by Faith" and "Wreath for Emmett Till," combine her passionate interests in African American history and in traditional poetic forms. Her approach to rhyme and meter import the techniques of the blues and jazz: loosely improvisatory slant rhymes, syncopated rhythms. Some of her best work evokes a deep contemplative silence, hiding mystery in near transparency, revealing through intimate and prosaic details a luminous and powerful vision. In 2001 she began a five-year appointment as Poet Laureate of Connecticut.

from Owning the Masters

I came of age as a reader of poetry during the early Sixties; the first contemporary poet I really read was LeRoi Jones. I was terribly moved by his public declaration, made in the middle of that tumultuous decade, of his decision to write against the white literary tradition, which he so clearly loved. Jones was a melancholy confessional Negro aesthete, confused in his identity, part of a new lost generation which called itself "Beat." He made a sudden about-face in about 1964, and changed his name and his style to become the poet of Black Nationalist rage. . . .

Though I was too timid and too thoroughly assimilated to follow Jones [subsequently Amiri Baraka] and other writers of the late Negro period into the literary separatism they called the Black Aesthetic, my heart went out to this struggling generation, and I think I felt my own perhaps toned-down version of the pain of their self-seeking. But Baraka's generation threw out the baby with the bathwater. In their single-minded quest for a revolutionary poetry they paid a great personal and artistic cost. . . .

How can a poet survive such a radical self-amputation? How can a poet survive without tradition? . . .

Though I'm embarrassed to ally myself with the forces of white old-dead boyism, I must confess that the title which came to me for this paper ("Owning the Masters") led me immediately to remember some MFA students I've had, who knew every poem in every book by whoever was pictured on the front page of the latest issue of a big-time little magazine, but drew a blank when I mentioned Matthew Arnold. Maybe they read "Dover Beach" in a class once? Oh, yeah: that Matthew Arnold. Student poets whose entire sense of the tradition was drawn from *The Norton Anthology,* shorter edition. Student poets who were never curious, or empassioned, or even angry enough to study the corpus of a dead white male poet. Student poets who measure themselves against each other and the pages of the latest issues of one or two literary journals, instead of against the old masters of our tradition.

Our tradition. I say this feeling like a woman wearing an ivory necklace and a mink coat at a national convention of Humans for Ethical Treatment of Animals. I know, I know: The tradition is the oppressor. The tradition doesn't include me because I'm black and woman. . . .

No writer wants to be treated as if she had grown up in an intellectual ghetto. But the fact is that Aframerican writers do grow up in a double tradition, savoring the words of Dunbar, Cullen, Johnson, McKay, Hughes, Brown, Hayden, and Brooks as well as those of the old dead white guys who've looked down on us from a tradition our old dead brown guys weren't allowed to enter for a long, long time. We are heirs of an alternate tradition, heirs of slave narratives, spirituals, great orators, jazz and blues. Yet the once enslaved are heirs to the masters, too. . . .

Many of my people—blacks, women—argue that we have no place in the tradition, because it excludes us. One of their problems with tradition is that they believe we're born into tradition the way we're born into gender and race. If your parents were Serbs, you're a Serb, and Serbs hate Croats. If you're a Hutu, you hate the Tutsi. It's one warlord against another out there, folks, and some of us want to play Hatfields and McCoys in the literary world, too. If you're a new formalist, you don't read free verse. If you're an Aframerican woman, you don't read Paul Celan. Elizabeth Barrett Browning says nothing to you about love if you're gay; *Paradise Lost* is an offense to womyn. Each group wants to redefine the tradition in its own image. . . .

Too often we ignore the fact that tradition is process. Believing that tradition is created in retrospect, we turn over boulders, stones, and pebbles in tireless quest of, for example, the unknown, unpublished great black lesbian poet of the Seventeenth Century. No doubt someday someone will find her, and that discovery will force us to make new maps of the literary landscape. But it will change not the landscape of the Seventeenth Century, but that of the generation which discovers her. For tradition, as process, is formed as we go forward. There is no doubling back, no taking that other fork in the road, no rewinding the tape. Some politically correct textbook editors have wanted to rewind and edit the tape, banning, for instance, the use of the word "slave," preferring instead the term "enslaved person." But no amount of politically correct sensitivity to potentially hurt feelings will erase the fact that African slavery played an essential role in the history and psychology of the New World. As, we must also admit, did the genocidal wars against Red injuns, or Indians, or American Indians, or Native Americans, or natives. As did the white man's war against the natural world. It has to do with time: Our tradition is what we inherit, not what we create.

Perhaps the tradition we pass on will be superior to the one that got dumped into our laps. Though I doubt it. One thing we can be sure of: It will be different. Our tradition is our shared understanding of encoded meanings, the history of our words. . . .

I don't believe the pleasures of poetry can be dissected and explained. But one of the pleasures of poetry must surely be its ability to give us a sense of community: We think along with someone else; the boundaries between two minds come down. And form itself is communal; it is, as Thomas Byers writes, ". . . one of the ways in which the poem participates in poetic, social, and historical dialogue." So a poem written with an ear to tradition enables us to think and sing along with many other minds: to join a sort of intergenerational silent interior Mormon Tabernacle Choir.

I'm convinced our inclination to create race-, gender- and ethnic-specific literary enclaves is dangerous; that it disinvites us from community. The Angloamerican tradition belongs to all of us, or should. As does the community into which the tradition invites us. That means the metrical tradition, too. . . .

"The master's tools will never dismantle the master's house," writes Audre Lorde in *Sister Outsider*. But why should we dismantle the house? Why toss the baby over the porch railing, with its bassinetteful of soapy water? Why don't we instead take possession of, why don't we own, the tradition? Own the masters, all of them. Wordsworth and Wheatley, Hughes, Auden. As we own the masters and learn to use more and more levels of this language we love, for whose continued evolution we share responsibility, the signifiers become ours. We must not stand, like trembling slaves, at the back door of the master's house. We must recognize, as Cornelius Eady does in a poem called "Gratitude," that "I am a brick in a house / that is being built / around your house." . . .

LISA ROBERTSON

Canadian writer Lisa Robertson (1961–)was born in Toronto and raised in a family of four children near Newmarket, Ontario. She migrated to British Columbia in 1979 in order to become a tree planter, a camp cook, then a bookseller, and was educated at Simon Fraser University and the Kootenay School of Writing, a collectively organized, writer-run center in Vancouver. She now lives in Paris and works as a freelance writer and teacher. Among the writers she says have influenced her work are Gertrude Stein, Djuna Barnes, Phyllis Webb, Lyn Hejinian, Dodie Bellamy, John Cage, Samuel Beckett, Erin Moure, and Denise Riley.

Robertson has published three books of poetry: *XEclogue, Debbie: An Epic* and *The Weather*. Each of these books is composed as a long poem, and explores the history and formal patterning of a classical literary genre (pastoral, epic, and georgic) from a contemporary, avant-garde influenced, and specifically feminist perspective. Her 2004 book, *Occasional Works and Seven Walks from the Office for Soft Architecture* is a linked series of prose walks and essays on city space, architecture, and the phenomenology of surfaces. This book explores the essay form in open relation to both prose poem and research paper, and stems from an ongoing practice of discussion and collaboration with visual artists.

Robertson also writes essays and reviews on poetry and essays on the visual arts. In the essay printed here, a preface to a "pastoral" poem, she explains her postmodern use of a form considered by some to be out of date. Her poetry has been awarded the Relit Award for Poetry, and she has taught at the University of Cambridge, the University of California at San Diego, and at Capilano College, North Vancouver.

from How Pastoral: A Manifesto

I wanted a form as obsolete yet necessary as the weather. I begin with the premise that pastoral, as a literary genre, is obsolete—originally obsolete. Once a hokey territory sussed by a hayseed diction, now the mawkish artificiality of the pastoral poem's constructed surface has settled down to a backyard expressivity. In the postpastoral poem (in evidence since the

English romantics and their modernist successors) the evocation of "feeling" in poet or reader obeys a parallel planting of "nature" in the poem. Translate backyard utopia as political mythology. Appearing to serve a personally expressive function, the vocabulary of nature screens a symbolic appropriation of the Land. Her cut sublimity grafts to the Human. I'd call pastoral the nation-making genre: within a hothouse language we force the myth of the Land to act as both political resource and mystic origin. A perversely topical utopia has always been the duped by-product of the ideology that blindly describes, thus possesses, a landscape in which people are imagined to be at peace with the economics of production and consumption. The dream of Liberty poses itself within the specificity of this utopian landscape. Certainly on this five-hundredth anniversary of the so-called New World, we must acknowledge that the utopian practice of Liberty stands now as a looming representation of degrading and humiliating oppressions to the (pastoral) majority and that pastoral utopias have efficiently aestheticized and naturalized the political practices of genocide, misogyny, and class and race oppression. I consider that now pastoral's obvious obsolescence may offer a hybrid discursive potential to those who have been traditionally excluded from Utopia. To begin with, we must recognize Utopia as an accretion of nostalgias with no object other than the historiography of the imaginary. But do not assume the imaginary to be merely the fey playground of children and the doomed. Consider that the imaginary generates landscapes for political futures. To people these landscapes with our own desires and histories, we must implement pastoral as a seedy generic artifice and deny it the natural and hegemonic position of political ideology.

Historically, from Virgil to Spenser to Goldsmith, the pastoral poem narrated the exigencies of land tenure, labor's relation to the state and capital, and the establishment of a sense of place as a ground for philosophical and aesthetic being and discourse. The trajectory of the pastoral poem has prepared a self-congratulatory site for the reproduction of power. We can follow this trajectory from Virgil's gorgeously ambivalent justification of the Roman Empire to the Elizabethan articulation of imperial utopias, Augustan parallels between English and classical pleasures of enlightenment, and late-eighteenth-century evocations of nostalgia for agricultural capitalism. "Beauty" clinched pastoral's edifying function. The quaint archaisms of the language, the dainty evocations of

springtime pleasures, the innocent characterization of the indolent shepherd: these niceties etched the pleasures of the genre as irrevocably sensual, masking imperialist ideology or at least couching it in the banalities
of conquest and repose. Yet the irony of loss remained the pastoral's central trope. The difficulties and pleasures of maintaining a primary, legal,
and productive entitlement to the land provided the pastoral subject since
Virgil's first eclogue politicized the theocratic idyll: "You, Tityrus, lie
under your spreading breech's covert, wooing the woodland Muse on
slender reed, but we are leaving our country's bounds and sweet fields.
We are outcasts from our country; you Tityrus, as ease beneath the shade,
teach the woods to re-echo 'fair Amaryllis.'"

Certainly, as a fin de siecle feminist, I cannot in good conscience perform even the simplest political identification with the pastoral genre.
Within its scope women have been reduced to a cipher for the produc-
tively harnessed land within a legally sanctioned system of exchange. In
pastoral the figure of woman appears as eroticized worker—the milk-
maid or shepherdess swoons in an unproblematic ecstasy with the land.
Moreover, she is pleased to give over her youthful presocial wildness to
the domesticating and enclosed tenure of the marriage contract. This
contract often gives occasion to the celebratory epithalamium, one of
the many possible moments in the pastoral montage. Pastoral plants the
agency of women's desire firmly within the patriarchal frame. And so
it is with a masochistic embarrassment that I confess to having been
seduced by the lure of archaic pleasures. Prime among these twist the
convoluted interleavings of those beckoning and luscious tropes, femininity and nature. Yet I shall release them from their boredom. . . .

GERTRUDE STEIN

Gertrude Stein (1874–1946) was born in Allegheny, Pennsylvania, where her parents, the children of German Jewish immigrants, owned a clothing store. After her birth, the family moved, first to Vienna, then to Paris, and finally to Oakland, California, when Gertrude, the youngest child, was five. Both of her parents died before she was eighteen. While she did not graduate from high school, she read widely on her own, and when her brother Leo went to Harvard, Stein was accepted at Radcliffe. There she studied with William James and graduated magna cum laude in philosophy. Although she attended Johns Hopkins Medical School, where she published essays about the effect of fatigue on the brain's attention span, Stein chose not to continue because of conflicts with the male faculty members over women's role in medicine. She moved to Paris and lived for nine years with her brother Leo, who had become an art critic and there, in 1912, met her lifelong partner, Alice B. Toklas. During World War II they remained in occupied France; their life there is central to Toklas's classic and only work, *The Alice B. Toklas Cookbook*. Stein died of cancer in 1946 in Paris.

Stein and her brother were among the first collectors of works by painters Picasso, Matisse, Braque, and others, and in Paris Stein hosted highly influential salons for these artists and expatriate writers. In her writing, especially *Tender Buttons* (1914), she attempted to replicate the effects of Cubist painting, concentrating on the present moment and using numerous slightly varied repetitions, simple elements (words), and a fragmented style. Her other works include *Three Lives* (1909), which focuses on three working-class women; the epic and difficult work *The Making of Americans* (written 1906–8, but not published until 1925); *Composition and Explanation* (1926), based on lectures about her theories of writing at Oxford and Cambridge; and the operas *Four Saints in Three Acts* and *The Mother of Us All,* based on the life of Susan B. Anthony, both with music by Virgil Thompson. *Wars I Have Seen* (1945) and *Brewsie and Willie* (1946) concern World War II. Stein's autobiography, called *The Autobiography of Alice B. Toklas* (1933), brought her the widest popular recognition, though she has entered the language most indelibly with the koan-like tautology "A rose is a rose is a rose is a rose." Stein is arguably the modernist writer who worked most radically with language, and her work had a huge influence on experimental poetry of the late twentieth century. "Patriarchal Poetry" uses repetition, rhyme, and syntactic fragmentation to defamiliarize and undermine the linguistic certainties and power structures of traditional poetics and to place words within a new, more liberating framework.

from Patriarchal Poetry

. . . How is it to be rest to be receiving rest to be how like it rest to be receiving to be like it. Compare something else to something else. To be a rose,

> Such a pretty bird.
>
> Not to such a pretty bird. Not to not to not to not to such a pretty bird.
>
> Not to such a pretty bird.
>
> Not to such a pretty bird.
>
> As to as such a pretty bird. As to as to as such a pretty bird.
>
> To and such a pretty bird.
>
> And to and such a pretty bird.
>
> And to as to not to as to and such a pretty bird.

. . . Was it a fish was heard was it a bird was it a cow was stirred was it a third was it a cow was stirred was it a third was it a bird was heard was it a third was it a fish was heard was it a third. Fishes a bird cows were stirred a bird fishes were heard a bird cows were stirred a third. A third is all. Come too.

Patriarchal means suppose patriarchal means and close patriarchal means and chose chose Monday Patriarchal means in close some day patriarchal means and chose chose Sunday patriarchal means and chose chose one day patriarchal means and close close Tuesday. Tuesday is around Friday and welcomes as welcomes not only a cow but introductory. This always patriarchal as sweet.

Patriarchal make it ready.

Patriarchal in investigation and renewing of an intermediate rectification of the initial boundary between cows and fishes. Both are admittedly not inferior in which case they may be obtained as the result of organisation industry concentration assistance and matter of fact and by this this is their chance and to appear and to reunite as to their date and their estate. They have been in no need of stretches stretches of their especial and apart and here now.

Favored by the by favored by let it by the by favored by the by. Patriarchal poetry and not meat on Monday patriarchal poetry and meat on Tuesday. Patriarchal poetry and venison on Wednesday Patriarchal poetry and fish on Friday Patriarchal poetry and birds on Sunday Patriarchal poetry and chickens on Tuesday patriarchal poetry and beef on Thursday. Patriarchal poetry and ham on Monday patriarchal poetry and pork on Thursday patriarchal poetry and beef on Tuesday patriarchal poetry and fish on Wednesday Patriarchal poetry and eggs on Thursday patriarchal poetry and carrots on Friday patriarchal poetry and extras on Saturday patriarchal poetry and venison on Sunday Patriarchal poetry and lamb on Tuesday patriarchal poetry and jellies on Friday patriarchal poetry and turkeys on Tuesday.

They made hitherto be by and by. . . .

. . . It can easily be returned ten when this, two might it be too just inside, not as if chosen: not as if chosen that not as if chosen, withal if it had been known to be going to be here and this needed to be as as green. This is what has been brought here.

Once or two makes that be not at all practically their choice practically their choice.

Might a bit of it be all the would be might be if a bit of it be all they would be if it if it would be all be if it would be a bit of all of it would be, a very great difference between making money peaceably and making money peaceably a great difference between making money making money peaceably making money peaceably making money peaceably.

Reject rejoice rejuvenate rejuvenate rejoice reject rejoice rejuvenate reject rejuvenate reject rejoice. Not as if it was tried. How kindly they receive the the then there this at all.

In change.

Might it be while it is not as it is undid undone to be theirs awhile yet. Not in their mistake which is why it is not after or not further in at all to their cause, Patriarchal poetry partly. In an as much to be in exactly their measure. Patriarchal poetry partly. . . .

ANNIE FINCH

Annie Finch was born in 1956 in New Rochelle, New York. She studied poetry and poetry writing at Yale, verse-drama with Ntozake Shange at the University of Houston's graduate creative writing program, and earned a PhD in English and American literature from Stanford University. She currently directs the Stonecoast Masters of Fine Arts program in creative writing at the University of Southern Maine.

Finch's books of poetry include *Eve, Calendars,* and *The Encyclopedia of Scotland,* as well as a translation of the *Complete Poems of Louise Labé.* Her musical collaborations include two opera librettos, "Lily Among the Goddesses" and "Marina," based on the life of Russian poet Marina Tsvetaeva, which premiered in New York in 2003.

Her writings on poetry have been collected in *The Ghost of Meter* and *The Body of Poetry: Essays on Women, Form, and the Poetic Self.* Finch has also edited several groundbreaking popular anthologies including *A Formal Feeling Comes* and *An Exaltation of Forms: Contemporary Poets Celebrate the Diversity of Their Art.*

Uniting all of Finch's work is a conception of poetry as essentially incantatory, performative, speaking to the body as much as to the mind. The themes of her poems draw upon earth-centered spirituality, myth, sex, and childbirth, and her poetry is inspired by the natural world, especially the landscapes of Maine, where she resides with her husband the environmentalist Glen Brand and her two children Althea and Julian.

In the essay from *The Body of Poetry* excerpted below, Finch balances her concerns with decentering subjectivity as a postmodern feminist poet with her political commitment to accessible language.

from Coherent Decentering:
Towards a New Model of the Poetic Self

Like many contemporary writers, I find the Romantic poetic construct of the fixed, central self and its point of view to be extraordinarily limited. Whether or not one accepts the Buddhist insight that the true self is a non-self, unconnected to transitory thoughts and emotions, if we look closely we are not likely to perceive our selves as discrete entities. . . .

I now see language as a Place where the poetic self can dissolve without throwing the world the poem represents into chaos. I appreciate poems that "problematize" the self, to use one common critical term, rather than pretending that the selves of the speaker of the poem and its reader are simple, solid entities. But, as the deconstructionists argue, the most apparently coherent syntax does not really create a simple point of view. And conversely, the usual avant-garde markers of the decentered poetic self—disjointed syntax, floating margins, random signifiers, clashing dictions, collage structure and found language, shifting or unidentifiable points of view—are, it needs to be said, literary conventions themselves. I believe that when contemporary poets disrupt syntax to convey the decentered self, it is the world, not the self, that they are representing as incoherent.

The incoherent worldview that is a *sine qua non* of much contemporary avant-garde poetics can be viewed as a direct descendant of the Romantic notion that Truth is a distant, absolute, and unreachable goal that is best approximated through some kind of "systematic derangement of the senses." . . .

The more I developed my poetic approach to subjectivity, the more the idea of the self as the point of reference around which everything else revolves—the lone conscious subjectivity in an objectified world— seemed wrong to me as person and poet. . . . Years later, when I began to study feminist poetics, I recognized the feminist critique of the traditional Romantic self of lyric poetry. I loved Keats, but I couldn't put my own lyric voice in that position with a straight face. As a woman, I knew too much about how it feels to be something—nightingale, urn, woman—that is an object in other people's eyes. . . .

Once I became more aware of poststructuralist theory and postmodern literary conventions, I experimented with pastiche and fragmented syntax in an attempt to convey the decentered self. But the more

I worked with language, the more I wanted to accept all of its common limitations. An effective shaman is able to return from a vision and live normally, to talk coherently and do business intelligently, to follow laws appropriate to each world. It seemed to me the strongest strategy was to work within the honestly conventional and artificial constraints of the language, twisting and turning their qualities to my advantage, rather than to pretend that those constraints didn't exist. . . .

A truism of today's avant-garde poetics is . . . that a fragmentary and disjointed style, defying the common mechanisms and necessities of language, is the only way to avoid positing a false unified self. This largely unexamined belief is one of the key dividing points between experimental and mainstream poetics. One of the tasks of my poems and criticism is to explore a third possibility: that . . . the decentered, multiple point of view . . . can thrive in the "mechanisms" of syntactic coherence—arguably the most crucial and uncompromising "necessity" of language.

The coherent methods of decentering the lyric self that I have explored include: syntactic density and innuendo; lexical and metaphorical subtext; and the questioning of "objects" and use of multiple speakers. Most of all, I have found my tools in the defamiliarizing representation of conspicuous word and sound patterns, or "form." When I began to write in patterns, I found a nonverbal vocabulary of coherent decentering and vatic containment that could channel the balance of energy and form, chaos and pattern, which I felt in nature and in language. . . .

I am aware that my method of coherent decentering substitutes one set of literary conventions for another. But for me it has two advantages over the accepted avant-garde practice. First, it avoids the mistake of confusing a fragmented worldview for a decentered self, and so it feels truer to my deepest experiences in nature. Second, it accepts consciously the artificial and contingent nature of language. All poems, however incoherent their syntax, posit a central self or speaker because poems are made of language. By defying common syntax, a fragmented poem focuses the reader's attention even more intently toward meaning-making. A coherently decentered poem, by contrast, respects the boundaries of common syntax and thereby addresses the reader's inevitable need for coherence— while, at the same time, pushing the boundaries of syntax so far that the reader's self may become unmoored, floating free within the confines of the poem.

PART 3

Mapping

EMILY DICKINSON

#448

This was a Poet—It is That

This was a Poet—It is That
Distills amazing sense
From ordinary Meanings—
An Attar so immense

From the familiar species
That perished by the Door—
We wonder it was not Ourselves
Arrested it—before—

Of pictures, the Discloser—
The Poet—it is He—
Entitles Us—by Contrast—
To ceaseless Poverty

Of Portion—so unconscious—
The Robbing—could not harm—
Himself—to Him—a Fortune—
Exterior—to Time—

Mapping

For the anonymous bard of tenth-century Iceland, the poet's role in society is clear: to keep history alive by telling the tales of great deeds, on behalf of the military leaders who support poetry with their patronage. The power of poetry to map out a place of living language in the face of death and oblivion is also a crucial aspect of its importance for Shakespeare in the Elizabethan era: "When wasteful war shall statues overturn, / And broils root out the work of masonry."

Poetry has always been a touchstone in the face of death or transience or the mutability that comes with upheaval. In the Romantic period Shelley, the first to name the poet as an "unacknowledged legislator," argues that "A man . . . must put himself in the place of another and many others; the pains and pleasures of his species must become his own. The great instrument of moral good is the imagination. . . . poetry is the root and blossom of all other systems of thought." Responding to him, Thomas Love Peacock asserts that "a poet . . . is a semi-barbarian in a civilized community. . . . The march of his intellect is like that of a crab backward." Their quarrel demonstrates how vividly oppositional two highly regarded poets can be while still holding poetry at the center of their universe. As Dickinson says, it takes a poet to "distill amazing sense / From ordinary Meanings."

The Victorian Matthew Arnold, in one of the most influential apologias of his time, defends the poet's role in the larger society: "more and more, mankind will discover that we have to turn to poetry to interpret life for us. . . . Without poetry, our science will appear incomplete; and most of what now passes with us for religion and philosophy will be replaced by poetry." Perhaps the most uncanonical poet in the history of American letters, Walt Whitman, despite writing in the dark years of the Civil War, is one of our most Dionysian and ecstatic poets. Superb and banal in the same stanza, Whitman is the spokesman for expanding America, in his role as self-appointed public poet celebrating every state and occupation. His inheritor, Muriel Rukeyser, shares Whitman's extremes of writing and his stance as public conscience. After being evacuated from Spain, she wrote extensively about the civil war there and lobbied on behalf of the Spanish Republicans. She wrote without regard for political or aesthetic theory, her freedom as a poet demanding fidelity to her own imagination and experience as an international non-partisan pacifist.

Vietnam War activist Denise Levertov also may have accomplished Arnold's aim by bringing together poetry and political action, a phenomenon we see taking place around us today. When Levertov is asked if she feels that she and other poets are "betraying [their] work as poets when [they] participate in sit-ins, marching in the streets, helping to write leaflets, talking to people about capitalism, Imperialism, racism, male chauvinism, oppression of all kinds," she answers, "we must fulfill the poet's total involvement in life in this aspect also."

But no one displays the growing certitude of this linkage more boldly than Gwendolyn Brooks. In a 1979 interview, Brooks, discussing her poetry with Steve Cape for *The Artful Dodge,* describes her chronological journey from self-expression to a stage in which her poems sought the goal of integration and finally to a black poetry written by, about, and to blacks. Moreover, the African writer Aimé Césaire fiercely asserts "that Europe for centuries has stuffed us with lies and swollen us with pestilence." Nobel Prize–winner Derek Walcott explains that for him poetry blends inescapably the personal and the political, keeping the language of the Caribbean alive within with his individual voice: "There is the buried language and there is the individual vocabulary, and the process of poetry is one of excavation and of self-discovery."

While for political poets, it is important for poetry to make sense and get a political message to an audience, for many contemporary poets, the responsibility of poetry is somewhat different. Some see poetry's mission as making a different kind of sense in a world of increasingly commodified and commercialized language. In a well-known essay, "The Obscurity of the Poet" from *Poetry and the Age,* Randall Jarrell points out that the common belief is that poetry is not read because it is difficult, but perhaps instead it is difficult because it is not read. Taking the argument one step further, Howard Nemerov explains that all poetry does not intend to communicate, and that if poetry were too accessible, that would be a sign of a weakening in the art. Nemerov would no doubt have agreed with contemporary experimental poet Charles Bernstein, who makes a convincing argument against the popular recent notion, National Poetry Month, on the same grounds.

Perhaps it is fair to say that poetry has most traditionally been both accessible AND difficult, common AND special, generally useful AND obscure. In non-literate societies, poetry often has a shamanic or spiritual function. After all, the technology of poetry developed to aid memorization before the invention of writing. Poetic language patterns give extra power to words that are used to heal, to invoke, to bless, and to remember ancestors and events. The nineteenth-century African poem "The Dead Man Asks for a Song" reminds us of poetry's connection with ritual and with accessing other states of mind, other worlds, through the combination of meaningful language and repeating rhythm. For poems to work as needed in a traditional culture, they must be able to enter daily life, but in a uniquely powerful way.

Perhaps because of poetry's long association with such supposedly primitive ways of looking at the world, the apparent conflict between poetry and science was an important challenge in the early twentieth century and gave rise to a long-running debate that still has important implications. As Muriel Rukeyser makes clear, poetry is not necessarily opposed to science and the logical view of the world. Still, poetry plays many opposing roles at once: to confound, to illuminate, to help keep us alive, and to reconcile us with death. Perhaps the embrace of such oppositions is the best way for poetry to offer a map of our condition.

ANONYMOUS

"Egil's Saga," sometimes called "Egla," was originally an oral poem, passed down from generation to generation of Icelandic poets for many centuries through memorization alone. It was finally written down between the twelfth and thirteenth centuries, possibly by Einar Skulason or by Snorri Sturluson, who is known to have recorded other similar poems. A tradition of oral poetry has existed in tribal cultures all over the world, from *Beowulf* in Britain to the *Iliad* in Greece to the *Kalevala* in Finland to *Mubila* in Zaire to the *Bhagavad-Gita* in India. Though oral epics can take days to recite, their strong rhythm and repeating metrical phrases make it possible for young poets to learn them by heart during years of apprenticeship and then to perform their own unique versions with their own creative changes.

Like many oral epics, the Icelandic Sagas have been a key source of pride and national identity among their people for centuries. The sagas describe supernatural events and political intrigues with humor and a blunt, succinct style. They narrate in great detail the settling of Iceland by political exiles, their pioneering industries of farming, fishing, whaling, and egg-gathering and their feasts and entertainment, magic and spells. Some of the passages are in prose and others in a highly complex and artificial poetic style. Like the meter of Anglo-Saxon poetry, Old Icelandic meter is insistent. It is based on the number of accents in each line and does not rhyme. Instead, the lines are held together by the alliteration of two or three initial word-sounds within every line. Since alliteration is more important than syntax, word order is often convoluted. The poems are filled with "kennings," concise metaphorical names, such as "wound-snake" for a sword, "sea-swan" for a ship, "song-pounder" for a tongue. "Egil's Saga" tells the many adventures of Egil Skallagrimsson, who grew up in Borg-a-Myrar and became a great poet and warrior, traveling widely in Scandinavia, Britain, and the Baltic. This passage describes the heroic approach to life in pre-Christian times: since "fame" and a good reputation among those to come were the chief value in life, the poet—as the only carrier of stories into the future—held enormous power.

from Egil's Saga

By sun and moon
I journeyed west,
My sea-borne tune
From Odin's breast,
My song-ship packed
With poet's art:
Its word-keel cracked
The frozen heart.

And now I feed
With an English king:
So to English mead
I'll word-mead bring,
Your praise my task,
My song your fame,
If you but ask
I'll sound your name.

These praises, King,
Won't cost you dear
That I shall sing
If you will hear:
Who beat and blazed
Your trail of red,
Till Odin gazed
Upon the dead.

The scream of swords,
The clash of shields,
These are true words
On battlefields:

Man sees his death
But Erik's breath
Frees battle-streams.

      *   *   *

And now my lord,
You've listened long
As word on word
I built this song:
Your source is war,
Your streams are blood,
But my springs pour
Great Odin's flood.

To praise my lord
This tight mouth broke
The word-floods poured,
The still tongue spoke,
From my poet's breast
These words took wing:
Now all the rest
May learn to sing.

WILLIAM SHAKESPEARE

William Shakespeare (1564–1616) was born in Stratford-upon-Avon, England. Although little is known of his early life, he is thought to have attended the local grammar school, which offered a sound classical education in Latin and Greek. At eighteen, he married Anne Hathaway. Their first child was born the following year, fraternal twins two years later. The first boy's early death at age eleven is thought to be the occasion for the lines in "King John" that begin "Grief fills the room of my absent child."

Around 1585 Shakespeare began his acting career, but because of the outbreak of the plague, the theaters were often shut down between 1592 and 1594. During this period he received patronage from the Earl of Southhampton and wrote two long narrative poems, *Venus and Adonis* and *The Rape of Lucrece*. His imaginative and sensual retelling of the story of Venus and Adonis was so popular that it was reprinted six times. In 1594 Shakespeare joined the Lord Chamberlain's acting troupe, which was highly acclaimed at Court; five years later, some of its members had the now-famous Globe theater designed and built.

Shakespeare was the foremost playwright of the Elizabethan age. He authored thirty plays: histories, comedies, tragedies, and romances. The tragedies, which include *Romeo and Juliet, Julius Caesar, Hamlet, Othello*, and *King Lear*, were for the most part written in the middle period of his career. His sonnets appear to have been written between 1593 and 1601, although they were not published until 1609. They were to leave an indelible mark on literature, establishing the form of three quatrains followed by a closing couplet composed in iambic pentameter known as Shakespearean or Elizabethan. Not much notice was taken of the sonnets until the last years of the eighteenth century. Even then, they were initially read not for art but in hopes of providing clues to the poet's life. Critics tend to divide them into two groups: sonnets 1–126 are addressed to a beloved friend, possibly a nobleman, and sonnets 127–152, addressed to the so-called Dark Lady, whose identity has been a puzzle for scholars ever since. The sonnet included here promises to immortalize the poet's beloved beyond the fame offered by statues or buildings. Shakespeare's sonnets almost invariably address the erosion of time and the longing for immortal beauty and love. The view of poetry as a means of conquering time derives from Spenser and was common in the Renaissance.

Sonnet LV

Not marble, nor the gilded monuments
Of Princes, shall out-live this powerful rhyme;
But you shall shine more bright in these contents
Than unswept stone besmeer'd with sluttish time.
When wasteful war shall statues overturn,
And broils root out the work of masonry,
Nor Mars his sword, nor war's quick fire shall burn
The living record of your memory.
'Gainst death and all-oblivious enmity
Shall you pace forth; your praise shall still find room
Even in the eyes of all posterity
That wear this world out to the ending doom.
    So, till the judgment that yourself arise,
    You live in this, and dwell in lovers' eyes.

THOMAS LOVE PEACOCK

Thomas Love Peacock (1785–1866), the only son of a London glass merchant who died when Peacock was three, grew up in his grandfather's house. His formal education ended when he was thirteen, but by then he was fluent in Greek and Latin and had become an omnivorous reader. An autodidact, he continued to study and broaden his knowledge of the arts. He entered the employ of the East India Company in 1818 and shortly after married Jane Griffith. When their third daughter died, Jane Peacock suffered a severe depression from which she never fully recovered. Although Peacock continued to work for the company until 1856—his supervisor was the father of John Stuart Mill—the position apparently allowed him ample time to write. As a poet, he wrote some neoclassical romantic pieces, but was at his best as a social satirist, keenly aware of the discrepancies between the well-to-do and the working poor. For example, his poem "A Bill for the Better Promotion of Oppression on the Sabbath Day" contains these lines: "And forasmuch as the laws heretofore / Have not sufficiently squeezed the poor / Be it therefore enacted by Commons, King / And Lords, a crime for any thing / To be done on the Sabbath by any rank / Excepting the rich. . . ."

Peacock was the author of seven novels, the first of which was *Headlong Hall (1816),* a so-called discussion novel in which conversation satirizing the ideals of the Romantic movement established a genre that proved successful and set the pattern for his subsequent works. In 1812 he met Shelley, and there ensued a warm lifetime relationship, often marked by friendly antagonism. He was a close friend of both of Shelley's wives, and Shelley appointed him his literary executor. Peacock's novels, frequently with historical settings, are best known for their comic discussions in which he lightheartedly satirized such mainstream writers as Byron, Coleridge, Wordsworth, and Shelley himself. Peacock's satirical essay on the value of poetry, excerpted here, provoked Shelley's famous *Defence of Poetry;* he argued that poets would be more usefully employed if they abandoned their muses and immersed themselves in the new sciences. Shelley's rebuttal claimed that poetry is always a force for the social good, that such poets as Chaucer and Milton are "the unacknowledged legislators of the World." Peacock's essay deserves close reading. He goes from tongue-in-cheek comments to some that are intended to be taken seriously.

from The Four Ages of Poetry

. . . A poet in our times is a semi-barbarian in a civilized community. He lives in the days that are past. His ideas, thoughts, feelings, associations, are all with barbarous manners, obsolete customs, and exploded superstitions. The march of his intellect is like that of a crab, backward. The brighter the light diffused around him by the progress of reason, the thicker is the darkness of antiquated barbarism in which he buries himself like a mole. . . . The philosophic mental tranquility which looks round with an equal eye on all external things, collects a store of ideas, discriminates their relative value, assigns to all their proper place, and from the materials of useful knowledge thus collected, appreciated, and arranged, forms new combinations that impress the stamp of their power and utility on the real business of life, is diametrically the reverse of that frame of mind which poetry inspires, or from which poetry can emanate. The highest inspirations of poetry are resolvable into three ingredients: the rant of unregulated passion, the whining of exaggerated feelings, and the cant of factitious sentiment . . . It can never make a philosopher, nor a statesman, nor in any class of life an useful or rational man. It cannot claim the slightest share in any one of the comforts and utilities of life of which we have witnessed so many and so rapid advances. But though not useful, it may be said it is highly ornamental, and deserves to be cultivated for the pleasure it yields. Even if this be granted, it does not follow that a writer of poetry in the present state of society is not a waster of his own time, and a robber of that of others. . . . There are more good poems already existing than are sufficient to employ that portion of life which any mere reader and recipient of poetical impressions should devote to them, and these having been produced in poetical times, are far superior in all the characteristics of poetry to the artificial reconstructions of a few morbid ascetics in unpoetical times. To read the promiscuous rubbish of the present time to the exclusion of the select treasures of the past, is to substitute the worse for the better variety of the same mode of enjoyment. . . .

PERCY BYSSHE SHELLEY

Shelley (1792–1822) was born to a privileged life as the eldest son of a member of Parliament whose baronetcy and seat in Parliament he could have inherited. He attended Eton and then Oxford, where his career of clashing with authority began, fostered by his reading of the works of Thomas Paine and William Godwin. His first publication was a Gothic novel *Zastrozzi* (1810) in which the villain voiced Shelley's own heretical and atheistic opinions. He was prolific in many genres during his first year at Oxford. Unfortunately, he was expelled for publishing a pamphlet coauthored with his friend Thomas Jefferson Hogg titled *The Necessity of Atheism,* which they distributed to heads of colleges, to their professor, and to university officials. Although he could have been reinstated through his father's influence if he renounced his atheism, he refused and, causing another scandal, eloped with sixteen-year-old Harriet Westbrook, his first wife and the daughter of a local tradesman. In Ireland he made radical speeches on religion and politics and wrote a pamphlet called "A Declaration of Rights on the French Revolution," then moved back to England to the Lake District. In two years he published his first serious work *Queen Mab,* a Godwinian vision and a long poem celebrating the merits of atheism, vegetarianism, and free love.

In 1814 Shelley ran away with Mary Godwin, the sixteen-year-old daughter of his colleague William Godwin and Mary Wollstonecraft, the author of the influential essay, *A Vindication of the Rights of Women.* Like William Godwin, Shelley was disdainful of marriage as an institution. He invited Harriet Westbrook, along with their two children, to join his new ménage as a platonic sister. Shelley and Mary were deep in debt and constantly moved about to avoid creditors and bailiffs. Despite the deaths of two of his children with Mary, and the loss of his two children with Harriet in the courts after Harriet's suicide, Shelley wrote prodigiously during the period from 1817 to 1819. At Lake Geneva, he and Mary met Lord Byron, and in a playful contest to write the best ghost story, Mary Shelley contributed an early draft of her novel *Frankenstein.* Back in England, the Shelleys settled in the village of Marlow where their friend Thomas Love Peacock lived. Both men became part of a literary circle that included Leigh Hunt and, at this time, John Keats. Inspired by Keats's death, Shelley wrote the great elegy, *Adonais.* Shelley planned a journal called *The Liberal* to be edited by Hunt, Byron, and himself that would provide a forum for their radical writings and a counterweight to conservative periodicals such as *Blackwoods*. Shelley spent the last four years of his life in Italy, during which he produced his major works, including *Prometheus Unbound*. Just before his thirtieth birthday, he drowned in a storm while sailing his schooner. His lengthy list of poetry and prose works express Shelley's views that the poet has an important political role to play, an idea developed in the famous essay excerpted here.

from A Defence of Poetry

. . . A man, to be greatly good, must imagine intensely and comprehensively; he must put himself in the place of another and of many others; the pains and pleasures of his species must become his own. The great instrument of moral good is the imagination; and poetry administers to the effect by acting upon the cause. Poetry enlarges the circumference of the imagination. . . .

Poetry is indeed something divine. It is at once the centre and circumference of knowledge; it is that which comprehends all science, and that to which all science must be referred. It is at the same time the root and blossom of all other systems of thought; it is that from which all spring, and that which adorns all. . . .

Poetry is the record of the best and happiest moments of the happiest and best minds. We are aware of evanescent visitations of thought and feeling sometimes associated with place or person, sometimes regarding our own mind alone, and always arising unforeseen and departing unbidden, but elevating and delightful beyond all expression: so that even in the desire and the regret they leave, there cannot but be pleasure, participating as it does in the nature of its object. It is as it were the interpenetration of a diviner nature through our own; but its footsteps are like those of a wind over the sea, which the coming calm erases, and whose traces remain only, as on the wrinkled sand which paves it. These and corresponding conditions of being are experienced principally by those of the most delicate sensibility and the most enlarged imagination; and the state of mind produced by them is at war with every base desire. The enthusiasm of virtue, love, patriotism, and friendship, is essentially linked with these emotions; and whilst they last, self appears as what it is, an atom to a Universe. Poets are not only subject to these experiences as spirits of the most refined organization, but they can colour all that they combine with the evanescent hues of this ethereal world; a word, or a trait in the representation of a scene or a passion, will touch the enchanted chord, and reanimate, in those who have ever experienced these emotions, the sleeping, the cold, the buried image of the past. Poetry thus makes immortal all that is best and most beautiful in the world; it arrests the vanishing apparitions which haunt the interlunations of life, and veiling them, or in language or in form, sends them forth among mankind, bearing sweet news of kindred joy to those with whom their sisters abide—abide, because there is no portal of expression from the caverns of the spirit which they inhabit into the universe of things. Poetry redeems from decay the visitations of the divinity in Man . . .

A poet, as he is the author to others of the highest wisdom, pleasure, virtue and glory, so he ought personally to be the happiest, the best, the wisest, and the most illustrious of men. As to his glory, let Time be challenged to declare whether the fame of any other institutor of human life be comparable to that of a poet. That he is the wisest, the happiest, and the best, inasmuch as he is a poet, is equally incontrovertible: the greatest Poets have been men of the most spotless virtue, of the most consummate prudence, and, if we could look into the interior of their lives, the most fortunate of men: and the exceptions, as they regard those who possessed the imaginative faculty in a high yet inferior degree, will be found on consideration to confirm rather than destroy the rule. . . .

The most unfailing herald, companion, and follower of the awakening of a great people to work a beneficial change in opinion or institution, is Poetry. At such periods there is an accumulation of the power of communicating and receiving intense and impassioned conceptions respecting man and nature. The persons in whom this power resides may often, as far as regards many portions of their nature, have little apparent correspondence with that spirit of good of which they are ministers. But even whilst they deny and abjure, they are yet compelled to serve, the Power which is seated on the throne of their own soul. It is impossible to read the compositions of the most celebrated writers of the present day without being startled with the electric life which burns within their words. They measure the circumference and sound the depths of human nature with a comprehensive and all-penetrating spirit, and they are themselves perhaps the most sincerely astonished at its manifestations; for it is less their spirit than the spirit of the age. Poets are the hierophants of an unapprehended inspiration; the mirrors of the gigantic shadows which futurity casts upon the present; the words which express what they understand not; the trumpets which sing to battle, and feel not what they inspire; the influence which is moved not, but moves. Poets are the unacknowledged legislators of the world.

ANONYMOUS

From the sixteenth century to the mid-twentieth century, a thriving oral poetry continued ancient traditions in African languages, even though most written African literature of those centuries is in European languages. Many of these oral poems may have existed for centuries in spoken form before they were first written down in the nineteenth or twentieth century. Forms of poetry included poetic forms for certain occupations, such as the *ijala* performed by Yoruba hunters, or the songs of the Ewe fishing communities; hymns to gods and goddesses; allusive, symbolic oracular poems, such as the Ifa used by the Yoruba for divination; and elegies, love songs, children's chants, war poems, and poems of praise. The griot, or praise singer, in West Africa was responsible for memorizing and remembering complicated traditional stories. He or she (a female griot was sometimes called a *jalimu*) traveled to share the stories with people in different villages.

Poetry was also used as a key element of the global tribal spiritual practice known as shamanism, from the Siberian word *Saman*. Archaeological and anthropological evidence shows that shamanism has been a healing and spiritual practice for twenty to thirty thousand years in the Americas, Asia, Africa, regions of Europe, and Australia. The role of the shaman in tribal society is to connect humanity with the natural and spiritual worlds. In altered states of consciousness induced with or without the aid of fasting, vigils, drugs, singing, drumming, chanting, or dancing, shamans regularly talk to animals, see visions, and converse with guardian spirits. In his or her capacity as the community's intermediary with other worlds, the shaman is responsible for maintaining traditional myths of death and rebirth. In "The Dead Man Asks for a Song," an oral poem transcribed during the nineteenth century, a dying person seems to be asking the shaman for a song that will help ease the transition to the underworld. The abiding importance of the elegy as a genre of contemporary poetry shows that poetry is still considered an appropriate tool to help people deal with death today, just as it was in traditional, non-literate tribal communities.

The Dead Man Asks for a Song

Sing me a song of the dead,
That I may take it with me.
A song of the underworld sing me,
That I may take it with me
And travel to the underworld.

The underworld says,
Says the underworld:
It is beautiful in the grave.
Beautiful is the underworld
But there is no wine to drink there.
So I will take it with me
And travel to the underworld
And travel to the underworld.

Sing me a song of the dead,
That I may take it with me.
A song of the underworld sing me,
That I may take it with me
And travel to the underworld.

WALT WHITMAN

Walt Whitman (1819–92), generally considered one of America's most influential and innovative poets, was born in a village on Long Island, New York, a member of the first generation of poets born in the United States. His father was a farmer and a carpenter; his parents and his siblings, uneducated and troubled, led difficult lives. Alcoholism, depression, and other forms of mental illness plagued the family. After his father's death, Whitman at times assumed responsibility for his mother and two of his brothers. He left school at eleven and, living in Brooklyn, rode the ferry back and forth across the East River to New York City, and made the acquaintance of people working on the ferries. His fascination with ferries, working people, and the act of crossing are evident in *Crossing Brooklyn Ferry* and other poems.

Whitman also educated himself in New York's museums, libraries, and public lectures, particularly those featuring Quaker thought. He worked as a laborer, an office boy, an apprentice on a liberal newspaper where he learned a printer's skill, and for five unhappy years a small-town schoolteacher. After beginning a successful career writing for magazines and newspapers, he published a temperance novel, a type of fiction popular at the time, which sold more than anything else Whitman published in his lifetime. As Emerson wrote in a letter, Whitman's work had "a long foreground." It was influenced by the City, by the operas Whitman loved to attend, by his exposure to slave auctions in New Orleans, and by Emerson's call for a poet equal to the richness and diversity of the United States.

At thirty-six, having for many years written conventional poems imitative of Shelley, Keats, and William Cullen Bryant, he composed twelve untitled poems which made up the first *Leaves of Grass*. Whitman's poems imagined an inclusive democratic society, one as open to African Americans, women, and homosexuals as to the white male majority. Although he encountered opposition to both his radical politics and his sexual agenda (John Greenleaf Whittier threw his book in the fire), he remained firm, rejecting Emerson's advice to delete the especially inflammatory sections of his poems. In the later *Calamus Poems* and *Live Oak, with Moss,* written after his years in Civil War hospitals dressing the wounds of soldiers and comforting them as they died, he wrote with increasing frankness about the bonds between men. His long musical lines, replete with many dactyls, appeared formless to many nineteenth-century readers and, along with his politics, alienated the public. In 1892, an impoverished Whitman died in New York City, having lived to witness the first solid recognition of his work. His ideas and poems were not appreciated fully until the middle of the twentieth century. In his preface, excerpted here, he, like Emerson, emphasizes the greatness of America and its need for an American poet commensurate with the nation.

from Preface to Leaves of Grass 1855

. . . Of all nations the United States with veins full of poetical stuff most need poets and will doubtless have the greatest and use them the greatest. Their Presidents shall not be their common referee so much as their poets shall. Of all mankind the great poet is the equable man. Not in him but off from him things are grotesque or eccentric or fail of their sanity. Nothing out of its place is good and nothing in its place is bad. He bestows on every object or quality its full proportions neither more nor less. He is the arbiter of the diverse and he is the key. He is the equalizer of his age and land . . . he supplies what wants supplying and checks what wants checking. If peace is the routine out of him speaks the spirit of peace, large, rich, thrifty, building vast and populous cities, encouraging agriculture and the arts and commerce—lighting the study of man, the soul, immortality—federal, state or municipal government, marriage, health, free trade, intertravel by land and sea . . . nothing too close, nothing too far off . . . the stars not too far off. In war he is the most deadly force of the war. . . .

The greatest poet hardly knows pettiness or triviality. If he breathes into any thing that was before thought small it dilates with the grandeur and life of the universe. He is a seer . . . he is individual . . . he is complete in himself . . . the others are as good as he, only he sees it and they do not. He is not one of the chorus . . . he does not stop for any regulations . . . he is the president of regulation. . . .

This is what you shall do: love the earth and sun and the animals, despise riches, give alms to every one that asks, stand up for the stupid and crazy, devote your income and labor to others, hate tyrants, argue not concerning God, have patience and indulgence toward the people, take off your hat to nothing known or unknown or to any man or number of men, go freely with powerful uneducated persons and with the young and with the mothers of families, read these leaves in the open air every season of every year of your life, re-examine all you have been told at school or church or in any book, dismiss whatever insults your own soul, and your very flesh shall be a great poem and have the richest fluency not only in its words but in the silent lines of its lips and face and between the lashes of your eyes and in every motion and joint of your body. . . . The poet shall not spend his time in unneeded work. He shall know that the ground is always ready plowed and manured . . . others may not know it but he shall. He shall go directly to the creation. His trust shall master the trust of everything he touches . . . and shall master all attachment. . . .

from Song of Myself, Stanza 2

Houses and rooms are full of perfumes, the shelves are crowded
    with perfumes,
I breathe the fragrance myself and know it and like it,
The distillation would intoxicate me also, but I shall not let it.

The atmosphere is not a perfume, it has no taste of the
    distillation, it is odorless,
It is for my mouth forever, I am in love with it,
I will go to the bank by the wood and become undisguised
    and naked,
I am mad for it to be in contact with me.

The smoke of my own breath,
Echoes, ripples, buzz'd whispers, love-root, silk thread, crotch
    and vine,
My respiration and inspiration, the beating of my heart, the
    passing of blood and air through my lungs,

The sniff of green leaves and dry leaves, and of the shore, and
    dark-colored sea-rocks, and of hay in the barn,
The sound of the belch'd words of my voice loos'd to the eddies
    of the wind,
A few light kisses, a few embraces, a reaching around of arms,
The play of shine and shade on the trees as the supple boughs
    wag,
The delight alone or in the rush of the streets, or along the fields
    and hill-sides,
The feeling of health, the full-noon trill, the song of me rising
    from bed and meeting the sun.
Have you reckon'd a thousand acres much? Have you reckon'd
    the earth much?
Have you practis'd so long to learn to read?
Have you felt so proud to get at the meaning of poems?

Stop this day and night with me and you shall possess the origin
    of all poems,
You shall possess the good of the earth and sun, (there are
    millions of suns left,)
You shall no longer take things at second or third hand,
    nor look through the eyes of the dead, nor feed on
    the spectres in books,
You shall not look through my eyes, either, nor take things
    from me,
You shall listen to all sides and filter them from your self.

MATTHEW ARNOLD

Matthew Arnold (1822–88), a major figure in Victorian letters, first as poet, then as literary critic, was the son of the headmaster of the famous Rugby School, where he won his first poetry prize. Arnold's haunting elegy for his father, "Rugby Chapel," is a memorable record of his father's great influence on him. He graduated from Oxford with a disappointing second, perhaps as a result of his active social life, and spent several years traveling and writing before publishing *The Strayed Reveller, and Other Poems* in 1849 and *Empedocles on Etna, and Other Poems* in 1852. In 1851 he married and was named inspector of schools, a post he held for thirty-five years. In 1853 he published *Poems,* a collection including excerpts from the first two books. This established Arnold as a leading poet of the day and included a preface outlining his expectations for the poetry of his age. Epic poetry drawn from stories and legends of the past was especially appealing to him; his "Sohrab and Rustum," based on an ancient Persian tale, is a prime example.

In 1857 he was named to the coveted professorship of poetry at Oxford, a post that he held for ten years. During this time he wrote little poetry but composed most of his best-known philosophical essays, including *Essays in Criticism* (1865) and *Culture and Anarchy* (1869) in which he argued for the preservation of knowledge "of the best that has been thought and said in the world"—that is to say, a high culture involving such virtues as beauty, intelligence, and order that would benefit a democratic society. He pleaded for religious belief apart from sectarian doctrines in the hope that it would ennoble those who came to live by it, although he himself was an agnostic, as evidenced in such famous poems as "To Marguerite" and "Dover Beach."

In 1883, Arnold, pensioned by Gladstone, was financially able to travel to the United States on a lecture tour and went as far west as St. Louis, giving three lectures that were later published as *Discourses in America.* An unnamed newspaper of the day described him, as he stooped to look at his manuscript, as "an elderly bird picking grapes on a trellis." Arnold died in 1888 while running to catch a trolley car in Liverpool where he had gone to meet his daughter.

from The Study of Poetry

"The future of poetry is immense, because in poetry, where it is worthy of its high destinies, our race, as time goes on, will find an ever surer and surer stay. There is not a creed which is not shaken, not an accredited dogma which is not shown to be questionable, not a received tradition which does not threaten to dissolve. Our religion has materialised itself in the fact, in the supposed fact; it has attached its emotion to the fact, and now the fact is failing it. But for poetry the idea is everything; the rest is a world of illusion, of divine illusion. Poetry attaches its emotion to the idea; the idea *is* the fact. The strongest part of our religion today is its unconscious poetry."

Let me be permitted to quote these words of my own, as uttering the thought which should, in my opinion, go with us and govern us in all our study of poetry. In the present work it is the course of one great contributory stream to the world-river of poetry that we are invited to follow. We are here invited to trace the stream of English poetry. But whether we set ourselves, as here, to follow only one of the several streams that make the mighty river of poetry, or whether we seek to know them all, our governing thought should be the same. We should conceive of poetry worthily, and more highly than it has been the custom to conceive of it. We should conceive of it as capable of higher uses, and called to higher destinies, than those which in general men have assigned to it hitherto. More and more mankind will discover that we have to turn to poetry to interpret life for us, to console us, to sustain us. Without poetry, our science will appear incomplete; and most of what now passes with us for religion and philosophy will be replaced by poetry. Science, I say, will appear incomplete without it. For finely and truly does Wordsworth call poetry "the impassioned expression which is in the countenance of all science"; and what is a countenance without its expression? Again, Wordsworth finely and truly calls poetry "the breath and finer spirit of all knowledge": our religion, parading evidences such as those on which the popular mind relies now; our philosophy, pluming itself on its reasonings about causation and finite and infinite being; what are they but the shadows and dreams and false shows of knowledge? . . .

The best poetry is what we want; the best poetry will be found to have a power of forming, sustaining, and delighting us, as nothing else can. A clearer, deeper sense of the best in poetry, and of the strength and joy to be drawn from it, is the most precious benefit which we can gather from a poetical collection such as the present. And yet in the very nature and conduct of such a collection there is inevitably something which tends to obscure in us the consciousness of what our benefit should be, and to distract us from the pursuit of it. We should therefore steadily set it before our minds at the outset, and should compel ourselves to revert constantly to the thought of it as we proceed.

Yes; constantly in reading poetry, a sense for the best, the really excellent, and of the strength and joy to be drawn from it, should be present in our minds and should govern our estimate of what we read. But this real estimate, the only true one, is liable to be superseded, if we are not watchful, by two other kinds of estimate, the historic estimate and the personal estimate, both of which are fallacious. A poet or a poem may count to us historically, they may count to us on grounds personal to ourselves, and they may count to us really. They may count to us historically. The course of development of a nation's language, thought, and poetry, is profoundly interesting; and by regarding a poet's work as a stage in this course of development we may easily bring ourselves to make it of more importance as poetry than in itself it really is, we may come to use a language of quite exaggerated praise in criticising it; in short, to over-rate it. So arises in our poetic judgments the fallacy caused by the estimate which we may call historic. Then, again, a poet or a poem may count to us on grounds personal to ourselves. Our personal affinities, likings, and circumstances, have great power to sway our estimate of this or that poet's work, and to make us attach more importance to it as poetry than in itself it really possesses, because to us it is, or has been, of high importance. Here also we over-rate the object of our interest, and apply to it a language of praise which is quite exaggerated. And thus we get the source of a second fallacy in our poetic judgments—the fallacy caused by an estimate which we may call personal.

Both fallacies are natural. It is evident how naturally the study of the history and development of a poetry may incline a man to pause over reputations and works once conspicuous but now obscure, and to quarrel with a careless public for skipping, in obedience to mere tradition and habit, from one famous name or work in its national poetry to another, ignorant of what it misses, and of the reason for keeping what it keeps, and of the whole process of growth in its poetry. . . .

The idea of tracing historic origins and historical relationships cannot be absent from a compilation like the present. And naturally the poets to be exhibited in it will be assigned to those persons for exhibition who are known to prize them highly, rather than to those who have no special inclination towards them. Moreover the very occupation with an author, and the business of exhibiting him, disposes us to affirm and amplify his importance. In the present work, therefore, we are sure of frequent temptation to adopt the historic estimate, or the personal estimate, and to forget the real estimate; which latter, nevertheless, we must employ if we are to make poetry yield us its full benefit. . . .

Indeed there can be no more useful help for discovering what poetry belongs to the class of the truly excellent, and can therefore do us most good, than to have always in one's mind lines and expressions of the great masters, and to apply them as a touchstone to other poetry. Of course we are not to require this other poetry to resemble them; it may be very dissimilar. But if we have any tact we shall find them, when we have lodged them well in our minds, an infallible touchstone for detecting the presence or absence of high poetic quality, and also the degree of this quality, in all other poetry which we may place beside them. Short passages, even single lines, will serve our turn quite sufficiently. . . .

Critics give themselves great labour to draw out what in the abstract constitutes the characters of a high quality of poetry. It is much better simply to have recourse to concrete examples;—to take specimens of poetry of the high, the very highest quality, and to say: The characters of a high quality of poetry are what is expressed *there*. They are far better recognised by being felt in the verse of the master, than by being perused in the prose of the critic. . . .

Only one thing we may add as to the substance and matter of poetry, guiding ourselves by Aristotle's profound observation that the superiority of poetry over history consists in its possessing a higher truth and a higher seriousness. . . . Let us add, therefore, to what we have said, this: that the substance and matter of the best poetry acquire their special character from possessing, in an eminent degree, truth and seriousness. We may add yet further, what is in itself evident, that to the style and manner of the best poetry their special character, their accent, is given by their diction, and, even yet more, by their movement. And though we distinguish between the two characters, the two accents, of superiority, yet they are nevertheless vitally connected one with the other. The superior character of truth and seriousness in the matter and substance of the best poetry, is inseparable from the superiority of diction and movement marking its style and manner. The two superiorities are closely related, and are in steadfast proportion one to the other. So far as high poetic truth and seriousness are wanting to a poet's matter and substance, so far also, we may be sure, will a high poetic stamp of diction and movement be wanting to his style and manner. In proportion as this high stamp of diction and movement, again, is absent from a poet's style and manner, we shall find, also, that high poetic truth and seriousness are absent from his substance and matter. . . .

ALLEN TATE

Allen Tate (1899–1979) was born John Orley Allen Tate in Winchester, Kentucky. His father's business interests, which included lumber and real estate, uprooted the family so frequently that Tate later remarked that he might as well have "been born, in a tavern at a crossroads." His parents divorced when Tate was twelve. At age seventeen Tate entered the Cincinnati Conservatory of Music to study violin but left to attend Vanderbilt University. In his senior year, while rooming with Robert Penn Warren, he was invited to assume the editorship of the *Fugitive,* a little magazine that promised to re-engage formalism in poetry and to revive the literary stature of the South.

In 1925 Tate married Caroline Gordon (the couple divorced in 1959). His first book, *Mr. Pope and Other Poems,* appeared three years later. A Guggenheim Fellowship followed; Tate went to London, where he met T. S. Eliot, and Paris, where he formed a lasting friendship with novelist Ford Madox Ford and poet John Peale Bishop. In 1929 he published a biography, *Jefferson Davis: His Rise and Fall.* Settling in Clarksville, Tennessee, Tate joined with other Southern Agrarians to champion the traditional rural economy of the South against the urban, industrialized North. It was 1937 before Tate brought out another collection of poems, *Selected Poems;* the next year he published his powerful Civil War novel, *The Fathers.* He taught at Princeton, served as Consultant in Poetry to the Library of Congress in 1943, edited the *Sewanee Review* from 1944 to 1947, and became professor of English at the University of Minnesota in 1951 until his retirement. He mentored many younger poets, among them Randall Jarrell and John Berryman. In 1959 Tate married the poet Isabella Gardner; after they divorced he married Helen Heinz, a former student at Minnesota.

Tate's essays reflect his close study of Baudelaire, Mallarmé and other French symbolists. His 1952 text, *Essays of Four Decades,* includes such formidable articles of intellectual prose as "The Present Function of Criticism" and "Literature as Knowledge" from which the essay excerpted here is taken. He rejects our technological society—even before the advent of computers—and describes the writer's task as overseeing the movement of language in a better direction.

from To Whom Is the Poet Responsible?

And for what? The part of the question that I have used as the title has been widely asked in our generation. I have seldom heard anybody ask the second part: *For what?* I shall have to assume, without elucidating it, a certain moral attitude towards the idea of responsibility which is perhaps as little popular in our time as the accused poetry that has given rise to the controversy. Thus I take it for granted that nobody can be held generally responsible, for if our duties are not specific they do not exist. It was, I think, the failure to say what the modern poet was responsible *for* that made it easy to conclude, from the attacks ten years ago by Mr. MacLeish and Mr. Van Wyck Brooks, that in some grandiose sense the poet should be held responsible to society for everything that nobody else was paying any attention to. The poet was saddled with a total responsibility for the moral, political, and social well being; it was pretty clearly indicated that had he behaved differently at some indefinite time in the near or remote past the international political order itself would not have been in jeopardy, and we should not perhaps be at international loggerheads today. We should not have had the Second World War, perhaps not even the first. . . .

If poetry makes us more conscious of the complexity and meaning of our experience, it may have an eventual effect upon action, even political action. The recognition of this truth is not in achievement of our own age; it is very old. Our contribution to it I take to be a deviation from its full meaning, an exaggeration and a loss of insight. Because poetry may influence politics, we conclude that poetry is merely politics, or a kind of addlepated politics, and thus not good for anything. . . .

I am sorry to sound frivolous; I confess that the political responsibility of poets bores me. I am discussing it because it irritates me more than it bores me. It irritates me because the poet has a great responsibility of his own: it is the responsibility to be a poet, to write poems, and not to gad about using the rumor of his verse, as I am now doing, as the excuse to appear on platforms and to view with alarm. I have a deep, unbecoming suspicion of such talking poets: whatever other desirable things they may believe in, they do not believe in poetry. They believe that poets should write tracts, or perhaps autobiographies: encourage the public, further this cause or that, good or bad, depending upon whose political ox is being gored.

My own political ox was at least driven into a fence corner when Mr. Pound thumped his tub for the Axis; but what I cannot easily forgive him was thumping any tub at all—unless, as a private citizen, dissociated from the poet, he had decided to take political action at some modest level, such as giving his life for his country, where whatever he did would be as inconspicuous as his ejaculatory political philosophy demanded that it be. But on Radio Rome he appeared as Professor Ezra Pound, the great American Poet. Much the same can be said of Mr. MacLeish himself. It is irrelevant that I find his political principles (I distinguish his *principles* from his *views*), insofar as I understand them, more congenial than Mr. Pound's. The immediate *views* of these poets seem to me equally hortatory, quasi-lyrical, and ill-grounded. We might imagine for them a pleasant voyage in one of Percy Shelley's boats. If society indicted and condemned poets for the mixture and the misuse of two great modes of action, poetry and politics, we might have to indict Mr. Pound a second time, as it could conceivably be done in some Swiftian social order; and we should have in fairness to provide an adjoining cell for Mr. MacLeish.

The relation of poetry and of other high imaginative literature to social action was not sufficiently considered in the attacks and counterattacks of the past ten years. No one knows precisely what the relation is; so I shall not try here to define it, though what I am about to say will imply certain assumptions. There is no doubt that poetry, even that of Mallarmé, has some effect upon conduct, insofar as it affects our emotions. To what extent is the poetry itself, even that of Mallarmé, an effect? The total complex of sensibility and thought, of belief and experience, in the society from which the poetry emerges, is the prime limiting factor that the poet must first of all be aware of; otherwise his language will lack primary reality, the nexus of thing and word. The failure to consider this primary reality produces willed poetry which usually ignores the human condition. The human condition must be faced and embodied in language before men in any age can envisage the possibility of action. To suggest that poets tell men in crisis what to do, to insist that *as poets* they acknowledge themselves as legislators of the social order, is to ask them to shirk their specific responsibility, which is quite simply the reality of man's experience, not what his experience ought to be, in any age. *To whom* is the poet responsible? He is responsible to his *conscience,* in the French sense of the word: the joint action of knowledge and judgment. This conscience has long known a severe tradition of propriety in discerning the poet's particular kind of actuality. No crisis, however dire, should be allowed to convince us that the relation of the poet to his permanent reality can ever change. And thus the poet is not responsible to society for a version of what it thinks it is or what it wants. *For what* is the poet responsible? He is responsible for the virtue proper to him as poet, for his special *arété* for the mastery of a disciplined language which will not shun the full report of the reality conveyed to him by his awareness: he must hold, in Yeats' great phrase, "reality and justice in a single thought."

We have virtually turned the argument of the attack around upon itself. For it was an irresponsible demand to ask the poet to cease to be a poet and become the propagandist of a political ideal, even if he himself thought it a worthy ideal. If the report of the imagination on the realities of western culture in the past century was as depressing as the liberal mind said it was, would not the scientist, the philosopher, and the statesman have done well to study it? They might have got a clue to what was wrong. They were, I believe, studying graphs, charts, and "trends"—the indexes of power—but not human nature. The decay of modern society is nowhere more conspicuous than in the loss of the arts of reading on the part of men of action. It was said at the beginning of the war that the traditions of modern literature represented by Proust had powerfully contributed to the collapse of Europe. It was not supposed that the collapse of Europe might have affected those traditions. If the politicians had been able to read Proust, or Joyce, or even Kafka, might they not have discerned more sharply what the trouble was and done something to avert the collapse? I doubt it; but it makes as much sense as the argument that literature can be a cause of social decay. If, for example, Mr. Churchill had been able to quote the passage about Ciacco from the *Inferno,* or the second part of *The Waste Land,* instead of Arthur Hugh Clough, might we have hoped that men would now be closer to the reality out of which sound political aspiration must arise?

I leave this subject with the observation that poetry had to be attacked for not having done all that men had expected of it at the end of the nineteenth century. "The future of poetry is immense," said Matthew Arnold. It had to be immense because, for men like Arnold, everything else had failed. It was the new religion that was destined to be lost more quickly than the old. Poetry was to have saved us; it not only hadn't saved us by the end of the fourth decade of this century, it had only continued to be poetry which was little read. It had to be rejected. The primitive Athenians, at the Thargelian festival of Apollo, killed two human beings, burnt them, and cast their ashes into the sea. The men sacrificed were called *pharmakoi:* medicines. We have seen in our time a powerful attempt to purify ourselves of the knowledge of evil in man. Poetry is one of the sources of that knowledge. It is believed by some classical scholars that the savage ritual of the *pharmakoi* was brought to Athens by barbarians. In historical times effigies made of dough were substituted for human beings.

RAINER MARIA RILKE
(Headnote in Part 1)

from Letters to a Young Poet

Three
Viareggio, near Pisa (Italy),
April 23rd, 1903

. . . read as little as possible of aesthetic criticism—such things are either partisan views, petrified and grown senseless in their lifeless induration, or they are clever quibblings in which today one view wins and tomorrow the opposite. Works of art are of an infinite loneliness and with nothing so little to be reached as with criticism. Only love can grasp and hold and be just toward them. Consider *yourself* and your feeling right every time with regard to every such argumentation, discussion or introduction; if you are wrong after all, the natural growth of your inner life will lead you slowly and with time to other insights. Leave to your opinions their own quiet undisturbed development, which, like all progress, must come from deep within and cannot be pressed or hurried by anything. *Everything* is gestation and then bringing forth. To let each impression and each germ of a feeling come to completion wholly in itself, in the dark, in the inexpressible, the unconscious, beyond the reach of one's own intelligence, and await with deep humility and patience the birth-hour of a new clarity: that alone is living the artist's life: in understanding as in creating.

There is here no measuring with time, no year matters, and ten years are nothing. Being an artist means, not reckoning and counting, but ripening like the tree which does not force its sap and stands confident in the storms of spring without the fear that after them may come no summer. It does come. But it comes only to the patient, who are there as though eternity lay before them, so unconcernedly still and wide. I learn it daily, learn it with pain to which I am grateful: *patience* is everything! . . .

Eight
Borgeby gård, Flädie, Sweden
August 12th, 1904.

I want to talk to you again a while, dear Mr. Kappus, although I can say almost nothing that is helpful, hardly anything useful. You have had many and great sadnesses, which passed. And you say that even this passing was hard for you and put you out of sorts. But, please, consider whether these great sadnesses have not rather gone right through the center of yourself? Whether much in you has not altered, whether you have not somewhere, at some point of your being, undergone a change when you were sad? Only those sadnesses are dangerous and bad which one carries about among people in order to drown them out; like sicknesses that are superficially and foolishly treated they simply withdraw and after a little pause break out again the more dreadfully; and accumulate within one and are life, are unlived, spurned, lost life, of which one may die. Were it possible for us to see further than our knowledge reaches, and yet a little way beyond the outworks of our divining, perhaps we would endure our sadnesses with greater confidence than our joys. For they are moments when something new has entered into us, something unknown; our feelings grow mute in shy perplexity, everything in us withdraws, a stillness comes, and the new, which no one knows, stands in the midst of it and is silent.

I believe that almost all our sadnesses are moments of tension that we find paralyzing because we no longer hear our surprised feelings living. Because we are alone with the alien thing that has entered into our self; because everything intimate and accustomed is for an instant taken away; because we stand in the middle of a transition where we cannot remain standing. For this reason the sadness too passes: the new thing in us, the added thing, has entered into our heart, has gone into its inmost chamber and is not even there any more,—is already in our blood. And we do not learn what it was. We could easily be made to believe that nothing has happened, and yet we have changed, as a house changes into which a guest has entered. We cannot say who has come, perhaps we shall never know, but many signs indicate that the future enters into us in this way in order to transform itself in us long before it happens. And this is why it is so important to be lonely and attentive when one is sad: because the apparently uneventful and stark moment at which our future sets foot in us is so much closer to life than that other noisy and fortuitous point of time at which it happens to us as if from outside. The more still, the more patient and more open we are when we are sad, so much the deeper and so much the more unswervingly does the new go into us, so much the better do we make it ours, so much the more will it be *our* destiny, and when on some latter day it "happens" (that is, steps forth out of us to others), we shall feel in our inmost selves akin and near to it. . . .

So for him who becomes solitary all distances, all measures change; of these changes many take place suddenly, and then, as with the man on the mountaintop, extraordinary imaginings and singular sensations arise that seem to grow out beyond all bearing. But it is necessary for us to experience *that* too. We must assume our existence as *broadly* as we in any way can; everything, even the unheard-of, must be possible in it. That is at bottom the only courage that is demanded of us: to have courage for the most strange, the most singular and the most inexplicable that we may encounter. That mankind has in this sense been cowardly has done life endless harm; the experiences that are called "visions," the whole so-called "spirit-world," death, all those things that are so closely akin to us, have by daily parrying been so crowded out of life that the senses with which we could have grasped them are atrophied. To say nothing of God. . . .

RANDALL JARRELL

Randall Jarrell (1914–65) was born in Nashville, Tennessee, took both his BA and MA degrees from Vanderbilt University, where he studied with John Crowe Ransom and Robert Penn Warren, poets active in the Fugitive group of writers that had originated in Nashville in the twenties. Jarrell showed no interest in southern political or social ideas, although Allen Tate, another Fugitive, was his mentor for a short time. Following graduation, Jarrell taught for two years at Kenyon College in Gambier, Ohio, where he roomed with Robert Lowell and became close friends with the novelist Peter Taylor. From Kenyon he went to the University of Texas, married, and published his first book, *Blood for a Stranger,* in 1942. In that same year, he enlisted in the Army Air Force and became a trainer of pilot navigators in Tucson, Arizona. He spent nearly four years in the service, during which he wrote extensively about World War II and army life, culminating in *Little Friend, Little Friend* (1945) and *Losses* (1948). After mustering out, Jarrell became literary editor of the *Nation* for a year and taught at Sarah Lawrence College, which became the model for the college in his novel, *Pictures from an Institution.* As a literary critic, Jarrell helped establish the reputations of such poets as Elizabeth Bishop, William Carlos Williams, and Marianne Moore. His collection, *Poetry and the Age* (1953), from which the essay excerpted here is taken, has become a classic for his postwar appreciations of these and many other poets.

In 1952, Jarrell remarried. His second wife, Mary von Schrader, remained his close companion for the rest of his life, accompanying him to his lectures and readings. He taught at the University of North Carolina in Greensboro, was Consultant in Poetry at the Library of Congress for two years, translated *Faust, Part I,* and wrote two children's books. Despite his ongoing struggle with bipolar disease, he published two major poetry collections, *The Woman at the Washington Zoo* (1960), which won the National Book Award, and *The Lost World* (1965), books that contain some of his best work. In narrative poems Jarrell captured the voices of women, trapped housewives, and the anxieties of children that were characteristic of the fifties and the emptiness of apparent prosperity. His one-time colleague and friend Robert Lowell said that Jarrell's work ranks "with the best lyric poets of the past." Jarrell was struck by a car and died in 1965, possibly a suicide.

from The Obscurity of the Poet

When I was asked to talk about the Obscurity of the Modern Poet I was delighted, for I have suffered from this obscurity all my life. But then I realized that I was being asked to talk not about the fact that people don't read poetry, but about the fact that most of them wouldn't understand it if they did: about the difficulty, not the neglect, of contemporary poetry. And yet it is not just modern poetry, but poetry, that is today obscure. *Paradise Lost* is what it was; but the ordinary reader no longer makes the mistake of trying to read it—instead he glances at it, weighs it in his hand, shudders, and suddenly, his eyes shining, puts it on his list of the ten dullest books he has ever read, along with *Moby Dick, War and Peace, Faust,* and Boswell's *Life of Johnson.* But I am doing this ordinary reader an injustice: it was not the Public, nodding over its lunch-pail, but the educated reader, the reader the universities have trained, who a few weeks ago, to the Public's sympathetic delight, put together this list of the world's dullest books.

Since most people know about the modern poet only that he is *obscure*—i.e. that he is *difficult,* i.e. that he is *neglected*—they naturally make a causal connection between the two meanings of the word, and decide that he is unread because he is difficult. Some of the time this is true; some of the time the reverse is true: the poet seems difficult *because* he is not read, *because* the reader is not accustomed to reading his or any other poetry. But most of the time neither is a cause—both are no more than effects of that long-continued, world-overturning cultural and social revolution (seen at its most advanced stage here in the United States) which has made the poet difficult and the public unused to any poetry exactly as it has made poet and public divorce their wives, stay away from church, dislike bull-baiting, free the slaves, get insulin shots for diabetes, or do a hundred thousand other things, some bad, some good, and some indifferent. It is superficial to extract two parts from this world-high whole, and to say of them: "This one, here, is the cause of that one, there; and that's all there is to it." . . .

If my tone is mocking, the tone of someone accustomed to help-lessness, this is natural: the poet is a condemned man for whom the State will not even buy breakfast—and as someone said, "If you're going to hang me, you mustn't expect to be able to intimidate me into sparing your feelings during the execution." The poet lives in a world whose newspapers and magazines and books and motion pictures and radio stations and television stations have destroyed, in a great many people, even the capacity for understanding real poetry, real art of any kind. The man who monthly reads, with vacant relish, the carefully predigested sentences which the *Reader's Digest* feeds to him as a mother pigeon feeds her squabs—this man *cannot* read the *Divine Comedy,* even if it should ever occur to him to try: it is too obscure. Yet one sort of clearness shows a complete contempt for the reader, just as one sort of obscurity shows a complete respect. Which patronizes and degrades the reader, the *Divine Comedy* with its four levels of meaning, or the *Reader's Digest* with its one level so low that it seems not a level but an abyss into which the reader consents to sink? . . .

I was sorry to see this conference given its (quite traditional) name of The Defence of Poetry. Poetry does not need to be defended, any more than air or food needs to be defended; poetry—using the word in its widest sense, the only sense in which it is important—has been an indispensable part of any culture we know anything about. Human life without some form of poetry is not human life but animal existence. Our world today is not an impossible one for poets and poetry: poets can endure its disadvantages, and good poetry is still being written—Yeats, for instance, thought the first half of this century the greatest age of lyric poetry since the Elizabethan. But what will happen to the public—to that portion of it divorced from any real art even of the simplest kind—I do not know. . . .

HOWARD NEMEROV

Howard Nemerov (1920–91) was born and grew up in New York City, where he graduated from the Ethical Culture's highly regarded Fieldston School. At the age of seventeen he entered Harvard College, earned his bachelor's degree in 1941, and became a pilot in World War II for the Royal Canadian Air Force. He married a young Englishwoman in 1944 and retired from the service as a first lieutenant after the war.

The couple returned to New York where Nemerov completed *The Image and the Law* (1947), his first book, to be followed by many others. His first teaching appointment was at Hamilton College. Later, he taught at Bennington College and Brandeis University before making his home in St. Louis, Missouri, as Mallinckrodt Disinguished Professor of English at Washington University. He was an associate editor of *Furioso* from 1946 to 1951, a magazine founded by two Yale undergraduates with the encouragement of Ezra Pound, who wrote enthusiastic letters of advice as "padre eterno or whatever." The first issue appeared in 1939 with poems by E. E. Cummings, Richard Eberhart, Horace Gregory, and a letter of encouragement from Archibald MacLeish. Only one issue appeared between 1941 and the end of World War II, but *Furioso* reappeared in 1946 with Nemerov and Reed Whittemore on the editorial board and continued to publish such major poetic voices as Richard Wilbur, Josephine Miles, and W. S. Merwin until its final issue in 1953.

Nemerov served as Consultant in Poetry to the Library of Congress in 1963 and 1964, before that post was renamed Poet Laureate. His list of awards and fellowships is lengthy, including induction into the American Academy and Institute of Arts and Letters in 1977. The following year, his *Collected Poems* won the National Book Award and the Pulitzer Prize for Poetry. *Trying Conclusions,* his new and selected poems, appeared in 1991.

Nemerov also wrote five works of fiction and four collections of non-fiction, including *Reflexions on Poetry and Poetics,* from which this excerpt is drawn. Ironic and idiosyncratic as critic, witty, meditative, and metrical as poet, Nemerov's voice is always distinctive. For example, this tidbit from an interview with Grace Cavalieri in 1988: "When I was starting to write the great influence was T. S. Eliot and after that William Butler Yeats. I got, of course, the idea that what you were supposed to do was be plenty morbid and predict the end of civilization many times. But civilization has ended so many times during my brief term on earth that I got a little bored with the theme and in old age I concluded that the model was really Mother Goose, and so you can see this in my new poems."

Nemerov was profoundly dedicated to his public role as poet and unwilling to cancel any obligation. Toward the end of his life he had his vocal cords sprayed with Teflon so that he could give his final reading. He died of cancer in 1991.

from The Difficulty of Difficult Poetry

PART ONE

1. The problem of difficulty in poetry, or "obscurity," is often thought to be exclusively a modern problem. When I began to study poetry the common assumption was that somewhere about 1910 poetry, which had formerly been clear and easy, became obscure and hard. More recently, a poet whose work I admire said that modern poetry stood to the poetry of the past as algebra did to arithmetic. Remembering my agonies with algebra, I shudder; but I don't believe this statement of the case to be entirely accurate, as I'll try to show.

2. "Obscurity" has always been, it seems, a standard accusation even against some of the most famous poets and celebrated poems in our language. . . .

3. . . . What one age finds obscure sometimes, not always, comes to seem perfectly plain to a later age. Note that if that very difficult poem "The Ancient Mariner," which seemed to contemporary opinion "a rhapsody of unintelligible wildness and incoherence," is at present taught in schools, that is because it is believed to be not a difficult poem at all but a very easy poem. . . .

In other words, difficult work, harsh and at first sight unpleasing work, work which offends against the taste of the age in which it appears, such work—sometimes, again, not always—slowly forms new elements of sensibility, inspires meditation and imitation until at last it is assimilated into the general complex of culture and a later audience is surprised and amused to find that this work once baffled and offended serious intelligences. This process may be observed in our own time to have brought "The Waste Land" from a poem of appalling obscurity to one which may be read, with a little help, by freshmen; and, even more striking, the resemblances between "The Love Song of J. Alfred Prufrock" and a monologue by Browning—the "Toccata of Galuppi's," for instance— have gradually come to seem as pronounced as the differences must have seemed in 1917. . . .

In English poetry this tension has generally been most visible in the manner of conceiving and making metaphors; that is, at some times metaphor is thought of and employed as an illumination or adornment of a discourse which essentially is regarded as existing separately, and as able to be perfectly understood, though less pleasurably understood, without the metaphors; at other times metaphor is regarded as itself the essence of poetry, and is thought to produce meanings which could not be arrived at by rational discourse at all. . . .

PART TWO

. . . There is a sort of reader who finds everything difficult if it happens to be written in verse. This need not keep us long, and would not need to be noticed at all were it not for the voluble arrogance with which such complaints are often expressed. Such readers really have a very simple problem: they don't like poetry, even though some of them feel they ought to; and they very naturally want poems to be as easy as possible, in order that there may be no intellectual embarrassment about despising them. These readers get their entire pleasure, not from reading poems, but from wrangling interminably over "communication," as though each of them lived in his own telephone booth.

2. There is a corresponding difficulty on the poet's side: the periphrastic habit which comes from the wish to make common matters singular, easy matters hard, and shallow thoughts profound; what Pope calls "the Art of Sinking in Poetry." . . .

5. Probably the difficulty which most vexes most readers, modern readers at any rate, has to do with the content of poems, and the quantity of knowledge required to make some poems intelligible. It is the poet's assumptions about his readers' information which have provoked the angriest outcries against modern poetry, as most particularly shown

by those who were enraged against the author of "The Waste Land" for using materials which they had not available—and even more enraged at him for making these materials available in the form of notes. One poet once said scornfully to me, "Why, if there were any value in all this esoteric stuff I could be much more esoteric than Eliot; I once translated Rumanian Folk-epics, and I could put in a lot of allusions to them." . . .

PART THREE

Beyond any limited and technical question concerning poetry stand the unlimited and possibly insane questions, "What Is Poetry?" and "What Is Poetry for?" . . .

My answers will be something to this effect.

1. Poetry is a means of contemplation, and it produces objects which help people to contemplate reality: objects in the same class with ikons, mirrors, prayer-wheels, and those glass paperweights containing, say, shells, pebbles, fish-hooks or feathers, common enough things which become uncommon by being sunken deep in a transparent medium.

2. So far as poetry is *for* anything beyond contemplation, we may say that it exists for the purpose of producing more poetry. . . .

The flat statement that poetry is or ought to be communication, even if it happened to be true, would be uninteresting. Some poetry, not necessarily the most interesting sort, has the clear intention of communicating—meanings. Other poetry has the clear intention of deepening the silence and space about itself ("The Tyger," for example, or the 12th chapter of Ecclesiastes). . . .

Archimedes, inventing the lever, cried, "Give me a place to stand and I will move the world."

Much later, Kierkegaard gave to the decisive commitment of Christianity—Incarnation, the idea that one's eternal happiness might depend on something which happened in history and in nature, at a time, in a place—this same name of The Archimedean Point.

The problem for poetry, as for all disciplines which interpret the world, resides likewise in the idea of the Archimedean point. Poems issue out of world, and then it is possible critically to refine further and think of meanings as issuing out of poems, but poems also flow back into world and become part of the continuum they sought to interpret; they suffer under and make the most of the Uncertainty Principle.

If poetry reaches the point which chess has reached, where the decisive, profound, and elegant combinations lie within the scope only of masters, and are appreciable only to competent and trained players, that will seem to many people a sorry state of affairs, and to some people a consequence simply of the sinfulness of poets; but it will not in the least mean that poetry is, as they say, *dead;* rather the reverse. It is when poetry becomes altogether too easy, too accessible, runs down to a few derivative formulae and caters to low tastes and lazy minds—it is then that the life of the art is in danger. . . .

JORIE GRAHAM

Jorie Graham (1951–)was born in New York City, raised in Italy and France, and studied philosophy at the Sorbonne in Paris. She then returned to New York and studied filmmaking at NYU, where she became interested in poetry when she overheard the end of T. S. Eliot's "The Love Song of J. Alfred Prufrock" being quoted in a classroom as she walked by.

Graham published her first book of poetry, *Hybrids of Plants and of Ghosts,* in 1980 to immediate acclaim and has since published eight more books of poetry including *The End of Beauty* and *The Dream of a Unified Field,* a selection of poems from five books, which received the Pulitzer Prize in 1996. She has edited several volumes of poetry and has won numerous awards including Whiting and MacArthur grants and the Academy of American Poets Lavan Award. Before becoming Boylston Professor at Harvard in 1999, the first woman to hold this position, Graham taught at Columbia and for many years at the Iowa Writers Workshop.

Graham's poetry reflects her fascination with art and philosophical questions as well as her European background. Her poems engage with metaphysical and historical questions. She intersperses quotes from Jonathan Edwards, Ralph Waldo Emerson, Wittgenstein, and Dante in her own work in ways that urge the reader to wrestle with the philosophical assumptions underlying Western culture. *Region of Unlikeness* explores the ramifications of the idea of history, and *The Errancy* questions the nature of learning in a relativistic world. Graham uses a process-oriented, collage-like, impressionistic method to tackle these questions, interspersing lyric and imagistic passages with metaphysical speculations. Her poetry is strongly influenced by postmodern writing techniques, while still being relatively accessible to those not accustomed to reading experimental work. In this essay she shows her appreciation for poetry's uniquely challenging qualities.

from Introduction to The Best American Poetry, 1990

. . . Yet surely the most frequent accusation leveled against contemporary poetry is its difficulty or inaccessibility. It is accused of speaking only to itself, or becoming an irrelevant and elitist art form with a dwindling audience. And indeed, contemporary poetry's real or apparent difficulty has made it seem somewhat like an intransigent outsider—or perhaps a high-minded purist—in the vast hungry field of American art. And this, in turn, affects how many poets conceive of their enterprise. For how often can we hear that "no one reads it," or that "no one understands it," without experiencing a failure of confidence, however inchoate? And how easily that failure of confidence converts to self-hatred, causing some of us to write articles about the death of poetry, or the horrors of creative writing programs, and others to turn on our own poems, prescribing rules, announcing remedies, saying narrative is all there is or should be, saying *self* should be ostracized, saying free verse is fatal, or all rhyme and meter reactionary, talking about elitism, about how poetry has failed to communicate to the common reader, until finally we cease to trust the power of poetry. We "accept the limitations" of the medium. We start believing that it is essentially anachronistic. We become anecdotal. We want to entertain. We believe we should "communicate" . . .

One problem might stem from the fact that poetry implicitly undertakes a critique of materialist values. It rests on the assumption that material values need to be seen through—or at least complicated sufficiently—in earnest or truer, or more resonant, more supple values. No doubt many of the attacks against poetry come from those of us who, uncomfortable with our slippery marriage to American materialism and its astounding arrogant excess, wish, however unconsciously, that poetry would avert its scrutiny. Or from those of us who turned to poetry at a more idealistic time in our lives and who now rage against it as we lose the capacity for idealism—dreamers turned insomniacs, accusing the dream of having failed them.

But, these basic issues aside, the difficulty of poetry, even for its most sympathetic readers, is a real one. Or rather it is both real and imagined. Much of it dissipates as one opens up to the experience of poetry. To comprehend poetry one must, after all, practice by reading it. As to "see" modern dance, one must at least know its vocabulary, its texture, what the choreographer chose *not* to do. As to understand good carpentry one must be able to grasp what the maker's options were, what the tradition is, what the nature of wood is, what the structural necessities were: what is underpinning, what flourish and passion, what *décor.* Of course, with woodworking or ballet, one can still enjoy what one barely grasps. And such pleasure would also be possible with poetry if intimidation didn't set in: intimidation created by its apparently close relation to the normal language of discourse; fear that one is missing the point or, worse, that one is stupid, blind.

* * *

Poetry can also be difficult, though, because much of it attempts to render aspects of experience that occur outside the provinces of logic and reason, outside the realm of narrative realism. The ways in which dreams proceed, or magic, or mystical vision, or memory, are often models for poetry's methods: what we remember upon waking, what we remember at birth—all the brilliant Irrational in the human sensibility. Poetry describes, enacts, is compelled by those moments of supreme passion, insight or knowledge that are physical yet intuitive, that render us whole, *inspired*. Among verbal events—which by their nature move horizontally, through time, along the lines of cause and effect—poetry tends to leap, to try to move more vertically: astonishment, rapture, vertigo—the seduction of the infinite and the abyss—what so much of it is after. "Ever more ancient and naked states" (Octavio Paz).

In fact, one could argue that poetry's difficulty for some readers stems from the very source of its incredible power: the merging of its irrational procedures with the rational nature of language. So that one mistake we often make is as simple as expecting poetry to be apprehended by the same reading methods and habits that "grasp" prose. While instead—mere practice and exposure to the art form aside—it's probably more a matter of avoiding the interference of fear in reading; more a matter of reading with one's most natural instincts and senses.

That's what is perhaps wrongheaded about the arguments often mounted today against poetry's alleged lack of accessibility to "ordinary" Americans. Aren't such accusations of elitism rather condescending to the people on whose behalf they are made? As if the non-literary men and women of America somehow didn't dream? As if associational logic were restricted to the educated? As if a portion of American readers were only able to read poems of narrative simplicity, having somehow— because of their work experience or background—lost all intuition and sensory intelligence? Isn't this line of thinking, in effect, another symptom of the distrust many of us feel regarding the very core of poetry, its inherent way of proceeding, its nature? I think of Umberto Eco in a recent radio interview: How do you explain that your books, so difficult, sell in the hundreds of thousands of copies in America? "Well," he replied, as if surprised by the question, "in my experience, people, ordinary people, like difficulty. They are tired of being treated like they can't get it. They want it. I give them what they want." . . .

*   *   *

As a collective emotion this distrust of [language] is, of course, one that each of us is free to subvert, override. But precisely because it is a collective emotion, it is one that much poetry inevitably incorporates, explores or enacts as not only an anxiety concerning its very reason to exist, but also as an anxiety concerning the nature and function of language, its capacity for seizing and transmitting . . . *truth?* Even that word seems tinged with regret, nostalgia, in such an atmosphere.

For isn't the essential characteristic of speech, and the particular virtue of its slowness, that it permits the whole fabric to be *received* by a listener—idea, emotion, fact, product, plot detail, motive—the listener having enough *time* to make up his or her mind?

Isn't to describe, to articulate an argument, to use language at the speed where the complexity and sonorousness of syntax and cadence reach the listener, to use it so that the free will of the listener is addressed —free will it is the very purpose of salesmanship to bypass? The genius of syntax consists in its permitting paradoxical, "unsolvable" ideas to be *explored,* not merely nailed down, stored, and owned; in its permitting the soul-forging pleasures of thinking to prevail over the acquisition of information called knowing. . . .

MURIEL RUKEYSER

Muriel Rukeyser (1913–80) was born into a wealthy family in New York City, attended the Ethical Culture School there, and then went to Vassar College. Although she dropped out after two years, determined to pursue a writing career, she continued to study at Columbia University. In 1935, her first book, *Theory of Flight,* was chosen by Stephen Vincent Benet for the Yale Series of Younger Poets Award. In the thirties, moved by the economic upheavals of the Depression, she worked as an editor for the *Student Review* and wrote for the Communist Party's *New Masses.* She went to Alabama to cover the Scottsboro Boys' trial and visited the silica mining site at Gauley Bridge in West Virginia. Her long poem, "The Book of the Dead," came out of this experience. On assignment for a British magazine to cover the anti-fascist Olympic Games in Barcelona in 1936, she was evacuated at the outbreak of the Spanish Civil War; many of her poems, most notably "Mediterranean," reflect her feelings at this time. Over the next few years her revolutionary stance gave way to a commitment to pacifism, in evidence in her third book, *A Turning Wind.*

Rukeyser was a constant target for foes on the extreme left and right but she continued to write and publish poetry the rest of her life. She also wrote biographies, fiction, film screenplays, and translated the poetry of Octavio Paz and Gunnar Ekelöff. In 1949, she published *The Life of Poetry,* partly in response to attack by the postwar faction of theorists and aestheticians, the New Critics. An excerpt from that work is reprinted here. In 1947, her only child, a boy, was born. As a single mother undoubtedly determined to be a better parent than her parents had been, she wrote less. Later, she came to refer to this period—from 1949 to 1964—as "the intercepted years," a difficult admission for an ardent feminist. Her staunch opposition to the Vietnam War attracted the college-age generation to her poetry. As president of the PEN American Center she fought for the human rights of writers around the world; as a role model for young women, she worked to break the taboos and coded silences that impeded their literary progress. In 1972, she and Denise Levertov undertook an unofficial peace mission to South Vietnam. These were very fertile years for Rukeyser; she published four more poetry collections. In 1975, representing the PEN Center, she traveled to South Korea to protest on behalf of poet Kim Chi-Ha. Her response to this protest is contained in the poem that forms the epicenter of her last book, *The Gates* (1976). Despite a stroke that affected her vision and speech, she continued to be an effective spokesperson for the generations of women writers who followed her.

from The Rare Union: Poetry and Science

. . . If there were no poetry on any day in the world, poetry would be invented that day. For there would be an intolerable hunger. And from that need, from the relationships within ourselves and among ourselves as we went on living, and from every other expression of man's nature, poetry would be—I cannot here say invented or discovered—poetry would be derived. As research science would be derived, if the energies we now begin to know reduced us to a few people, rubbing into life a little fire.

However, there is this poetry. There is this science. The farther along the way we go in each, the more clearly the relationship may be perceived, the more prodigal the gifts.

The definitions of Western culture have, classically, separated these two disciplines. When Darwin wrote of Humboldt that he displayed the rare union between poetry and science, he set the man in a line of heroes of that meeting-place—a line which includes Lucretius and Goethe and Leonardo, but which for the last centuries has been obscured in the critical structure which insists that the forms of imagination are not only separate, but exclusive.

The scientist has suffered before the general impoverishment of imagination in some of the same ways as the poet. The worker in applied science and the inventor might be thought of as the town crackpots, but there was always the reservation of an audience, like children lined up before a holiday conjuror, waiting to be shown. The theoretical scientist, like the poet, could never "show" his audience: they lacked language, and in another way, so did he. Unless the law could be translated into an image, it kept the pure scientist in a position remote from his society. He would be called "abstract," "obscure": he would be a freak of intellect, even to the members of his house.

The explosion of a bomb ended that period. The function of science was declared, loudly enough for the unborn to hear. The test on the bombing range at Alamogordo proved one series of devoted researches; Hiroshima, Nagasaki, Bikini, Eniwetok, acted out others. Only the human meanings were left to explore: the power for life.

That dramatizing of poetry, in a shock of annunciation, can never take place. For poetry is, at every instant, concerned with meaning. The poet—of the kind of poetry for which I hope—knows that consciousness and creation are linked, and cannot be postponed. The scientist of the science I hope for knows that too. And more than this recognition is shared, even in our flawed reality. The union Darwin named is true.

Kronecker said of mathematicians, "We are all poets!" The remark provoked assent and sneers: it was noticed. . . .

A REMARK BY BAUDELAIRE

When Baudelaire said that the imagination "is the most scientific of the faculties because it alone understands the universal analogy," he set the trap and sprung it in one phrase. The trap is the use of the discoveries of science instead of the methods of science. Woodrow Wilson was caught there, when he called for a Darwinian, rather than Newtonian, system of government.

The coherence of one kind of discovery is not the coherence of another. We recognize constantly; but in that recognition, we are lost unless we realize that there is little uniformity.

The biased abstraction which is all experience as well as all classification (in D. L. Watson's phrase) carries us to the creative process. And here Baudelaire does spring his trap, for the analogy is *universal*. Imagination finds, and combines, to make its work more human. Knowledge and effective action are met here, too, in one gesture; the gesture of understanding the world and changing it.

Sometimes the conclusions meet, and we prove each other. I remember a visit that Charles Biederman, the "abstract" artist in metals and plastic and concrete, made to the early work in Chicago on the cyclotron. Biederman was shown through by a friend of his, a scientist who out of courtesy asked him what he thought of the structural design. The scientist expected an uncritical answer, and was startled into rudeness when the artist said, "It would be *very good*, according to my standards, except for one thing: that joint—if you put a sphere in, just there, it could really be called perfect." On his next visit, months later, he met the scientist who said, "Do you remember what I called you, last time? Well, you'd better know what's happened. Things kept going wrong, and the trouble was traced to just that joint. They put a sphere in; everything's smooth now."

One of the most fully realized connections between the forms of imagination was made in the writing of Henry Adams, who entered the century consciously, having absorbed the relationships he would need as working instruments. He brought the definitions of unity and multiplicity to Chartres, to the work of Gibbs, to the discovery of radium, and to political history, the image which he predicted would be the crucial one for our period: the image of the bomb. Writing of science and the rush of phase, he found himself—with Melville in his way, with Jeffers in his—cold and lost before annihilation. The languages are not the same: for one it is the devouring of evil and the sea, for one the black crystals of inhuman space and inhuman destruction, for one the heat-death, entropy. But they consider annihilation.

From where do the answers come? The next answers, that must come in the form of questions?

We know what Galileo muttered. What is our *E pur si muove?*

Is there a clue in the idea of the unity of imagination, the meeting-place between science and poetry and between one man and another?...

LÉOPOLD SÉDAR SENGHOR

One of twenty children of a well-to-do peanut trader, Senghor (1906–2001) was born in Senegal, attended Catholic mission school, and planned to become a priest. However, while attending the seminary in Dakar, he was expelled for taking part in a protest against racism. Nevertheless, his grades earned him a coveted scholarship to the Sorbonne in Paris, where he counted among his close friends Georges Pompidou, who was later to become president of France, and wrote his dissertation on exoticism in the poetry of Charles Baudelaire. Politics and surrealism, a rare combination, were to come together in the mind and output of this unusual poet-statesman. The years in Paris exposed Senghor to the heady intellectual ferment of the period. Black writers and artists from the Caribbean, North America, and Africa were gradually defining their opposition to colonial rule. The Harlem Renaissance and the writings of W. E. B. Du Bois were popular influences.

One cannot speak of Senghor without acknowledging his close ties with Aimé Césaire, whom he also met at the Sorbonne, where they were both studying for their *agrégation* in the thirties. Together with Léon Damas, they formulated the concept of *négritude,* a call to young black intellectuals everywhere to come together to enunciate the development of African cultural values and to celebrate their racial identity. The three founded a student newspaper, *L'étudiant noir.* While serving in an all-African unit of the French army in World War II, Senghor was captured and interned in a Nazi prison camp, where he wrote *Chants d'ombres (Shadow Songs).* A number of other poetry volumes followed. At the same time, Senghor was deeply involved in the tumultuous politics of his era. He served in the French parliament, representing what was then the French colony of Senegal, and was instrumental in persuading President Charles de Gaulle to grant Senegal its independence in 1960. Senghor became not only the first president of Senegal but the first Christian presiding over a predominantly Muslim country. It could be said that his negritude enabled him to unify his people despite these internal disharmonies.

Senghor, over his long life as a democratic and socialist statesman and poet, was a prolific writer. His poems have been widely translated and anthologized. Senghor's poetry highlighted the identity crisis of the educated African. His best work dramatizes the confrontation between the old and the new Africa. He has been compared to Walt Whitman for his rhythmic strength and spontaneity. These lines are taken from *Nocturnes* and provide a glimpse of his fascination with a black muse with blue eyes, although the poem itself is untitled:

> I turn sometimes in the street and see again
> A palm tree smiling in the Trade Winds.
> Her lisping brushes against me with a light touch of wings,
> And I say 'Yes, it is Signare!' I have seen the sun set
> In the blue eyes of a blond black woman.
> At Sèvres-Babylone or Balangar, her perfumes
> Of amber and "gongo" spoke to me.

The black woman, the black muse with white traits, seems to speak to the existing tensions between African paganism and Christianity, a thread that can be traced through much of Senghor's poetry. While president, he wrote less but never forsook poetry. In 1980, he resigned from his post, a rare event on a continent where rulers seldom relinquish power voluntarily. He retired to Normandy, in France, the home of his second wife, where in seclusion he continued to write poetry and composed his memoir, *ce que je crois* (What I Believe). He died in 2001 at the age of ninety-five.

from Elegy of Midnight

> . . . I carry in my blood a river of seeds
> That can fertilize all the plains of Byzantium
> And the hills, the austere hills.
> I am the Lover and the locomotive with a well-oiled piston.
> Her sweet strawberry lips, her thick stone body,
> Her secret softness ripe for the catch, her body
> A deep field open to the black sower.
> The Spirit generates under the groin, in the matrix of desire[.]

The sex is one antenna among many where flashing messages
    are exchanged.
Love music no longer can cool me down, nor the holy rhythm
    of poetry.
Against this despair, Lord, I need all my strength
—A soft dagger in the heart as deep as remorse.
I am not sure of dying. If that was Hell: the lack of sleep
This desert of the Poet, this pain of living, this dying
From not being able to die, the agony of shadows, this passion
For death and light like moths on hurricane lamps at night,
In the horrible rotting of virgin forests.

  . . .

from Elegy of the Trade Winds

  . . .

My negritude is not the inertia of race but the sun of the soul,
My negritude is view and life, a trowel in my hand
And a spear in my fist, a scepter.
It is not a question of drinking and eating the passing moment.
Too bad if I am moved by the roses of Cape Verde!
My duty is to awaken my people to the blazing future,
My joy is to create nurturing images, Oh rhythmic lights
Of the Word! Now that our granaries are full
And the bulls shiny, now that fish abound in our waters
And on the edge of ocean currents,
It would feel so good to sleep under the Trade Winds . . .
Here I am all bright with oil like red gold,
Like the Sine champion at the start of the wrestling season,
Honey in the voices of young girls—prizes fought over
For spring weddings. But I mean marriage
With my people and I prepare for it by keeping watch
And by fasting. . . .

ADRIENNE RICH

Adrienne Rich (1929-) was born in Baltimore, Maryland, daughter of a doctor father and a gifted pianist mother. In 1951, Rich received her BA from Radcliffe and won the prestigious Yale Series of Younger Poets Prize for her first book, selected by W. H. Auden, *A Change of World*. He praised Rich for her chiseled formalism and emotional restraint. Rich married a Harvard economist, Alfred Conrad, and they had three sons over the next five years.

In 1963, *Snapshots of a Daughter-in-Law* was published to mixed reviews. This book marks the watershed in Rich's poetic career. The language is freer and more intimate, beginning to express her inchoate feelings about sexual alienation and political oppression, themes made more explicit in *Necessities of Life* (1966). That same year, Rich and Conrad moved to New York, where she taught remedial English to third-world and poor students preparing for college. Since the 1960s Rich has been involved in the civil-rights and anti-war movements, in the continuing resistance to racism, militarism, and anti-Semitism, and as a lesbian in the women's liberation movement. In the essay excerpted here, she addresses "the poetry of cultural re-creation" among people of color, poets born to other mother tongues, lesbian and gay poets, and others.

Rich's honors and awards are many, including the National Book Award in 1974 for *Diving into the Wreck,* two Guggenheim fellowships, the first Ruth Lilly Prize, the Lambda Book Award, the Human Dignity Award of the National Gay Task Force, the William Whitehead Award for Lifetime Achievement, the Academy of American Poets Wallace Stevens Award, the Bollingen Prize, the Lannan Foundation Lifetime Achievement Award, and the Award in Literature of the National Foundation for Jewish Culture. Since 1984, she has lived in California with her partner, the writer Michelle Cliff.

from "What would we create?"

. . . For a long time I've been trying to write poems as if, within this social order, it was enough to voice public pain, speak memory, set words in a countering order, call up images that were in danger of being forgotten or unconceived. In a country where, even among the arts, poetry is the least quantifiable, least commoditized, of our "national products," where the idea of "political poetry" is often met with contempt and hostility, this seemed task enough. But I've also lived with other voices whispering that poetry might be little more than self-indulgence in a society so howling with unmet human needs—an elite art, finally, even when practiced by those among us who are most materially at risk. It's been possible to consider poetry as a marginal activity, of passionate concern to its practitioners perhaps, but as specialized, having as little to do with common emergency, as fly-fishing.

But there's been a missing term. I saw, or thought I saw, that poetry has been held both indispensable and dangerous, one way or another, in every country but my own. The mistake I was making was to assume that poetry really is unwanted, impotent, in the late twentieth-century United States under the system known as "free" enterprise. I was missing the point that precisely because of its recognitive and recollective powers, precisely because in this nation, created in the search for wealth, it eludes capitalist marketing, commoditizing, price-fixing, poetry has simply been set aside, depreciated, denied public space.

This is the difference between the United States and Turkey in the late 1930's, when the revolutionary poet Nazim Hikmet was sentenced to twenty-eight years in prison "on the grounds that the military cadets were reading his poems." This is the difference between the United States and Greece, where, both in the 1930's and after World War II, the socialist poet Yannis Ritsos was interned in concentration camps, exiled, placed under house arrest, his writings burned. This is the difference between the United States and the Stalinized Soviet Union, when the poet Osip Mandelstam (among countless other writers, in Russian and Yiddish, murdered in those years) was persecuted and exiled for an anti-Stalin poem, or, in the 1970's, the poet Natalya Gorbanevskaya sent to a "penal mental institution," or, in the 1980's, the poet Irina Ratushinskaya to a prison for "dangerous state criminals." This is the difference between the United States and Chile in 1973, where the junta who came into power the day of Pablo Neruda's death sacked the poet's house and banned his books.

In the United States, depending on who you are, suppression is qualitatively different. So far, it's not a question of creating human martyrs, since the blacklisted writers of the McCarthy era, although artists denied state and federal funding as "obscene" are under government censorship, and efforts to deport the writer Margaret Randall, based on her writings, were vigorously pursued for five years by the INS. Instead, poetry itself—I mean not words on paper only, but the social recognition and integration of poetry and the imaginative powers it releases—poetry itself is "banned" (in the terminology of the South African apartheid laws: forbidden to speak in public, forbidden to be quoted, to meet with more than one or two persons at the same time). Poetry itself, in our national life, is under house arrest, is officially disappeared. Like our past, our collective memory, it remains an unfathomed, a devalued resource. The establishment of a national "Poet Laureateship" notwithstanding, poetry has been set apart from the practical arts, from civic meaning. It is irrelevant to mass "entertainment" and the accumulation of wealth—thus, out of sight, out of mind.

So the ecology of spirit, voice, and passion deteriorates, barely masked by gentrification, smog, and manic speech, while in the mirrors of mass-market literature, film, television, journalism, our lives are reflected back to us as terrible and little lives. We see daily that our lives are terrible and little, without continuity, buyable and salable at any moment, mere blips on a screen, that this is the way we live now. Memory marketed as nostalgia; terror reduced to mere suspense, to melodrama.

We become stoical; we hibernate; we numb ourselves with chemicals; we emigrate internally into fictions of past and future; we thirst for guns; but *as a people* we have rarely, if ever, known what it is to tremble with fear, to lament, to rage, to praise, to solemnize, to say *We have done this, to our sorrow;* to say *Enough,* to say *We will,* to say *We will not.* To lay claim to poetry. . . .

AIMÉ CÉSAIRE

Aimé Césaire (1913–) was born on the island of Martinique in the Caribbean. He and his six siblings were raised in an educated but marginally poor household. Nevertheless, his mother, a seamstress, and his father, a local administrator, sent their precocious son to Paris in 1931 to prepare for entrance exams to the prestigious École Normale Supérieure. There, among other intellectuals, he met the Senegalese poet, Léopold Sédar Senghor. Together with another Martinican student, they launched a journal called *L'etudiant noir.* Césaire published his famous tract against assimilation in this journal in 1935, coining the term *négritude,* a call for young blacks to take pride in their racial identity. The long poem for which he is best known and from which the excerpt in this book is drawn, *Cahier d'un retour au pays natal (Notebook of a Return to the Native Land),* a passionate narrative about the Martinique of his boyhood, appeared in 1939. He was inspired to write it by the view of an offshore island while on a brief holiday on the then-Yugoslavian coast and stayed up most of the night drafting it. The next morning, upon inquiry, he learned that the island's name was Martinska. With his Martinican wife, Suzanne Roussy, who was also a student in Paris, Césaire then returned to his native land, where the couple took up teaching posts, and he continued to promote his increasingly radical views in a new publication, *Tropiques.* Unfortunately, the new magazine, which sought to merge Marxism, surrealism, and negritude, was launched in the midst of a repressive authoritarianism as France itself, and its Caribbean island colonies, fell to the fascist Vichy government in 1941. Nevertheless, employing various ruses such as pretending their journal was simply devoted to folklore, *Tropiques* survived the war and went on to promote its anticolonial stance.

In 1960, Césaire published a collection of poems, *Ferrements,* about black liberation and the hopeful future he saw for an Africa bursting the chains of slavery to take independent control of its countries. He saw African countries rising in their metaphoric armor to bring together all those who had been displaced by the slave diaspora. But it was not to be.

Over the next forty years, Césaire continually raised his voice against colonialism, racism, and the violence and intimidation by which they functioned. In addition to composing socio-historical studies, he was more and more drawn to drama as a means of conveying his convictions. *La tragédie du roi christophe* (1963) depicts the initial success of Toussaint L'Ouverture's slave revolution in Haiti in 1791–93, which was followed by his arrest by Bonaparte's troops and his deportation to prison in France. The long tyranny of the Haitian François Duvalier, who took power there in 1957, is also a prescient element in the play. Another failed rebellion, that of Patrice Lumumba, is the subject of his next play, *Une saison au Congo* (1965). But his best-known work is the 1969 adaptation of Shakespeare's *The Tempest*. Here, he casts Caliban and Ariel as Prospero's colonial subjects. Caliban is the rebel; Ariel the temporizer, seeks in vain to awaken his master's moral fiber. Caliban's final speech is widely quoted for its expression of the radical intelligentsia's moral outrage as it came to realize how it had been duped and emasculated by colonial education. For the next three decades Césaire focused less on the fury elicited by colonialism and moved closer to the surrealism that first surfaced in his student poems. His collection, *Noria*, (1976) and his play, *Moi, laminaire* (1982) both explore the workings of the unconscious, especially as seen through dream material. In the words of the critic Robin Kelley, "The weapon of poetry may be Césaire's greatest gift to a modern world still searching for freedom."

from Notebook of a Return to the Native Land

And we are standing now, my country and I, hair in the wind, my hand puny in its enormous fist and now the strength is not in us but above us, in a voice that drills through the night and the hearing like the penetrance of an apocalyptic wasp. And the voice complains that for centuries Europe has force-fed us with lies and bloated us with pestilence, for it is not true that the work of man is done
that we have no business being on earth
that we parasite the world
that it is enough for us to heel to the world whereas the work of man has only begun
and man still must overcome all the interdictions wedged in the recesses of his fervor
and no race has a monopoly on beauty, on intelligence, on strength

and there is room for everyone at the convocation of conquest
and we know now that the sun turns around our earth lighting
the parcel designated by our will alone and that every star falls from the
sky to earth at our omnipotent command.

I now see the meaning of this trial by the sword: my country is the "lance of night" of my Bambara ancestors. It shrivels and its point desperately retreats toward the haft when it is sprinkled with chicken blood and it says that its nature requires the blood of man, his fat, his liver, his heart, not chicken blood.

And I seek for my country not date hearts, but men's hearts which in order to enter the silver cities through the great trapezoidal gate, beat with warrior blood, and my eyes sweep my kilometers of paternal earth I number its sores almost joyfully and I pile one on top of another like rare species, and my total is ever lengthened by unexpected mintings of baseness.

And there are those who never get over being made in the likeness of God but of the devil, those who believe that being a nigger is like being a second-class clerk; waiting for a better deal and upward mobility; those who beat the drum of compromise in front of themselves, those who live in their own oubliette; those who say to Europe: "You see, I *can* bow and scrape, like you I pay my respects, in short I am not different from you; pay no attention to my black skin: the sun did it."

And there is the nigger pimp, the nigger askari, and all the zebras shaking themselves in various ways to get rid of their stripes in a dew of fresh milk.

And in the midst of all that I say: right on! my grandfather dies, I say right on!
the old negritude progressively cadavers itself.
No bones about it: he was a good nigger a really good nigger,
massa's good ole darky.
The whites say he was a good nigger,
I say right on!
He was a good nigger indeed,

poverty had wounded his chest and back and they had stuffed into his poor brain that a fatality impossible to trap weighed on him; that he had no control over his own fate; that an evil Lord had for all eternity inscribed Thou Shall Not in his pelvic constitution; that he must be a good nigger; must sincerely believe in his worthlessness, without any perverse curiosity to check out the fatidic hieroglyphs. . . .
He was a very good nigger

and it never occurred to him that he could hoe, burrow, cut anything, anything else than insipid cane

He was a very good nigger.

And they threw stones at him, chunks of scrap iron, broken bottles, but neither these stones, nor this scrap iron, nor these bottles . . .

O peaceful years of God on this terraqueous clod!

and the whip argued with the bombilation of the flies over the sugary dew of our sores.
I say right on! The old negritude
progressively cadavers itself
the horizon breaks, recoils and expands
and through the shredding of clouds the flashing of a sign
the slave ship cracks everywhere . . . Its belly convulses and resounds . . .
The ghastly tapeworm of its cargo gnaws the fetid guts of the strange suckling of the sea!
And neither the joy of sails filled like a pocket stuffed with doubloons, nor the tricks played on the dangerous stupidity of the frigates of order prevent it from hearing the threat of its intestinal rumblings.

In vain to ignore them the captain hangs the biggest loudmouth nigger from the main yard or throws him into the sea, or feeds him to his mastiffs.

Reeking of fried onions the nigger scum rediscovers the bitter taste of freedom in its spilled blood

And the nigger scum is on its feet.

AUDRE LORDE

Audre Geraldine Lorde (1934–92), whose parents were Caribbean immigrants from Grenada, was born in New York City and educated at Catholic schools. Her first act of self-determination at a young age was to drop the "y" from her first name. Poetry came to her early; while in high school she submitted a poem to a literary magazine only to be told it was too "romantic" to qualify. She sent it to *Seventeen*, which accepted it for publication. Lorde graduated from Hunter College in 1959 and received a master's degree in library science from Columbia University in 1961. The following year she married a lawyer, Edward Rollins; they had two children but divorced in 1970. Lorde joined the Harlem Writers Guild, but resigned from it because of what she viewed as the group's overt homophobia. In 1968, she was awarded the first of two National Endowment for the Arts fellowships and became poet-in-residence at Tougaloo College in Jackson, Mississippi, where she witnessed nightly violence against civil-rights workers. At Tougaloo she met Frances Clayton, who became her lifetime partner. It was here that she linked her poetic talent and her dedication to the struggle against injustice. Her first book of poetry, *The First Cities*, was published in 1968, followed in 1970 by *Cables to Rage*. Neither of these books expressed any lesbian sentiments; Lorde "came out" in 1971, publicly reading a lesbian love poem, which *Ms.* magazine then printed. Her third collection, *From a Land Where Other People Live*, was nominated for a National Book Award; the award went to Adrienne Rich, who accepted it only as part of a joint statement with Lorde and Alice Walker "in the name of all women whose voices have gone and still go unheard in a patriarchal world."

Coal, published in 1976, was Lorde's first collection released by a major New York publisher, Norton; this house subsequently published her next three poetry collections and brought her a wider audience. Of *The Black Unicorn*, 1978, Adrienne Rich wrote, "refusing to be circumscribed by any simple identity, Audre Lorde writes as a Black woman, a mother, a daughter, a Lesbian, a feminist, a visionary; poems of elemental wildness and healing, nightmare and lucidity." In 1979 Lorde was the featured speaker at the first national march for gay and lesbian liberation in Washington, D.C. Lorde was professor of English at John Jay College of Criminal Justice from 1979 to 1981 and poet and professor of English at Hunter College from 1981 to 1987. She was the cofounder of Kitchen Table: Women of Color Press and founder of Sisters in Support of Sisters in South Africa. She found no contradiction between motherhood and lesbianism, feminism and raising a son, being black and having a white partner. In addition to her ten books of poems, her autobiographical *Cancer Journals* appeared in 1980 and won the American Library Association Gay Caucus Book of the Year in 1981. In 1994, after a fourteen-year battle against cancer, Lorde died in St. Croix.

from Poetry is Not a Luxury

The quality of light by which we scrutinize our lives has direct bearing upon the product which we live, and upon the changes which we hope to bring about through those lives. It is within this light that we form those ideas by which we pursue our magic and make it realized. This is poetry as illumination, for it is through poetry that we give name to those ideas which are—until the poem—nameless and formless, about to be birthed, but already felt. That distillation of experience from which true poetry springs births thought as dream births concept, as feeling births idea, as knowledge births (precedes) understanding.

As we learn to bear the intimacy of scrutiny and to flourish within it, as we learn to use the products of that scrutiny for power within our living, those fears which rule our lives and form our silences begin to lose their control over us.

For each of us as women, there is a dark place within, where hidden and growing our true spirit rises, "beautiful / and tough as chestnut / stanchions against (y)our nightmare of weakness / and of impotence."

These places of possibility within ourselves are dark because they are ancient and hidden; they have survived and grown strong through that darkness. Within these deep places, each one of us holds an incredible reserve of creativity and power, of unexamined and unrecorded emotion and feeling. The woman's place of power within each of us is neither white nor surface; it is dark, it is ancient, and it is deep.

When we view living in the european mode only as a problem to be solved, we rely solely upon our ideas to make us free, for these were what the white fathers told us were precious.

But as we come more into touch with our own ancient, noneuropean consciousness of living as a situation to be experienced and interacted with, we learn more and more to cherish our feelings, and to respect those hidden sources of our power from where true knowledge and, therefore, lasting action comes.

At this point in time, I believe that women carry within ourselves the possibility for fusion of these two approaches so necessary for survival, and we come closest to this combination in our poetry. I speak here of poetry as a revelatory distillation of experience, not the sterile word play that, too often, the white fathers distorted the word *poetry* to mean—in order to cover a desperate wish for imagination without insight.

For women, then, poetry is not a luxury. It is a vital necessity of our existence. It forms the quality of the light within which we predicate our hopes and dreams toward survival and change, first made into language, then into idea, then into more tangible action. Poetry is the way we help give name to the nameless so it can be thought. The farthest horizons of our hopes and fears are cobbled by our poems, carved from the rock experiences of our daily lives.

As they become known to and accepted by us, our feelings and the honest exploration of them become sanctuaries and spawning grounds for the most radical and daring of ideas. They become a safe-house for that difference so necessary to change and the conceptualization of any meaningful action. Right now, I could name at least ten ideas I would have found intolerable or incomprehensible and frightening, except as they came after dreams and poems. This is not idle fantasy, but a disciplined attention to the true meaning of "it feels right to me." We can train ourselves to respect our feelings and to transpose them into a language so they can be shared. And where that language does not yet exist, it is our poetry which helps to fashion it. Poetry is not only dream and vision; it is the skeleton architecture of our lives. It lays the foundations for a future of change, a bridge across our fears of what has never been before.

Possibility is neither forever nor instant. It is not easy to sustain belief in its efficacy. We can sometimes work long and hard to establish one beachhead of real resistance to the deaths we are expected to live, only to have that beachhead assaulted or threatened by those canards we have been socialized to fear, or by the withdrawal of those approvals that we have been warned to seek for safety. Women see ourselves diminished or softened by the falsely benign accusations of childishness, of nonuniversality, or changeability, of sensuality. And who asks the question: Am I altering your aura, your ideas, your dreams, or am I merely moving you to temporary and reactive action? And even though the latter is no mean task, it is one that must be seen within the context of a need for true alteration of the very foundations of our lives.

The white fathers told us: I think, therefore I am. The Black mother within each of us—the poet—whispers in our dreams: I feel, therefore I can be free. Poetry coins the language to express and charter this revolutionary demand, the implementation of that freedom.

However, experience has taught us that action in the now is also necessary, always. Our children cannot dream unless they live, they cannot live unless they are nourished, and who else will feed them the real food without which their dreams will be no different from ours? "If you want us to change the world someday, we at least have to live long enough to grow up!" shouts the child.

Sometimes we drug ourselves with dreams of new ideas. The head will save us. The brain alone will set us free. But there are no new ideas still waiting in the wings to save us as women, as human. There are only old and forgotten ones, new combinations, extrapolations and recognitions from within ourselves—along with the renewed courage to try them out. And we must constantly encourage ourselves and each other to attempt the heretical actions that our dreams imply, and so many of our old ideas disparage. In the forefront of our move toward change, there is only poetry to hint at possibility made real. Our poems formulate the implications of ourselves, what we feel within and dare make real (or bring action into accordance with), our fears, our hopes, our most cherished terrors. . . .

DENISE LEVERTOV

Denise Levertov (1923–97) was born in England of Welsh and Russian parentage. Her father, a pious Hasidic Jew, converted to Anglicanism and became a pastor before her birth. She and her older sister Olga were home-schooled by their mother, an avid reader, who introduced them to such authors as Cather, Dickens, and Tolstoy. A precocious child, Levertov began to write poems at the age of five. She claimed that she knew at this early age that she would become a writer.

During the bombings of London in World War II, Levertov, seventeen years old, became a civilian nurse. She wrote her first book, *The Double Image* (1946), before she was twenty-two; it won her recognition as one of a poetic group known as the New Romantics. In 1947 she married an American, Mitchell Goodman (they later divorced), and the following year the couple moved to New York City, where Levertov came under the influence of William Carlos Williams and Robert Duncan. Without Williams, she said, "I could not have developed from a British Romantic with an almost Victorian background to an American poet of any vitality." Levertov was also influenced by the Black Mountain School of poets, particularly by Robert Creely, but did not consider herself attached to any school. Her poetry moved away from fixed forms and evolved in an open, experimental style in which content and form were meant to attain a state of dynamic, intuitive interaction.

In 1949, Levertov's son was born. She subsequently taught at Vassar, MIT, and Tufts, and for a decade at Stanford University. Poetry editor of the *Nation* and later of *Mother Jones,* Levertov's own poetry took up such social issues as the Vietnam War, the trial of Nazi war criminal Adolf Eichmann, the white students shot at Kent State, the black students shot in Orangeburg, women's rights, protests at nuclear sites, motherhood, love, and nature. She wrote twenty books of poems as well as translations from Jean Joubert and four essay collections. The sixties and early seventies saw Levertov join the War Resisters League. She lectured and wrote against the war; themes of feminism and activism were prominently visible in her work, and many critics attacked what they saw as her propagandistic poems. She addresses this issue in the excerpt that follows. Her voice acquired a fresh lyric intensity with *Freeing the Dust* (1975), which won the Lenore Marshall prize. Her many awards include the Shelley Memorial Award, the Robert Frost Medal, and Guggenheim and National Endowment of the Arts fellowships.

Levertov moved to Seattle, Washington, where she spent the final decade of her life. Here, looking out on Mount Rainier, which she sought fiercely to defend from the encroachments of civilization, she completed six books of poems before succumbing to complications from lymphoma.

from Horses with Wings

. . . Poets—not, let it be emphasized, in their personal human aspect (or not in any greater degree than for any other individuals in whom the imagination is alive), but as poets, in the activity of poem-making— possess like Pegasus some inherent power of exaltation. But it is equally important to recognize that Pegasus was not constantly airborne. It was by striking his sharp hoof hard upon the rocky earth that Pegasus released the fountain of Hippocrene, the fountain of poetic inspiration henceforth sacred to the Muses. (Some say, too, that it was not until the moment that Medusa's blood, spurting from her neck, *touched earth* that he became manifest.) Poet and poem must strike hard and sink deep into the material to tap spiritual springs or give new birth to "the winged fountain."

In poetry we may observe traits of the parents as well as of Pegasus himself. There are poems vast, restless, almost formless, yet powerful, which evoke the character of Poseidon and the ocean's tidal rhythms. There are Medusan poems of rage and hatred, sharp-clawed with satire, writhing with serpentine humor, and flashing forth venomous tongues of denunciation of despair.

And then there are those, far more numerous, which in various pro-portions combine, like Pegasus himself, earth and air; and it is these, not those in which the traits of Poseidon or Medusa dominate, which are most representatively poems. They may walk, trot, or gallop, but they have the inherent power to soar aloft. Some poets hold this power in reserve, keeping Pegasus on a tight rein; others avail themselves of it with more or less frequency. Such flights are not to be equaled with abstraction, as may too easily be done if one assumes that the earthy [*sic*] horse represents the concrete and the wings the abstract. Pegasus as horse does indeed present the sensual, the sensuous, the concretely specific, but that physicality is itself related to the unconscious; that is, not only to the instinctive but the intuitive. And his wings, which do not deform but increase and enhance his equine characteristics of speed and strength of motion, express not the abstractions of linear intellection but the transcendent and transformative power of imagination itself.

But it would be no service to the understanding of poetry's essential nature and the poet's vocation to smooth over its stern or daimonic aspects. Pegasus, sired by a ruthless god, born in violence of an abhorrent monstrosity, is himself a daimon, a force, an energy. He is not, as Heine put it, a virtuous utilitarian hack; nor is he a children's pet. Bellerophon only tames him with the help of a magical golden bridle, the gift of Athene. It is a beneficent act to help destroy the devastating Chimaera, whose three heads—of a goat, a snake, and a lion—embody licentiousness, insidious venom, and ruthless dominance; and the story reveals in parable that inspiration, not courage and strategy alone, overcomes these evils. Yet, not himself destructive, Pegasus, by lending to Bellerophon his indispensable swiftness and power to rise aloft, has become accessory to the performance of a killing. As a flying cloud, he may carry life-giving showers but can also bring the devastation of flash floods. And after Bellerophon's hero-deed is done, it is the speed and levitational power of his steed that tempt him to hubris. Extreme speed is a way of referring to a kind of excessive eloquence, the words tumbling out too fast for coherence, and too many for each to be just and indispensable. A poet flying high and swiftly becomes a kind of bird, whose speech is not intelligible to humankind; or a breath of the storm wind, which breaks what it sweeps over. Pegasus, anciently known as accursed as well as blessed, in latter days can perhaps be seen in this aspect as the steed of poets willfully abstruse or brutally verbose. Finally, Bellerophon attempts to fly upon him to Olympus—and then Pegasus throws him. Whether or not Zeus sent a gadfly to sting him into this action, or whether he himself resented Bellerophon's presumption, the glorious familiar becomes instrumental in the hero's fall from grace, both by being that which (innocently) tempts and that which, misused, rejects further cooperation. Thereafter he himself is translated to the Olympian stables and becomes the bearer of thunder and lightning "at the behest of prudent Zeus"—of those tremendous words from an apparent nowhere ("out of the sky," as we say), whether sounding within the mind or out in the bustling world, which come sometimes to strike us with terror or remorse and in a flash to illuminate an obscure history or reveal an abyss at our feet.

Eos, the dawn, sometimes rides Pegasus, bringing a saffron shimmer of first light. This daybreak appearance may bring to mind the astonishing poetry occasionally uttered (and occasionally written down) by young children, and also the poetic efflorescence that often takes place in adolescence. But like that of early morning sunshine, these promises are not always fulfilled. The poet of extraordinary gifts who early produces major work and dies very young is, or has become, a rarity; and the earliest work of those who live longer is even more rarely of more than historical interest. It is the pristine value of initial inspirations that Pegasus more aptly signifies when regarded as the horse of dawn. No matter what metamorphoses poem or stanza or image within them may have to pass through to become all that it can, its source and first appearance should not be despised. . . .

GWENDOLYN BROOKS

Gwendolyn Brooks (1917–2000) was born in Topeka, Kansas, but grew up in Chicago. While still in her teens, she accumulated a sheaf of her poems that had appeared in the *Chicago Defender*. After she married the writer Henry Blakely in 1938, the couple moved to a cramped apartment on the South Side. A son was born in 1940 and a daughter in 1951. In 1943, Brooks won the Midwestern Writers' Conference Poetry Award, and in 1945 Harper & Row published her first book of poems, *A Street in Bronzeville*, which received critical acclaim. There followed in short order a Guggenheim fellowship, election as a fellow to the American Academy of Arts and Letters, and her selection as one of *Mademoiselle's* Ten Young Women of the Year. Her second book, *Annie Allen*, won the Pulitzer Prize in 1949, making her the first African American to receive that honor.

Other honors succeeded these. President Kennedy invited her to read at a Library of Congress poetry festival in 1962; she was appointed Consultant in Poetry to the Library of Congress (a post that was later renamed Poet Laureate of the United States) in 1985, and in 1994 she delivered the Jefferson Lecture for the National Endowment for the Humanities. Other awards include the Frost Medal, the Shelley Memorial Award, a grant from the National Endowment for the Arts, and half a hundred honorary doctor of letters awards. Brooks wrote more than twenty volumes of poetry as well as a novel and an autobiographical fragment. Her career veered from an initial position of literary integrationist to that of protest poet. Strongly influenced by the works of Countee Cullen and Langston Hughes, she absorbed the racial consciousness of the Harlem Renaissance and brought her voice to the Chicago School of writing, with its emphasis on urban commitment and the dichotomy of a city divided between black and white. Never strident, Brooks was always forceful, as the piece excerpted here, an interview with Steve Cape, attests. Stylistically, her work embraces ballads, the rhythm of the blues, sonnets, and unrestricted free verse. Sometimes she utilizes E. E. Cummings's lower-case and hyphenated structures; sometimes her stanzas are formal, even Spenserian. When she was asked by George Stavros in an interview published in *Contemporary Literature* (1970) whether "We Real Cool" was modeled after Ezra Pound, she burst out, "My gosh, no! I don't even admire Pound. . . . When I start writing a poem, I don't think about models or about what anybody else in the world has done." Her obituary in the *San Francisco Chronicle* contained this Brooksian quotation: "If you have one drop of blackness in you—yes, of course it comes out red—you are mine, you are a member of my family."

from The Future of Black Poetry

. . . SC: In the short manual on black poetry writing that you wrote . . . you comment on poetry being a transient thing and it serving an immediate purpose more than a person intentionally trying to write for posterity or for something that will be permanent.

BROOKS: That does not express what I have been doing; whatever I said to that effect was about those black poets in the late sixties, some of whom, not all but some of whom felt that black poetry shouldn't be written with an eye to posterity billions and trillions of years from now. They felt, some of them, that if they wrote a poem that worked for black people today, it would have served its purpose. . . . I'm afraid that I'm weak enough to think that it would be very nice if somebody could get some nourishment or healing or just plain rich pleasure out of poems I'm writing today.

SC: Another thing from *Black Poetry Writing* that I'd like to get a comment on. You broke black poetry down into three stages, a first stage that was a statement of condition, and then moving to a poetry of integration, and then the present poetry being more an assertive, positive, individualistic thing.

BROOKS: I was describing my own three stages of creativity. One, I call my "express myself" stage, because I was writing about anything and everything in my environment just because I wanted to express myself—flailing about. And second, my "integration flavoring" stage when I wrote a lot of poems which I hoped would bring black people and white people and all people together, and they didn't seem to be doing that (laughter) in great numbers at any rate, and a third stage governed by that little credo that some of the Black poets had in the late sixties, "Black poetry is poetry written by blacks, about blacks, and to blacks," and then, I'm trying very seriously now to create for myself, develop for myself a kind of poem that will be immediately accessible and interesting, immediately interesting, to all manner of blacks, not just college students though they're included too. That kind of poem will feature song, will be *songlike,* and yet still properly called poetry.

SC: Is that where you—?

BROOKS: Are now.

SC: What about the future of black poetry in America, do you see any trends which you think are going to be developed?

BROOKS: I believe that events will dictate what turns black poetry takes next. A lot of black poetry is being written now that seems to be interior poetry, poetry that goes deeper into the interior to explore, but I believe that the writing concern will be coming back outdoors just as soon as some things become blatantly obvious. A lot of stuff is happening now that I believe will involve us all, and the poets, their writing, will reflect what they're experiencing, just as it did in the late sixties.

SC: What would a few of these things be?

BROOKS: Well, I'm sure your imagination can help you there—when you look at the headlines and you listen to television, and you hear our various leaders urging Carter to get over there and drop a few bombs (laughter).

SC: Everything getting more conservative. . . .

BROOKS: Well, I think that is what *has* been happening, but Conservatism can go—look, I'm no sociologist but at least I think I can say this—Conservatism goes just so far and then there's a reaction against it, wouldn't you agree to that? At least that's what's been happening so far and I don't expect the future to be much different. I do know that the people, the blacks on the African continent, don't seem inclined to lie down. They're getting fiercer and fiercer, and more and more interested in protecting themselves. I don't expect that to have a reverse. If you just let your imagination go you'll see that we're in for some very lively poetry. . . .

CHARLES BERNSTEIN

Charles Bernstein (1950–)was born in New York City to a second-generation Russian Jewish immigrant family employed in the garment industry. He received his BA from Harvard College, where he studied philosophy, discovered an affinity for Gertrude Stein, and was active in radical theater. After a brief period in California, where Bernstein became connected with writers of experimental poetry, he and his wife, artist Susan Bee, moved to New York, where in 1978 he co-founded the influential journal $L=A=N=G=U=A=G=E$, dedicated to a poetry that rejected "received and beloved notions of voice, self, expression, sincerity, and representation." One of contemporary poetry's major entrepreneurs, he has since founded the Electronic Poetry Center at SUNY Buffalo, where he taught for many years, New York's Ear Inn series, and other literary institutions. Bernstein has published over twenty books of poetry, most recently *Republics of Reality: 1975–1995* (2000). He has collaborated on projects with his wife and with composers of opera. His three books of essays include *A Poetics* (1992), and he has also edited several anthologies on poetics. He has won numerous honors, including Guggenheim and National Endowment for the Arts fellowships and is a professor at the University of Pennsylvania.

Believing that "Official Verse Culture" reflects a narrow stylistic orthodoxy, Bernstein has devoted his career to building alternative formations that provide a space for difference. Bernstein has said that in his formative years, " I was trying to get away from the literary, from any preset idea of poetry or of the aesthetic." His work has been strongly influenced by film, theater, performance art, and painting. Of his current work he has said, "I for one am happy to embrace the description of my work as ungainly solipsistic incoherence that has no meaning. No meaning at all." In his diatribe against the popular recent program National Poetry Month, Bernstein argues that poetry should not be brought into mass culture, but kept apart from it as "a crucial alternative."

Against National Poetry Month As Such

And they say
If I would just sing lighter songs
Better for me would it be,
But not is this truthful;
For sense remote
Adduces worth and gives it
Even if ignorant reading impairs it;
But it's my creed
That these songs yield
No value at the commencing
Only later, when one earns it.

—*translated from Giraut de Bornelh (12th century)*

April is the cruelest month for poetry.

As part of the spring ritual of National Poetry Month, poets are symbolically dragged into the public square in order to be humiliated with the claim that their product has not achieved sufficient market penetration and needs to be revived by the Artificial Resuscitation Foundation (ARF) lest the art form collapse from its own incompetence, irrelevance, and as a result of the general disinterest among the broad masses of the American People.

The motto of ARF's National Poetry Month is: "Poetry's not so bad, really."

National Poetry Month is sponsored by the Academy of American Poets, an organization that uses its mainstream status to exclude from its promotional activities much of the formally innovative and "other-stream" poetries that form the inchoate heart of the art of poetry. The Academy's activities on behalf of National Poetry Month tend to focus on the most conventional of contemporary poetry; perhaps a more accurate name for the project might be National Mainstream Poetry Month. Then perhaps we could designate August as National Unpopular Poetry Month.

Through its "safe poetry" free verse distribution program, the Academy of American Poetry's major initiative for National Poetry Month is to give away millions of generic "poetry books" to random folks throughout the country. This program is intended to promote safe reading experiences and is based on ARF's founding principle that safe poetry is the best prophylactic against aesthetic experience.

Free poetry is never free, nor is free verse without patterns.

Oscar Wilde once wrote, "Only an auctioneer admires all schools of art." National Poetry Month professes to an undifferentiated promotion for "all" poetry, as if supporting all poetry, any more than supporting all politics, you could support any.

National Poetry Month is about making poetry safe for readers by promoting examples of the art form at its most bland and its most morally "positive." The message is: *Poetry is good for you.* But, unfortunately, promoting poetry as if it were an "easy listening" station just reinforces the idea that poetry is culturally irrelevant and has done a disservice not only to poetry deemed too controversial or difficult to promote but also to the poetry it puts forward in this way. "Accessibility" has become a kind of Moral Imperative based on the condescending notion that readers are intellectually challenged, and mustn't be presented with anything but Safe Poetry. As if poetry will turn people off to poetry.

Poetry: Readers Wanted. The kind of poetry I want is not a happy art with uplifting messages and easy to understand emotions. I want a poetry that's bad for you. Certainly not the kind of poetry that Volkswagen would be comfortable about putting in every new car it sells, which, believe it or not, is a 1999 feature of the Academy's National Poetry Month program.

The most desirable aim of the Academy's National Poetry Month is to increase the sales of poetry books. But when I scan some of the principal corporate sponsors of the program of the past several years, I can't help noting (actually I can but I prefer not to) that some are among the major institutions that work actively against the wider distribution of poetry. The large chain bookstores are no friends to the small presses and independent bookstores that are the principal supporters of all types of American poetry: they have driven many independents out of business and made it more difficult for most small presses (the site of the vast majority of poetry publishing) to get their books into retail outlets, since by and large these presses are excluded from the large chains. I also note this year that *The New York Times* is a major sponsor of National Poetry Month; but if the *Times* would take seriously the task of reviewing poetry books and readings, it would be doing a far greater service to poetry than advertising its support for National Poetry Month. The whole thing strikes me as analogous to cigarette makers sponsoring a free emphysema clinic. Indeed, part of the purpose of the Academy's National Poetry Month appears to be to advertise National Poetry Month and its sponsors—thus, the Academy has taken out a series of newspapers ads that mention no poets and no poems but rather announce the existence of National Poetry Month with a prominent listing of its backers, who appear, in the end, to be sponsoring themselves.

The path taken by the Academy's National Poetry Month, and by such foundations as Lannan and the Lila Wallace—*Reader's Digest,* have been misguided because these organizations have decided to promote not poetry but the idea of poetry, and the idea of poetry too often has meant almost no poetry at all. Time and time again we hear the official spokespersons tell us they want to support projects that give speedy and efficient access to poetry and that the biggest obstacle to this access is, indeed, poetry, which may not provide the kind of easy reading required by such mandates.

The solution: find poetry that most closely resembles the fast and easy reading experiences of most Americans under the slogans—Away with Difficulty! Make Poetry Palatable for the People! I think particularly of the five-year plan launched under the waving banners of Disguise the Acid Taste of the Aesthetic with NutriSweet Coating, which emphasized producing poetry in short sound bites, with MTV-type images to accompany them, so the People will not even know they are getting poetry.

This is the genius of the new Literary Access programs: the more you dilute art, the more you appear to increase the access. But access to what? Not to anything that would give a reader or listener any strong sense that poetry matters, but rather access to a watered down version that lacks the cultural edge and the aesthetic sharpness of the best popular and mass culture. The only reason that poetry matters is that is has something different to offer, something slower on the uptake, maybe, but more intense for all that, and also something necessarily smaller in scale in terms of audience. Not better than mass culture but a crucial alternative to it.

The reinvention, the making of a poetry for our time, is the only thing that makes poetry matter. And that means, literally, making poetry *matter*, that is making poetry that intensifies the matter or materiality of language—acoustic, visual, syntactic, semantic. Poetry is very much alive when it finds ways of doing things in a media-saturated environment that only poetry can do, but very much dead when it just retreads the same old same old.

* * *

As an alternative to National Poetry Month, I propose that we have an International Anti-Poetry month. As part of the activities, all verse in public places will be covered over—from the Statue of Liberty to the friezes on many of our government buildings. Poetry readings will be removed from radio and TV (just as it is during the other eleven months of the year). Parents will be asked not to read Mother Goose and other rimes to their children but only . . . *fiction*. Religious institutions will have to forgo reading verse passages from the liturgy and only prose translations of the Bible will be recited, with hymns strictly banned. Ministers in the Black churches will be kindly requested to stop preaching. *Cats* will be closed for the month by order of the Anti-Poetry Commission. Poetry readings will be replaced by self-help lectures. Love letters will have to be written only in expository paragraphs. Baseball will have to start its spring training in May. No vocal music will be played on the radio or TV or sung in the concert halls. Children will have to stop playing all slapping and counting and singing games and stick to board games and football.

As part of the campaign, the major daily newspapers will run full page ads with this text:

Go ahead, don't read any poetry.

You won't be able to understand it anyway: the best stuff is all over your head.

And there aren't even any commercials to liven up the action.

Anyway, you'll end up with a headache trying to figure out what the poems are saying because they are saying NOTHING.

Who needs that.

Better go to the movies.

JUDITH ORTIZ COFER

Judith Ortiz Cofer (1952–) was born in Hormigueros, Puerto Rico. She came to the United States as a two-year-old, when her military father, stationed at the Brooklyn Navy Yard, chose Paterson, New Jersey, where he had relatives, as a home base. His fleet went to Europe frequently; every time he sailed, her mother took her and her brother back to Hormigueros. In prose and in poetry Cofer describes the experience of the immigrant, focusing on the Puerto Rican's sense of psychological exile, which she feels is just as problematic as actual political and economic separation from the mainstream. Wherever they lived, her mother, who refused to assimilate, made that place into a microcosm of the island. As a child, Cofer had to serve as her mother's translator and interpreter. Being dislocated and relocated geographically she feels made her into a silent observer. This material provides the nexus for her three books of poems, *Reaching for the Mainland* (1987), *Terms of Survival* (1987), and *The Latin Deli: Prose and Poetry* (1993). Cofer has also written fiction and essays. Her collection of short stories, *An Island Like You,* was named Best Book of the Year (1995–96) by the American Library Association. *The Year of Our Revolution*, stories and poems, was awarded a Paterson Book Prize in 1998. In an interview published in the *Kenyon Review* in 1992, Cofer said, "Poetry is what connects me to my memory, to my imagination, to my subconscious life, and to my original language."

In addition to the Puerto Rican immigrant experience, Cofer writes about the particular difficulties and gifts of the writer who is a woman. Her poems reflect this feminist concern, as does her anthology, edited with Marilyn Kallett, *Sleeping with One Eye Open: Women Writers and the Art of Survival* (1999), which presents stories and essays about women who lead effective lives as artists. Cofer's title essay relates the ways in which a mythological story from her Puerto Rican culture gave her her writing.

Cofer has received fellowships from the National Endowment for the Arts, the Witter Bynner Foundation, and the Rockefeller Foundation. She is now Franklin Professor of English at the University of Georgia.

from And May He Be Bilingual

. . . Before his image they kneel,
Margarita, Josefina, Maria, and Isabel
All fervently hoping
That if not omnipotent
At least He be bilingual.

In this early poem I express the sense of powerlessness I felt as a non-native speaker of English in the United States. Non-native. Non-participant in the mainstream culture. Non, as no, not, nothing. This little poem is about the non-ness of the non-speakers of the ruling language making a pilgrimage to the only One who can help, hopeful in their faith that someone is listening, yet still suspicious that even He doesn't understand their language. I grew up in the tight little world of the Puerto Rican community in Paterson, New Jersey, and later moved to Augusta, Georgia, where my "native" universe shrank even further to a tiny group of us who were brought to the Deep South through the military channels our fathers had chosen out of economic necessity. I wrote this ironic poem years ago, out of a need to explore the loneliness, the almost hopelessness, I had felt and observed in the other non-native speakers, many my own relatives, who would never master the English language well enough to be able to connect with the native speakers in significant ways as I did. . . .

I teach American literature as an outsider in love with the Word —whatever language it is written in. They, [Cofer's students] at least some of them, come to understand that my main criterion when I teach is excellence and that I will talk to them about so-called minority writers whom I admire in the same terms as I will the old standards they know they are supposed to honor and study. I show them why they should admire them, not blindly, but with a critical eye. I speak English with my Spanish accent to these native speakers. I tell them about my passion for the genius of humankind, demonstrated through literature: the power of language to affect, to enrich, or to diminish and destroy lives, its potential to empower someone like me, someone like them. The fact that English is my second language does not seem to matter beyond the first few lectures, when the students sometimes look askance at one another, perhaps wondering whether they have walked into the wrong classroom and at any moment this obviously "Spanish" professor will ask them to start conjugating regular and irregular verbs. They can't possible know this about me: in my classes, everyone is safe from Spanish grammar recitation. Because almost all of my formal education has been in English, I avoid all possible risk of falling into a discussion of the uses of the conditional or of the merits of the subjunctive tense in the Spanish language. Hey, I just *do* Spanish, I don't explain it. Spanish language.

Likewise, when I *do* use my Spanish and allude to my Puerto Rican heritage, it comes from deep inside me where my imagination and memory reside, and I do it through my writing. My poetry, my stories, and my essays concern themselves with the coalescing of languages and cultures into a vision that has meaning first of all for me; then, if I am served well by my craft and the transformation occurs, it will also have meaning for others as art. . . .

As I travel around this country I am constantly surprised by the diversity of its peoples and cultures. It is like a huge, colorful puzzle. And the beauty is in its complexity. Yet there are some things that transcend the obvious differences: great literature, great ideas, and great idealists, for example. I find Don Quixote plays almost universal; after all, who among us does not have an Impossible Dream? Shakespeare's wisdom is planetary in its appeal; Gandhi's and King's message is basic to the survival of our civilization, and most people know it; and other voices that are like a human racial memory speak in a language that can almost always be translated into meaning.

And genius doesn't come in only one package. The Bard happened to be a white gentleman from England, but what about our timid Emily Dickinson? Would we call on her in our class, that mousy little girl in the back of the room squinting at the chalkboard and blushing at everything? We almost lost her art to neglect. Thank God poetry is stronger than time or prejudices. . . .

What I'm trying to say is that the phenomenon we call culture in a society is organic, not manufactured. It grows where we plant it. Culture is our garden, and we may neglect it, trample on it, or we may choose to cultivate it. In America we are dealing with varieties we have imported, grafted, cross-pollinated. I can only hope the experts who say that the land is replenished in this way are right. It is the ongoing American experiment, and it has to take root in the classroom first. If it doesn't succeed, then we will be back to praying and hoping that at least He be bilingual.

LI-YOUNG LEE

Li-Young Lee (1957–) was born in Jakarta, Indonesia, of Chinese parents. His father, a deeply religious Christian, had been Mao Zedong's personal physician, and his mother traced her ancestry to Chinese royalty. In 1949 when the People's Republic of China came to power, the family fled to Indonesia. Ten years later they again went into exile to escape rising hostility against Chinese settlers (Lee's father was jailed for a year by Sukarno) and trekked through Hong Kong, Macau, and Japan before taking up residence in the United States in 1964. Lee, who taught at Northwestern University and the University of Iowa, now lives in Chicago with his wife and two sons. His extended family lives in the same building.

Lee's books of poetry are *Rose* (1986), *The City in Which I Love You* (1991), and *Book of My Nights* (2001), a title alluding to his frequent battles with insomnia. Lee is a well-liked poet and sought-after reader of his poems and has won numerous poetry awards including the Lamont Prize and the Delmore Schwartz Memorial Poetry Award. His memoir, *The Winged Seed: A Remembrance* (1995), received an American Book Award. His other honors include a Lannan Literary Award, a Whiting Writer's Award, grants from the Illinois Arts Council, the Commonwealth of Pennsylvania, the Pennsylvania Council on the Arts, the National Endowment for the Arts, and a Guggenheim Foundation fellowship. Lee's poetry takes the form of direct, anecdotal free verse focused on images. His subject matter encompasses the cultural traditions of his extended family, and several of his best-known poems focus on imagery drawn from traditional Chinese meals. His poetry finds deep emotion and meaning in paying close attention to the specific incidents of daily life—meals, tasks, and relationships—as well as in the sleepless spiritual searching of his inner self. In this interview, he explores the spiritual responsibility of poetry.

from Interview with Marie Jordan

JORDAN: When you speak of breath, how are breath and poems related?

LEE: Poems and breath are related in basically the same way that breath and utterance are related. That is, when we speak we use the outgoing breath, the exhaled breath. The exhaled breath is the dying breath, while the inhaled breath is the in-feeding breath. So all human utterance is our dying breath articulated.

JORDAN: And the inhale? Do we inhale the poem with our breath?

LEE: Well, let me back up and try to answer it this way. Breathing is a wheel. It turns in and out, inhale, exhale. Now, I don't want to get too esoteric here, but I'll mention the fact that as we inhale, our bones and muscles actually get very compacted, harder. When we exhale, on the other hand, our bodies become very soft. Ancient Daoists, so I'm told, believed that upon inhalation our ego-self becomes very inflated, while during exhalation our sense of ego and body diminishes and we become more open to a deeper, bigger presence. What I find of interest, though, is this: As we speak, what we mean gets disclosed in opposite ratio to the expelled breath. That is, as breath dies in exhalation while we speak, more and more of the meaning of what we're saying gets divulged. Frost calls this the tribute of the current to the source. Was it Blake who called it proceeding by contraries? Meaning is born as the breath dies. In the case of poetry, the meaning that gets born is manifold, saying one thing but meaning many things. And in this way, a poem is a paradigm of human living. As we perish, the meaning of our lives is revealed.

JORDAN: Theodore Roethke said he wanted poetry to extend consciousness as far as it can go. He said that he sought to write poems that try in their rhythms to catch the very movement of the mind itself. Do you think along the lines of Roethke, in terms of the mind?

LEE: I do. But let me say that I understand all poems to be projections. And to study those projections is to begin to understand the projector, the mind, or ground, of the projection. Let me add here that by the word mind I mean what the Chinese mean when they use the word *shin*. That is, mind and heart. A poem is an image of the maker, as a human being is an image of God. But a poem doesn't simply transpose being. It also proposes possibilities of being. A poem is also a proposition. It isn't just a naturalistic copy of the projector. Or maybe it is, and an integral aspect of human being is its tendency to speculate or propose certain ideal modes of being. Poems make very important propositions by their enactment of certain presences we may never envision if it weren't for the poems. Does this make sense?

JORDAN: This seems especially true in *Book of My Nights*. In your two previous books, *Rose* and *In The City in Which I Love You,* there seems to be an underlying wrestling with self and God. Now you seem to be far more intimate with the unknown, and with God. That wrestling, like Jacob's pulling at the thigh of God, is missing. Did you feel that when writing these poems?

LEE: I felt it in my life. I think that because when I was young I deified my parents, so I projected or transferred all the god-presence onto my parents and the world around me. Part of my own evolution or development as a person is to try to recognize that presence is in my being, too. God's presence is in the cells of my body and deep in my subconscious. God's presence is not only out there in the world in trees and oceans and birds and people, but it's in me, I hope. In the new poems I was more successful at that. I was more open to what somebody called, "the invasion from the inside."

JORDAN: Your new poems appear at once semiotic and mimetic. They are fluid, diffused, and disseminated, yet you maintain an analysis of universal relationships. Do you see your poems as being beyond language, or metalanguage?

LEE: The thing that obsesses me is always beyond language. Language is almost an inconvenience. I have a feeling that no matter what kind of art we're practicing, at some point we become hyper-aware of our medium. If we're painting it's paint and if writing it's the language. But if we don't at some point move beyond our hyper-consciousness of language, we're stuck in the land of the medium. On that plane, only the relationships of words to other words is available, while the relationships of words to their ground, mother-silence, on the one hand, and to the concepts they name, on the other hand, gets abandoned.

That would be like seeing the significance of people only in relationship to other people, in other words, only as social units. Meanwhile, their relationship to the ground of their being and to their individuality is disregarded.

JORDAN: You have said that we are all guests in language and once we start speaking our language we bow to that language and bend that language to us. What do you mean when you say that we bend language to us?

LEE: The beautiful Mexican poet, Octavio Paz, said something like— the difference between prose and poetry is that in prose you use language and in poetry, you yield to language. It feels like there's this weird dialectic between us and the language. I can't tell whether we just yield to it or we bend it. Maybe both. Sometimes it feels like we're bending the language. Maybe it's a process of self-making. I can't tell.

JORDAN: What, aside from language, does the poet have to work with?

LEE: It's not just language that we use to write poems. We use silence, too. In fact, I think we use language to inflect silence so we can hear it better. I suppose that's why I love Emily Dickinson. I love her the most when I don't have the feeling she's fooling around with language, but up against something she can hardly say. What we're actually seeing is the language straining to say something.

JORDAN: What do you mean by inflecting silence?

LEE: Inflected silence could be explained by the way everything seems quieter after you hear a bell ring. After church bells ring everything seems more quiet. It's almost as if we're using language, but the real subject is silence. The silence is primal. I hope that after a line or stanza there's a silence imparted to the reader. That's my worry.

JORDAN: Aren't there different kinds of silences?

LEE: Yes. Different colors and shades. The deepest possible silence is the silence of God. I feel a poem ultimately imparts silence. That way it's again disillusioning. It disillusions us of our own small presence in order to reveal the presence of this deeper silence—this pregnant, primal, ancient, contemporary, and imminent silence, which is God. I don't know another form of language where this is possible except in poetry.

JORDAN: I see a circular form in your new poems, going toward and
coming back, and the life-death tension between poles. You take
risks moving from deeper to more daring levels of consciousness, including the dream-state subconsciousness. There remains
a tension between poles, a day-night, child-parent, and light-
darkness. You call it "miles of the sea arriv[ing] at a seed . . ."

LEE: It feels true when I'm writing the poems.

JORDAN: What do you mean by the silence being God?

LEE: Do you know the verse in the Bible that reads, "Be still and
know that I am God?" That kind of stillness, and silence. I think
a really good poem can impart a stillness which is God—which
is also awe. I would say that disillusionment is revelation and
revelation is apocalypse and every poem is apocalyptic. On the
one hand we have ecliptic things that hide and on the other hand
we have apocalyptic things that reveal. The writing of poetry is
writing that reveals, but doesn't just reveal a personal presence,
it reveals a transpersonal presence and the dualities of that presence is silence, stillness, and the saturation of presence. . . .

NAOMI SHIHAB NYE

Naomi Shihab Nye (1952–), poet, essayist, author of children's literature, and songwriter, was born in St. Louis, Missouri. Nye's Palestinian father had arrived in the United States at eighteen and married her mother, an American artist of Swiss-German descent. Both parents encouraged Nye's writing from an early age, and at seven she published her first poem. In 1966, when Nye was fourteen, her family moved to her father's native village of Sinjil in the West Bank where her father edited the *Jerusalem Times*. In Sinjil, Nye met her paternal grandmother, Sitti Khadra, with whom she shared a close relationship until her Sitti Khadra died at age 106. Nye earned her BA from Trinity University in San Antonio, Texas, and since then has stayed in San Antonio, working as a visiting writer with students of all ages. She lives with her husband and son.

Nye has published numerous books of poems, including *19 Varieties of Gazelle: Poems of the Middle East* (2002), *Fuel* (1998), *Red Suitcase* (1994), and *Hugging the Jukebox* (1982) and edited several anthologies. *Sitti's Secrets* (1995), whose main character is based on Sitti Khadra, received the Jane Addams Children's Book Award. In 1988, the Academy of American Poets gave Nye the I. B. Lavan Award for her third anthology, *I Feel a Little Jumpy Around You*. Other works include *Lullaby Raft* (a picture book) and *Never in a Hurry* (a collection of essays). Her first novel, the autobiographical *Habibi*, Arabic for "dear one" or "my dear," was published in 1998. She has received three Pushcart Prizes and two poetry prizes from the Texas Institute of Letters. She has appeared on the PBS television specials *The Language of Life with Bill Moyers* and *The United States of Poetry*. Nye's poetry reflects her commitment to a simple life close to the earth. She gets her material from the sights, sounds, and smells of daily life, and her direct, strongly imagistic poems have a wide appeal. "Lights in the Windows" exemplifies Nye's belief in the unifying power of poetry and of human power to heal ourselves and each other through openness to life and to literature.

from Lights in the Windows

Years ago a girl handed me a note as I was leaving her proud town of Albany, Texas, a tiny, lovely place far in the west of our big state. "I'm glad to know there is another poemist in the world," the note said. "I always knew we would find one another someday and our lights would cross."

Our lights would cross. That girl had not stood out to me, I realized, among the other upturned, interested faces in the classroom. How many other lights had I missed? I carried her smudged note for thousands of miles. . . .

If American students are provincial about the literary histories of other places, imagining themselves to be the primary readers and writers on the planet, it is up to us to help enlighten them. When I first traveled to India and Bangladesh as a visiting writer for the Arts America program of the U.S. Information Agency, friends commented helpfully upon our departure, "Why do you suppose people over there will care about poetry? They can barely get enough to eat!" Stereotyping ran rampant among even my educated community. In India, poems were shared with us which were 7,000 years old. In Bangladesh, an impromptu poetry reading was called one evening and 2,000 enthusiastic listeners showed up. Could either of those things happen in the United States?

Anyone who feels poetry is an alien or ominous form should consider the style in which human beings think. "How do *you* think?" I ask my students. "Do you think in complete, elaborate sentences? In fully developed paragraphs with careful footnotes? Or in flashes and bursts of images, snatches of lines leaping one to the next, descriptive fragments, sensory details?" We *think* in poetry. But some people pretend poetry is far away.

Probably some of us were taught so long and hard that poetry was a thing to *analyze* that we lost our ability to find it delicious, to appreciate its taste, sometimes even when we couldn't completely apprehend its *meaning.* I love to offer students a poem now and then that I don't really understand. It presents them with the immediate opportunity of being smarter than I am. Believe me, they always take it. They always find an interesting way to look through its window. It presents us all with a renewed appetite for interpretation, one of the most vibrant and energetic parts of the poetry experience.

I'm reminded of a dear teacher I had in high school who refused to go on to the next poem in our antiquated textbook until we had all agreed on the same interpretive vision of each poem—*her* vision. Wearily we raised our hands. Yes, yes, that poet was just about to jump off a cliff. Onward! If we can offer each other a cognizance of *mystery* through the poems we share, isn't that a greater gift? Won't a sense of inevitable mystery underpinning our intricate lives serve us better than the notion that we will each be given a neat set of blanks to fill in—always?

Poems offer that mystery. Poems respect our ability to interpret and translate images and signs. Poems link seemingly disparate parts of experience—this seems particularly critical at the frenzied end of the 20th century. I have yet to meet one person in all my travels who doesn't say they are too busy, they wish they had a little more time. If most of us have lost, as some poets suggest, our meaningful, deep relationships with the world of nature, poems help us to see and feel that world again, beyond our cities and double-locked doors. I have learned as much about nature from the poems of Mary Oliver as I have ever learned walking in the woods.

And since we now live in a world where activities in one person's woods have a direct relationship on countries far away—the disappearing rain forests in southern Mexico and Hawaii and the changing weather everywhere, for example—we need to know one another. It is an imperative, not a luxury. What will we recognize? As the daughter of a Palestinian immigrant, steeped since early childhood in Palestinian folktales, I found it critical the older I grew to read Israeli Jewish writers too. I had to know how many links we had. When Yehuda Amichai of Israel writes, ". . . the field needs it: *wildpeace* . . . ," he is talking about the same fields my ancestors wept over for years. I have no doubt these cousins of the human race could learn to work in them together.

During the Gulf War, I carried poems from writers in Iraq into classrooms I was visiting. It seemed important to remember that there were real people in Iraq, real fears and hopes, real chimneys and children and shoes and bread. A friend warned me, "You won't get away with it," but the exact opposite response occurred. Teachers said, "Where can we get more of these?" Did it matter that a third grader said, "I wonder what those little children in Iraq are thinking about today. I wonder if they slept at all last night." It mattered to me. Did it matter that high school girls ended up discussing the coldness of media euphemisms—"collateral dam-age" for innocent people dead, for example—how the television made everything seem somehow cold and distant, but the poems written in a personal human voice made that so-called enemy feel very close? That was the *job* of poems, we decided. To give us a sense of others' lives close up. Poems could be a zoom lens in a world of wide-angle sweeps. And the teachers at Hockaday School in Dallas said, "Do a book for us, okay? Give us a lot of voices from everywhere—we'll be waiting." . . .

And the poems came flying in, some stitched together at the top, some on thick, old-country paper, some fully illustrated with 20-page autobiographies accompanying. One fellow from a remote island asked if I could please nominate him for the Nobel Prize. . . .

As will happen with collections, the poems ended up gathering them-selves into sections that felt almost organic—related to family, or words and silences, or losses, or human mysteries. The sky seemed to occur sur-prisingly often as a universal reference point, which gave us the title. I loved receiving the autobiographical notes almost as much as the poems. An example from Amanda Aizpuriete: "I'm raising four children and translating Emily Dickinson into Latvian in my spare time." Or a note on Shuntaro Tanikawa by one of his translators, Harold Wright: "He entered a poetry contest because he didn't want to study for his college entrance exams and went on to become one of Japan's best-known contemporary poets." When Al Mahmud of Bangladesh describes his early life with poetry—"Poetry was . . . carefully collected bird's eggs / fragrant grass, the runaway calf of a sad-looking young farm wife, / neat letters on secret writing pads in blue envelopes."—he gives us a world we can touch and smell and share. When Benilda Santos of the Philippines describes the elaborate, loving way her little son said goodbye to her when he was in kindergarten and she left him at school, and the way he says goodbye to her now, years later—"his standard reply's / a tight smile / an eyebrow's twitch or sometimes / the slightest of nods. / Nothing remains of the old goodbyes . . ."—I cry every time because I am a mother now, and because I was also a daughter saying goodbye in both ways, and because human beings need to be reminded of themselves simply to see who we all are and how we fit together. . . .

RICHARD JACKSON

Richard Jackson (1946–) was born in Lawrence, Massachusetts and educated at Merrimack College (BA), Middlebury College (MA), and Yale University (PhD). He began his career as a high-school English teacher in North Adams, Massachusetts, but soon moved to the University of Tennessee at Chattanooga where he teaches in the English and University Honors departments and directs the Meacham Writers' Conference. He also teaches in the Vermont College MFA program and has won teaching awards at both schools.

Since a Fulbright year in the former Yugoslavia, Jackson has been a member of the Sarajevo Committee organized by P.E.N. International and has worked with groups concerned with the Balkan wars and fund raising for refugees. In 2000 he was awarded the Order of Freedom Medal for literary and humanitarian work in the Balkans by the president of Slovenia. Each year he returns to Slovenia with a group of students, introducing them to its culture and to its writers and poets.

Jackson is the author of five books of poems, *Heartwall* (Juniper Prize, 2000), *Alive All Day* (Cleveland State Prize, 1992), a *Selected Poems* in Slovene, and *Unauthorized Autobiography: New and Selected Poems* (2003). He has also published four chapbooks of adaptations from Petrarch and other Italian poets. *Half Lives: Petrarchan Poems* (2004), and his own poems have been translated into a dozen languages. He has edited two anthologies of Slovene poetry, *The Fire under the Moon* and *Four Slovenian Poets*, and edits an eastern European chapbook series and two journals, *Poetry Miscellany* and *mala revija*. He is also the author of a book of criticism, *Dismantling Time in Contemporary American Poetry* (winner of the Agee Prize) and *Acts of Mind: Interviews with Contemporary American Poets* (winner of Choice Award). He has received Guggenheim, National Endowment for the Arts, National Endowment for the Humanities, and Witter-Bynner fellowships; a *Prairie Schooner* Reader's Choice Award; the Crazy Horse Prize; and four Pushcart Prizes and appeared in *Best American Poems* 1997.

Jackson is married to Terri Harvey and has a daughter and two granddaughters.

from Why Poetry Today?

"And what are poets for in a difficult time?" asks Holderlin. And in our own age, Czelaw Milosz seems to echo the question: "What is poetry which does not save / Nations or people?" And, we might ask today, what sort of poetry can do this and not participate in its own self-made imperialism? What sort of poetry can do this and not attempt to establish itself from an falcon's perspective, from a distant and austere Parnassus, looking down upon the very people it should serve? These are questions as important for readers as they are for writers. Here is the great Slovene poet, Edvard Kocbek:

> If all the seven hundred million Chinese,
> each weighing fifty kilos, say,
> were simultaneously to jump
> from a height of 2 meters
> onto the land of their foe,
> it would make for an earthquake of magnitude Four.
> And if the Chinese were then to repeat this leap
> every fifty-four minutes,
> when the waves of the earthquake returned from around the world,
> they would raise the tremor to such a pitch
> it would raze the land of their foe.
> All this would be true to the style of Mao Zedong.
> Their enemies could stifle the quake
> only by catching precisely the interfering waves
> with counterleaps of their own.
> The unknown is only the size of the population.
> We, Slovenians, for instance, would need to jump
> from such a height that we would all be killed.
> That is why we have to sign up with our neighbors.

There is a lot to be learned from this, but most important is the sense of self irony. Perhaps most obvious is that to speak the last line one must have the confidence, self assurance, and independence—as a poet and as a people—to be able to speak this irony. In terms of the numbers set up by the poem's images it is true; in terms of the spirit portrayed in the poem, the savage wit, it is false. Here is a poem of great power, a political poem for our difficult times, and yet it has a large enough vision to be able to poke a little fun at itself, to give us a sense of irony and perspective —to suggest a way of embracing other cultures, not just fighting them. Yes, on the surface it suggests "signing up" as a mode of losing national identity, but surely the tone I have suggested, and the satire against others earlier in the poem, suggests "signing up" as also a way of committing oneself and one's culture, freely, to the concerns of all cultures for freedom and integrity.

When poetry goes bad it is usually because it becomes so ideological and rigid, so lacking in the kind of essential irony, self questioning, self evaluation, that I have suggested is part of Kocbek's vision: bad excludes rather than embraces us. It becomes dehumanized as the revolutionary forces given in language become institutionalized and static, as they begin to participate in the given power structure. . . . The poem is a unique form of discourse, always subverting the accepted view of things, always proposing new and unique perceptions and visions, based on desires, hopes. . . .

The problem for the poet, then, becomes an ethical one. The poem itself must question its own procedures and perspectives—perhaps by shifting stylistic gears, asking questions, suggesting alternatives, changing tone or course in the middle, keeping an ironic tone, understating or overstating for effect. The technique of the poem ought to call itself into question, ought to turn its own revolutionary spirit on its own vision so that it does not become static. This is especially true when the subject of a poem with political aspirations deals with others, with observations, with witnessing. . . .

. . . [A]ll poetry, but more overtly, political poetry, is always written from the point of view of desire, of someone denied something—an outsider—yet must also be written within the tradition of poetry: the resulting double vision is itself something that can give this poetry its power, as witness poets such as Neruda and Vallejo, Dimitrova and Popa, Kosovel and Holub. As an outsider trying not to be exclusionary him or herself, the poet tries to discover and create a world—with all the political inferences in that statement—that includes and embraces us. It is a form of history making. That is why the great Mexican poet Octavio

Paz said: "The language that nourishes the poem is, after all, nothing but history, name of this or that, reference and meaning. . . . Without history—without men, who are the origin, the substance and the end of history—the poem could not be born or incarnated, and without the poem there could be no history either, because there would be no origin or beginning." . . .

DEREK WALCOTT

Derek Walcott (1930–) was born in Castries, Saint Lucia, a small island in the Antilles chain in the Caribbean. His mother, who had been born in the Dutch half of the island of Saint Maarten, taught at the Methodist school in Saint Lucia; his father, a watercolorist and free spirit, died when Derek and his twin, Roderick, were very young. Derek attended St. Mary's College in Castries, then went on scholarship to the University of the West Indies in Kingston, Jamaica. At age eighteen he published his first collection, *25 Poems;* five years later he moved to Trinidad. After teaching school, he began writing feature articles and drama reviews for newspapers in Jamaica and Trinidad. A Rockefeller fellowship in 1957 enabled him to move to New York for two years to study American theater; in 1959 he returned to Trinidad to found its theater workshop, which produced some of his early plays. His best known drama, *Dream on Monkey Mountain,* commissioned by the Royal Shakespeare Company in the sixties, was actually performed in the United States.

Walcott's 1964 poetry collection *In a Green Night* brought him considerable recognition. Succeeding collections—*The Fortunate Traveller* (1981), *Midsummer* (1984), *The Arkansas Testament* (1987)—explore his sense of loneliness and isolation, his roots in the Caribbean, his African origins, and the English language still peppered with British idioms from Saint Lucia's years as a British colony in a string of French-speaking islands. The multicultural melange of identities continues to hold his interest, as his epic poem *Omeros* (1990) attests, reworking the stories of the *Iliad* and the *Odyssey,* recast in the West Indies. A hugely ambitious and worldly text, *Omeros* mingles references to Mayakovsky and Poe, Brodsky and the Beatles as he deftly weaves all sixty-four chapters into one vivid tapestry. Walcott writes in the English of an educated colonial as well as in the dialect of the Caribbean. His poems are richly metaphorical. In his Nobel lecture 1992, excerpted here, he declares, "There is the buried language and there is the individual vocabulary, and the process of poetry is one of excavation and of self-discovery."

In addition to the Nobel Prize in Literature, Walcott won a MacArthur "genius" award in 1981. He is an honorary member of the American Academy and Institute of Arts and Letters. He divides his year between teaching at Boston University and his home in Trinidad.

from The Antilles:
Fragments of Epic Memory. Nobel Prize Lecture, 1992

. . . Break a vase, and the love that reassembles the fragments is stronger than that love which took its symmetry for granted when it was whole. The glue that fits the pieces is the sealing of its original shape. It is such a love that reassembles our African and Asiatic fragments, the cracked heirlooms whose restoration shows its white scars. This gathering of broken pieces is the care and pain of the Antilles, and if the pieces are disparate, ill-fitting, they contain more pain than their original sculpture, those icons and sacred vessels taken for granted in their ancestral places. Antillean art is this restoration of our shattered histories, our shards of vocabulary, our archipelago becoming a synonym for pieces broken off from the original continent.

And this is the exact process of the making of poetry, or what should be called not its "making" but its remaking, the fragmented memory, the armature that frames the god, even the rite that surrenders it to a final pyre; the god assembled cane by cane, reed by weaving reed, line by plaited line, as the artisans of Felicity would erect his holy echo.

Poetry, which is perfection's sweat but which must seem as fresh as the raindrops on a statue's brow, combines the natural and the marmoreal; it conjugates both tenses simultaneously: the past and the present, if the past is the sculpture and the present the beads of dew or rain on the forehead of the past. There is the buried language and there is the individual vocabulary, and the process of poetry is one of excavation and of self-discovery. Tonally the individual voice is a dialect; it shapes its own accent, its own vocabulary and melody in defiance of an imperial concept of language, the language of Ozymandias, libraries and dictionaries, law courts and critics, and churches, universities, political dogma, the diction of institutions. Poetry is an island that breaks away from the main. The dialects of my archipelago seem as fresh to me as those raindrops on the statue's forehead, not the sweat made from the classic exertion of frowning marble, but the condensations of a refreshing element, rain and salt.

Deprived of their original language, the captured and indentured tribes create their own, accreting and secreting fragments of an old, an epic vocabulary, from Asia and from Africa, but to an ancestral, an ecstatic rhythm in the blood that cannot be subdued by slavery or indenture, while nouns are renamed and the given names of places accepted like Felicity village or Choiseul. The original language dissolves from the exhaustion of distance like fog trying to cross an ocean, but this process of renaming, of finding new metaphors, is the same process that the poet faces every morning of his working day, making his own tools like Crusoe, assembling nouns from necessity, from Felicity, even renaming himself. The stripped man is driven back to that self-astonishing, elemental force, his mind. That is the basis of the Antillean experience, this shipwreck of fragments, these echoes, these shards of a huge tribal vocabulary, these partially remembered customs, and they are not decayed but strong. They survived the Middle Passage and the *Fatel Rozack,* the ship that carried the first indentured Indians from the port of Madras to the cane fields of Felicity, that carried the chained Cromwellian convict and the Sephardic Jew, the Chinese grocer and the Lebanese merchant selling cloth samples on his bicycle.

And here they are, all in a single Caribbean city, Port of Spain, the sum of history, Trollope's "non-people." A downtown Babel of shop signs and streets, mongrelized, polyglot, a ferment without a history, like heaven. Because that is what such a city is, in the New World, a writer's heaven.

Ours are not cities in the accepted sense, but no one wants them to be. They dictate their own proportions, their own definitions in particular places and in a prose equal to that of their detractors, so that now it is not just St. James but the streets and yards that Naipaul commemorates, its lanes as short and brilliant as his sentences; not just the noise and jostle of Tunapuna but the origins of C. L. R. James's *Beyond a Boundary,* not just Felicity village on the Caroni plain, but Selvon Country, and that is the way it goes up the islands now: the old Dominica of Jean Rhys still very much the way she wrote of it; and the Martinique of the early Césaire; Perse's Guadeloupe, even without the pith helmets and the mules; and what delight and privilege there was in watching a literature— one literature in several imperial languages, French, English, Spanish— bud and open island after island in the early morning of a culture, not timid, not derivative, any more than the hard white petals of the frangipani are derivative and timid. This is not a belligerent boast but a simple celebration of inevitability: that this flowering had to come. . . .

There is a force of exultation, a celebration of luck, when a writer finds himself a witness to the early morning of a culture that is defining itself, branch by branch, leaf by leaf, in that self-defining dawn, which is why, especially at the edge of the sea, it is good to make a ritual of the sunrise. Then the noun, the "Antilles" ripples like brightening water, and the sounds of leaves, palm fronds, and birds are the sounds of a fresh dialect, the native tongue. The personal vocabulary, the individual melody whose metre is one's biography, joins in that sound, with any luck, and the body moves like a walking, a waking island.

This is the benediction that is celebrated, a fresh language and a fresh people, and this is the frightening duty owed.

I stand here in their name, if not their image—but also in the name of the dialect they exchange like the leaves of the trees whose names are suppler, greener, more morning-stirred than English—*laurier canelles, bois-flot, bois-canot*—or the valleys the trees mention—*Fond St. Jacques, Mabonya, Forestier, Roseau, Mahaut*—or the empty beaches—*L'Anse Ivrogne, Case en Bas, Paradis*—all songs and histories in themselves, pronounced not in French—but in patois.

One rose hearing two languages, one of the trees, one of school children reciting in English:

> I am monarch of all I survey,
> My right there is none to dispute;
> From the centre all round to the sea
> I am lord of the fowl and the brute.
> Oh, solitude! where are the charms
> That sages have seen in thy face?
> Better dwell in the midst of alarms,
> Than reign in this horrible place . . .

While in the country to the same metre, but to organic instruments, handmade violin, chac-chac, and goatskin drum, a girl named Sensenne singing:

> *Si mwen di 'ous ça fait mwen la peine*
> *'Ous kai dire ça vrai*
> (If I told you that caused me pain

You'll say, "It's true.")

Si mwen di 'ous ça penetrait mwen

'Ous peut dire ça vrai

(If I told you you pierced my heart

You'd say, "It's true.")

Ces mamailles actuellement

Pas ka faire l'amour z'autres pour un rien.

(Children nowadays

Don't make love for nothing.)

It is not that History is obliterated by this sunrise. It is there in Antillean geography, in the vegetation itself. The sea sighs with the drowned from the Middle Passage, but butchery of its aborigines, Carib and Aruac and Taino, bleeds in the scarlet of the immortelle, and even the actions of surf on sand cannot erase the African memory, or the lances of cane as a green prison where indentured Asians, the ancestors of Felicity, are still serving time.

That is what I have read around me from boyhood, from the beginnings of poetry, the grace of effort. In the hard mahogany of woodcutters: faces, resinous men, charcoal burners; in a man with a cutlass cradled across his forearm, who stands on the verge with the usual anonymous khaki dog; in the extra clothes he put on this morning, when it was cold when he rose in the thinning dark to go and make his garden in the heights—the heights, the garden, being miles away from his house, but that is where he has his land—not to mention the fishermen, the footmen on trucks, groaning up mornes, all fragments of Africa originally but shaped and hardened and rooted now in the island's life, illiterate in the way leaves are illiterate; they do not read, they are there to be read, and if they are properly read, they create their own literature. . . .

CZESLAW MILOSZ

Czeslaw Milosz (1911–2004) was born into a family of Roman Catholic Polish gentry in the rural town of Szetejnie, Lithuania, under Czarist control, only a few years before the outbreak of World War I. At its conclusion, he attended high school, and later, university in Vilno, which had become a part of the new but shaky democratic regime of Poland. His first book of poems appeared in 1933; the following year he completed law school, then spent a year in Paris with his uncle, the French poet Oscar Milosz. Back in Vilno, he worked at a radio station but lost his job there because of his increasingly leftist views. He moved to Warsaw where he rose to prominence in the Catastrophist school of poetry, which stressed the decline of European culture and predicted cosmic disaster. He rejected the poetic philosophy of art for art's sake as well as nationalism, anti-Semitism, and any doctrinaire stance. With the German invasion of Poland in September 1939, which triggered the outbreak of World War II, the catastrophist version of history came true.

In Warsaw, where he worked for various underground presses and was a horrified witness to the Holocaust, Milosz kept a low profile as a janitor at the university. In 1944 he married Janina Dluska, who had worked at the same radio station in Vilno. The couple had two sons. (Dluska died in 1986 and Milosz married Carol Thigpen in 1992.) During this bleak time, appropriately enough, he translated *The Waste Land* into Polish. In 1945, the newly formed communist government of Poland appointed him attaché to Washington, D.C., and Paris, but the ever darkening cloud of totalitarian ideology he was forced to work under caused him to seek political asylum in Paris in 1951. His work was subsequently banned in Poland but it circulated widely in secret publications and over time, Milosz came to be regarded reverentially as a major literary figure. For the next ten years, Milosz lived in Paris working as a freelance writer. He accepted an appointment at the University of California at Berkeley in 1960, although none of his poetry was translated into English until 1973 and taught there until his retirement in 1984.

In 1980, at the Gdansk shipyard in Poland where the Solidarity movement originated, a monument memorializing the workers killed in the riots was unveiled. These lines from Milosz's poem, "You Who Were Wronged," are engraved there: "Do not feel safe. The poet remembers.

You can kill one, but another is born." In that same year, he was awarded the Nobel Prize in literature.

Nobel Prize Lecture, 1980

I.

My presence here, on this tribune, should be an argument for all those who praise life's God-given, marvelously complex, unpredictability. In my school years I used to read volumes of a series then published in Poland—*The Library of the Nobel Laureates.* I remember the shape of the letters and the color of the paper. I imagined then that the Nobel laureates were writers, namely persons who write thick works in prose, and even when I learned that there were also poets among them, for a long time I could not get rid of that notion. And certainly, when, in 1930, I published my first poems in our university review, *Alma Mater Vilnensis,* I did not aspire to the title of a writer. Also much later, by choosing solitude and giving myself to a strange occupation, that is, to writing poems in Polish while living in France or America, I tried to maintain a certain ideal image of a poet, who, if he wants fame, he wants to be famous only in the village or the town of his birth.

One of the Nobel laureates whom I read in childhood influenced to a large extent, I believe, my notions of poetry. That was Selma Lagerlöf. Her *Wonderful Adventures of Nils,* a book I loved, places the hero in a double role. He is the one who flies above the Earth and looks at it *from above* but at the same time sees it in every detail. This double vision may be a metaphor of the poet's vocation. I found a similar metaphor in a Latin ode of a Seventeenth-Century poet, Maciej Sarbiewski, who was once known all over Europe under the pen-name of Casimire. He taught poetics at my university. In that ode he describes his voyage—on the back of Pegasus—from Vilno to Antwerp, where he is going to visit his poet-friends. Like Nils Holgersson he beholds under him rivers, lakes, forests, that is, a map, both distant and yet concrete. Hence, two attributes of the poet: avidity of the eye and the desire to describe that which he sees. Yet, whoever considers poetry as "to see and to describe" should be aware that he engages in a quarrel with modernity, fascinated as it is with innumerable theories of a specific poetic language.

Every poet depends upon generations who wrote in his native tongue; he inherits styles and forms elaborated by those who lived before him. At the same time, though, he feels that those old means of expression are not adequate to his own experience. When adapting himself, he hears an internal voice that warns him against mask and disguise. But when rebelling, he falls in turn into dependence upon his contemporaries, various movements of the avant-garde. Alas, it is enough for him to publish his first volume of poems, to find himself entrapped. For hardly has the print dried, when that work, which seemed to him the most personal, appears to be enmeshed in the style of another. The only way to counter an obscure remorse is to continue searching and to publish a new book, but then everything repeats itself, so there is no end to that chase. And it may happen that leaving books behind as if they were dry snake skins, in a constant escape forward from what has been done in the past, he receives the Nobel Prize.

What is this enigmatic impulse that does not allow one to settle down in the achieved, the finished? I think it is a quest for reality. I give to this word its naive and solemn meaning, a meaning having nothing to do with philosophical debates of the last few centuries. It is the Earth as seen by Nils from the back of the gander and by the author of the Latin ode from the back of Pegasus. Undoubtedly, that Earth *is* and her riches cannot be exhausted by any description. To make such an assertion means to reject in advance a question we often hear today: "What is reality?", for it is the same as the question of Pontius Pilate: "What is truth?" If among pairs of opposites which we use every day, the opposition of life and death has such an importance, no less importance should be ascribed to the oppositions of truth and falsehood, of reality and illusion.

II.

Simone Weil, to whose writings I am profoundly indebted, says: "Distance is the soul of beauty." Yet sometimes keeping distance is nearly impossible. I am *A Child of Europe,* as the title of one of my poems admits, but that is a bitter, sarcastic admission. I am also the author of an autobiographical book which in the French translation bears the title *Une autre Europe.* Undoubtedly, there exist two Europes and it happens that we, inhabitants of the second one, were destined to descend into "the heart of darkness" of the Twentieth Century. I wouldn't know how to speak about poetry in general. I must speak of poetry in its encounter with peculiar circumstances of time and place. Today, from a perspective, we are able to distinguish outlines of the events which by their death-bearing range surpassed all natural disasters known to us, but poetry, mine and my contemporaries', whether of inherited or avant-garde style, was not prepared to cope with those catastrophes. Like blind men we groped our way and were exposed to all the temptations the mind deluded itself with in our time.

It is not easy to distinguish reality from illusion, especially when one lives in a period of the great upheaval that began a couple of centuries ago on a small western peninsula of the Euro-Asiatic continent, only to encompass the whole planet during one man's lifetime with the uniform worship of science and technology. And it was particularly difficult to oppose multiple intellectual temptations in those areas of Europe where degenerate ideas of dominion over men, akin to the ideas of dominion over Nature, led to paroxysms of revolution and war at the expense of millions of human beings destroyed physically or spiritually. And yet perhaps our most precious acquisition is not an understanding of those ideas, which we touched in their most tangible shape, but respect and gratitude for certain things which protect people from internal disintegration and from yielding to tyranny. Precisely for that reason some ways of life, some institutions became a target for the fury of evil forces, above all, the bonds between people that exist organically, as if by themselves, sustained by family, religion, neighborhood, common heritage. In other words, all that disorderly, illogical humanity, so often branded as ridiculous because of its parochial attachments and loyalties. In many countries traditional bonds of *civitas* have been subject to a gradual erosion and their inhabitants become disinherited without realizing it. It is not the same, however, in those areas where suddenly, in a situation of utter peril, a protective, life-giving value of such bonds reveals itself. That is the case of my native land. And I feel this is a proper place to mention gifts received by myself and by my friends in our part of Europe and to pronounce words of blessing.

It is good to be born in a small country where Nature was on a human scale, where various languages and religions cohabited for centuries. I have in mind Lithuania, a country of myths and of poetry. My family already in the Sixteenth Century spoke Polish, just as many families in Finland spoke Swedish and in Ireland—English; so I am a Polish, not a Lithuanian, poet. But the landscapes and perhaps the spirits of Lithuania have never abandoned me. It is good in childhood to hear words of Latin liturgy, to translate Ovid in high school, to receive a good training in Roman Catholic dogmatics and apologetics. It is a blessing if one receives from fate school and university studies in such a city as Vilno. A bizarre city of baroque architecture transplanted to northern forests and of history fixed in every stone, a city of forty Roman Catholic churches and of numerous synagogues. In those days the Jews called it a Jerusalem of the North. Only when teaching in America did I fully realize how much I had absorbed from the thick walls of our ancient university, from formulas of Roman law learned by heart, from history and literature of old Poland, both of which surprise young Americans by their specific features: an indulgent anarchy, a humor disarming fierce quarrels, a sense of organic community, a mistrust of any centralized authority.

A poet who grew up in such a world should have been a seeker for reality through contemplation. A patriarchal order should have been dear to him, a sound of bells, an isolation from pressures and the persistent demands of his fellow men, silence of a cloister cell. If books were to linger on a table, then they should be those which deal with the most incomprehensible quality of God-created things, namely being, the *esse*. But suddenly all this is negated by demoniac doings of History which acquires the traits of a bloodthirsty Deity. The Earth which the poet viewed in his flight calls with a cry, indeed, out of the abyss and doesn't allow itself to be viewed *from above*. An insoluble contradiction appears, a terribly real one, giving no peace of mind either day or night, whatever we call it, it is the contradiction between being and action, or, on another level, a contradiction between art and solidarity with one's fellow men. Reality calls for a name, for words, but it is unbearable and if it is touched, if it draws very close, the poet's mouth cannot even utter a complaint of Job: all art proves to be nothing compared with action. Yet, to embrace reality in such a manner that it is preserved in all its old tangle of good and evil, of despair and hope, is possible only thanks to a distance, only by soaring *above* it—but this in turn seems then a moral treason.

Such was the contradiction at the very core of conflicts engendered by the Twentieth Century and discovered by poets of an Earth polluted by the crime of genocide. What are the thoughts of one of them, who wrote a certain number of poems which remain as a memorial, as a testimony? He thinks that they were born out of a painful contradiction and that he would prefer to have been able to resolve it while leaving them unwritten.

III.

A patron saint of all poets in exile, who visit their towns and provinces only in remembrance, is always Dante. But how has the number of Florences increased! The exile of a poet is today a simple function of a relatively recent discovery: that whoever wields power is also able to control language and not only with the prohibitions of censorship, but also by changing the meaning of words. A peculiar phenomenon makes its appearance: the language of a captive community acquires certain durable habits; whole zones of reality cease to exist simply because they have no name. There is, it seems, a hidden link between theories of literature as *Écriture*, of speech feeding on itself, and the growth of the totalitarian state. In any case, there is no reason why the state should not tolerate an activity that consists of creating "experimental" poems and prose, if these are conceived as autonomous systems of reference, enclosed within their own boundaries. Only if we assume that a poet constantly strives to liberate himself from borrowed styles in search for reality, is he dangerous. In a room where people unanimously maintain a conspiracy of silence, one word of truth sounds like a pistol shot. And, alas, a temptation to pronounce it, similar to an acute itching, becomes an obsession which doesn't allow one to think of anything else. That is why a poet chooses internal or external exile. It is not certain, however, that he is motivated exclusively by his concern with actuality. He may also desire to free himself from it and elsewhere, in other countries, on other shores, to recover, at least for short moments, his true vocation—which is to contemplate Being.

That hope is illusory, for those who come from the "other Europe," wherever they find themselves, notice to what extent their experiences isolate them from their new milieu—and this may become the source of a new obsession. Our planet that gets smaller every year, with its fantastic proliferation of mass media, is witnessing a process that escapes definition, characterized by a refusal to remember. Certainly, the illiterates of past centuries, then an enormous majority of mankind, knew little of the history of their respective countries and of their civilization. In the minds of modern illiterates, however, who know how to read and write and even teach in schools and at universities, history is present but blurred, in a state of strange confusion; Molière becomes a contemporary of Napoleon, Voltaire, a contemporary of Lenin. Also, events of the last decades, of such primary importance that knowledge or ignorance of them will be decisive for the future of mankind, move away, grow pale, lose all consistency as if Frederic Nietzsche's prediction of European nihilism found a literal fulfillment. "The eye of a nihilist"—he wrote in 1887—"is unfaithful to his memories: it allows them to drop, to lose their leaves; . . . And what he does not do for himself, he also does not do for the whole past of mankind: he lets it drop." We are surrounded today by fictions about the past, contrary to common sense and to an elementary perception of good and evil. As The Los Angeles Times recently stated, the number of books in various languages which deny that the Holocaust ever took place, that it was invented by Jewish propaganda, has exceeded one hundred. If such an insanity is possible, is a complete loss of memory as a permanent state of mind improbable? And would it not present a danger more grave than genetic engineering or poisoning of the natural environment?

For the poet of the "other Europe" the events embraced by the name of the Holocaust are a reality, so close in time that he cannot hope to liberate himself from their remembrance unless, perhaps, by translating the Psalms of David. He feels anxiety, though, when the meaning of the word Holocaust undergoes gradual modifications, so that the word begins to belong to the history of the Jews exclusively, as if among the victims there were not also millions of Poles, Russians, Ukrainians and prisoners of other nationalities. He feels anxiety, for he senses in this a foreboding of a not distant future when history will be reduced to what appears on television, while the truth, as it is too complicated, will be buried in the archives, if not totally annihilated. Other facts as well, facts for him quite close but distant for the West, add in his mind to the credibility of H. G. Wells' vision in *The Time Machine*: the Earth inhabited by a tribe of children of the day, carefree, deprived of memory and, by the same token, of history, without defense when confronted with dwellers of subterranean caves, cannibalistic children of the night.

Carried forward, as we are, by the movement of technological change, we realize that the unification of our planet is in the making and we attach importance to the notion of international community. The days when the League of Nations and the United Nations were founded deserve to be remembered. Unfortunately, those dates lose their significance in comparison with another date which should be invoked every year as a day of mourning, while it is hardly known to younger generations. It is the date of 23 August 1939. Two dictators then concluded an agreement provided with a secret clause by the virtue of which they divided between themselves neighboring countries possessing their own capitals, governments and parliaments. That pact not only unleashed a terrible war; it re-established a colonial principle, according to which nations are not more than cattle, bought, sold, completely dependent upon the will of their instant masters. Their borders, their right to self-determination, their passports ceased to exist. And it should be a source of wonder that today people speak in a whisper, with a finger to their lips, about how that principle was applied by the dictators forty years ago.

Crimes against human rights, never confessed and never publicly denounced, are a poison which destroys the possibility of a friendship between nations. Anthologies of Polish poetry publish poems of my late friends—Wladyslaw Sebyla and Lech Piwowar, and give the date of their deaths: 1940. It is absurd not to be able to write how they perished, though everybody in Poland knows the truth: they shared the fate of several thousand Polish officers disarmed and interned by the then accomplices of Hitler, and they repose in a mass grave. And should not the young generations of the West, if they study history at all, hear about the 200,000 people killed in 1944 in Warsaw, a city sentenced to annihilation by those two accomplices?

The two genocidal dictators are no more and yet, who knows whether they did not gain a victory more durable than those of their armies. In spite of the Atlantic Charter, the principle that nations are objects of trade, if not chips in games of cards or dice, has been confirmed by the division of Europe into two zones. The absence of the three Baltic states from the United Nations is a permanent reminder of the two dictators' legacy. Before the war those states belonged to the League of Nations but they disappeared from the map of Europe as a result of the secret clause in the agreement of 1939.

I hope you forgive my laying bare a memory like a wound. This subject is not unconnected with my meditation on the word "reality," so often misused but always deserving esteem. Complaints of peoples, pacts more treacherous than those we read about in Thucydides, the shape of a maple leaf, sunrises and sunsets over the ocean, the whole fabric of causes and effects, whether we call it Nature or History, points towards, I believe, another hidden reality, impenetrable, though exerting a powerful attraction that is the central driving force of all art and science. There are moments when it seems to me that I decipher the meaning of afflictions which befell the nations of the "other Europe" and that meaning is to make them the bearers of memory—at the time when Europe, without an adjective, and America possess it less and less with every generation.

It is possible that there is no other memory than the memory of wounds. At least we are so taught by the Bible, a book of the tribulations of Israel. That book for a long time enabled European nations to preserve a sense of continuity—a word not to be mistaken for the fashionable term, historicity.

During the thirty years I have spent abroad I have felt I was more privileged than my Western colleagues, whether writers or teachers of literature, for events both recent and long past took in my mind a sharply delineated, precise form. Western audiences confronted with poems or novels written in Poland, Czechoslovakia or Hungary, or with films produced there, possibly intuit a similarly sharpened consciousness, in a constant struggle against limitations imposed by censorship. Memory thus is our force, it protects us against a speech entwining upon itself like the ivy when it does not find a support on a tree or a wall.

A few minutes ago I expressed my longing for the end of a contradiction which opposes the poet's need of distance to his feeling of solidarity with his fellow men. And yet, if we take a flight *above* the Earth as a metaphor of the poet's vocation, it is not difficult to notice that a kind of contradiction is implied, even in those epochs when the poet is relatively free from the snares of History. For how to be *above* and simultaneously to see the Earth in every detail? And yet, in a precarious balance of opposites, a certain equilibrium can be achieved thanks to a distance introduced by the flow of time. "To see" means not only to have before one's eyes. It may mean also to preserve in memory. "To see and to describe" may also mean to reconstruct in imagination. A distance achieved, thanks to the mystery of time, must not change events, land-scapes, human figures into a tangle of shadows growing paler and paler. On the contrary, it can show them in full light, so that every event, every date becomes expressive and persists as an eternal reminder of human depravity and human greatness. Those who are alive receive a mandate from those who are silent forever. They can fulfill their duties only by try-ing to reconstruct precisely things as they were, and by wresting the past from fictions and legends.

Thus both—the Earth seen from above in an eternal now and the Earth that endures in a recovered time—may serve as material for poetry.

IV.

I would not like to create the impression that my mind is turned toward the past, for that would not be true. Like all my contemporaries I have felt the pull of despair, of impending doom, and reproached myself for succumbing to a nihilistic temptation. Yet on a deeper level, I believe, my poetry remained sane and, in a dark age, expressed a long-ing for the Kingdom of Peace and Justice. The name of a man who taught me not to despair should be invoked here. We receive gifts not only from our native land, its lakes and rivers, its traditions, but also from people, especially if we meet a powerful personality in our early youth. It was my good fortune to be treated nearly as a son by my relative Oscar Milosz, a Parisian recluse and a visionary. Why he was a French poet, could be elucidated by the intricate story of a family as well as of a coun-try once called the Grand Duchy of Lithuania. Be that as it may, it was possible to read recently in the Parisian press words of regret that the highest international distinction had not been awarded half a century earlier to a poet bearing the same family name as my own.

I learned much from him. He gave me a deeper insight into the reli-gion of the Old and New Testament and inculcated a need for a strict, ascetic hierarchy in all matters of mind, including everything that pertains to art, where as a major sin he considered putting the second-rate on the same level with the first-rate. Primarily, though, I listened to him as a prophet who loved people, as he says, "with old love worn out by pity, loneliness and anger" and for that reason tried to address a warning to a crazy world rushing towards a catastrophe. That a catastrophe was imminent, I heard from him, but also I heard from him that the great conflagration he predicted would be merely a part of a larger drama to be played to the end.

He saw deeper causes in an erroneous direction taken by science in the Eighteenth Century, a direction which provoked landslide effects. Not unlike William Blake before him, he announced a New Age, a second renaissance of imagination now polluted by a certain type of scientific knowledge, but, as he believed, not by all scientific knowledge, least of all by science that would be discovered by men of the future. And it does not matter to what extent I took his predictions literally: a general orientation was enough.

Oscar Milosz, like William Blake, drew inspirations from the writings of Emanuel Swedenborg, a scientist who, earlier than anyone else, foresaw the defeat of man, hidden in the Newtonian model of the Universe. When, thanks to my relative, I became an attentive reader of Swedenborg, interpreting him not, it is true, as was common in the Romantic era, I did not imagine I would visit his country for the first time on such an occasion as the present one.

Our century draws to its close, and largely thanks to those influences I would not dare to curse it, for it has also been a century of faith and hope. A profound transformation, of which we are hardly aware, because we are a part of it, has been taking place, coming to the surface from time to time in phenomena that provoke general astonishment. That transformation has to do, and I use here words of Oscar Milosz, with "the deepest secret of toiling masses, more than ever alive, vibrant and tormented." Their secret, an unavowed need of true values, finds no language to express itself and here not only the mass media but also intellectuals bear a heavy responsibility. But transformation has been going on, defying short term predictions, and it is probable that in spite of all horrors and perils, our time will be judged as a necessary phase of travail before mankind ascends to a new awareness. Then a new hierarchy of merits will emerge, and I am convinced that Simone Weil and Oscar Milosz, writers in whose school I obediently studied, will receive their due. I feel we should publicly confess our attachment to certain names because in that way we define our position more forcefully than by pronouncing the names of those to whom we would like to address a violent "no." My hope is that in this lecture, in spite of my meandering thought, which is a professional bad habit of poets, my "yes" and "no" are clearly stated, at least as to the choice of succession. For we all who are here, both the speaker and you who listen, are no more than links between the past and the future.

APPENDIX

Thematic Index

ABSTRACTIONS

Ezra Pound (1885–1972), "A Few Don'ts by an Imagiste," 172

Stanley Kunitz (1905–), *from* "Table Talk, A Paris Review Interview with Chris Busa," 207

Maxine Kumin (1925–), *from* "Coming Across: Establishing the Intent of a Poem," 73; *from* "Closing the Door," 74

Frank O'Hara (1926–66), "Personism: A Manifesto," 225

AFRICAN AND AFRICAN AMERICAN POETICS

Phillis Wheatley (1753–84), "On Imagination," 27

Langston Hughes (1902–67), *from* "The Negro Artist and the Racial Mountain," 222

Léopold Sédar Senghor (1906–2001), *from* "Elegy of Midnight," 359; *from* "Elegy of the Trade Winds," 360

Aimé Césaire (1913–), *from Notebook of a Return to the Native Land,* 365

Gwendolyn Brooks (1917–2000), *from The Future of Black Poetry,* 377

Derek Walcott (1930–), *from* "The Antilles: Fragments of Epic Memory. Nobel Prize Lecture, 1992," 402

Audre Lorde (1934–92), *from* "Poetry Is Not a Luxury," 369

Lucille Clifton (1936–), "when i stand around among poets . . ." 96

Marilyn Nelson (1946–), *from* "Owning the Masters," 294

Yusef Komunyakaa (1947–), *from* "Control Is the Mainspring," 291

Nathaniel Mackey (1947–), *from* "Cante Moro," 81

Harryette Mullen (1953–), *from* "A Conversation with Harryette Mullen," 283

ARAB AND ARAB-AMERICAN POETICS

Naomi Shihab Nye (1952–), *from* "Lights in the Windows," 394

ASIAN AND ASIAN AMERICAN POETICS

Po Chu-I (772–846), "Madly Singing in the Mountains," 15

Theresa Hak Kyung Cha (1951–82), "Diseuse," 108

Li-Young Lee (1957–), *from* "Interview with Marie Jordan," 389

ENDINGS

FAME

FEMINIST POETICS

FORMALISM. *SEE ALSO* METER AND RHYTHM, SONNET

FREE VERSE. *SEE ALSO* LINE

INNOVATIVE POETICS

INSPIRATION. *SEE ALSO* IMAGINATION, MUSE, DUENDE

INTELLIGIBILITY

LENGTH OF POEMS

LINE. *SEE ALSO* FORMALISM, METER AND RHYTHM

LOVE

MANIFESTOES

MEMORY

PLEASURE AND POETRY

POETIC TRADITION

TROPES: METAPHORS AND SIMILES

WONDER

INDEX OF AUTHORS AND TITLES